# HONOUR, FAMILY, AND PATRONAGE

Conversation

# HONOUR, FAMILY
## AND
# PATRONAGE

J. K. CAMPBELL

OXFORD UNIVERSITY PRESS
New York and Oxford

© Oxford University Press 1964
First American printing 1974
Printed in the United States of America
printing, last digit: 10 9 8

# PREFACE

I THINK it is useful and necessary to explain at once the particular point of view from which I describe in this study the life of a community of Greek Sarakatsan shepherds. I begin with an analysis, in some detail, of kinship institutions and the structure of the family, which emphasizes how an individual's moral obligations are concentrated almost exclusively within family and kindred at the expense of his relations with people outside that relatively limited circle. Families not connected by kinship or marriage are related through institutions of mutual hostility and competition; and unrelated persons view one another at all times with intense distrust. A system of social values based on concepts of honour, strength, and pride is associated with these institutions and attitudes, and together they guide the conduct of Sarakatsani in the apparent anarchy of their communal life. Inevitably these institutions and values severely limit the possible forms of economic and civic cooperation. Further, they considerably affect the character of the relations between this community of mutually opposed family commonwealths and the rest of Greek society. Given a centralized administration, and parliamentary government with a universal franchise, an implication of the internal structure of the community is that these relations tend to take certain forms of political and social patronage. Honour, Family, and Patronage represent a pattern of interrelated institutions and values.

In this book I have attempted to abstract for the purposes of analysis a particular complex of institutions and values which are not peculiar to the Sarakatsani. Very similar formal elements are critical for the study of society anywhere in the Greek provinces, and even, in many respects, in the cities. Moreover, the social forms which are described here have many interesting parallels in other parts of the Mediterranean world, and it is principally as a contribution to the study of social structures in this area that I offer my study.

It follows that this is in no sense a complete ethnographic account of even one community of Sarakatsani, let alone a survey of Sarakatsan culture in general. Mme Chatzimichalis has published the first volume of a work which will represent, when it is completed, the fullest possible account of Sarakatsan folklore and material culture. It is a pleasure to acknowledge my debt to her work which goes far beyond the few references noted in this book. Where there appear to be disagreements between us these are generally accounted for by the circumstance that, as a folklorist, Mme Chatzimichalis' object is to describe Sarakatsan life and culture in its most traditional form. My own study, on the other hand, is concerned with only certain aspects of a particular community of Sarakatsani as I discovered it in 1954 and 1955.

Various incidents in this book describe the illegal acts of some individuals, or the social humiliation of others; and most of the information I received from Sarakatsani was certainly regarded by them as confidential. I have therefore taken what steps I can to cover personal identities. Although I lived among Sarakatsani in a number of villages in Zagori, the greater part of the material used in this study concerns the Sarakatsani who graze the land of one particular village in central Zagori. To this village I have given the fictitious name of Neochori. Similarly I have changed all personal names.

It is impossible, unfortunately, to acknowledge all the many instances of help and hospitality I have received at various times. There are original debts of gratitude to Mr. W. A. Camps who persuaded the Ministry of Education to support my research when they had virtually decided otherwise; and to my father who supplemented this grant at times of crisis to make it barely possible to carry out the necessary fieldwork. At an early moment of indecision in Greece I received a letter from Professor E. E. Evans-Pritchard which advised me to join the Sarakatsani. In retrospect, I owe much to this. I have to thank Dr. J. G. Peristiany for his constant encouragement, and for many discussions which have radically affected the form of this book particularly in connexion with my analysis of Sarakatsan values. My gratitude is due to Dr. J. M. Beattie and Dr. Rodney Needham who read the manuscript and offered many invaluable criticisms and suggestions. I also wish to thank Sir Maurice

Bowra, Dr. K. O. L. Burridge, Mr. E. Katsaros, Dr. R. G. Lien-hardt, Mr. Zisimos Lorenzatos, and Dr. Philip Sherrard who read and commented on particular chapters. And to the Warden and Fellows of St. Antony's College I express my appreciation for their patient support and encouragement.

It was my misfortune that feelings over the Cyprus issue became particularly embittered shortly after I began my fieldwork, with the result that my relations with the local authorities were always difficult. My movements were restricted and under surveillance. I was seldom able to persuade local officials to provide me with, or to help me obtain, any kind of quantitative or statistical information. Indeed, it is certain that without the generous support of the deputy Prime Minister Mr. Panayiotis Canellopoulos, I would not have been allowed to remain. Within a week of his leaving office I was ordered to remove myself from the area and on this abrupt note my fieldwork ended. If one remembers the unhappy atmosphere which then existed, it would be unreasonable to complain of the reaction of some Greek officials and individuals to my presence and my suspect work. It is with all the more gratitude that I remember the kindness and practical assistance of many Greek friends, which they did not always give without risk. Particularly I wish to mention Mr. Sotiris Dakaris of the Greek Archaeological Service, and his wife. My debt to the Sarakatsani will be obvious from this book; and to none is it greater than to my friend Theodoros Gogolos.

I dedicate this book to my wife, Sheila Campbell, who shared the fieldwork in physical and political conditions which were often unpleasant, and who first won the confidence of a secretive people.

J.K.C.

*Kifissia.*
*May* 1962.

During my fieldwork I was visited by the Greek photographer 'Dimitri' and I am grateful for permission to use some of the photographs he took on those occasions. I am similarly grateful to Mr. Roger Vaternelle who prepared the map; and to Professor Bernard Kayser who made it possible for him to do so.

# CONTENTS

# LIST OF ILLUSTRATIONS

# HONOUR, FAMILY, AND PATRONAGE

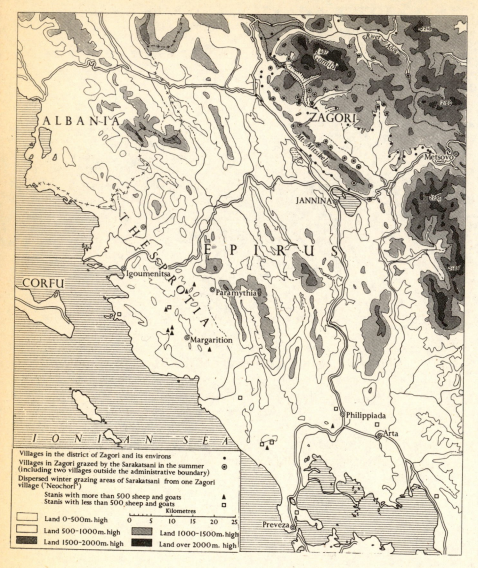

Villages in the district of Zagori and its environs
Villages in Zagori grazed by the Sarakatsani in the summer
(including two villages outside the administrative boundary)
Dispersed winter grazing areas of Sarakatsani from one Zagori
village ('Neochori')
Stanis with more than 500 sheep and goats
Stanis with less than 500 sheep and goats

Kilometres
0    5    10    15    20    25

Land 0-500m. high
Land 500-1000m. high          Land 1000-1500m. high
Land 1500-2000m. high         Land over 2000m. high

Map of the Epirus Indicating Summer and Winter Grazing Areas
of the Zagori Sarakatsani

# I

# HISTORICAL AND GEOGRAPHICAL INTRODUCTION

## 1. VLACHS

IN continental Greece north of Corinth the observant traveller is soon aware of communities of Greek-speaking transhumant shepherds known as Sarakatsani (Σαρακατσάνοι, or Σαρακατσαναῖοι). In the plains it is unnecessary even to leave the main roads to see small groups of circular, domed, huts of wood and thatch, or flocks of sheep and goats guarded by shepherds dressed in rough black suits and immense goat-hair capes woven from the fleeces of their own animals. From May until the first days of November these semi-nomad shepherds graze their considerable flocks on the higher slopes of the mountains, generally 3,000–6,000 feet above sea level; during the remainder of the year they live in the coastal plains. Simple facts of climate and relief, snow on the high ground in winter, in the summer burning heat in the plains, encourage this transhumance in a geographical area physically dominated by the ranges of the Pindus massif and the southern extremity of the Rhodope mountains. Epirus, Thessaly, Macedonia, and Thrace are the provinces in which they are most numerous but communities are found further south in continental Greece and some groups are established in the north of the Peloponnese and Euboea. In the whole of Greece their number, perhaps, approaches eighty thousand,[1] a population which was possibly absolutely greater a hundred years ago, but was certainly relatively more considerable as a fraction of the total inhabitants of the area.

The Greek villagers generally refer to the Sarakatsani simply as Vlachs (βλάχοι), that is shepherds who, in step with the rhythm of the seasons, lead their animals alternately down to the plains and up to the mountains. The occupational reference of the word, Vlach,[2] is an old one, already in use during the

---

[1] Mme Chatzimichalis arrives at a total of 81,473. Ἀγγελικὴ Χατζημιχάλη, Σαρακατσάνοι, Athens, 1957, vol. i, Part A, p. νβ'.

[2] See e.g. Anna Comnena, Ed. Bonn., i, p. 395. One of a number of references quoted by Mme Chatzimichalis, op. cit., vol. i, Part A, p. νς'.

Byzantine period. But it may also be used, in its original and
more specific sense, to describe Koutsovlachs (Κουτσοβλάχοι)
an ethnic minority group speaking a romance language akin to
Rumanian, or the related groups of Albanian Vlachs ('Αρβανι-
τοβλάχοι) who are trilingual, speaking the Koutsovlach language
as their mother tongue and Greek and Albanian for political
and commercial reasons. These different connotations of the
word, Vlach, have led to some confusion, which has been all
the greater because many Koutsovlachs lead a transhumant
shepherd life, identical in its general outline with that of the
Sarakatsani. To the uninitiated eye they may appear to dress
alike, to build the same type of thatched hut, and many of their
communities graze their flocks in areas of the Pindus mountains
neighbouring on those used by the Sarakatsani. The result has
been that many nineteenth-century travellers, and even some
Greek observers, failed to realize the existence of the Sarakatsani and imagined that all 'nomad' shepherds were Koutsovlachs of one kind or another.

But although many Koutsovlachs are transhumant shepherds, many are not. For instance, in the eastern half of the
Zagori district in Epirus, a majority of the Koutsovlach villagers
make their living from timber and agriculture. Probably since
the sixteenth century[3] a considerable number of Koutsovlachs
have been established in their own villages in the high Pindus.
They have pretensions to culture, and for generations sons of
rich Koutsovlach families have been prepared for commerce,
politics, and the professions. In these respects the Koutsovlachs
differ from the Albanian Vlachs who, in so far as they continue
to be recognized as 'Albanian', are generally concerned only
with shepherding. Some of these Albanian Vlachs have grazing
areas close to the Albanian frontier which until 1930 they were
able to cross in their search for winter pastures.

With both these ethnic minority groups, Koutsovlachs and
Albanian Vlachs, the Sarakatsani are culturally contrasted.
They speak only Greek; their values, institutions, and art forms
are in many respects markedly dissimilar from those of the
Koutsovlachs and Albanian Vlachs. They themselves claim
that the klephtic heroes Katsandonis and Karaïskakis were

[3] See A. J. B. Wace and M. S. Thompson, *Nomads of the Balkans*, London,
1914, p. 147.

Sarakatsani, and they believe that in blood and heroism their own contribution to the freedom of Greece was incomparable. At the same time they explicitly question the loyalty of the Koutsovlachs[4] or Albanian Vlachs, accusing them in the recent wars of collaboration or communist affiliations. Although they share a similar type of economy there is no sympathy between Sarakatsani and these other shepherds. They envy the Koutso-vlachs for their relative affluence and their established villages. And they are hostile to the Albanian Vlachs, because it is particularly with these groups that many Sarakatsani must compete for the limited areas of winter grazing land. Even the flesh of an Albanian Vlach, they say, does not smell like that of a Christian.[5] Intermarriage with these people is unknown and between the more traditional Sarakatsani and Koutsovlachs it is, at least, very rare.

In recent decades the problem of the origin of the Sarakatsan communities has provoked a considerable amount of writing. Interest was aroused more particularly after the publication in 1925 of a brilliant linguistic study of the Sarakatsan dialect by the Danish scholar, Carsten Höeg.[6] In the opening chapters of this work Höeg gives some ethnographic details of the communities he visited and presents a theory that these shepherds are the descendants of primitive pastoral tribes, which he believes must always have existed in this part of Greece from pre-classical times.[7] This view was naturally well received by Greek folklorists and historians. For equally obvious reasons it was strongly disputed by a number of Rumanian writers and publicists, of whom perhaps Theodor Capidan is the best known. Before the 1939–45 war these writers, continuing in a long tradition of Rumanian nationalist propaganda, were eager to stress the relationship between Rumanians and Koutsovlachs. (Indeed, even before the beginning of this century schools had been subsidized by Rumanian funds in the larger Koutsovlach

[4] In fact, from the period of the Revolution the contribution of the Koutsovlachs to the Greek State both in wealth and talent has been very considerable.

[5] Chatzimichalis, op. cit., vol. i, Part A, p. νη΄.

[6] Carsten Höeg, *Les Saracatsans*, Étude linguistique, 2 vols., Paris and Copenhagen, 1925 and 1926.

[7] P. Aravandinos had already made this claim in 1905. Π. Ἀραβαντινός, *Μονογραφία περὶ Κουτσοβλάχων*, Athens, 1905, p. 38.

villages.) But Capidan[8] and his followers also claimed that the Sarakatsani, far from being the descendants of ancient Greek tribesmen, were not Greeks at all, but Rumanian Koutsovlachs who in comparatively recent times had become hellenized.[9] The complete absence of any reference in Byzantine authors, or in writers of chronicles as late as the eighteenth century, to any communities of shepherds known as Sarakatsani, only increased the temptation to wild flights of speculative fancy by both sides to this controversy. In the absence of any certain historical data much of the argument centred around the interpretation of what little the Sarakatsani themselves had to say about their past, and a number of ingenious but quite improbable solutions to the etymology of the name Sarakatsanos.[10]

The various problems which surround the origins of the Sarakatsani may never find definitive solutions. The affairs of unlettered shepherds were not considered important by classical, Byzantine, or mediaeval writers. The probability that, as a consequence of the existing conditions of climate and relief, transhumant pastoralism of one kind or another has, from the earliest times, been a feature of Greek country life, has no doubt discouraged curiosity and comment. A hundred years ago a significantly higher proportion of the country people lived by the herding of sheep and goats, whether they belonged to genuinely transhumant communities, or to established villages which sent away their animals for six months of the year under the care of shepherds whose families remained in the village. It is only in the last fifty years that, with closer settlement and more intensive agriculture, groups of transhumant shepherds have become a somewhat anomalous element in Greek country life. But the emergence of the different Balkan nationalities is the factor which essentially explains this sudden interest in wandering shepherds. Before and after the Balkan Wars (1912–13),

[8] See Theodor Capidan, 'Saracacianii', *Dacoromania*, 1924–6, vol. 4, pp. 923-59.

[9] Cf. C. Jirec'ek, *Das Fürstentum Bulgarien*, Vienna, 1891, p. 118.

[10] A lucid review of these different solutions is found in an article by Δημ. Γεωργακᾶς, «Περὶ τῶν Σαρακατσαναίων τῆς Θράκης», Ἀρχεῖον τοῦ Θρακικοῦ Λαογραφικοῦ καὶ Γλωσσικοῦ Θησαυροῦ, 1945–6, vol. 12, pp. 105–28. The second part of this article, 1947–8, vol. 14, pp. 193 ff., is concerned with other aspects of the problem of origin.

folklorists and historians struggled with patriotic inventiveness to provide historical and ethnological evidence for the advance or validation of their various national frontiers in areas which under the unity imposed by the Byzantine and Ottoman Empires had become an inextricable patchwork of different ethnic and religious groups. The Sarakatsani were one element in this complex pattern. For under Turkish rule their seasonal migrations had led many of them across limits that were later to become the frontiers of Greece, with Albania, Yugoslavia, Bulgaria, and Turkey.

In these debates the Greeks and their supporters present the more convincing argument. They suggest that if the Sarakatsani were recently hellenized Koutsovlachs they would preserve at least some traces of a foreign origin in their language and customs. But Höeg has shown[11] that neither phonetically, nor in terms of grammatical structure, are there traces of Koutsovlach elements in the dialect spoken by the Sarakatsani. He also claims that the dialects of the Sarakatsani in Epirus, Macedonia, and Thessaly present a linguistic unity.[12] If the various groups of Sarakatsani had, indeed, been recently hellenized one would have expected them to speak the local dialect of the province in which they now find their grazing lands; and this is not the case. And he properly adds to these linguistic arguments information about the different marriage customs of the two groups.[13]

Where Höeg has used linguistic and ethnographic criteria, Mme Chatzimichalis also emphasizes the unity of Sarakatsan art forms,[14] which are simple, static, and geometric, do not vary from one province to another, and in the absence of naturalistic expression differ radically from those of the Koutsovlachs.

But the rebuttals by both these authors of the opinion that Sarakatsani are hellenized Koutsovlachs are only the preliminaries to their own more general theory that the Sarakatsani are the direct descendants of shepherd communities of preclassical Greece—a claim which it is equally difficult to prove

---

[11] Höeg, op. cit., vol. i, p. 78.
[12] Ibid., vol. i, preface, p. VIII.
[13] Ibid., vol. i, p. 81.
[14] Chatzimichalis, op. cit., vol. i, Part A, p. ρϛ′.

or disprove. Mme Chatzimichalis believes that they are a people, who, in their pastoral way of life, social organization, and art, show forth certain prototypical elements of early Greek culture.[15] She is much impressed, for instance, by the similarities between the motifs of Sarakatsan decorative art and those of the 'geometric' style of pre-classical Greece.

Professor Höeg claims that a comparison of the Sarakatsan dialect with the other dialects of continental Greece[16] suggests that it was formed some four or five centuries ago. Arrived at this point in time he observes that although the peoples which invaded the Balkans during the Middle Ages, i.e. the Slavs, Bulgars, Turks, and Tartars, were all of nomadic origin, they rapidly changed to an agricultural economy as soon as they were established in Europe. Further, it is only in quite exceptional circumstances that sedentary populations revert to nomadism. The Sarakatsan material culture, he argues, shows no trace of sedentary origins; on the contrary it follows with precision and simplicity from the conditions of transhumant life in a particular physical environment. And on the other hand Höeg is able to supply literary evidence[17] that forms of transhumance existed in classical and Hellenistic Greece; particularly in northern and north-western Greece. By a form of argument *ex ignorantia* we arrive at the conclusion that the Sarakatsani, a people without history, must always have lived in more or less the same conditions and areas as we find them today.

As is proper for a social anthropologist not concerned with the problem of origins, my own more limited conclusion is that in their social values and institutions, the Sarakatsani, as they exist today, provide no evidence of a past history that was ever anything but Greek. They still hold to what villagers now describe as 'the old customs', moral attitudes in family and community which a hundred years ago were general throughout Greek mountain communities, and still persist today, although now in conflict with other values of urban and alien origins.

---

[15] Ibid., vol. i, Part A, in the section 'Sarakatsani, nomads since ancient times?'

[16] Höeg, op. cit., vol. i, pp. 82 ff.

[17] For instance; Sophocles, Oedipus Rex, line 1135 ff.; Arrian, Anabasis, VII.9.2.

## 2. THE SARAKATSANI OF ZAGORI

The community of Sarakatsan shepherds which I describe in this study numbers about 4,000 souls.[18] In summer they are found in Zagori, a mountainous district north-east of the town of Jannina on the western limits of the Pindus range in the province of Epirus. Here they graze their sheep and goats from May until the early days of November; or as they would calculate it, between the feast-days of St. George and St. Demetrius which mark their seasonal migrations between plain and mountain (and are celebrated according to the old Julian calendar, that is, on the 6th May and the 8th November by the new calendar). In each Zagori village with high grasslands there is a local gathering of Sarakatsan families which exploit the grazing land of the community and add to it a summer population of 100–300 men, women, and children. Since 1938 the majority of these shepherd families have enjoyed the same citizenship and grazing rights as the sedentary villagers of Zagori from whom previously they had to rent their pastures. There are 152,000 sheep and goats in the Zagori of which 85,000 sheep and 13,000 goats belong to the Sarakatsani.[19] Although the eastern villages of the district are Koutsovlach in speech and sentiment very few of their inhabitants are, any longer, transhumant shepherds, and the pastures of these villages are used by the Sarakatsani, who indeed occupy almost all the higher pastures of the district, grazing their flocks on the lands of 30 of the 43 villages which today constitute Zagori; the remaining villages are low lying (where it is easier to keep animals throughout the year), or they are without extensive areas of grass.

In the winter the community is more widely dispersed. The Sarakatsani move down from the mountains to the coastal plains and valleys over an area which extends from the Albanian frontier as far south as the towns of Arta and Preveza and even

[18] There are no census details for the Sarakatsani as such. And police restriction on my movements prevented me from carrying out a complete survey of all the sheep villages in Zagori. However, on the basis of my own incomplete figures and information supplied by the Ministry of Agriculture for pastoralism in Zagori generally, this figure is most unlikely to be far from the truth.

[19] Thus there are 24·5 sheep and goats per head of population among the Zagori Sarakatsani.

beyond. Here many of the shepherds have no grazing rights and they must rent pasture sometimes at great cost from village communities or private individuals. Since the first world war the settlement of refugees and more intensive farming techniques have progressively reduced the area of grassland in the plains. Each year the search for winter grass by the Sarakatsani becomes wider and more desperate. But quite apart from the greater geographical dispersion of the community in winter, the problems of weather and lambing isolate the shepherds of each flock whose only concern during these months is the care of their animals. In summer, although the Sarakatsani are still dispersed over 390 square miles of mountainous country, there is time to visit kinsmen who live at a distance, weddings and festivals are celebrated, and in general there is a greater awareness of the community and its life. Winter in the plains is a kind of exile; the return in spring to the mountains of Zagori is the return home.

The pattern of social groupings in this community is extremely simple. The most restricted unit is the most important. This is the family, whether in its elementary or extended form. To this small group the individual owes almost exclusively his or her time, energy, and loyalties. However, the family group is normally unable to manage its flocks without some assistance from outside and, in these circumstances, two, three, or more families related by kinship or marriage, associate to form 'a company' (παρέα), or stani (στάνη)[20], which for functional reasons must include at least four adult males and generally numbers between 15 and 50 persons of all ages. But the duties which the individual assumes as a member of the 'company' are specific and have an obvious relation to the welfare of his family. The relationship between the constituent families of the group is contractual; any family may elect to leave the association whenever it wills, any family may be expelled by the decision of the other members. Apart from this participation in a group of co-operating and related families, the shepherd normally has no membership in other social groupings which might conflict with his exclusive duties to the family.

[20] I shall employ these terms interchangeably, generally using 'company' when the emphasis is on the relations of co-operation between the constituent families of the group, and 'stani' when the context refers to the undifferentiated group with its huts, flocks, and grazing land.

It is believed by the Sarakatsani that the interests of unrelated families are opposed and, indeed, mutually destructive. The local gathering of families which in summer happen to graze the pastures and enjoy citizenship rights of the same village, has little cohesion as a group except when on a rare occasion, such as a village festival, it breaks into brief and violent opposition to the villagers; and it has no organization beyond the ephemeral political combinations which appear at the time of local village elections. The idea of the total community is, of course, important; it represents a way of life in opposition to the ways of peasants, merchants, and bureaucrats. But the community, too, lacks any structure of authority or effective organization; and, in part, for the same reasons, that is to say the solidarity, exclusiveness, and mutual opposition of the families which form it.

While it is true that the total community (or the local gathering of families as a segment of it) is not an organized social group, it nevertheless defines a social space within which values are shared and the conduct of men and women is evaluated by other Sarakatsani. These values concern, especially, right ways of acting in family and kinship roles and the sex-linked moral characteristics which a man or woman ought to exhibit when he, or she, stands forward as the protagonist of the family and the guardian of its honour. Such evaluations imply a hierarchy of prestige. And it is precisely through mutual competition in terms of strength, wealth, and a reputation for honour, that the opposed families, and groups of related families, are associated with one another in a coherent and regular manner.

To these general features of the community it is necessary to add a brief consideration of particular geographical and historical factors which help to explain the presence of the Sarakatsani in the Zagori. Geographically Zagori is the western flank of the Pindus range immediately north of the approaches to the Metsovo pass, which forms its southern boundary; the mountain Mitsikeli is its western limit, and the sweep of the river Aóös contains it from the east and the north. The ridges of the Pindus, which effectively separate the eastern and western coastal plains of continental Greece, run in a north-west to south-east direction. The vast pressures which created these folds came from the east so that the escarpments present extremely abrupt precipices and tend to 'lean over' towards the west. Thus, in general, the western slopes of the Pindus, as in parts of Zagori, present an extremely difficult terrain over which movement is not easy. Many of the valleys are narrow and steep-sided and the two principal rivers Aóös and Vikos lie in deep and formidable ravines. The canyon of Vikos is a remarkable natural feature 4,000 ft. in depth.

The most important sheep grazing area of the Zagori is the Gamila feature whose highest peak is 8,140 ft. above sea level. On the higher slopes of this mountain the important sheep villages of Papingo, Tsepelevo, Kapesovo, Vradeto, and Skamneli, to mention only the villages on its western flank, graze 33,000 sheep and goats. The rocks of this mountain, as of the other high peaks in Zagori, are of limestone formation; but the smaller features and the valleys are mostly rocks of sandstone. At the contact lines between the permeable limestone and the sandstone there are often springs and streams fed by the melting snows and the abundant rain, for this is the wettest area of Greece with, in places, an annual rainfall of 50 inches. The limestone slopes produce a sparse but fine grass which the shepherds claim is the best grazing for the milking or pregnant ewe. On some of the lower slopes in the eastern Zagori, especially those which face eastwards, there are considerable forests of silver fir and Corsican pine and a grass which is more luxuriant. The shepherds, however, prefer the thin grasses of the open limestone slopes, and comparative figures of milk yields appear to support this preference.

The more important grazing villages of the Zagori are situated 3,000–4,000 ft. above sea level and the pastures are generally found above the village to an altitude sometimes as high as 6,000 ft. Snow falls on the higher pastures as early as the first days in November and the villages themselves are often deep in snow from Christmas until the middle of March. These are the physical and climatic conditions which lead to the transhumant economy—abundant and, generally, well watered summer grasslands with maximum day temperatures which seldom exceed 80°F. in the village, or 70°F. on the higher pastures, but snow and bitter cold which force the shepherds to take their animals to the plains in winter. In the higher villages of Zagori a few sheep and goats are kept under cover during the winter, but there is neither enough hay nor sufficient steading to attempt this on any considerable scale. Similarly, villagers in the plains may keep some sheep through the summer despite a smothering heat and parched grazing. But the condition of these animals is meagre.

Yet it was the Sarakatsani rather than the people of Zagori who exploited, and continue to exploit, these pastoral resources of grass and water; and this is a fact that has to be explained on historical grounds.

The Turks under Sinan Pasha captured Jannina in 1430, and that part of Epirus which now lies between the Albanian frontier and the town of Arta remained an Ottoman possession until its cession to Greece as recently as 1913. From the earliest period of the occupation a majority of these lands were divided into military fiefs. The fief-holders, tenants-in-chief, in exchange for certain military commitments enjoyed the revenue from a number of taxes including the tithe of one-tenth, but the cultivators, mainly Christians, possessed a right of secure tenure in their land which lapsed only if they did not cultivate it over a period of three years. From time to time, however, and by various methods (often through the expropriation of the rights of peasants who had fallen into debt), fiefs were converted into private properties, chiftliks, on which the villagers became métayers, conceding half the produce of their cultivations to the landowner and possessing no certain rights of tenure which the latter did not choose to recognize.

The villages of Zagori, however, succeeded not only in defending their limited rights as Christian villagers in military fiefs but also in persuading the Turks to grant them other and more important privileges. By the eighteenth century the forty-six villages had developed a confederate alliance. Each village elected a representative to a council which in turn appointed a general intendant for Zagori who was established in Jannina as administrator of the confederation's affairs in liaison with the Ottoman authorities. There were three essential privileges which it was the task of this representative to defend; the right of the confederation to collect and deliver to the imperial government taxes owed by the member villages (other than the dues payable to the fief-holders); the right of Zagori villages to administer their own affairs, to hear cases of civil law between citizens of Zagori, and to maintain a small force of village guards; an undertaking by the Turkish Governor not to establish Government representatives within the boundaries of the district. There were reciprocal benefits in these arrangements. The Zagori was protected from the capricious exploitation of direct administration and tax collection which threatened the villages with indebtedness, conversion into private estates, and the consequent loss of private and communal rights to land. The Turkish authorities, whose principal concerns were internal security and regular fiscal supplies, gained as faithful and dependent allies a community in an area difficult to police, along whose southern boundary ran the important but hazardous line of communication to Metsovo and Thessaly.[21]

In the late eighteenth and throughout the nineteenth century the Zagori was, by the standards of Greek country life, rich. But the source of this wealth was not local. Sons whose presence was not urgently needed at home travelled to the more prosperous towns of the Empire particularly in Rumania. In these places they established businesses of various kinds from humble bakeries to important merchant houses. Others became doctors and teachers. A man once established created openings for kinsmen. These migrants were known as 'travellers' (ταξιδιῶτες); for the implication was that they would eventually return. A man generally returned to his village when he was about 25 years of age and took a wife from his own or another Zagori village. He remained with his new wife for perhaps three or four months, generally until her pregnancy was established. He then returned to his business or professional position abroad leaving his wife behind in his parents' home. Every four or five years he paid further visits to the village to see his family and perhaps to increase it, until he had amassed enough wealth to build a substantial house and fill it with elegant carpets, furniture, and icons. Into this he retired from his business or profession and passed the later years of his life playing the role of a 'notable' in village life and politics.

This curious form of emigration was practised in other parts of Greece but perhaps nowhere more intensively than in Zagori. But the degree to which it was developed was dependent upon

[21] Ἰωάννης Λαμπρίδης, «Ζαγοριακά» in Ἠπειρωτικὰ Μελετήματα, Athens, 1889, gives a useful but sometimes uncritical account of Zagori history.

the privileges of self-administration that have been described and which were not finally abrogated until 1866. So many men could not have left their families and villages unprotected, nor would there have been any security for the wealth they amassed, had the reciprocal rights and obligations of the authorities and the Zagori villages not been clearly acknowledged on both sides. In this situation an important sanction was the presence in Constantinople of a number of rich Zagori notables able to communicate the grievances of their compatriots directly to the Sultan. Not only were they able to dispense bribes to high officials on behalf of the confederation but they supplied the central Government with intelligence about the movements and intentions of the local governor in Jannina who was not infrequently intriguing against his own masters in Constantinople. Even in the case of Ali the Lion, the most powerful and greedy of Jannina's rulers, an awareness of this introduced some restraint into his dealings with the Zagori.

This concern with commerce and the professions, and the imperial ambience in which their local politics were implicated, gave the inhabitants of these villages a cosmopolitan rather than a peasant outlook. It is true that until 1912 they assiduously worked the small pockets of cultivable land and tended their vines and fruit trees, but generally with the manpower of gipsies or families of lower status. A few men of Zagori possessed large flocks of sheep but no self-respecting citizen of this district could himself lead the life of a shepherd. Consequently by the nineteenth century, if not earlier, shepherding in central, western, and much of eastern Zagori, whether of village sheep or their own, was in the hands of the Sarakatsani.

The villages in the plains of Jannina, Arta, and Preveza were in a different and less enviable situation. Originally many of their lands had been military fiefs. In terms of agricultural wealth they were richer than mountain villages but geographically they were more vulnerable to intimidation and exploitation. By the kind of process that has been described, most of these fiefs in time became private estates, chiftliks. By the early nineteenth century these areas had been considerably depopulated as a consequence of the capricious administration of chiftlik proprietors or their agents, and through looting by Albanian bands in the frequent disturbances of civil order during this period. Both in the chiftliks and the extensive monastery lands there were considerable tracts of uncultivated grassland.

Therefore, the very different fortunes of the villagers in the Zagori mountains and those living in the plains, both, alike, encouraged the transhumant sheep economy of the Sarakatsani throughout the nineteenth century and until 1922. The inhabitants of Zagori were primarily interested in the life abroad, not in fully exploiting the pasturage resources of their villages. And the influx of wealth had aroused various pretensions to education and social status which could scarcely be accommodated with a life of transhumant nomadism. In the higher villages, apart from the few animals which it was possible to keep under cover through the winter, the pastures were generally empty, and the villages were willing to rent large tracts of grazing land to wealthy Sarakatsan shepherds who might lead groups of families controlling two or three thousand sheep. This arrangement brought revenue to the village. And it sometimes established relations of patronage through which the villagers were informed about the movements of brigands who periodically descended on their rich houses; or when hostages had been taken shepherds were often the channel of mediation and negotiation. Similarly, in the plains, monasteries and chiftlik owners were equally ready to lease their uncultivated grassland in the winter, often for a nominal payment when the Sarakatsani undertook to graze the sheep of the monastery or chiftlik as well as their own. These conditions of adequate grassland in summer and winter, and in certain respects a complementarity of interests between Zagori villages and the Sarakatsani in the mountains, and in the plains between the Sarakatsani and the owners or administrators of large estates, persisted generally until the period of the first world war.

But in 1922 the military defeat in Asia Minor led in the years which followed to the exchange of population between Greece and Turkey. One of the measures taken by the Government for the re-settlement of refugees was the division of chiftlik and monastery lands into peasant holdings and the building of new villages. By 1927 the old winter pastures of the Zagori Sarakatsani had largely vanished. Some of the richer shepherds had the foresight to buy small properties in the Arta and Preveza plains and reduced the size of their flocks. Others found small pastures in the area around Paramythia and until 1930 some families, at least, were able to cross the Albanian frontier for their winter grass. In 1944 the flight into Albania of the Muslim villagers of Thesprotia opened new areas of grazing to the Sarakatsani of Zagori, but these, too, are now less extensive after the settlement of refugees from Northern Epirus and the claims of Christian villagers who live in the district. Generally since 1927, when the division of chiftlik lands was substantially effected, the difficulties over winter grazing have grown more acute each year. By 1955 it was seldom possible to find winter grazing for a flock of more than 1,000 sheep in one area. One consequence has been the reduction in the size of the flocks of leading Sarakatsan families. Before 1922 it was not exceptional for a man to own 2,000 sheep; today a flock of 500 is considerable.

The disappearance of winter grassland threatened the basis of transhumant pastoralism not only in Epirus but also in the other provinces of continental Greece. Although they could do little to alter fundamentally the new conditions they had created by the distribution of winter grassland for cultivation, the Government attempted in 1930 to protect the position of the shepherds by a law[22] establishing rights of protected lease (δικαιώματα ἐνοικιοστασίου), so that a shepherd who had enjoyed a grazing lease on a pasture during one winter had the right to return to it in the following autumn (and at a price determined by the Government). There remained, however, various conditions under which such leases might lapse, and the area of available grazing continued to decrease, although now at a less disastrous pace.

After 1922 grazing conditions did not change radically in the Zagori. The temporary emigration of Zagori men to other parts of the Ottoman Empire was replaced by the permanent emigration of whole families of Zagori villagers to the towns and cities of the Greek kingdom. But the grasslands remained to be exploited by the Sarakatsani. In 1938, however, a law[23] was passed by the Government of Metaxas that was to have important

---

[22] Law 4818 of 14/16 July 1930, 'Concerning the lease of grazing lands'.
[23] Decree 1223 of 3/4 May 1938, 'Concerning the settlement of Pastoralists'.

consequences. It instructed that the names of semi-nomad shepherds should be added to the citizenship roll of either the summer or the winter village of their grazing grounds. A majority of the Sarakatsani with grazing in the western and central Zagori elected to write their names on the roll of their summer village.[24] The purpose of the central government was to control an untidy and potentially disorderly element in a state based on the village community of settled peasantry. However, the proud villagers of Zagori with their inherited pretensions were deeply dismayed at this act of arbitrary legislation. While their own youth left for the town and city, rights of citizenship in the villages were by law extended to uncivilized and uneducated shepherds. Traditionally the Sarakatsani had built their summer huts on the grazing land they leased. But now possessing the rights of village citizenship, some bought houses in the depopulated village and others began to build their groups of huts on its outskirts. Daily contact between the two communities in these circumstances intensified their traditional antipathy. Yet at the same time the newly acquired local voting rights necessarily integrated the Sarakatsani into the village patronage system, and the villagers' attitude of open contempt forced them slowly but certainly to a growing conformity with village habits at least in their more outward and material aspects.

There were also important changes in the forms of co-operation between families within the community. Previously the grazing of areas carrying two or three thousand sheep had been sold each year by Zagori villages to the leading families of Sarakatsani. For these alone had the wealth and experience to carry through the negotiation. Through the lease of this grazing, the head of such a family, the tselingas (τσέλιγγας), also controlled a number of other families who contracted to work with him for the summer or winter period. The nucleus of the group was co-operating families (σμίχτες) often related by kinship or marriage; but a number of unrelated men with few or no animals of their own were also associated as wage shepherds.

---

[24] However, a village could resist the application if it was able to show that grazing land was not available. Since the pressure on grazing land was greater in the plains, Sarakatsani often had no other choice but to apply for citizenship in a mountain village.

In its physical aspect as a complex of flocks, grazing lands, huts, and sheep-folds it was referred to as a stani (στάνη), or when the speaker was more concerned with the relations of dependence and co-operation between the tselingas and his followers, as the 'tselingato' (τὸ τσελιγκᾶτο); 50–150 men, women and children were the approximate human limits of the traditional stani. Although the co-operating families paid at the end of each period of six months for a share of the grazing land in proportion to the size of their flocks, the power of the tselingas was great. Since the lease was his own, a family unwilling to accept his authority could be expelled. The sale of milk, meat, and wool, the purchase of flour, salt, and other essential needs of the stani, were entirely in his hands. Through the six-month period the other families lived on his credit, and at its close his detailed calculations of profit and debt were necessarily taken on trust since he was often the only literate man in the group.

The measures of 1930 concerning protected leases had already modified the power of the tselingas since not only he but all his associated shepherds were individually protected under the law. But the regulations of Metaxas radically reinforced this trend since now each shepherd citizen was firmly entitled to graze his sheep for six months on the communal grassland of his own village. Thus in the summer pastures of the Zagori villages where a majority of the community had claimed their rights of citizenship, the size of the stani became more narrowly related to the simple needs of sheep management. In general, it became smaller in numbers, seldom exceeding 30 men, women, and children, but sometimes including only the members of a single family; its members were now almost exclusively kinsmen and affinal relations; its structure was looser and more egalitarian. There were parallel changes in the size and form of the winter stani. The winter groups, however, remained somewhat larger (up to 50 persons of all ages and sometimes more), since with lambing and milking more hands are needed in winter than summer. Moreover, with the shortage of winter grazing any man with land at his disposal, which for one reason or another was not subject to a protected lease, was still able to hold in a position of dependence as many sheep and men as his land would carry.

A further consequence was that the poorer shepherds.

relieved from the various pressures that the tselingas had previously been able to apply, and now entitled to secure grazing rights, were able gradually to increase their flocks or, if they were wage shepherds, to build up a small flock that had not previously existed. At the same time the impossibility of finding considerable tracts of winter grazing forced the rich tselingas to reduce the size of his flocks below the formerly modest limit of a thousand. The conjunction of these trends has led to a more even distribution of wealth in the community.

I have indicated some of the geographical and historical conditions that help to explain the presence of the Sarakatsani in Zagori. And I have referred to more recent developments that have introduced important changes in the internal structure of the community and in its relation to the outside world. But these general considerations also emphasize the inherent vulnerability of a transhumant shepherd community in a society of settled villages. Historically, and still today, the village is the important political and social unit in rural Greece. Its elected officials are used by the Greek Government in many matters (as they were by the Ottomans) as the final link in the bureaucratic hierarchy. They are a channel of government and a channel of patronage. Yet many of the Sarakatsani of Zagori still have no secure political rights in the plains where their difficulties are greatest. There, many stand outside the political body of the village, membership of which would grant them each year the right on which their survival as a community depends, the right to graze.

# II

## OF SHEEP AND SHEPHERDS

### 1. THE FLOCKS

SARAKATSANI are deeply concerned about three things; sheep, children (particularly sons), and honour. It is a common feature of many pastoral peoples with simple material cultures that they are highly dependent on their physical environment[1] and that the care of herds, the structure of the community, and its social values, form a coherent pattern of activities and sentiments which presents few inconsistencies. The three concerns of the Sarakatsani are mutually implicated. The sheep support the life and prestige of the family, the sons serve the flocks and protect the honour of their parents and sisters, and the notion of honour presupposes physical and moral capacities that fit the shepherds for the hard and sometimes dangerous work of following and protecting their animals.

In the winter and spring the Sarakatsani divide their animals into four flocks. The most important of these divisions is the flock of pregnant ewes or, after lambing, the milking ewes (τὰ γαλάρια). In the second flock are the rams, and the sterile ewes which were not successfully mated in the summer (τὰ στέρφα). The third division is a small flock of the last season's ewe lambs (τὰ ζυγούρια).[2] And finally there are the goats. Although sheep and goats are the property of families, and are identified by different ear-signs, the constituent families of a stani do not separate their animals. One flock of pregnant ewes is formed from all the stock of the different families; and similarly for the other categories. These dispositions are influenced partly by the difficulty of shepherding efficiently more than 250 animals in a single flock on grazing land which is often broken ground, always without fencing, and where wolves and wild dogs make frequent raids by night. But an even more important factor is that since grassland is generally natural, not cultivated, the

---

[1] See E. E. Evans-Pritchard, *The Nuer*, Oxford, 1940, p. 16.

[2] The Sarakatsani also keep a few wethers (τὰ γκιουσέμια), which grow larger in stature than entire animals and are used as leaders of the various flocks.

quality of any tract of grazing land is seldom homogeneous. In these circumstances the best grass must be reserved for the pregnant ewes to strengthen them before lambing, and afterwards to maintain their milk yield at the highest possible level. For the prosperity of the stani depends on the crop of lambs and the amount of milk that is sold to the cheese merchant.

The physical plan of a stani in winter varies in detail with the character of the grazing but certain features are almost always present. The huts of the stani, the group of co-operating families, are established on or close to the best grassland, on flat ground, sheltered from the prevailing wind, and as near as possible to water, although in practice a spring or well may be a mile away and sometimes farther. The huts are generally close together but in no regular pattern; although if brothers, as is generally the case, form the nucleus of the group, they build their homes next to one another with the huts of cousins and other relatives on the periphery. The size of the winter stani varies. It is restricted, as I have suggested in the previous chapter, by the difficulties of finding enough winter grazing land. But a lower limit is also drawn by the minimum requirement of four active adult shepherds and a young goatherd, a working force that makes it barely possible to work the scheme of shepherding that has been described.

In November, when the sheep arrive from the mountains, the pregnant ewes are not allowed to pasture indiscriminately on the better grasslands (γαλαροτόπι) reserved for their use after lambing. Until Christmas, when the lambing period begins, they graze only on the rougher and higher sections of this grassland perhaps a mile, or more, from the huts. In this area the women help the shepherds to build a circular sheep-fold (γρέχι) constructed from bundles of brushwood tied to one another and sometimes secured to posts. In this the ewes sleep and find some relief from the cold and the driving rain. Outside the women erect a small refuge of branches and thatch (χαλατζούκα) for the two shepherds who guard them.

In the early days of December the women tie together branches to make wooden frames, 5 ft. 6 in. in height and 4 ft. wide (λισιές), on which they interlace other more pliable branches and bind bundles of reeds, grass, or ferns. With these portable frames the shepherds and their women set up another circular sheep-fold on level well-drained land close to the huts. Each frame leans towards the centre at an angle of 60° to the ground and is supported by a forked branch. In the lee of this inclined wall the animals press together for warmth and protection. During the last days of December and the first ten days of the New Year most of the lambs are born. As each ewe drops its lamb, the two animals are brought down from the pen on the rough pasture at dawn and dusk by relays of unmarried girls, and are placed in the new sheep-fold close to the huts. By the middle of January the whole flock of ewes with their lambs is together once more. Once the lambs are born the yield of milk becomes the main concern. The ewes are now grazed intensively on the best grassland which is divided into plots or strips (ἀπολυσιές) used in daily rotation. Under present conditions, however, few stanis possess enough winter grassland, and for some weeks before lambing and until the move to the mountains in the spring, the milking ewes are also fed each morning with weighed quantities of maize, oats, or cotton-cake.

On the first of February the cheese merchant sets up his station (μπατζαριό) close to the grassland of the largest stani in the neighbourhood. In return for this convenience the women of this stani build two thatched huts; in one the cheese-maker and his assistant sleep, work, and keep their equipment, cauldrons, churns, and the cream separator; the other, which is entered only through a low trap-door from the first hut, and is sunk three feet below the surface of the ground, is used for the storage of the cheeses[3] on beds of fern leaves under the necessary conditions of stillness and humidity. The women must also supply the cheese-maker with water and firewood.

Cash and credit at this time of year are very short for the Sarakatsani and there is now a great urgency to sell milk. Every effort is made to wean the male lambs quickly. The ewes are seldom allowed to suckle these lambs for longer than four weeks before they are sold to an animal dealer for the spring lamb market; a few only are kept back to maintain the right proportion of rams to ewes in the flock. This sale of lambs brings

[3] Cheese merchants separate some of the cream to make butter. From the separated milk they make a hard cheese known as κεφαλοτύρι; and, then, from the remaining liquid a form of cheese known as μυζήθρα.

in an immediate sum of money, and if the quantity of milk then
released is an encouraging amount the merchant may be persuaded to make another advance of credit. Before the first of
February the shepherds will have prepared the milking pen
(στρούγκα) as close as possible to the cheese-maker's station.
The pen is a circular or elliptical enclosure of stones or brushwood with a wide opening, or 'mouth', at one end through
which the sheep are driven in, and a narrow opening, or 'eye',
at the other end through which the sheep are taken in turn to
be milked by the shepherds who sit on flat stones on either side
of this narrow passage. At first in the early days of February only
a little milk is taken, for the ewes are still with their lambs. But
the amount steadily increases after the sale of the male lambs.
However, none of the ewe lambs is sold unless the family is in
great difficulty. And anxious as the Sarakatsani are to sell all
their milk they will not endanger their development by weaning
them too quickly; for the future of the flock depends upon the
condition of these animals, which in two years' time produce
their first lambs. The ewes are allowed to suckle them for seven
or eight weeks and it is not until early March that they are
finally weaned or 'cut', and that the flow of milk to the cheese-
maker becomes considerable.

The three other flocks of the stani divide the remaining
grazing according to their needs. The best of this is allotted to
the young 'zigouria', the lambs of the previous season. The flock
of rams, with the ewes which remained sterile after the summer
mating, go to the highest and roughest grazing since they are
strong and resistant to cold, and this is generally the most
distant flock of sheep from the huts. In both cases a sheep-fold
of brushwood, and refuges of branches and thatch for the shepherds, are built to protect animals and men from the winter
storms and rain.

The goats guarded by one or two young and nimble goatherds feed on whatever is unsuitable or inaccessible to the sheep,
especially the leaves of scrub-oak and other trees and bushes.
Since goats seldom represent more than 20 per cent of the total
stock of Sarakatsan families from Zagori no attempt is made to
form more than one flock. At the end of November after they
have repaired or remade the family huts the women begin to
build the elaborate goat-pen with latticed sides at least six feet

high, and a narrow three-foot wide roof of thatch inclined towards the centre of the pen, which has an elliptical form. Goats
are less resistant to cold weather than sheep, and the kids which
are born towards the end of December very easily contract
pneumonia during the first six weeks of life. After the kids are
born the goats graze during the day on rough ground not too
far distant from the pen which is itself positioned close to the
huts but away from the sheep-fold. They return in the evening
to feed their kids during the night, but the latter remain in the
pen during the day enclosed for warmth in a small conical
thatched shelter (τσάρκος) built into the wall at the far end of
the pen. But the Sarakatsani add that a further reason for
keeping them in the pen during the day is that they are greedy
and ferocious feeders. After four weeks the women begin to
feed the kids with the leaves of bushes which they cut and
carry into the pen. Each day they are grazed for an hour
or two on any convenient piece of rough ground. Finally, in the
early days of March the goatherds 'cut' the kids from their
mothers, and the flock returns to its distant pastures. The kids
sleep alone in the pen each night and are grazed by a young
boy during the day.

The summer dispositions of the stani are different and simpler.
The leader of a stani is allotted by the president of the village
two areas of grazing: one for milking ewes, and another for the
remainder of his flock—the rams and sterile ewes, and the
winter's ewe lambs (the 'sterpha', and the 'zigouria') which are
now merged into one flock. The two areas are not necessarily
adjacent and both are generally far from the village, two or three
hours' steep climbing away. The families remain in the village
in houses or huts and are able to turn away from their exclusive
concern for the animals which held every moment of their
attention during the winter months. The difficult period of the
year is over and they now turn outwards, as it were, to the
affairs of the total community, to betrothals, marriages, quarrels,
and mutual criticism; and to their relations of clientage and
hostility to the villagers of Zagori.

Meanwhile, however, the Sarakatsani continue to sell their
milk throughout June and until the last days of July. A cheese
merchant sets up a station positioned to serve a number of
neighbouring grazing areas. And where the boundaries of these

grazing areas permit the arrangement, four or five milking pens of different stanis may be conveniently within sight of the cheese-maker's hut.

Summer is not entirely without its anxieties. In June the rams are allowed to run with the milking ewes, each ram, on average, covering twenty-five ewes. An early and successful mating season (μαρκάλος) is important because it promises few sterile ewes, lambing before the hard winter weather sets in, and earlier supplies of milk. Before the end of July the cheese-maker departs, and the shepherds begin to enjoy a period of relative ease. What milk the ewes continue to give during the early days of August before lactation finally ceases, is used, like the milk that is taken before the first of February and during the ten days of the journey to the mountains, to make a rough 'feta' cheese for the family's own use.

\* \* \*

The needs of the sheep in a particular physical and political environment, and the arrangements made by the Sarakatsani to meet them, have certain consequences for Sarakatsan social life. One of these concerns seasonal differences. In the winter the community is geographically more dispersed, stanis travel far in different directions to find their winter grass and very often they do not have other Sarakatsani as their immediate neighbours. On the other hand the stani itself is physically more concentrated. A sheep requires only a quarter of an acre of good grass in the plain as against half an acre or more in the mountains. The stani is turned in on its own affairs. The huts of the stani are on the grazing land and the group of families is concerned almost exclusively with the problems of lambing, milk, and the protection of the animals against cold and wolves. In the summer, for reasons which have been mentioned in the previous chapter, stanis are generally smaller, and sometimes may be no larger than a single family. The stani is also dispersed. The families live in houses or huts in the village, the shepherds with the two flocks of sheep and the goats are far above the village, and are separated from one another. Yet the community itself is more concentrated than in winter. In the local group of families that graze the land of the same village, the huts or houses of the different families are in sight and often sound of one another. And although the grazing areas high above the village are spatially more extensive than in winter, they are, however, overstocked. Shepherds have a common grazing boundary with the sheep of two or three other stanis on whose grass they systematically trespass. Between families unconnected by kinship or marriage, relations, acted out during these months in terms of reciprocal hostility and theft, are more intense than in winter. Summer, indeed, is the time for quarrels. It is also the season of festivals. It is true that, if the total community is less dispersed than in winter, this is a relative difference since it is still disposed over an area of some 390 square miles. But summer shepherding conditions allow shepherds the possibility of visiting kinsmen who live at a distance. At weddings and village festivals kinsmen are able to meet and exchange their news, and unrelated men have the opportunity to observe one another critically. In summer, generally, social exchanges whether friendly or hostile are both more frequent and more ardent.

Practical arrangements for the care of the flock have a further consequence. Personal and family honour and pride, which are fundamental values of the community, breed a spirit of intense and aggressive competitiveness that sometimes threatens even the relations of unmarried brothers, more commonly the co-operation between more distant kin in the same stani, and frequently provokes verbal or physical quarrels between shepherds unrelated by kinship or marriage. Yet the simple circumstance that within the one stani each shepherd is physically isolated, or with only a single companion, in the service of the different flocks which have been described, limits the potential moments of disharmony in the family and the stani. The animals allow their protectors no rest except when they sleep themselves; otherwise they must continually graze to remain alive and the shepherds must continually follow them because of the absence of fencing and the presence of wolves and sometimes of human thieves. Each shepherd is insulated, as it were, by his work. In the winter, moreover, the shepherds may be more or less isolated from contact with other unrelated shepherds since there is often no grazing boundary with another stani. In the summer, it is true, there may be common grazing boundaries with two or three different stanis across which shepherds face one another on terms of hostility and reciprocal trespass. Yet even then, if we consider the community as a whole, the directions in which the shepherds of one stani may show active aggression are limited, as also are the form and degree of its expression, simply because a shepherd cannot leave his sheep. And this also makes it possible for unrelated shepherds to feel, but not very often to express, an intensity of hostility for one another that would otherwise reduce a vulnerable community of shepherds to a condition of anarchy if confrontations were more numerous than, in fact, they are.

## 2. THE SHEPHERDS

For the Sarakatsani, sheep and goats, men and women, are important and related oppositions with a moral reference. Sheep are peculiarly God's animals, and their shepherds, made in His image, are essentially noble beings. Women through the particular sensuality of their natures are inherently more likely to have relations with the Devil; and goats were originally the animals of the Devil which Christ captured and tamed for the service of man. It is consistent with these ideas that sheep and shepherds in their respective animal and human worlds display ideal moral characteristics. Sheep are docile, enduring, pure, and intelligent. When the shepherd carries out a small veterinary operation or when the ewe gives birth, the animal suffers in silence. To match this purity and passive courage shepherds ought to be fearless and devoted guardians, and clean in the ritual sense. After sexual intercourse a shepherd must carefully wash his hands before milking sheep and it is generally preferable that the two shepherds of the flock of milking ewes should be unmarried men.

Whether or not shepherds require quite the degree of courage that the values of the community insist they do, is open to doubt. Perhaps devotion, endurance, and a head for heights, would be a more objective assessment. Two experienced shepherds, preferably men between twenty-five and thirty years of age, guard the pregnant or milking ewes. Another young and active shepherd follows the flock of last season's lambs, the 'zigouria'. One or two older but not necessarily intelligent men watch the rams and sterile ewes, the 'sterpha'. Young shepherds before their military service often serve their apprenticeship with the goats, a severe enough test of agility and endurance. One goat-herd is normally sufficient but he needs a companion when the kids begin to be born. If the manpower of the stani is sufficient a young shepherd will graze and work the mules and horses. And often an old grandfather will graze the flock of lambs near the huts for a few weeks after they have been weaned, or will relieve a son or nephew with one of the flocks so that he may take a day's rest at the huts. Although the myth is cultivated that shepherds are particularly skilled in those tasks which they happen to be performing and that each of these tasks is equally necessary for the well-being of the stani, in fact any adult Sarakatsanos can do the work of any other; there are no specialists.

It is tacitly understood that the post of honour is the care of the milking ewes, for the future of the stani depends on the lambs and the milk. In the autumn these shepherds set out each day at dawn from the sheep-fold which may be a mile or more from the huts, grazing the ewes on the outlying areas of the better grassland. The sheep are not as intelligent as the Sara-katsani claim and the shepherds must constantly move around the flock whistling, shouting, and guiding the animals with their crooks to the better patches of grass, urging them on at a steady but not too rapid pace so that they gain the maxi-mum benefit from the grazing. At dusk the sheep return to the sheep-fold to rest (μουδιάζουν) until midnight when the shepherds again take them out to graze for two or three hours before they sleep again until dawn. On nights when there is driving rain or no moon the midnight grazing (ὁ σκάρος) is a situation which tests the shepherd's nerves and ability. If a ewe is cut off from the flock it may fall an easy victim to a wolf. Two or three ferocious dogs assist the shepherd to give him warning of wolves or thieves and by their barking to repel various aerial manifestations of the Devil which also threaten the flock.

Lambing is the crisis of the shepherd's year. During these weeks the shepherds work almost without sleep. They must be constantly vigilant because a ewe generally strays from the flock to drop its lamb and may then abandon it after the birth. A shepherd must be at hand immediately after the birth to ensure that the ewe cleans the lamb, that the lamb finds the udder and that the ewe and lamb recognize one another by smell. For this reason, too, the sheep-fold must be moved to dry ground when it becomes fouled by mud and excrement since this makes recognition by smell difficult. Sometimes when a ewe has a difficult delivery the shepherd must try to manipulate the lamb into the correct position to ease its passage. At night, in bad weather, and with the ever present menace of wolves, these various operations are exceedingly difficult.

With the establishment on the first of February of the cheese-maker's station the ewes whose lambs have been weaned are milked twice a day at dawn and dusk. Any men of the stani, including the tselingas, who are not away with the other flocks, come to assist the two shepherds of the milking ewes. There is competition to discover who is the strongest milker, who draws off most milk into his bucket and milks the greater number of sheep without suffering cramp in his hands. But there is a more general anxiety about the total quantity of milk taken at each milking and the shepherds watch apprehensively for symptoms of a disease that attacks the udder and turns milk to water (παρμάρα). The Sarakatsani say that shepherds have a great σεβντάς for lambing and milking, a word perhaps impossible to translate, which includes the ideas of love and longing, anxiety and envy. It follows that the milking-pen is the part of the stani most threatened by the evil eye of other shepherds, and also the part of the stani where the shepherds are careful to deploy different objects such as a viper's head or an egg dyed red on the Thursday of Easter week which have the power to neutralize this pervasive and destructive force of envy, as well as more direct attacks by the Devil.

The next demand upon the strength of the shepherd comes in the early days of May when the stani sets out for the mountains. This is a moment almost of festival. The sheep again carry their bells which are not worn in the winter. As well as their practical function of identifying the flock they express the joy of the stani that the difficult winter period is over and its pride in the appearance of its flock. But the journey itself is not pleasurable for the shepherd. Particularly in recent years it has become difficult to find grazing on the road and there are hostile and sometimes violent encounters with villagers and agricultural guards. The sheep travel eight to ten miles each night on a road which is often congested with the flocks of other stanis. In the dark and on ground he does not know the shepherd must try to graze his sheep where he can, prevent them from mixing with the animals of other flocks, and guard them from village or Sarakatsan thieves for whom the conditions are an opportunity and a temptation. At dawn they try to find some grass, and here the mule-train (καραβάνι) with the older men, women, and children, overtakes them to prepare a temporary milking-pen. After the animals have been milked the women at once begin to turn the milk into cheese, and later to bake bread. Meanwhile the shepherds graze the sheep until about 11 a.m. when the animals lie down to rest in the heat of the day. They are milked again in the evening before setting out on the next leg of their journey. But the women remain to make the cheese for the second time in the day, and to take a few hours of sleep before they move swiftly through the night to overtake the sheep once again. After a journey of perhaps ten days they finally reach their homeland, the high mountains of Zagori.

In the mountains shepherding practice changes. The sheep graze at night in the cool air when their appetite is stronger. At dawn the animals are watered and about 9 o'clock they are milked. They then 'sleep in the shade' (σταλίζουν) until the late afternoon when they are milked again before setting out to graze in the fresh evening air. About once in every eight days salt is spread on flat stones. They eat this greedily and are watered immediately afterwards, a treatment which increases their will to graze in the summer heat, and is believed to strengthen them for successful mating.

The quality of physical courage, on which the Sarakatsani put so much emphasis in their list of the ideal attributes of the shepherd, is perhaps more necessary in summer than winter. Moving along, or over, the broken limestone ridges in the darkness from one plateau of grass to another requires a very sure foot and steady nerves. Sheep sometimes get into difficulties and have to be rescued. If an animal falls into a crevasse and breaks a leg it must be extricated, the limb bound and splinted, and the animal carried down the mountain to the village.

Immediately before or after the migration to summer pastures, the animals are shorn. Already at the end of March some wool has been taken from their legs and haunches but the full shearing is delayed until the warmer weather. Shearing, too, marks the passing of the winter and is considered a festival. On the final day there is meat, wine, and dancing. Like the journey from the plains it is also hard work for the shepherd, giving him, however, an opportunity to prove his expertise and strength. In a highly competitive atmosphere before the appraising eyes of each other and the women, the men of the stani gather in the sheep-fold to clip the fleeces of the different flocks. A strong and skilful man may shear sixty animals in a day.

The cycle of shepherding activities continues with the mating season in June or July, the date depending on the condition of the animals. Then, in the last days of July, the cheese merchant closes his station and gradually with the reduced flow of milk from the pregnant ewes the shepherds milk their animals less frequently until, some time in the first half of August, lactation ceases. At length the shepherds pause and rest.

When the shepherds arrive in the mountains their mood changes almost abruptly from an expectation of the worst to guarded optimism. Since the autumn they have suffered anxiety, crisis, and frequently physical exhaustion in their efforts to avoid disaster to the lambs, a small milk yield, or disease. These dangers do not exist, or are less considerable, in the summer. At this season the systematic practice of reciprocal grass theft, the sometimes accidental trespass, the intermingling of two flocks when they converge on the cheese-maker's station at milking time, are all situations which may precipitate quarrels with unrelated shepherds that threaten life and honour, but they are not possibilities that cause the shepherd much apprehensive concern. In personal oppositions he is confident in his own strength and courage, he depends on nothing outside himself. On the other hand, whatever skill a shepherd may possess, the dangers which threaten the flock in winter often depend on factors or elements beyond his individual control. Yet extreme poverty, which is a possible consequence of such a disaster, destroys honour and sometimes takes the lives of small children.

The Sarakatsan shepherd identifies himself with his animals. Their condition is almost as personal a concern as his own health and appearance. If a sheep is stoned by another man, the shepherd's honour is touched. In numbers and quality sheep are the prerequisite of prestige. He is aware of their dependence on him and of the dependence of his whole family on what the flock is able to supply. He knows each animal, its history, and peculiarities. There is an extensive descriptive vocabulary of sheep terms. Skilled shepherds do not count their sheep, they scan them, recognizing at once the absence of an animal identified by a particular combination of markings, colours, and idiosyncrasies. Sick sheep are tended with care and compassion. A shepherd may sleep with the animal under his cape to give it warmth. He is neither gentle nor sentimental towards his sheep but between the man and his animals there exists an evident solidarity.

## 3. THE WOMEN

Women and goats are conceptually opposed to men and sheep. Goats are unable to resist pain in silence, they are cunning and insatiate feeders. Greed and cunning are important characteristics of the Devil and Sarakatsani will often say that although Christ tamed these animals the Devil still remains in them. Sarakatsani keep some goats to exploit that part of their grazing land which is unfit for sheep. But as animals they are despised, and a stani with too high a proportion of goats to sheep loses prestige. Women are not, of course, simply creatures of the Devil but the nature of their sexuality which continually threatens the honour of men, makes them, willingly or unwillingly, agents of his will. It is consistent, therefore, that in the practical division of labour women rather than men care for the goats. Although it is unfitting for women to graze these animals, they alone are responsible for building the goat-pen, for cutting and carrying to the pen the branches of tender leaves to wean the kids, often for watching the kids in the first days when they graze without their mothers, always for milking the goats, for carrying the milk to the cheese-maker, for shearing their fleeces, and for collecting and sacking the goat dung which is sold to the villagers.

Conversely, women, particularly married women involved in sexual intercourse, or girls during their menstrual periods, do not approach the sheep unnecessarily. A woman is careful not to cross directly in front of a flock, partly for the practical reason that it breaks the smooth rhythm of its grazing but also because her presence in some way affronts the sheep and might cause disease. *A fortiori* a woman never milks a sheep. Yet there is no rigid avoidance. And, in fact, women regularly do the heavy work in building sheep-folds or moving them to a new site when they are fouled with mud and dung. And relays of women at dawn and dusk bring down the newly born lambs with their mothers from the flock to the clean and better protected sheep-fold near the huts. They are, however, by preference, unmarried girls (τσοῦπρες).

But in relation to the division of labour, the complementary opposition of the sexes in fact turns less upon the opposition of sheep and goats and is more concerned with a wider and more important distinction. Men are occupied with their extensive duties of grazing and protecting the flocks, women within or immediately around the hut, with its central hearth and fire which gives physical warmth and spiritual protection, are concerned with the intensive tasks of the care of children and the provision of food, clothes, and shelter for their family. The expressive role of the woman within the family hut accentuates the quality of motherhood, not sexuality, and it is consistent with this aspect of her social personality that the shepherd brings a sick sheep to his hut to be nursed and cared for by the women. It is a woman who ties a ewe which has lost its lamb to the wall of the hut by a short cord so that it cannot sit, and patiently persuades it to accept the lamb of another ewe which has borne twins.

The assistance women give in the care of the animals is their direct contribution to the stani. Their work within the hut concerns only their own family. These tasks are manifold. They care for the children, cook, bake bread on the open hearth, cut wood or bushes for the fire, carry water in barrels from the spring, sometimes from a very considerable distance. In the stream, or spring, they also wash the clothes of their family. They search the mountain slopes for wild vegetables and herbs and in the summer villages they cultivate a small vegetable garden in which onions, beans, and lettuces are grown. They also keep a few hens. Some of the eggs are kept for the children but the majority are bartered in the village shop for dyes and other small needs. A man may occasionally give his wife a kid

1. Milking

to sell but otherwise chickens and eggs are her only source of cash income.

The huts which protect the Sarakatsani from the weather and the curiosity of other families, are of two principal kinds, circular and domed (τουρλωτά), or rectangular and 'arched' (ἀψιδωτά). Except that in the case of rectangular huts the men help the women to erect the posts and crossbeams the building of the hut is entirely the work of women. They cut, select, and tie into position the pliable but strong branches which form the framework of the circular hut. They collect, dress, and tie on to the wooden skeleton the bundles of reeds, grasses, or ferns with which the hut is thatched. They level the floor inside and plaster both the floor and the walls to a height of three feet with a mixture of mud and mule-dung. They form the central hearth. Five or six women working continuously are able to erect a hut of conventional size[4] in two to three days, although it will have taken them at least as many days to find and prepare their materials.

The treatment of the wool from which the Sarakatsani make the greater part of their clothing and all their blankets is also, naturally, in the hands of the women. The wool is divided into three categories according to the fineness and length of the staple. It is washed in hot water and beaten with a wooden implement to free it from surplus grease. After the wool has been dried in the sun and disentangled with a carding tool (λανάρι) it is spun by hand from a distaff (ρόκα). This is a lengthy process and when a woman's hands are not otherwise employed she is either spinning or knitting. Finally, the spun thread is woven into cloth on the simple wooden loom which the women operate continuously during the months of August and September when the flocks and the shepherds make fewer demands on their energies. On the loom are made the blankets, the shepherd's capes woven from a mixture of wool and goats' hair, and the cloth for jackets, skirts, and trousers. Today professional village or town tailors cut and sew the suits of the men, but the cloth remains their own. Only shoes, shirts, and cotton material (for the young girls' dresses at the summer festivals) are bought from the shops of Jannina and other towns.

[4] A circular hut for a family of 6 or 7 adults generally has a diameter of 14 or 15 feet. Height and diameter are approximately the same.

From this brief and summary description of Sarakatsan methods of animal husbandry and the other associated tasks which provide the shepherds with food, clothes, and shelter, it is evident that the flocks of a stani are an object of attention and daily routine about which the working activities of men and women in the group are co-ordinated. The complementarity of the different contributions of the various members of the stani or family, the symbiotic relationship between the people of the stani and their animals, are a source of strength and solidarity. And the physical needs of men and animals in a given physical and political environment are satisfied by the organization and division of labour which I have briefly outlined.

But the relation between the environment, the animals, and their shepherds must be seen not only in terms of utilitarian satisfaction or social function. Shepherding has intrinsic value; it is a way of life, not merely one way of remaining alive. This appears best perhaps in the shepherds' conception of time. Time is not for the Sarakatsani a homogeneous medium, units of which may be saved or lost.[5] In one aspect, it is a succession of activities concerned directly or indirectly with the flocks and determined by the ecological rhythms of the different seasons and the changing conditions of temperature, grass, and water. The cycle of the year is related, of course, to the succession of calendrical months, but the months themselves are associated with particular activities rather than the reverse. Within the cycles of the day, the week, and the year different moments in time have different qualities, sacred or profane, of ill fortune or good fortune, to which the work and the life of the shepherd is accommodated. For example, shearing may not begin on a Sunday which is sacred, nor on a Tuesday or Friday which are inauspicious. Time in another aspect is measured against the progress of the individual through his life considered as a succession of statuses in the family. This paradigm of statuses, also, has a circular appearance in the replacement of one generation by another. Time then is not a scale marking a linear progress, or a means of dividing life into portions of work and leisure, it is a continuum of activity within the family and in the service of the flock. The family and the flock are both forms divinely

[5] Cf. R. B. Onians, *Origins of European Thought*, Cambridge, 1951, p. 411; and Evans-Pritchard, op. cit. p. 103.

confirmed, the earthly family being a refraction of the Holy archetype Family, while the sheep is a sacred animal blessed by God. These things have always been so, they always will be so. Life is sheep, children, and honour, mutually implicated elements none of which requires any justification of utility or profit. The family is the form in which these three elements are fused; and it is to a consideration of this circumstance and its consequences that the analysis now proceeds.

# III

# KINSMEN AND AFFINES

## 1. THE SIGNIFICANCE OF KINSMEN

THE kindred (τὸ σόϊ) includes only those blood kinsmen of a man (or woman)[1] who are formally recognized for social purposes. The Sarakatsani recognize as members of the kindred all cognatic relatives as far as the degree of second cousin, whether these links are traced through the father's or mother's side of the family. In this system, all those persons descended from a man's four grandparents and their brothers and sisters are his kinsmen, except the children of his second cousins, the grandchildren of his first cousins, and the great-grandchildren of his own siblings, who are not members of his kindred. To express this in more general terms, the recognition for social purposes of collateral relations is relatively wide in a man's own generation and subsequently becomes, from his point of view, relatively less wide in each descendant generation. As a man passes through life, critical events, such as his marriage and the birth of children, the marriages of these children and the birth of grandchildren, direct his obligations and interests to his own immediate descendants to the exclusion of collaterals.

Kindred relationships are considered by the Sarakatsani to be extensions from the family. Naturally, it is always a member of a man's elementary family who mediates his various relationships in the kindred, parents providing the links with grandparents, uncles, aunts, and cousins; siblings those with nephews and nieces. And although the kindred is a system of personal relationships while the family is a corporate group,[2] the systematic character of the former, and the structure of the latter, are necessarily interdependent and consistent.

[1] Except where there is ambiguity I shall not repeat this cumbersome qualification.

[2] Perpetuity is a quality often premised of corporate kinship groups, whereas Sarakatsan families are limited to a life of some 40 years, i.e. the period which normally elapses between a man's marriage and the division

The Sarakatsan family is not only a domestic association of individuals with mutual affections based on blood relationship, it is a corporate group owning in common all significant property; and of this the leader, whether father or brother, is the trustee not the owner. Economically it struggles to become a self-sufficient unit with a division of labour organized about the service of its flocks; politically its members invariably act together. The individual in his work and behaviour is entirely committed to his family, whose prestige and reputation for honour are his foremost concern.

The family is also a religious community with its own 'sacra', icons, and other objects. In the popular mind it is an earthly reflection of the Heavenly Family of God the Father, the Mother of God, and Christ. Relations between members of a family ought to be modelled on the attitudes which, it is imagined, inspire the relations of the Heavenly archetype Family and its members. A father ought to have wisdom and foresight, a mother compassion, a son courage and respect, a daughter virginity, and so on.[3] Through grace, which descends in the sacrament of the Eucharist and through the icons, and in other ways, they are helped to achieve these modes of being, and in achieving them they partake, in a sense, of the condition of the Holy Family and are therefore less vulnerable as a group to material disaster or the spiritual attacks of the Devil. Through reference to a divine model, a man or woman in family life participates in a reality that transcends individuality; the harsh and ceaseless struggle to survive, even simple and often repeated actions such as carrying water or milking sheep, come to possess a validity which is absolute and intrinsic.

of the joint household by his married sons. Yet so long as it does last, the family group has in other respects a corporate jural existence and personality. Cf. Sir Henry Maine, *The Early History of Institutions*, London, 1893, p. 78.

The Sarakatsan family is a system of closed relationships and a group with a recognized leader. It holds all property in common and controls the productive powers of all its members and the reproductive capacities of its women. In principle all its members are held to be responsible for the action of any other member. It is with regard to these characteristics that I describe this group as 'corporate'.

[3] In the different aspects of her person, the Mother of God provides a model for both the mother and the daughter in the earthly family.

The family is, indeed, the centre of the shepherd's world. Inside its limits he finds support, affection, and a sense of moral obligation. With certain qualifications these attitudes are extended to all the relations of the kindred. But outside the family and the kindred a man meets and expects only hostility and suspicion. There are conventions of conduct, but there is no general conscience of obligation to others. From the point of view of each individual, the community is divided into those who are kinsmen, a man's own people (δικοί), and those who are not kinsmen, that is strangers (ξένοι). There is a third intermediate category of persons, the affines (συμπέθεροι), strangers with whom a man or his kinsman has become related through a contract of marriage. Confidence, trust, and an altruistic concern about another individual's welfare can only exist between kinsmen, and it is only in a kinship relationship that a man is able to abandon the outlook of self-interest which normally guides him in relations outside the family.

It follows that a man looks towards his kinsmen for practical support. As we have seen, unrelated families are mutually opposed. The family, with reference to which the individual must act in almost all contexts of behaviour, faces a hostile community. Therefore this support is peculiarly important. Yet, in relation to the community's population of about 4,000 souls, the average size of an individual's kindred is small, seldom exceeding 250 men, women, and children of whom some 160 will be second cousins, a category of relations who are on the margin of kinship. Kinsmen are relatively few and correspondingly precious. In summer the kindred is scattered over 390 square miles of difficult and tortuous country, and a man does not, generally, live within an hour's walk of more than one-fifth of his kinsmen. This, in part, is the practical importance of kinship connexions; they offer a certain freedom of social manœuvre. Kinsmen established at strategic points through a community, which is numerically not small and geographically very dispersed, are able to offer hospitality and local information which pride and distrust prevent a man asking of unrelated persons. The network of a man's kinship relations provides him with a system of information and intelligence without which he cannot conduct his affairs efficiently or profitably. The price that he should ask for his milk, his wool, and animals for slaughter, the intrigues of others with merchants and officials, which often vitally affect his own affairs, the ever pressing problem of where winter pasture is to be found, this is the kind of information a man exchanges with his kinsman or, more rarely, with a close and trusted affine.

Kinsmen are indispensable in the delicate negotiations of 'match-making'. Before a girl is sought in marriage, very careful inquiries have to be made concerning her virtue, industry, health, and temperament. A kinsman who lives near the girl's family will be in a position to give accurate details; his information will be trusted, and he will treat the affair with the discretion it demands. For marriage involves a contract between two hostile groups, and offence, given or received by either side, is a question of honour and may lead to violence and killing.

I have introduced the notion that the opposed families of this fragmented community are related through competition for prestige. Certainly, it is impossible to miss the competitive flavour of social life outside the home. Men care passionately about their prestige, the prestige of their families, and of their kinsmen. Indeed all these reputations are parts of a single complex. And in a paradoxical fashion they depend upon the opinions of enemies. Whenever there is some incident or affray, the news of it travels with remarkable rapidity to all quarters of the Zagori. Within a matter of forty-eight hours small groups of Sarakatsani throughout the area will be passing judgement on the behaviour of the people involved, as this is evaluated according to the values of the community. They will analyse minutely what a man is reported to have said and done, and they will decide whether he was justified in what he did and whether he displayed manliness (ἀνδρισμός) in defending his honour. In such discussions a man's kinsmen will take his side, acting as advocates and apologists for his behaviour. Furthermore, the mere numerical size of a man's kindred is a matter of prestige, because, other things being equal, it means that he is a man who will be taken notice of, assisted, and well-informed wherever he goes. In discussing kinship the Sarakatsani often say, 'Nobody takes account of a man without kinsmen'. They use, in this context, a word, λογαριάζω, which expresses both the idea of esteeming another man and of being obliged to take him into consideration before proceeding to some course of action.

Consultation between trusted kinsmen about their various affairs is continual. The enterprise itself may be of almost any kind, the marriage of a son or daughter, a decision whether or not to sell sheep to raise money for the payment of a debt, or the acceptance or non-acceptance of an offer of winter pasture. Similarly, when a man is involved in some crisis, a fight with another shepherd, a brawl at a marriage feast, or a difficult court case, kinsmen come to him of their own accord with advice and criticism. In this way he learns which courses of action will enjoy the moral support of his kin and which will not. And since a man loses prestige if his kinsman acts wrongly, he will always exhort him to an honourable course of action however difficult the circumstances. For his part, the principal actor is influenced by the fear of losing the support of his kinsmen, as he may do if he takes decisions which lose him prestige. His kinsmen can then only protect their own prestige by isolating themselves to a greater or lesser degree from social contact with him. Consequently this consultation between kinsmen is not only to a man's advantage in terms of his own prestige, but it is also a subtle sanction for right ways of acting in the community as a whole.

In economic matters, too, a shepherd looks to his kinsmen for help and co-operation. Quite apart from the deep distrust which divides unrelated persons, shame prevents a man from seeking assistance outside the kindred, since this would be a tacit admission that he had been rejected by his own kinsmen. Thus sentiment and convention lead in the same direction. A shepherd lives from one monetary crisis to another. When he needs a small money loan for an operation fee at a Jannina hospital or for the expenses of a wedding, he is often unable to persuade a merchant to grant him an additional advance; but he seldom fails to raise it from his kinsmen if they have the money in hand. Economic co-operation may take other forms. The condition of the family's flocks is not only the basis of its physical existence but the source of pride and prestige. A man fears to meet the appraising eyes of another if his animals are in a meagre and spindle-shanked condition. But grazing, both in the Zagori and in the winter pastures, varies considerably from place to place and from year to year. Therefore, if a kinsman has some grass which is good for fattening lambs or restoring weakened ewes, a man may ask him to take some of his weaker animals which are in difficulties. For this service he will have to pay, but he would not in any circumstances trust his sheep to the care of an unrelated shepherd.

But the most intimate form of economic association between kinsmen occurs where a number of autonomous but related families join together for the co-management of their flocks and, in particular, to discover and negotiate for winter pastures. The solution of this problem requires that the group should reach an understanding, whether direct or through an inter-mediary, with persons of influence in villages and government departments. The leader of such a 'company' is known as the tselingas (ὁ τσέλιγγας). In a majority of cases the nucleus of the group he leads may be descibed as a simple fraternal association, that is a number of married brothers with families, each of whom maintains his own household, his own purse, and has his own animals clearly marked. But, in addition, such groups often include uncles, nephews, brothers-in-law, pater-nal and maternal cousins, and it would be possible to produce many examples of different combinations of kinsmen and affinal relatives. At this point, it is sufficient to stress that they are founded upon ties of kinship and marriage, that they are voluntary and often unstable associations in which each family retains its own independent social personality, its own budget, and its own animals.

In these ways kinsmen give each other moral and practical support in facing a hostile and competitive world where one man delights openly and with little inhibition in the misfor-tunes of another. A man co-operates with his kinsmen because he trusts them. There is a sense of security within the kindred which is significantly absent outside its limits. One may not steal from a kinsman's flock, nor cheat him in monetary settle-ments, nor seduce his sister, nor gossip about his private affairs. But it is necessary to stress that there are definite limits to what may be expected from kinsmen. When honour demands a vengeance killing, kinsmen outside the family will lend moral support but none of them is obliged to pull the trigger or thrust home the knife. Again, money may be loaned between kinsmen but repayment after a reasonable interval is expected, and in almost all cases is met, even where it leads to the sale of sheep. It amounts to this, that a man will help his kinsman and indeed is morally obliged to do so, so long as this assistance does not conflict with the interests of his own family.

## 2. THE KINDRED

The kindred of the Sarakatsani has three important formal characteristics. It is bilateral, the limits of its extension are precisely defined, and within these limits a man may not marry.

There is a sense in which almost all kinship systems may be described as bilateral, or to speak more accurately, filiation is normally bilateral and complementary.[4] But in describing the Sarakatsan kindred as bilateral it is my intention also to suggest a certain, though not exact, symmetry in the relations of a man to the family of origin[5] of his father on the one hand, and to the family of origin of his mother on the other; and to indicate further that, in principle, a man has equivalent confidence in, and similar rights over and obligations towards, more distant collateral kinsmen such as first or second cousins, whether the relationships with these persons are traced through the father or through the mother.[6] There is always a very strong moral obligation to assist any collateral kinsman. For instance, it often

[4] Meyer Fortes, 'Structure of Unilineal Descent Groups', *American Anthropologist*, 1953, vol. 55, p. 33.

[5] This is Lloyd Warner's familiar distinction between the family of orientation and the family of procreation. I prefer the terms 'origin' and 'marriage'; in the family of origin the individual is a child and a sibling, in the family of marriage a spouse and a parent.

[6] The bilateral form of the kindred is plainly reflected in the terminology. The word σόϊ, kindred, applies, of course, to both maternal and paternal relations; and the words for kinsman συγγενής and relationship συγγένεια are both used in the same way. The terms which are used to describe kinship relationship outside the family do not differentiate between maternal and paternal kinsmen. Thus the term θεῖος, uncle, is used for both mother's brother and father's brother as well as for all male first cousins of both parents whether these are connected through male or female links. The same may be said about the other terms for παππούλης, grandfather, βάβω, grandmother, θεία, aunt, ἐξάδερφος, ἐξαδέρφη, male and female cousin, ἀνεψιός, ἀνεψιά, nephew and niece, and ἐγγόνι, ἐγγονή, grandchild, grand-daughter.

happens at weddings that quarrels develop between unrelated guests. Insults, curses, and blows are exchanged, and sometimes knives are drawn. These events have a certain pattern. A man is insulted, or imagines that he has been insulted, by another. At once all the relatives of either man range themselves alongside their kinsman; and those who are unrelated to either party, as well as others embarrassed by an equal allegiance to both sides, throw themselves between the two antagonists. But the paternal or maternal origin of relationship neither increases nor diminishes the obligation to support a kinsman in this or any other situation.

Property and prestige are passed from one generation to the next according to customary rules of inheritance in the one case, and canons of popular judgement in the other, which reflect the symmetry of an individual's relations to the families of origin of his father and mother. Property is itself an element in prestige, while wealth without prestige loses its significance. Individual and family reputation, as I have already indicated, is a self-evident value; without it social life has no meaning. This prestige is inherited both from the father's family and the mother's. It is true that the prestige of paternal connexions is greater; but the quality of the mother's family of origin is also critical, for criticism of the mother, who contributes important moral qualities to the characters of her children, is a peculiarly effective method of denigrating a family. The individual, of course, may increase or diminish his reputation by his own acts but it is on the basis of a reputation inherited from both parents that he at first faces the judgements of the community. And if this inherited reputation is unsatisfactory, it will be exceedingly difficult for the individual by his own efforts to redeem it. It is partly for these reasons that the choice of a wife is a matter which is approached with delicacy and deliberation. Many personal qualities of a prospective bride are taken into consideration but invariably the crucial question to be debated is the quality and prestige of the girl's family and close kin. The Sarakatsani use a Turkish word, νταμάρι, of which the primary meaning is a vein, to indicate the general quality of a man's immediate maternal and paternal ancestors.[7] And if either the

[7] The more general meaning of νταμάρι in modern Greek is 'stone quarry'.

bride or the bridegroom is from a family of lower prestige than the other, it is said that he (or she) 'destroys' the νταμάρι of the other partner. For it is thought that in the family which results from a marriage both partners have contributed their blood 'to make one blood' which is unique and on whose purity the prestige and honour of the new family depends.

In a similar manner both husband and wife contribute wealth to the elementary family which they establish. The corporate property of a family is a common stock of animals, money, and goods, from which sons and daughters must be endowed. Daughters receive their portion as dowry at the moment of marriage, but the married sons normally continue to live in an extended family group where family wealth is still held in common. In the eventual partition of this joint household and its property, which is delayed until all the daughters have been married, and generally occurs five to ten years after the marriage of the eldest son, equal shares of stock and other assets are received by each son; but in the case of the youngest son an extra half-share is provided for the maintenance of each surviving parent who by custom remains in the household of this son. When an elementary family leaves the joint household of married brothers, the husband's family has probably contributed about 100 sheep and goats and one or two mules while the wife's family has supplied in the form of her dowry (προικιό) the furnishings of the hut and sufficient clothes and finery for the bride to wear or display for a period of ten years or more. The value of such a dowry is about £150, or the equivalent of 50 sheep. Since 1945, however, the practice has grown up of demanding from the bride's family about forty sheep or their equivalent in gold sovereigns in addition to the traditional dowry. Thus approximately under the traditional convention, and more rigorously today, there exists a certain balance between the wealth that passes into a new family from the husband's family of origin and that which is contributed by the wife's family of origin. It would be wrong to think of the dowry merely as a payment made by a bride's family to obtain a husband for her. Certainly there have been cases where girls who had physical or moral deficiencies have had to pay large dowries to get any kind of husband at all. It is also true that calculations of family prestige are concerned in the size of the dowry. But the implicit purpose of the dowry is to complement the wealth with which the new family is or will be endowed by the husband's family. In this sense the handing over of the dowry is the first act of socially regulated co-operation between two previously unrelated and therefore hostile families. The two parties to the marriage contract co-operate to establish a new group. Each side contributes one of its members and a certain amount of property. And, under the traditional custom at least, the contribution of each side appropriately reflects the complementary activities of the two partners. The husband provides the animals, the wife the furnishings of the hut. And this bilateral endowment of a new family with property from both families of origin is also observed in the limiting case where a man has no sons and marries his youngest girl to a bridegroom who is willing to live in his father-in-law's home. In this instance it is the bridegroom who contributes wealth at the moment of marriage, bringing with him his share in the flocks of his family of birth, while the property of the wife's family of origin, which may be considerable, does not formally come under the control of the new family until the wife's father has retired from active work.

Just as the elements of wealth and prestige are inherited through both the mother and the father, so the Sarakatsani also believe that a child inherits the elements of its moral character from both parents, although, since the important moral qualities in this community are sex-linked, sons are thought to form their moral character essentially after the pattern of their fathers, especially with reference to manliness, while daughters particularly inherit those qualities of the mother which affect their sense of sexual shame. Nevertheless the pattern of character and behaviour, which a son partly inherits and partly learns from his father, may be modified by elements which he receives from his mother; and in the same way a girl may inherit some character traits from her father. Sometimes facets of character which are passed from or through the parent of opposite sex may be referred to the individual's χούι. This is an aspect of personality to which one may attribute those idiosyncratic actions and attitudes which are in some way unusual or even deviant. The Sarakatsani insist that this is as likely to be inherited from one side of the family as from the other. John Charisis tears his shirts to shreds when he dances at weddings. This odd behaviour is not approved, but in terms of χούι it may, at least, be explained; and it is remembered that his mother's brother, although he did not tear his shirts, used to waste his substance in another way by gambling at cards for high stakes, which he could not afford.

It is clear, then, that the elements of wealth, prestige, and character pass into a family from both the families which enter into the original betrothal contract. This not only reflects the bilateral and symmetrical form of the kindred but in some measure helps to maintain it. For, if a man has contracted a judicious marriage with a girl from a family of at least equivalent prestige, the children will be anxious to associate with their matrilateral kin. On the other hand, it is noticeable that where a man has married into a family of lower prestige than his own (that is, where prestige has not been equally inherited from both sides), his children tend to evade obligations to their mother's kinsmen while they carefully cultivate kinsmen of the father. However, if a wife brings a substantial dowry (that is, where a newly established family is equally endowed with wealth from both sides), the husband is obliged to be particularly helpful to the family and kinsmen of his wife, and this leads to close relations between his children and their maternal cousins.

The bilateral structure of the kindred implies, of course, that this association of kinsmen is not a corporate group. Its definition must always be relative to a particular group of siblings.[8] At a wedding, when representatives of all sections of the bridegroom's kindred gather round him in support against the kindred of the bride, the illusion is created that two solidary corporate groups of kinsmen are involved. But in fact they are only united in the particular context of the wedding and by reason of each individual's personal kinship relation to the bridegroom. Indeed since any particular kindred comprises descendants of four pairs of unrelated great-grandparents, only the sibling group which is central to this kindred is related to all

---

[8] This has long been recognized. See Bertha Phillpotts, *Kindred and Clan*, Cambridge, 1913, pp. 3, 275. However, it should be clear that corporate associations of kinsmen may exist in this kind of community. But other criteria will be involved, not merely kinship relationship.

its members.[9] It is only through the marriages of their grand-parents and parents that a man and his siblings are related to the four component groups of collaterals in his kindred. Kindred relations are personal, not corporate, relations. And the Sarakatsan kindred in no way acts as a property-holding group since, besides the fact that it is relative to a particular sibling group, it has no continuity from generation to generation.

In drawing attention to this bilateral and symmetrical form of the kindred I have been careful to avoid speaking of bilateral descent. In anthropological writings principles of descent normally refer to rules which determine membership in corporate lineal descent groups. Such groups are bodies of kinsmen whose members may be recruited through filiation to a line of descent exclusively through males (patrilineal), or exclusively through females (matrilineal).[10] Descent from a common ancestor or group of ancestors defines membership in the group and identifies the interests of its members, which may concern political and ritual rights and obligations as well as inheritance and succession. It is possible to talk of a corporate bilateral descent group where membership depends upon filiation through both parents but in such an instance the group would have to practise obligatory endogamous marriage. But the Sarakatsan kindred is not an endogamous group. Corporate descent groups imply a principle of perpetual succession, a feature which the kindred entirely lacks; and they also imply that individuals have categorical rights and obligations outside the elementary or extended family, whereas in the Sarakatsan kindred this is not so. Not descent, but filiation of a man or woman to his or her family of origin is the factor which

---

[9] Any two kinsmen other than siblings have kindreds which to a greater or lesser degree overlap. A man may find himself in a situation where two men, both related to him but unrelated to one another, are in some form of conflict in which both appeal to him for support. In this predicament the only solution is to remain neutral, since it would be sinful to act against a kinsman except under great provocation. But generally such a situation extends rather than restricts the range of kinship obligations; towards a person who, although not a kinsman himself, is closely related to a kinsman, a man ought to act with more consideration and less hostility than is usual between men who are unrelated.

[10] There are other possibilities, viz. bilineal or dual descent, parallel descent, and alternating descent.

determines status, categorical rights and obligations, and membership in the family group, which is the only solidary kin grouping in this system of kinship and marriage. Hence in a description of the Sarakatsan kindred it seems preferable not to speak, even loosely, of any principle of descent.[11]

It is true that the kindred of any man includes the descendants of four pairs of great-grandparents. It is, therefore, possible to represent the kindred diagrammatically as four interlocking pyramids of cognatic descent. But this kind of abstraction bears no relation to the mental image which a Sarakatsanos forms of his kindred, in which relations are conceived in terms of extension from the family of origin, not descent from a common ancestor. There is mutual affection and moral obligation between my second cousin and myself because my grandparent and his grandparent were siblings rather than because we are both descendants of common great-grandparents. I prefer, then, to speak of equivalent bilateral extension, for this describes precisely the constitution of the kindred. The qualification of bilateral extension by the notion of equivalence is intended to underline both the fact that collateral kinsmen are recognized to the degree of second cousin on either side of the family, and also the equipotential character of matrilateral and patrilateral relationships.

The second formal characteristic of the kindred is the definition of its limits, which, in this case, are drawn in a man's own generation at the collateral degree of second cousin, a span of collateral kinship which is calculated by recognizing as kinsmen the descendants of his four grandparents and their siblings. Thereafter, as we have seen, the recognition of collaterals is increasingly restricted in descendant generations. This limitation, considered together with equivalent bilateral extension, leads to a simple process within the kindred whereby the range of collateral relationship which a child may inherit from either parent is severely delimited. The second cousins of his parent are not, in a formal sense, a man's kinsmen and, therefore, he

---

[11] In some general remarks about the concept of descent in bilateral systems Professor Firth has adopted a similar viewpoint. Raymond Firth (editor), *Two Studies of Kinship in London*, London, 1956, p. 15. Cf. also W. H. R. Rivers, *Social Organisation*, London, 1924, p. 86, and G. P. Murdock, *Social Structure*, New York, 1949, p. 15.

may marry a kinswoman of this degree. In other words, the children of a marriage throw away, as it were, perhaps three-quarters[12] of those kinsmen who are recognized collateral relations of the parents. The father, when he identifies himself with the interests of his own children, at once creates a certain kinship distance between himself and any one of his own siblings, the kindred of whose children only partly coincides with the kindred of his own children. Since the descendants of the father's second cousins are no longer kinsmen of his children, they also cease to be significant for him and are not recognized as kinsmen; similarly in the case of the grandchildren of first cousins, and the great-grandchildren of siblings. And the same considerations apply in the case of the mother and her collateral kin. With the passage of time parents turn their loyalty and interest from the collateral kinsmen of their own generation to their direct descendants and to only those collateral descendants who remain relevant for their own descendants; these are necessarily fewer in each descendant generation.

From one point of view a man's kinsmen are the descendants of the four sibling groups of his two grandfathers and two grandmothers. Sarakatsan kinship finds its source in the unity of the sibling group born and nurtured within a legitimate family. Collateral kinsmen see themselves as the descendants of such a group and it is this sentiment which provides the basis of the personal moral solidarity with a kinsman. Thus the Greek word for cousins (ἐξάδερφοι) means literally 'from brothers'. But Sarakatsani are, also, conscious that it is through marriages in which the interests of siblings or cousins cannot be mutually identified that kinsmen become separated. For a man is related more closely to a particular kinsman than to the kinsman's child; thus, with the close identification of a father's interests with those of his children and the exclusive concentration of categorical obligations in the family of marriage, the marriages of collaterals inevitably lead to change and a measure of disintegration in the individual's kindred. In a phrase, marriage joins strangers while it separates those who are already kinsmen. The consequences for the children and grandchildren of siblings are that a man has approximately only half his kindred

[12] The exact size of this fraction depends upon the size of the various sibling groups in the kindreds.

in common with his first cousin and only one quarter in common
with his second cousin. It shows with what rapidity in this kinship system the common interests of the descendants of a sibling
group disappear. With the passage of only three generations
these descendants are formally unrelated and there is no restriction on the marriage of third cousins. A man says of this third
cousin, 'The kindred has left the house' (βγῆκε τὸ σόϊ ἀπὸ τὸ
σπίτι).

The third formal characteristic of the kindred is that a man
may not marry within its limits. This means that the two families
who form a marriage alliance are unrelated[13] and that the
kindred of the groom will not considerably overlap with the
kindred of the bride although they may claim some kinsmen in
common. A kindred in which maternal and paternal kinsmen
normally form mutually exclusive categories naturally has a
wider span than a kindred in which these categories overlap;
and to that extent, the marriage prohibition is consistent with
the need to have many kinsmen in many places.

We have seen that the principle of equivalent bilateral extension together with the defined limits of the kindred acts over a
period of time to force collaterals apart. A second consequence
of the prohibition on marriage in the kindred is that it makes it
impossible to counteract this process by confirming in a later
generation a relationship which has already been established.
Thus the practice of either first- or second-cousin marriage such
as is reported from Spain by Pitt-Rivers,[14] where it is favoured
as a means of conserving property within the family, is not
possible among the Sarakatsani. This leads to a third consequence of the marriage prohibition. It forces a man who wishes
to marry off his son or daughter to face, as it were, outwards
from his kindred towards the total community. Thus while non-
kinsmen are rivals and even enemies, they are also in a sense
potential affines. This is peculiarly significant in a community
where men unrelated by kinship are associated mainly through
institutionalized forms of hostility and rivalry. A contract of
marriage is normally the only instrument which may bring two
unrelated families into positive association and co-operation.
Indeed, a sense of the community's endogamy is an important

[13] Except in the cases of marriage between third cousins.
[14] J. A. Pitt-Rivers, *The People of the Sierra*, London, 1954, pp. 103–6.

element in their consciousness of being a community at all. Sarakatsani, when they wish to stress their solidarity in opposition to villagers or other outsiders, often claim that, if full records of their marriages had been preserved through the generations, it would be clear that they are all kinsmen, although they are quick to add the qualification that such kinship has long ago 'left the house'. The same principles of kinship extension and marriage prohibition which from the point of view of the individual tend towards the loosening of his relations with collaterals within the kindred, at the same time lead to a measure of cohesion within the community considered as a system of actual and potential kinship relations. Kin and non-kin, actual relations and potential relations, are opposed but also complementary categories.

Of these three formal features of the Sarakatsan kindred the dominant is, without doubt, equivalent bilateral extension. The distinctive consequence of this principle is that the only possible corporate group based upon kinship alone which can exist in such a system over a period of time as long as a generation is the elementary family. For since there is no unilineal principle of descent grouping, there can be no corporate kinship group of higher order, which either includes the elementary family, or cuts across it by including some of its members and excluding others. Nor are there non-unilineal corporate kin groups in which membership is based on optional or alternate filiation or on the choice of residence after marriage.[15] Such arrangements would conflict with the symmetrical affiliation of Sarakatsani to all kinsmen through all lines and the equivalence of obligation to all kinsmen of the same degree. Although the association of an elementary family, for the first five to ten years of its existence, with the husband's extended family of origin may obscure the situation, the newly established elementary family is influenced by both the families of origin of the husband and wife.

An interesting recognition of this occurs on the very day of marriage when in other respects the bride's family feel that they

[15] For a review of non-unilineal descent groups, see William Davenport, 'Nonunilinear Descent and Descent Groups', *American Anthropologist*, 1959, vol. 61, pp. 557–72. Cf. also J. D. Freeman, 'The Family System of the Iban of Borneo', *Cambridge Papers in Social Anthropology No. 1*, Cambridge, 1958.

have been defeated and plundered. The Greek Orthodox
marriage service is in two parts, the first being the rite of
Betrothal (ἀρραβῶνας), the second the rite of 'Crowning'
(στεφάνωσις); and normally they are celebrated in church as one
ceremony. The Sarakatsani, however, bring a priest to the huts
of the bride's family to perform the religious betrothal ceremony
which the shepherds name 'the half wedding' (ὁ μισὸς γάμος),
and consider to be equal in importance to the office of 'Crowning'.
The bride's kinsmen will not surrender her to the groom's
retinue until this ceremony is performed, and equally the
marriage ceremony cannot be completed until the bride is
brought to the home of the bridegroom. In effect, each side
celebrates half the marriage service.

This double attraction is eventually resolved by the new
family's relative emancipation from both the old families. Once
the young family has parted from the husband's extended
family of origin, it stands on its own without categorical rights
over, or obligations towards, other related elementary families.
It neither gives nor receives unconditional support of the kind
that involves physical violence or economic assistance. In these
important respects the family, even within the kindreds of its
members, is, in a sense, isolated.

This isolation of the elementary family is accurately reflected
by the kinship terminology, although in this respect it does not
differ from the general form of European kinship terminologies.
It is significant that the terms for the kinship personalities in a
man's elementary families of origin and marriage, that is in his
inner circle of kinship, are not extended to more distant kinsmen as is the case in many societies with systems of unilineal
descent. The family (οἰκογένεια) which may refer, according to
context, to either or both elementary families in which the individual has or had corporate membership, and to any surviving
grandparents, is part of the kindred, yet at the same time is
clearly distinguished from it. In its widest connotation the
'family' is, of course, a class of relations and not a residential
group. The principles which essentially relate members of the
family are parental obligation and filiation, while the kindred is
based on collateral extension. Between these two classes of kinsmen siblings are the bridge, since at the same time they are
directly descended from the same parents and grandparents and

occupy, before marriage, a socially equivalent status, but become, after their marriages, the points of departure of distinct collateral lines of descent.

At the beginning of this chapter I described the multiform character of the family. It is a domestic group, an economic and property-owning unit, a quasi-political association, a religious communion, and so on. It is now evident that the elementary family group is the only stable solidary unit associated with the kindred and that while it enjoys important support from collateral kinsmen, it is also, in a sense, isolated from them. The immense importance, then, of this social group on the one hand, and its lack of continuity through time on the other, mean that the institutionalized arrangements for its establishment or dissolution, for the transference of categorical rights and obligations from an old family to a new, are of critical importance. Underlying the nature of these arrangements is the simple fact that each individual during some part of his lifetime is almost always the member of two families: one of origin, the other of marriage.[16] A man is a son and brother in one family, a father and husband in the other; a woman is a daughter and sister in the family of origin, a mother and wife in the family of marriage. It is obviously important that the rights and duties of these different roles, when played by the same individual, should not conflict. This is a problem for all systems of kinship, but it is especially acute in this community because all the individual's significant rights and obligations inhere in the family and in no other group. The individual passes from his first family to his second through marriage. In the case of the woman the solution of the problem of conflicting roles is radical; she leaves the home of her father, who ceases to have any rights over her except the residual right of resuming his power over her if she becomes a widow before the birth of children. The protection of her honour is no longer the concern of her brothers, and her working services now belong exclusively to the husband's family. When later she pays one of her rare visits to her original home, she may not spin even a handful of her mother's wool. The husband does not shed the categorical obligations of his roles as son

[16] An individual may have membership in a third family; for the grandparents, after the division of the joint household, normally live as members of the family of marriage of their youngest son.

and sibling quite so rapidly, though it is significant that after his marriage and even before the birth of his children he is unlikely to undertake a vengeance killing for a murdered brother or a dishonoured sister. Eventually, after five to ten years, but often sooner, he parts from the extended family and from all his remaining categorical rights and obligations as son and brother.

Thus siblings before their marriages are a unity for a person outside the group. If he injures or insults any member of the group, he attacks the whole group, every male member of which is under equal obligation to retaliate. At this stage siblings of the same sex are socially equivalent as to status, there is an almost complete identity of interest, and their mutual relations are governed by a consciousness of their common filiation to the same parents. After the marriages of the brothers and sisters of a sibling group the situation entirely changes. They no longer form a unity against the outsider nor are they socially equivalent; they have become differentiated by their marriages and young families. Their interests are no longer identified, and siblings both in form and effect are now merely collaterals. There is a growing tendency to isolation from all collateral lines, not only those of the individual's own siblings. The supreme value in a man's life now becomes the economic welfare and social prestige of his children. He is, therefore, not always free to give unreserved and unthinking aid to his brothers and cousins as he used to do. Moreover, he is now forced, also for the sake of his children, who derive the half of their kindred through their mother, to consolidate his relationship with his affines. This he can only do by weakening to some degree the previously exclusive solidary relations between himself and his brothers and sisters.

Always implicit in Sarakatsan kinship relations is the interplay of the two notions of sibling solidarity and parental obligation. Parental obligation, of course, is established through legitimate marriage and the resulting conjugal relationship, but the very strength of the latter relation is founded on the sacred character of parental love and duty. In the elementary family the two principles of sibling solidarity and parental obligation are complementary and together guide its members in their duties and exclusive affections. But in the relations of married siblings and collaterals the two principles are opposed, sibling solidarity being the source and justification of relationship and moral obligation between collaterals, while parental obligation is the principle which, within the limits of a bilateral kindred, isolates the family from other kinsmen and their families. At the risk of some repetition, and in summary form, the critical aspects of these relationships are: (1) before marriage siblings are bound to one another by categorical obligations; (2) after marriage, the purpose of which is the begetting of children, this nexus is gradually dissolved; (3) after marriage the supreme value in a man's life becomes the welfare of his children; (4) parenthood forces a man for the sake of his children to cultivate his affines; this weakens to some extent the relationship with his siblings; (5) brothers after living together for a few years after marriage as a united extended family divide the common flock and the common household; after partition brothers generally continue to co-operate in the management of their sheep, but on a basis of strict accountancy; (6) collateral kinship is conceived by the Sarakatsani themselves as an extension from the family of origin which relates kinsmen to an original pair of siblings; thus collaterals see themselves as united by derivation from a once united sibling group but divided as a result of the marriages contracted by the members of that group and their children.

I must now introduce a consideration which to some small extent qualifies the symmetry which I have claimed to be a feature of the bilateral kindred. The absence of a unilineal principle of descent grouping does not prevent the Sarakatsani from having a very strong sentimental interest in their patriline and a formal preference for those kinsmen who are related through the father, especially those who bear the same name. The cousins with whom a man often shares his early childhood years in an extended family are agnatic cousins. And while the obligation to carry out blood vengeance does not extend beyond the elementary family, it is significant that when a man voluntarily avenges a kinsman beyond this narrow circle it is almost always an agnatic first cousin. Yet it must be said again that outside the elementary family moral obligations to kinsmen of the same collateral degree are the same however the relationship is mediated. The man, who states categorically that 'we prefer relatives through the father', may name a maternal cousin as his most trusted friend.

When a Sarakatsanos talks loosely of his 'fathers and fore-fathers', he is probably thinking of a vague body of ancestors in the agnatic line. But in fact a man seldom knows very much about his direct ancestors in any line beyond the generation of his grandparents unless they have some claim to particular fame or infamy. Ascendant kinsmen are only relevant as individual personalities to the extent that they affect the inheritance of physical and moral attributes and social prestige. And it is the families of origin of the man's parents, presided over by his four grandparents, which essentially affect his social standing. The lines of descent from the two pairs of grandparents are the kinship co-ordinates, as it were, which intersect and define the unique position of a group of siblings within the community. Naturally the preference for the kinsmen of the father implies that in this evaluation the qualities of paternal kin have more weight, but this is not to be confused with the presence of a patrilineal descent principle.

A man is more interested in his sons than in his daughters simply because they are males and not because they are specific-ally agnatic links ensuring continuity in an exclusively agnatic descent line. It is important to a man to beget male children be-cause in so doing he accentuates his own masculinity, extended in time. A man wants sons 'so that his name will be heard' (νὰ ἀκούεται τ'ὄνομά του), not simply the surname which is in-herited patrilineally, but for it to be said that this is George Carvounis son of John Carvounis. Sons bring prestige, daughters do not. When the husband enters the hut for the first time after the birth of a daughter, his wife turns her head away and lowers her eyes in shame.

This formal preference for the father's kinsmen is consistent with, and indeed is, in the area of kinship, a reflection of the greater value placed upon the male sex. This is a fundamental value of Greek culture, whose essential masculinity can be re-marked at all stages in its development from Homeric times until the present day. Thus, in the Sarakatsan community it is the behaviour of the ideal man that provides the dominant value patterns of honour and pride. The sexes divide the com-munity into opposite yet complementary categories, categories which are moral as well as biological. The behaviour which is considered appropriate for the male and female stereotypes is at many points antithetical, and relations between the sexes are hostile although this hostility cannot generally be given overt expression. The male sex is held to be unambiguously superior not only in power but also in worth to the female, to which the stigma of original sin is closely attached. The female is a constant threat to the honour and integrity of the male, and must be disciplined and dominated. In the absence, therefore, of a unilineal descent principle, it is reasonable to suppose that these attitudes and beliefs of the Sarakatsani concerning the relation of the sexes are significantly connected with the preference for paternal kinsmen.

Patrilocal marriage fits consistently into the pattern of these preferences. A man brings his bride into the household of his father or if he has retired, into the household of his elder brother. The extended family of origin remains a single corporate unit until such time as one or more of the brothers decide to contract out, claiming then, as is their inalienable right, their equal shares in the flock. A brother begins to press for partition precisely when the claims of his children for special attention begin to be felt. Normally this occurs when the eldest child of the second son in a family is about five years old.

But the presence of extended families needs to be explained on other grounds than a preference for paternal kinsmen. Elsewhere in the Greek world, where masculine values and preference for paternal kin are equally strong, the residential pattern is often neolocal, that is to say the newly married couple set up house in a home of their own, independent of either family of origin. Such arrangements are, of course, exactly those we might expect to find associated with a bilateral kindred. Amongst the Sarakatsani there seem to be three important reasons why separation does not take place immediately after marriage. First there is the solidarity of the elementary family of origin built up over a period of about 25 years of mutual devotion and mutual responsibility in face of a hostile and critical world. It is difficult to describe adequately the quality of this solidarity, except perhaps to say that even by the standards of Greek family life it is remarkable—proof against appalling adversities and unyielding to the weaknesses of individuals.

Secondly, the marriage ceremony does not set the seal upon an already established relationship, it only creates the necessary legal and religious conditions for its inception. This is a pertinent fact in a community where, although a man may sometimes have seen his bride before the marriage day, it is most unlikely that he has ever spoken to her. It requires the passage of time and the birth of a child before it can be said in any real sense[17] that an elementary family has been founded. The third reason introduces an economic factor. The Sarakatsan technique of grazing sheep demands for optimum efficiency the co-operation of certainly not fewer than four adult males. An undivided household means an undivided flock, and generally sufficient shepherds to look after it. It is true that after partition brothers normally continue to run their sheep together, but sheep must then be branded, accounts kept, and in different ways the possibility of friction between the associated brothers is greater than when the flock is undivided.[18, 19]

[17] As opposed to its formal establishment at the religious ceremony of marriage.

[18] Parts of this chapter appear in an essay, 'The Kindred in a Greek Mountain Community', included in *Mediterranean Countrymen*, edited by Julian Pitt-Rivers, Mouton and Co., The Hague, 1963. This volume has been published in the series 'Recherches Mediterranéennes' of La Maison des Sciences de L'Homme. I am grateful for permission to reprint this material.

[19] The degree to which my analysis of the Sarakatsan kindred is valid for Greek rural communities in general may be judged by comparing it with Ernestine Friedl's lucid account of kinship usage in her book, *Vasilika: A Village in Modern Greece*, New York, 1962.

# IV

## THE EXTENDED FAMILY

### 1. THE STATUS OF THE BRIDE

I HAVE said that the Sarakatsan family is an isolated and autonomous social group and I have stressed the moral solidarity which characterizes the relations of its members. But the Sarakatsan family, like all domestic groupings, passes through a cycle of development which in this instance begins with the marriage of a man with a woman and normally ends with the final division of the family's flocks between their sons one or two years after the youngest has married. An examination of some aspects of this process makes it possible to give an account of the institutions governing the redistribution of rights over property and persons which accompanies the development of new families and the dispersion of the older groups which have brought them into being. But the autonomy, solidarity, and isolation of the family make this transition difficult and critical. It is not only that it causes individuals real psychological distress when a girl at her marriage must abandon the family of her birth or when another family must receive a strange woman into the circle of their close and exclusive relationships. The marriages of any group of siblings have to be arranged in such a way that the family derives the maximum of prestige from them; and also that individuals relinquish their obligations to the family of origin only when these have been fulfilled, or have been safely delegated to another unmarried member of the group.

A description of the cycle of family development serves a second purpose. It documents the changing relations in the sibling group which are precipitated by the marriages of its members. The solution of the conflict between parents' newly assumed obligations to infant children and their long established duties and affections to siblings and parents in the family of origin, illustrates the distinction between the relatives of the family and the collateral relatives of the kindred. Indeed, this conflict is, as it were, the growing point of the distinction.

In a formal sense the elementary family is established on the

day of marriage when the groom and his retinue of kinsmen
and affines arrive to claim the bride at the huts of her father.
After the celebration of the religious ceremony of betrothal in
her own home the groom and his train escort the bride and her
dowry back to the huts of the groom's family; there, after a
short rest, for the journey is often long and rough, the wedding
ceremony is performed by the priest on the afternoon of the
same Sunday. None of the bride's family or kindred accompanies her to the home of the groom or witnesses the marriage
service.[1] The physical severance from her family and kinsmen
is complete and dramatic, the more so when it is remembered
that since the day of her birth feelings of affection, co-operation
at work, and even ordinary conversation, have only been possible for her inside the circle of the family and her kindred.

Many points of wedding custom reflect the character of her
new status as a member of her husband's family of origin. When
the groom arrives at the home of the bride and immediately
before the religious ceremony of betrothal takes place, three
gifts are presented to her by members of the groom's family.
First the brother of the groom places at her feet a pair of new
shoes; and in the right shoe he leaves a coin, preferably a gold
sovereign. For now she enters a new pathway of her life, and it
is hoped she will bring prosperity both to the family she is
founding and to the family of her mother-in-law where she will
live and work, at least for some years. Having placed the shoes
at her feet the brother of the groom then greets her by taking
her right hand in his. She returns his greeting with a demure
and scarcely audible 'Thank you' and bending low over his
outstretched hand carries it to her lips, then touches it to her
forehead and once more to her lips. The other gift-bearers are
sisters of the groom, or, if these are lacking, wives of his
brothers. Their gifts are generally pieces of gold or silver
jewellery, earrings, bracelets or necklaces with pendant crosses.
The women greet the bride by kissing her first on the right
cheek and then on the left and the bride responds by kissing their
hands in the manner already described.

The moment comes when the bride must kiss the hands of
her parents and leave them. Together with her brothers and

---

[1] However, where a family is related both to bride and groom, they will
generally send a representative to support each side.

sisters, her cousins and the wives of her brothers, she walks some two hundred yards to the place where the groom's party await her. As they walk they chant a song which with brevity and unspoken inference expresses her grief.

> Mother, bless me on this my first journey away from you.
> Daughter, go with my blessing, may God bring you fortune.[2]

The bride is surrendered, and the eldest brother of the groom mounts her on a chosen animal. The horse is led by a sister of the groom while the other sisters, brothers, and brothers' wives surround and support her on all sides; for she is not only frightened and desolate but physically weak after long hours of standing, and the lack of food and sleep which she has endured since the beginning of the customary ceremonies on the Friday. At the end of the journey the bride is led to the door of the bridegroom's hut where his parents stand to receive her. The father assists her to dismount and she kisses his hand. She kisses the mother's hand, too, and is embraced by her. Then, as she enters the hut, crossing the threshold with her right foot forward, the mother of the groom passes over her wrists two bracelets of bread and gives her a cup of wine in either hand which she pours in her steps as she moves to the far side of the hut. There she is greeted by and kisses the hands of those kinsmen and affines of the groom who did not make the journey to escort her from her home. Finally, they bring to her all the children; and in the same way and with the same respect she kisses their hands also. In the presentation of the gifts, and later of bread and wine, which are the elements of communion and commensality; in the concern the groom's family show for her on the journey to her new home; and in the bride's first ceremonial, but simple, exchange of greetings with people to whom she has never spoken, but to whom she is now irrevocably bound, there is symbolized the initial pattern of their relations, submission and respect on her part, and acceptance and protection on theirs.

---

[2] Εὐχήσου με μανούλα μου στὸ πρῶτο κίνημά μου.
Μὲ τὴν εὐχή μου, τσούπρα μου, Θεὸς νὰ σὲ προκόψῃ.

From Sunday until the evening of Tuesday, by which time the guests have all departed, the bride remains secluded inside the bridegroom's hut, where she is attended by relays of the groom's close female kinswomen. This seclusion fits the feelings of shyness and shame which a bride is expected to experience at the thought of the various implications of her new status; but it also protects her from the dangers of the evil eye, the destructive force of envy whether consciously or unconsciously exercised to which both the marriage partners are thought to be peculiarly susceptible at this time. In the groom's hut she is guarded and supported by the women with whom her lot is now cast and by the icons and other ritual objects which belong to the family. Whenever a stranger or a member of the family comes into the hut she at once stands up to show respect, gazing fixedly with expressionless stare at the ground in front of her. It is not unusual for a bride to stand transfixed in this way for three or four hours. It is with the greatest difficulty that from time to time she is persuaded to sit down and rest, or to eat a mouthful of wheaten bread dipped in wine.

On the Monday, however, she must leave the hut about midday to lead the dance. She dances in turn with the marriage sponsor (ὁ κουμπάρος), her husband, father-in-law and mother-in-law, brothers-in-law and sisters-in-law, and other prominent guests. On the Tuesday morning she prepares in silence cups of sweet coffee for her parents-in-law. They wish her long life and sons, and she thanks them. At midday she makes a rice pie. Later that day the guests, who night and day have been drinking, dancing, and feasting since Saturday morning, depart. Before they leave, the guests, almost all of whom are kinsmen or affines of the groom, take their leave of the bride, the men taking her hand, the women kissing her on the cheeks; and she with respect kisses their hands. Each guest makes her a small money gift and she in return gives each man a small wedding bag (τροβάς) of black and white check material woven by herself, in which is placed some bread, meat, and cheese for the homeward journey. Each female guest receives a smaller embroidered bag. To the sponsor the bride gives the choicest blanket (βελέντζα) of her dowry after he has presented her with a money gift of about 100 drachmas (twenty-five shillings). The bride, at this point, also exchanges gifts with the members of her husband's immediate family. She gives shirts or socks to her father-in-law and brothers-in-law. To her husband's sisters and sisters-in-law she presents embroidered bodices. As a rule the father-in-law presents the new bride with a blanket and the other members give her various articles of clothing, such as skirts or blouses.

All the guests have now left and on the Tuesday night the bride and groom sleep together for the first time. But the ceremonial introduction of the bride to her new family and the tasks she must perform is not yet completed. On the Wednesday the women of the family escort the bride to the well. With them walks a youth carrying the wedding standard. This standard attests the virginity and purity of the two partners and, except on the Sunday when it is borne in front of the bridegroom on his journey to claim the bride, it has flown above the thatch of the bridegroom's hut since the Saturday evening.[3] On the Wednesday morning, since the marriage has now been consummated in the physical union of the bride and groom, the standard is taken down from the roof. At the spring or well the shaft of the standard is thrust upright into the water and abandoned, while the standard is cut free and put away until the marriage of another son. In the minds of the Sarakatsani this is the definitive moment when the bride finally enters the ranks of the married women.[4] At once the bride fills and carries to the huts of her new home her first barrel of water. This is an appropriate task to open her new life of service; for carrying water is rightly considered by the women to be their hardest work. Bent double under their enormous load they must often stagger as far as a mile from the well to the huts. On the afternoon of the same day she takes up her distaff for the first time and spins a little red wool, red the colour which represents virility in her husband, strength and fertility in herself. On the Thursday, under the supervision of her mother-in-law and with some help from the other women, she washes the clothes of the whole family as well as her own undergarments stained with the blood of her virginity. During these first few days all the women of the family make a conscious effort to put the bride at ease in

[3] When it replaces a smaller flag made with a handkerchief, placed there at the beginning of the marriage preparations.

[4] Cf. Höeg, op. cit., vol. i, p. 52.

her new surroundings. They can appreciate her feelings of despair and loneliness; it is an ordeal which one day every Sarakatsan woman must face. But such sentiments can be afforded only a brief indulgence. From the Friday the bride undertakes the full routine of work allotted to her by her husband's mother.

The ceremonial induction into the family of the groom during and immediately after the wedding, the symbolic acts which she must perform, and the exchange of gifts with her close affines, all indicate the quality of her initial status within the extended family. The essential fact is that the new bride is subordinate to all other adults in the extended family. Even the five-year-olds try with varying success to boss the new 'bride'. As a worker her services belong to the whole group. She is, as they often say, 'our bride'. Not only does she care for the comfort of her own husband but she is responsible for washing, mending, and darning the clothes of all his unmarried brothers. In general, it can be said that any hard or unpleasant work will be delegated to her. A mule to be rounded up, water to be carried—the new bride is certain to be sent. 'She must learn our ways,' the other women explain, 'and must take root in her new family. Besides, she has no children to care for.' The bride takes most of her orders from her mother-in-law under whose critical and watchful direction she works. But she must be prepared to carry out requests from any brother, sister, or other more senior bride of the extended family. Yet despite her subordinate status she is accepted as a full member of the group. This is the implication of the exchange of gifts with members of the family; for in this community gifts are never exchanged with unrelated persons. 'She is one of us', they say. Membership carries with it the possibility of a growing comradeship, and the right to protection against insult and injury from outsiders. Her behaviour is extremely modest. She speaks only if she is addressed, and then her replies are made with the utmost show of respect. She addresses her husband's brothers as ἀφέντη, 'master', and his sisters as κυρά, 'mistress'. She follows her husband in his modes of address to all senior relatives, father, mother, uncle, aunt, and so on. The family and kinsmen address the newcomer as simply νύφη, 'bride'. In the first months the bride will rise to her feet and remain standing when a man of the

2. The Women

family comes into the hut and will not sit down unless specifically requested to do so.

The young bride is punctilious in providing all these expressions of respect and humility. In this new situation what is
important for her is that her formal membership in the extended
family shall in as short a time as is conventionally possible
become a more spontaneous acceptance of herself by the other
members of the group. Yet even at this early stage, when as an
individual she counts for very little, she is aware that her person
separates her husband from his family of origin. The dowry
wealth which she has brought, and in which the whole family
takes pride, is property held in trust for her unborn children;
it may not be alienated for the benefit of her husband's brothers.
The distaff, with which she spins her first wool on the Wednesday, is a gift from her husband, preferably carved by himself or,
if he has not the skill, at least commissioned by him.[5] The bride
may not bring a distaff from her own home nor may she receive
one as a gift from her mother-in-law or anybody else in her
husband's family. This is an object with mystical power which
will protect her children from evil forces. In these respects it is
a symbol of the solidarity and future autonomy of her family
which as yet scarcely exists but whose full development only
death or sterility can hinder. Her awareness of the odd contradiction in her new situation, the humility required of her on the
one hand, the assurance of her ultimate triumph on the other,
only increases the bride's feelings of shyness and shame, attitudes
which on other grounds she is anyway expected to express.

During the early months of the marriage the young husband
gives the minimum of overt public attention to his bride. He
may, in stern, almost harsh, tones, make some simple request of
her for food and drink or dry clothes, but he does not make
conversation. For her part, a bride will never address her husband before other members of the family. If she requires anything she arranges it through her husband's brother. There is
not, during this period, the slightest inclination on the part of
the husband to champion his wife in any dispute which she
may have with the other women of the family. Nor does he
show the least annoyance when a brother, in his presence,

---

[5] See Chatzimichalis, op. cit., vol. i, Part B, p. 410.

gives his wife some peremptory order. The husband's obligations and affections are still entirely contained within his own family of origin. Indeed his behaviour reflects an almost compulsive assertion that 'this is how it will always be'. Clearly if this fiction is to be maintained for even a short space of time, the husband must not display any affective interest in his bride, since this would inevitably disturb the equilibrium in the old pattern of his relations with his siblings and his parents. Therefore in his general behaviour the husband attempts to deny the importance of his exclusive sexual relationship with his bride and he makes every effort to conceal the occurrence and frequency of sexual intercourse. However, since all the members of a family sleep together in the same hut, this is not easy.

Before the marriage ceremony a temporary hut is built for the bridal pair, or sometimes a space is cleared in the hut which is otherwise used as a store-shed. Customarily the bridegroom does not go with the sheep for eight days from the Sunday of his marriage and he is thus able to sleep in privacy with his bride for six nights. Although this initial privacy is granted to him, the whole progress of these marital events is shared by the groom with his brothers; some of this information also leaks through to the female members of the family. In this first sexual communion the entire family identifies itself with the young husband. There is no question at this stage of his having any affection for his bride. This may emerge later partly as a result of the intimacies now initiated. It is something of an ordeal and a matter of considerable anxiety for all Sarakatsan bridegrooms that they should be able to effect a technically successful assault upon this strange woman and uphold their reputation for manliness in its most literal sense, a reputation which affects the prestige of the entire family. The stress on physical and moral manliness (ἀνδρισμός) in the stereotype of the ideal man encourages in the Sarakatsani a deep-seated fear of sexual impotence on this critical occasion which is, indeed, almost a public ceremony of initiation. In the morning, success or failure on the previous night is discussed with brothers in embarrassed monosyllables and, if there has been difficulty, they try to give advice and encouragement. Any lack of sexual prowess almost inevitably reaches the ears of the bride's family and the possibility of a leakage farther afield cannot be overlooked.

But with the return of the young shepherd bridegroom to his sheep this co-operative interest in his sexual relations ends. He may continue to sleep with his bride in privacy for one or two months but if he prolongs this period unduly it represents a clear breach in the solidarity of the family. Sexual intercourse becomes now progressively associated not with the proof of manliness, but with conjugal intimacy and solidarity. And in his attempt to maintain his relations with his family of origin unaltered and intact he uses great care to avoid any demonstration of this kind of interest in his bride. Sarakatsan sleeping arrangements are simple. Velenzas, thick woollen carpet-like blankets, are spread on the ground. The Sarakatsanos removes his shoes and his jacket, and another velenza is placed over him. It is the duty of the young bride to place the heavy enveloping velenzas over each member of the family in turn and then to put out the oil lamp before making her way to her husband's side. It is not generally very long before a concert of snores indicates that the family is asleep and it is then possible for the bride and groom under their heavy covering to exchange silent embraces. Silence, of course, is necessary to avoid discovery but in any case the Sarakatsani believe that speech during intercourse is shameful. At first light the bride is first on her feet to blow the embers on the hearth into a blaze and prepare the coffee. With these conventional arrangements it is possible for the physical solidarity of the family to remain relatively unimpaired, and for the bride and groom to enjoy marital intimacy without directly affronting the sensibilities of the husband's family of origin.

However, there is a further complication. Before his marriage the young shepherd returned from the sheep to spend a night at the family hut perhaps once in every three weeks; then he changed his clothes, had the luxury of a night under cover, and heard the family news and gossip. After his marriage he comes openly to the huts more frequently; but he cannot return more than once in every twelve or thirteen days without feeling some embarrassment that he is showing too much interest in a person who is still an interloper in the family circle, and a sense of shame that his sexual desires and intentions must be very evident. He therefore supplements his fortnightly visits with other clandestine meetings. The bride sleeps near the door, a cold and draughty part of the hut not favoured by more senior members of the family. The groom arrives at the huts some time after midnight when the family is asleep, slips into the hut, remains with his young wife for an hour or so and then, well before dawn, is already on his way back to the sheep which may be two or three hours' walking distance away. Naturally the family are aware that these visits occur. Stories are told about grooms who tripped over milk cans as they entered the pitch dark hut or failed to convince the dogs of their true identity. They are considered to be hysterically funny; perhaps an indication of the ambivalent feelings which this conflict of loyalties provokes.

If the newly married shepherd is the eldest son the developing pattern of relations has certain rather specific nuances. The family take an excessive pride in the first bride. They also take some trouble to make her feel at home, although at the same time their sensitivity to the attitude of the groom towards her is greater than in the case of the marriages of younger brothers. This after all is the first intrusion of an outsider into the hitherto exclusive family circle. More importantly the relationship between a father and his eldest son frequently shows signs of strain during this period. A father cannot in accordance with customary right long delay his retirement beyond the time when his eldest son has his first child, for it is an important value of this community that a man who is married and a parent should be the 'master' (νοικοκύρης) in his own household. But after the son's marriage and before the birth of the first child the father insists that he should continue to control the affairs of the extended family while the son is learning under his guidance the elements of his future role. Until the pregnancy of his wife is well established, the irritating uncertainty about the transfer of power, which will confer on him the status and prestige of a family leader in the community, sometimes tempts the son to show a lack of respect[6] to his father which previously he would not have dared to express so freely.

The retirement of the father resolves tensions between proximate generations in the extended family which are considerably aggravated by the influence of the prestige values of the wider

---

[6] Such lack of respect, however, is seldom shown in public.

community. A man who, although married and a parent, remained for a number of years under the day-to-day direction of an elderly father, however vigorous, would lose prestige and find himself the butt of comic satire. The fact that the younger married brothers work for a time under the direction of an elder brother in a common household is a different matter. The relations of brothers after marriage are based on free association. Policy decisions are a matter of consensus rather than direction. The suspicion against the man who does not relieve his father of his burden of responsibility (whether he wants to be relieved of it or not) is that he is nervous, diffident, lacking in self-assertion, and unable to be a 'capable protector' (ἱκανὸς προστάτης) of his family.

In summary, then, the first phase of the development of the elementary family is a latency period in which conjugal solidarity, although gradually developing, is subordinate to the sibling solidarity between the husband and his brothers and sisters. In general it may be said to last until the birth of the first child. Also, although there is no formal change in the relation of father and eldest son during this period, competitive friction between them tends to increase.

## 2. BROTHERS AND THEIR WIVES

After one or two years most brides have become mothers. This, naturally, brings about a great change in the bride's position in the extended family. Previously, although full membership of the group was extended to her, yet in an affective sense she remained a stranger even in the eyes of her own husband. After the birth of her first child it is said that the new bride 'takes root in the new family'. Not only does she take root, as it were, in the extended family but more significantly the new elementary family, consisting of herself, her husband, and the infant child, takes a definitive form. The arrival of the child is received with joy by the whole extended family whose attitude towards the bride shifts from tolerance to acceptance and affection for her as the mother of their tiny kinsman.

It is from the moment when the members of the extended family first feel this new affection for the bride that their control over her begins to diminish. So long as the extended family remains undivided and a younger brother of her husband does not also bring a wife into the group, the bride continues to work very hard carrying water, and gathering firewood for the family. But she will now receive, necessarily, more assistance from the other women in the family and often the demands of her child for the breast, as well as the other attentions it requires, will take priority over all other considerations.

At this time the husband's behaviour towards his wife undergoes fundamental changes. He now begins to talk with her more freely before other members of the family. She is not any longer merely the conjugal partner with whom he has sexual relations, which even in marriage possess a suspect if not exactly shameful quality. She is now the mother of his child; and in this role, especially if her infant is a son, the husband openly recognizes his wife without the ambivalence which previously attached to their relationship. For the child represents his own social individuation; it stresses his separation even from his siblings with whom his common interests have previously been almost undifferentiated. As a father he must now assert himself in the world, and even within his own extended family, if he is to carry out adequately his parental obligations.

After the birth of the first child the bride does not usually continue to address her husband's brothers and sisters as respectively, ἀφέντη, 'master', and κυρά, 'mistress'; instead she uses their christian names. And if, by this time, a younger brother of her husband has been married, the family no longer address her as νύφη, 'bride', but use the name of her husband with the suffix '-ina' added; thus Pericles, Periclina. With these changes it is openly recognized that a new elementary family group has emerged; and they reflect, too, the growing equality in the relationships of the wife with the members of her husband's family of origin who are of her own generation. It is also significant that no member of the extended family, except the parents-in-law, any longer orders her about in peremptory fashion in the presence of her husband, let alone attempts to scold or discipline her.

Parallel to the diminished control of the family over the bride, is the tacit understanding that the husband/father of the new elementary family is no longer able to fulfil critical obligations of his roles as son and brother in his family of origin; specifically, he is not expected to risk his life in any form of vengeance killing even if it concerns the death of a brother or the dishonour of a sister. Under the conditions of social life in a patrilocal extended family it is inevitable that there will be some conflict between a man's roles as son and brother in his family of origin and his roles as husband and father in his family of marriage. In important matters the Sarakatsani solve this problem by holding to the principle that obligations to direct lineal descendants always take priority over obligations to either direct ascendant or collateral kin. It is, then, not marriage but the birth of children which breaches the unity of the group of brothers.

The Sarakatsani claim that brothers would undoubtedly live together all their lives were it not for the quarrels of their wives. This is a rather too simple explanation of the causes which eventually lead to the separation of brothers; yet it is true that the differences between wives often provide the occasions for separation. There are two proverbs which the Sarakatsani often quote when discussing this subject. 'Women make the house and they destroy it' (οἱ γυναῖκες φχιάνουν τὸ σπίτι καὶ τὸ χαλᾶν). 'Wives are like nuts from forty different walnut trees' (ἀπὸ σαράντα καρυδιὲς καρύδια). The second proverb implies that wives are all alike, yet each comes from a different home. 'Each wife', said one informant, 'has her own mother. They cannot come to an understanding.' The Sarakatsani expect the wives of brothers to quarrel and on the whole they are not disappointed in their expectations. Yet, fundamentally, the growing distance between brothers is due to the obligations and affections which they owe to their children and which replace their former attachment to the sibling group. Quarrels between wives are not simply the result of incompatibility of temperament or some innate Greek sense of individuality. They arise because wives identify themselves with the rights and interests of their children. That this exclusive identification occurs, follows from the logic of the kinship system based on equivalent bilateral extension. As we have seen, the elementary family is the only corporate kinship group which is relatively enduring in this bilateral system. The children of each brother have in common with their cousins only half of their kindred. Through their affiliation to the kinsmen of their mother, they have certain affective interests and moral obligations they cannot share with their cousins. In many unilineal descent systems, on the other hand, the interests and rights of a woman's children are so intimately related to those of the children of their father's brothers that irrespective of personal feelings, her duty to her own children demands loyal co-operation with all members of the lineage. The weak extended family of the Sarakatsani does not provide a framework with continuity in time in which units segmented in one context may yet be united in another. When the joint flock of animals has been divided, co-operation between married brothers, and therefore contractual obligation, generally continues, but categorical obligations deriving from common membership in the family of origin are no longer valid. An index of this instability of the extended family is the relatively early retirement of the father, which has already been discussed.

An important characteristic of the extended family is that it is based on consent rather than authority. The flock and everything connected with it is held as common property, and since brothers have equal interests in the flock, decisions which concern its welfare are based on a general consensus of opinion. The eldest brother, who normally acts as the executive head, implements the general decision of the group. He also acts as its treasurer and all money is controlled by him. When business affairs take him to Jannina he does the shopping for the whole group, returning with perhaps a pair of shoes for the wife of one of his brothers, a cotton frock for his daughter, and a new jacket for one of his nephews. If one of his brothers wants cigarettes or requires money to play cards in the coffee-shop he comes and states his needs without embarrassment. The younger brother knows from experience what is reasonable and he does not usually make impossible demands on the family's slender resources. If he injures his family, he injures himself. The solidarity of brothers in such matters, even after marriage and the birth of children, is remarkable. Yet gradually, and in most cases with the greatest reluctance, they come to realize that their several obligations to their new families of marriage preclude the possibility of their living together indefinitely in a single domestic household. Observation of the conduct of their wives may often assist them in arriving at this conclusion.

The attitudes of wives towards one another are far less

reasonable. Unless their requirements happen to be similar, what is given to one wife is by definition not given to the other. Inevitably each believes that the other is the better treated. An elder brother often makes a conscious effort to treat his younger brother's wife with particular consideration and tact, supplying from the family purse without debate the money required for all her children's needs; shoes, a new jacket, medicine and so on. This may merely infuriate the elder brother's wife who sees herself and her children sacrificed to her husband's wish to maintain intact the relationship with his brother. On the other hand, the younger brother's wife is seldom grateful. She may not believe that she is being favourably treated and, at best, she will still resent the fact that she must apply to her husband's brother for the requirements of her children.

Yet the break-up of the united group of brothers is not due to the quarrels of the wives alone. As his children pass out of infancy, a father's thoughts are increasingly concerned with the problem of how to provide for their future. For instance, it may be necessary to practise extreme economy for a number of years, or even to borrow money to buy additional sheep, in an attempt to build up a flock large enough to support his sons and provide for his daughters' dowries. Obviously such operations can only be carried through efficiently and equitably when each brother has command of his own share of the family's stock.

The affairs of the family group led by Theodoros Ferendinos (see Chart, page 74) illustrate these problems. After thirteen years together in an extended family the five brothers are considering the need to divide their household and the flocks. It is a family of moderate wealth and prestige owning 365 sheep and goats. The five brothers are known to be resolute, brave, and mutually devoted. Yet although I never observed an open quarrel between these brothers, friction is evident. Four of the brothers are married, two of them have children nearing school age while three of the eldest brother's children are already at school. They are all concerned as to how they will support these growing families. Theodoros the elder brother has four children, but the second and third brothers have only two each. While the group lives in one household it is clear that to some extent the younger brothers are carrying part of the burden of

CHART

## EXTENDED FAMILY LED BY THEODOROS FERENDINOS

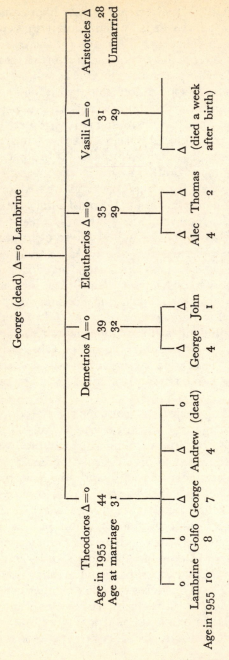

George (dead) Δ=0 Lambrine

Theodoros Δ=0
Age in 1955          44
Age at marriage  31

Lambrine  Golfo  George  Andrew (dead)
Age in 1955  10    8       7       4

Demetrios Δ=0
                    39
                    32

George  John
   4       1

Eleutherios Δ=0
                    35
                    29

Alec  Thomas
  4       2

Vasili Δ=0
            31
            29

(died a week
 after birth)

Aristoteles Δ
                28
Unmarried

N.B. There are also two sisters not shown in this chart. They were, in 1955, respectively 42 and 40 years of age; the elder sister was married three years before, the younger one year after, the marriage of Theodoros.

supporting Theodoros' children, particularly as the three children who are at school must be well dressed and well shod to uphold the family's prestige before the children of the villagers and the other Sarakatsani who are trying to emulate them. Dissatisfaction, it must be stressed, is not expressed by those brothers who have no children. The attitude of the unmarried brother, or even of the married brother without children, remains one of common identification and mutual sharing without the keeping of any conscious account. But the brother who has become a parent must adopt a more calculating attitude if he is to fulfil this new role according to accepted expectations.

For the same reasons, although brothers in an earlier phase of the extended family's development willingly delegate the control of a common purse to the senior brother, they find this arrangement less congenial at a later stage when the pressure of anxieties about the future of their families of marriage begins to be felt. The different spending habits of brothers, which within limits were formerly merely an incident in the common identification of siblings, later become difficult to ignore. Theodoros himself admits that 'he wastes money easily' by standing drinks in the coffee-shop and playing cards, whereas Demetrios the second brother has a reputation for being tight-fisted and careful. Eleutherios the third brother is somewhat uncouth and feels ill at ease in the coffee-shop. Vasili and Aristoteles resemble their eldest brother and like to drink and play cards when the opportunity presents itself. Demetrios admits that Theodoros must spend money in the coffee-shop to keep in with people and to know what is going on. But he thinks that often he spends more money than is necessary. No doubt his drinking companions account him a fine fellow, but this hardly assists Demetrios in his problems. Demetrios privately grumbled to me when Theodoros bought a fifty shilling pocket watch for Aristoteles the youngest brother. Aristoteles was the favourite of Theodoros, Demetrios complained. The boy had herded his sheep well enough for several years by using the sun and stars. The truth was that he wanted a watch because some of the other young shepherds had watches. Had I not observed how he now rushed up to everybody and asked them if they wanted to know the time and, before they could answer, pulled out the new watch simply to show them that he had one? Admittedly every man must have some 'self-regard' (ἐγωϊσμός) but the family had to pay fifty shillings for this watch.

During the summer of 1954 Vasili worked for a Thessaly merchant who had come to the Epirus looking for wool. Vasili travelled around the Zagori countryside as his agent, buying up wool wherever he found it. By entering a price in his account book somewhat in excess of the amount he actually paid out, but still below the maximum buying price laid down in the merchant's instructions to him, he was able to make a very pleasing profit in addition to his weekly wage. When he returned to the family he gave almost all the profit to Theodoros but secretly withheld six pounds for himself. Vasili had been married only two years at the time, but his wife was expecting a child in the next month. His conscience was clearly troubled at the deception he was practising and in his confession to me he explained that three years ago there would have been no point in keeping any of the money to himself, but now he was married, his wife was about to have a child, and he vaguely felt the need to have some reserve of money which was entirely under his own control.

The wives of the four married brothers live together in one domestic unit and work under the direction of their mother-in-law. There are many practical advantages in this situation of which they are not unaware. When one wife is cooking the communal meal, another is collecting firewood or carrying water while the old mother-in-law watches over the children. There are goats to be milked, wild herbs to be collected, clothes to be washed. There is the whole lengthy process of spinning and weaving. In all these multifarious domestic tasks the collaboration of the five women makes for companionship and a certain economy of time and energy. But while the joint operations of the brothers with the sheep are based on a relationship of common identification, the co-operation of their wives is of a contractual character. The partnership works smoothly so long as each wife is thought to be pulling her weight in relation to her seniority. This clearly may often be a matter rather of opinion than obvious fact. And while the brothers are usually careful not to express any displeasure they may feel for one another, wives are only too ready to criticize one another in public.

Theodorina, the wife of Theodoros, is criticized because of

her lack of physical robustness. About three years ago she lost a baby girl. She was prostrate with grief and never fully recovered. She has been to a number of different doctors who have agreed that she is suffering from 'weakness' but have variously diagnosed this as due to infected tonsils, bad heart, and anaemia. She has had her tonsils and adenoids removed and a number of courses of injections; this treatment has cost a considerable sum of money and has produced no visible improvement. Demetrina, the wife of the second brother, is particularly scornful of Theodorina. 'Theodorina is down on the ground (κατὰ γῆς) again', she complains, and goes on to explain that she is leaving her children in the ditch to fend for themselves just because of an idea in her head. This refers to her grief for her little girl. It is right to grieve, but not to this extent where she is unable to care properly for her sons and daughters for whose existence she ought to thank God. No doubt what really annoys Demetrina and the other women is the money wasted on medicines, and the extra work which they have to do when Theodorina periodically says she is too sick to go about her tasks.

Demetrina, herself, is disliked by all the other wives and her mother-in-law because of her sharp tongue and her dogmatic holier-than-thou attitude. Her own family of origin is on the worst of terms with her husband's brothers and she is suspected, not without reason, of passing on information about the conduct of affairs in the extended family into which she has married. She is a storm centre in many quarrels with the other wives on account of her four-year-old son, an unpleasant and physically tough blonde-headed bully, who maltreats his young cousins by hurling stones and hitting them over the head with pieces of wood. They note that this child resembles his maternal kin.

The third wife, Eleutherina, is a good worker but graceless in body and personality. She suffers from some catarrhal complaint which makes her speech almost unintelligible and causes her nostrils to drool with mucus. Behind her back the other wives mock her for these defects and she is conscious of this. Her small son Alec, who is four years old, suffers from the same catarrhal complaint, appears to be mentally backward, and is subject to periodic fits. She is held responsible for the disabilities of the child which affect the prestige of the whole family.

Vasilina the youngest wife has been married for about two years. She gave birth to a son, but the child was weak and died. Since she has scarcely advanced from the status of being a new bride, she does not assert herself. She is a willing worker but slow and without much intelligence. For these reasons the other women have little patience with her and criticize her freely.

The wives openly admit that they live in anticipation of the day when their husbands will separate the single household and each wife will become 'mistress' (νοικοκυρά) in her own home. Their imputation of various short-comings to the other wives is merely a way of demonstrating their fundamentally opposed interests in respect to their different families. Each wife/mother is in herself a symbol of the kinship distance which separates her children from their paternal cousins, and therefore her husband from his siblings. The worst quarrels between wives are about their children. And such quarrels are particularly dangerous to the unity of the brothers. Two married brothers frequently stand together and verbally or even physically chastise their wives who make trouble in the family by quarrels over personal differences; but when the issue between the wives concerns their children (however trivial its origin may be), the two sibling/fathers, out of loyalty to and identification with their children, are inevitably committed to the support of their wives.

Therefore a circumstantial factor of some importance in deciding the moment when brothers must separate is the increasing difficulty of maintaining discipline in a joint household without causing offence to the constituent elementary families. When Theodoros on occasions shook a worried head and said, 'We are eighteen individuals (νομάτοι) in this house', this was the cause of his anxiety. As head of the house he could directly discipline only his own wife and children. He would not verbally reprimand a brother's wife in her husband's presence, unless she was a newly married bride or without children; in his absence he would certainly scold her if she did not comply with some instruction which concerned the general running of the joint household; but he could not interfere in her relations with her children. No brother would ever strike another brother's wife. Even the control of the mother-in-law over her sons' wives, though it is still considerable, becomes less complete after three or four years of marriage. In this household there are eight young children and babies playing, fighting, and screaming. Except in the early evening when a sleep of exhaustion stills their activities, the scene is one of constant tumult. In this situation a brother cannot strike the children of another. *A fortiori* one wife cannot in any way interfere with the children of another wife. When a father separates two embattled cousins he pushes the child which is not his own out of the way telling it to go to its mother, and then turns to deal his own child a slap across the face. Clearly these symptoms of disorder and indiscipline in the extended family result from the growing isolation of each of the constituent elementary families. The autonomy of each elementary family in regard to all its internal relationships and the control of its children is not compatible with the co-existence of the families in a single domestic unit.

When an extended family of several brothers and their wives has lived as a single household for a number of years it **is** not unusual to hear in the gossip of other families some criticism of this arrangement. In fact, few extended families survive for longer than ten years without the separation of at least some brothers. No doubt the criticism of the extended family which does remain united beyond this limit may be attributed, in some measure, to the jealousy of other groups in which brothers have not been able to show quite the same mutual devotion. Yet, if they have succeeded in living up to one kinship value, their detractors are right to point out that they have failed to maintain other and more important values. Thus one critic of the Ferendinos family said that it was not right that the second and third brothers in the family, who each had two children, were not yet complete masters in their own households. They were assisting their elder brother with his larger family to a degree which was scarcely honourable when they had their own children to care for. Moreover, it was added, everybody knew that the wives were at each others' throats. It was dangerous to allow this state of affairs to continue because it would inevitably end in quarrels between the brothers themselves.

## 3. SEPARATION

There is no precise formalized rule as to when brothers ought to separate. Some informants say that when an elder brother has a family of his own, and his younger brother is also married

and has had two children born to him, the elder brother ought
to leave the extended family. Others state that an elder brother
with a family should not share a common household with a
younger brother after the latter's eldest child approaches school
aged (5–6 years of age). It is also said that it is necessary for
brothers to remain united in one household until all the sisters
are married. All agree that in any individual family the course
of events depends upon the particular circumstances.

An examination of field data reveals that broadly speaking
there are two modes of separation. Either a group of brothers
waits until all the brothers are married before any separation
occurs, or, from time to time, individual brothers leave the
extended family to set up their own households and withdraw
their share of the stock from the common flock before the whole
group has completed its marriages.

TABLE I

## THE SEPARATION OF BROTHERS

| Number of brothers in a sibling group | 2 | 3 | 4 | 5 | 6 | |
|---|---|---|---|---|---|---|
| Groups united until all are married | 8 | 4 | 1 | 1 | 0 | 14 |
| Groups divided before all are married | 0 | 3 | 4 | 1 | 1 | 9 |
| | 8 | 7 | 5 | 2 | 1 | 23 |

In this simple table, data is presented on twenty-three groups
of brothers which in recent years completed their marriages.
Of these twenty-three groups, nine did not wait until all the
brothers were married before some division occurred. On the
other hand, of the fourteen groups which have waited until all
the brothers were married before dividing their sheep and
households, eight had only two brothers and a further four,
three brothers. Thus it would appear that there is a correlation
between the size of the group of brothers and the method of
separation. In groups of four or more brothers, it is generally
not possible to wait until all the brothers are married before
some division occurs.

Where the division of the household is effected in a single
operation after all the brothers have been married, and where it
occurs 'with good heart' (μὲ καλὴ καρδιά), the whole group

co-operates in the erection of new dwellings, each brother setting up a separate household in a new hut. The common treasury is used to furnish the new homes with the necessary simple domestic equipment. Articles of dowry such as blankets, mirrors, trays, drinking glasses, which may have been in communal use in the extended family, accompany each wife to her new hut. The youngest son with his parents, if they are alive, and his bride remain in the hut of the former joint household.

When these arrangements have been completed, the animals are massed and penned. The animals of each category, rams, ewe lambs, 2-year-old ewes, 3-year-old ewes, and so on are driven in turn through a narrow opening. As each animal passes through the opening, it is nominated to a particular brother, each brother taking animals in a fixed rotation. Or sometimes the animals of each category are divided by the drawing of lots. In either case, as the animals are assigned to each brother, he effects some variation on the existing ear-sign. The youngest brother, who receives an additional half-share of stock for each of his surviving parents, also retains the original ear-sign.

This operation is a severe test of brotherly love. A brother who finds that he has an undue number of indifferent animals in his share is unlikely to believe that the division of stock has been just. Therefore, in some cases, a disinterested relative, generally an uncle, is persuaded to hold the ring and preside over a fair distribution. The separate flocks which result from this division are unlikely to be equal in numbers. For, apart from the extra animals which the youngest son receives for the maintenance of the old parents, any animals and their natural increase which came into the flock as dowry of the brothers' wives are never under any circumstances included in the equal distribution, but remain the property of the brothers concerned.

For the other method of separation, in which individual brothers leave the main body of the extended family to set up their own households, the procedure is similar; but in this case only one share is separated out from the joint property. If this process is continued to its logical conclusion, the operation is finally completed when the youngest brother finds himself alone with his bride and surviving parents in the original extended family hut. In fact, what occurs more frequently in separations of this type, is that after the first two or three brothers have contracted out of the extended family, the remaining two or three younger brothers hold together until the youngest is married and established before a further and final division is made.

It is now necessary to introduce a further complicating factor. The groups of brothers we have been considering have sisters to whom they owe certain categorical obligations. We are here mainly concerned with two of these obligations. They must, as members of the family, contribute their share towards her dowry, and they must defend her honour (τιμή). The marriage of the sister represents for the brother the successful and honourable accomplishment of these tasks: her virginity has been conserved intact and the dowry has been handed over. In logical order these obligations are prior to any that a man later acquires through marriage in the new elementary family which is then formed. Thus, ideally, it is held that all the sisters in a family should marry first, before even the eldest brother takes a wife. In this way, duties which a man has in the role of brother in the family of origin do not come into conflict with his duties as a father and husband in the family of marriage. Generally speaking, men marry when they are about thirty or thirty-one years of age, whereas their sisters hope to find a bridegroom when they are in their mid-twenties. Table II gives an indication of these general trends.

The age at which any girl marries depends on a number of different considerations. Normally, her own family do not wish to lose her before she is about twenty-five years of age. It requires the labour of years to accumulate a worthy dowry; and this is important for reasons of prestige. Further, the family does not want to be deprived of her working services prematurely. Despite the stated ideal that all the sisters should marry before the eldest brother, this is seldom realized since it would destroy the balance of female labour in the group. Generally at least one sister remains unmarried until the bride of the eldest brother is brought into the family. Another factor which delays the marriage of a girl is the real distress which this causes her parents and siblings in a group where affective loyalties are so remarkably strong. However, a family may accept a proposal of marriage for a daughter in her early twenties if it helps the general arrangement of the marriages of a sibling group or if it is an attractive offer for prestige reasons. But it has to be remembered that although it may be hinted through the mediation of kinsmen that a girl is ready to marry, it is always the man's family who must make the approach. If a girl is poor, ugly, unhealthy, or from a family of low social standing, she may wait

TABLE II

## THE AGE OF MARRIAGE (1945-55)

| Age at Marriage | | Brides | Grooms |
|---|---|---|---|
| Over | 32 | 2 | 13 |
| | 32 | 2 | 12 |
| | 31 | 6 | 27 |
| | 30 | 7 | 21 |
| | 29 | 10 | 17 |
| | 28 | 17 | 13 |
| | 27 | 14 | 9 |
| | 26 | 22 | 4 |
| | 25 | 25 | 5 |
| | 24 | 16 | 2 |
| | 23 | 6 | 0 |
| | 22 | 5 | 0 |
| | | 132 | 123 |

many years without receiving an offer; and, in the end, she may be forced to accept the proposal of a widower or a man with some physical or mental incapacity.

But, providing that all the brothers are not born first and all the sisters last, or that there are two sisters very much younger than the rest of the sibling group, it is often possible to marry off all but one of the sisters before the eldest brother has had to wait beyond the age when he might normally expect to marry. Although the late age of marriage of brothers is not unconnected with the duty of first discharging obligations towards the sisters before a man acquires a family of his own, it is not a simple correlation. It is also related to the balance of power between father and son. If a man marries at the age of 30 and his first son is born a year later, this son will in turn reach the age of 30 when his father is in his early sixties, an age at which he becomes physically incapable of the strenuous life that the executive head of a shepherd family necessarily leads. And even if his physique remains unimpaired he cannot delay the marriage of his first son beyond his thirty-first year without suffering considerable and growing criticism in the community. He must, then, bow to the inevitable, arrange the marriage of his son and in a short time (at the birth of the first grandchild) hand over control; for, as we have stressed, it is not compatible with the values of this community for a married man with a child to be still under parental control and not master in his own house. But fathers do not normally hand over control until they have to. An elder brother, who has no sisters to guard or provide for, may marry a year or two sooner, but the difference is not marked.

Old age, then, and the fear of public criticism and ridicule generally force a man to arrange the eldest son's marriage before his thirty-second birthday. No consideration of the needs of sisters will normally delay this event. And the marriage of other brothers in the middle of the birth order of the sibling group are arranged with the same upper limit in mind. On the other hand, the youngest brother will almost certainly not marry until all the sisters have found husbands. Through the social equivalence of brothers, the duty of watching over and, if need be, avenging the honour of the sisters, is delegated to the unmarried member of the group of brothers. This arrangement recognizes the conflict between the roles of father/husband and brother when they are played simultaneously by the same person; a conflict which, according to Sarakatsan kinship values, can only be resolved in favour of the father/husband. It is an arrangement which, on occasion, may delay considerably the marriage of the youngest brother.

TABLE III

## CHILDREN OF EUTHYMIOS CARVOUNIS

| Group of Siblings | | Age at marriage | Age in 1955 |
| --- | --- | --- | --- |
| Demetrios | (M) | 31 | 42 |
| George | (M) | 30 | 38 |
| Michael | (M) | 32 | 36 |
| Elias | (M) | Unmarried | 35 |
| Amalia | (F) | 24 | 32 |
| Evangelike | (F) | 28 | 28 |

The children of Euthymios Carvounis (Table III) are one of those unfortunate sibling groups where all the brothers were born first and the sisters afterwards. The youngest sister has just been successfully married to a villager. But the youngest brother, Elias, is 35 and only now becomes free to find himself a wife.

Naturally, under these conventions, a sister may sometimes find herself without an unmarried brother to act as guardian of her honour. Apart from sibling groups with no brothers, this is likely to be the case where there is only one brother with sisters who are considerably younger and a father who is incapacitated. Pericles Gogolos, for instance, had to marry and succeed his father at the age of 27, when his two younger unmarried sisters, Erasmia and Machoula, were respectively only 23 and 19 years of age.

It appears, then, that the solidarity of the sibling group, as this is manifested in the obligations of brothers towards sisters, ideally demands that all sisters should be married before any of their brothers. In practice, we find that while the ideal is approached, though seldom achieved, when the ages and birth order of the siblings are not an obstacle, in less favourable circumstances it is only the youngest brother who may have to wait some time before marrying. But while the obligations to a sister do not in the main delay the marriages of brothers, the presence of unmarried sisters in the house does effectively prevent married brothers from dividing the extended family household. It is true that in most families, by the time the second brother has married and has children approaching school age, the sisters because of their earlier age of marriage will have left their family of origin. But where this is not so, it is held to be wrong for married brothers to break up the united family group before the sisters are married. In the first place, it is said that brothers who live in a united household are accustomed to reaching unanimous decisions. If each brother has become used to making various decisions for himself, it is less likely that they will agree about whom the sister should marry, and how much dowry in sheep and money should be conceded. Moreover, the traditional element in the dowry, the heavy blankets and personal clothing, claims the better grades of wool from all the sheep of all the brothers for a number of years before the marriage takes place. In a united extended family this presents no difficulty; but if wool had to be collected from a number of autonomous households, it would certainly lead to friction between the wives with reciprocal accusations of sharp practice. Finally, in a large household which has many women the honour of the sister is more efficiently safeguarded. It is not sufficient to have an unmarried brother to take revenge if the sister suffers rape or insult. This is certainly a deterrent, but it does not ensure complete security. It is equally important that whenever a sister goes out on some errand, to gather firewood or carry water, she has a companion to go with her. In the popular mind wells and illicit sexual intercourse are linked together. If a man for any reason wants to see the local girls, he has only to sit by the well and by and by he will see them all. (The wells used by the Sarakatsani traditionally were never, and today are often not, village wells, but remote mountain springs.) If an unmarried girl goes to the well too frequently alone, the gossips are quick to suggest that her object is to collect something more than a barrel of water. But if she always has a companion, she is protected both from the danger of assault which is probably, in fact, remote, and from the danger of slander which is much more real.

For these reasons, then, brothers do not divide the extended household until all the sisters are married. Afterwards, the brothers are free to complete their own marriages and separate their households in the manner that has been described. Each is now the leader of an autonomous family. But when the division of the joint household occurs with 'good heart', and where there is sufficient grazing, they will normally remain together in a 'company' under the general leadership of the eldest brother. But working operations are now on a basis of strict accounting. Brothers often point out that the relative peace and goodwill which prevails between their wives and children after the division of the extended family household is bought at the price of a hitherto unknown element of calculation in their own relations. This is true. However, they sometimes forget that just before division took place it was often precisely the lack of calculation in their relations that they themselves had been complaining about.

In describing the process of development which occurs

within and between the elementary family of marriage and the extended family of origin, it has been possible to document a number of statements about kinship relations which were presented rather more formally in the previous chapter. During this review, a constant theme has been the inherent conflict between the sibling bond and the conjugal relation. It becomes clear that the conjugal relationship only takes priority over the long established relations between siblings after the birth of children; and this is because, in the Sarakatsan view, the obligations of parents towards their children possess an absolute and sacred quality. Indeed, it is the conflict between the individual's roles in his families of origin and of marriage which provide the key to the understanding of Sarakatsan kinship usages. The individual's withdrawal after marriage from categorical obligations to the other members of the sibling group marks the isolation of the family of marriage; and the increasing kinship distance which separates the husband or wife from brothers and sisters and other collateral kinsmen. And these processes are consistently related to the bilateral form of the kindred and the prohibition on marriage within its limits.

It is also apparent that the processes we have been discussing are not unaffected by the dominantly competitive values of the community. We have seen how the belief that a married man with a family ought to be master in his own household so that he may assert the interests of his own elementary family of marriage, influences the decision of a brother to set up his own household. It is not merely a question of material interest. Prestige is also involved. This is clear in the case of the eldest son, who puts pressure on his father to hand over the administration of family affairs. For in this instance there is no immediate fission of the unit into two or more parts, merely a redistribution of roles. The assumption of the status of head of household is in itself a matter of prestige. It makes a man in principle the equal, in that particular respect, of all the other heads of household in the community, and enables him to compete with them in all those situations where the prize is approval of a man's conduct and ability as worthy of the ideal type family protector. Therefore, in so far as the absolute quality of the parental obligation is institutionalized in the kinship system in the separation of brothers' households, the kinship system is consistent with the competitive values. On the other hand, two factors have been noted which tend to hinder the young shepherd from attaining the status of head of household as soon as might otherwise be the case. First, an eldest son must show respect to his father and accept his leadership as long as he is physically active and capable; or until the son is about thirty years of age. This is another way of saying that normally an eldest son cannot take a wife and expect to be in charge of family affairs until he is about thirty years of age. Secondly, brothers, although married, must remain as a united extended family until their sisters are safely married. This, of course, reflects the original unity of the sibling group. Thus, so far as respect and obedience towards an active father, or the unity of the sibling group (which are both important values of the kinship system), delay the young shepherd from assuming the role of a head of household, the kinship system and the competitive values of the community are in some measure of conflict.

## 4. THE 'COMPANY' OF RELATED FAMILIES

It is some consolation to brothers who may feel a genuine distress at the necessary development of their relationship, if after the dissolution of the extended family they continue to manage their sheep together in a 'company'. It is also a practical convenience since the elementary family is not, normally, the sheep management unit in the winter unless it happens to possess at least 200 sheep and the services of four active shepherds. As we have seen in chapter two, the Sarakatsani prefer, in winter, to divide their sheep and goats into a number of different flocks. Where grassland is natural and scarce, the advantage of this division is that the optimum use is made of the pasture offered by any particular stretch of country. The lower limit of 200 sheep follows from the difficulty of renting very small areas of grazing from village communities. Also it is damaging to the pride of a shepherd if he is seen standing on watch over a flock of only forty or fifty 'zigouria', 'sterpha', or 'galaria'. Nevertheless, if poorer families with less than a hundred animals are unable to find or persuade kinsmen to accept them into their 'company', they are forced to work during the winter as wage shepherds for villagers, or occasionally for richer Sarakatsani, a situation which emphasizes their poverty and suggests the inadequacy of their kindreds. Six of the forty-two households at Neochori find themselves in this position.

The requirements of a particular system of sheep management, then, often result in the association of two or more elementary or extended families in a 'company'. However, to explain the size and constitution of a particular 'company' it may be necessary to consider other factors as well. One of these is the difficulty of finding winter grazing. Where a tselingas owns or controls, by whatever means, grazing land in excess of the requirements of his own family, he almost inevitably leads a 'company' of kinsmen whose number is determined simply by the size of their flocks and the carrying capacity of his land.

Another factor is security. One of the larger 'stanis' in Thesprotia represents the interests of eighty persons with two thousand head of sheep and goats. They occupy a continuous tract of grazing land but although the different families are now individually entitled to their occupancy they still prefer to manage their affairs together in what represents, in fact, a confederation of three 'companies'. The stani had originally arrived in the area in the winter of 1944–5 after the Muslim landowners had fled to Albania, an exodus which left considerable areas of grassland untenanted. The Christian villagers of the district who claimed the abandoned lands strongly resented this immigration of shepherds while the final distribution of the land was still in doubt. Yet they were impressed by the strength and armament of the group and were not unpleased, at a time when food was short, to barter the grazing land for quantities of cheese in the first winter and olive oil in the second. However, difficulties soon arose between the two groups. After the Sarakatsani had refused to sell a proportion of their own lambs to replace the village flocks which had been destroyed or stolen in the war, they were peremptorily ordered, in January 1946 at the height of the lambing, to leave the village boundaries; an ultimatum which the villagers must have known they would refuse. Shortly afterwards a desperate attempt to burn down the Sarakatsan huts was also unsuccessful. In the six years which followed these incidents, 1947–53, the Muslim lands were administered by the Ministry of Finance and the Sarakatsani continued to graze them in relative peace. But in 1954 the land used by the stani became village common land and without village citizenship the

Sarakatsani no longer had any rights to grazing which the village council did not choose to recognize. They were warned not to return in the autumn.

The stani commissioned two patrons, who are influential lawyers in Jannina, to present their case to the Governor-General of the Epirus. Their plea was simply that their clients had nowhere to go; that they were simple men but easily tempted to violence in a crisis. In October the Nomarch (or Prefect) of Thesprotia was ordered to arrange for the compulsory admission of the shepherds to the same winter grazing. But the Nomarch (it was alleged) had received gifts from the villagers and did not wish to comply. He replied that the size of the villagers' own flocks made the administration of the order very difficult. Delay in correspondence and the endless discussion of practical difficulties are the time-honoured methods by which a junior officer in the hierarchy may evade the instruction of a senior official without becoming guilty of direct disobedience. But by late October the sheep were already on the road. The tselingas now appealed to his cheese merchant who suggested a present of fifty pounds to be passed by himself to his friend the Nomarch's Chief of Staff. It is impossible to say how this money was used, or if indeed it ever left the pocket of the merchant. But early in November, when the sheep had almost reached the village, an order was sent by the Nomarch to the President of the village that he must again receive the sheep of the Sarakatsani into the pastures.

It seems very probable that the relative success of this stani in facing these threats owes something to its size. If the stani had been smaller it is possible that the villagers would have resisted its initial lodgement in 1944 or that the later attempt to drive it out by force would have been more effective. It is certain that in 1954 the most impressive argument which their patrons were able to advance to the authorities was the simple fact that this large body of persons and animals had to be accommodated somewhere to avoid violence and political embarrassment. Furthermore, no stani of moderate size and resources could have easily afforded the expenses of these struggles in fees and bribes.

The composition of co-operating 'companies' in the winter and summer pastures is not necessarily the same. Often those

who are grouped together in a co-operative 'company' in the
winter do not have their summer grazing rights at the same
village. But, apart from this contingency, two factors which
lead to a modification in co-operative arrangements for the
summer are first, that most families have secure grazing rights
in the Zagori villages where their members are enrolled as
citizens, and secondly, that in the summer a group which owns
more than 200 sheep disposes them in two flocks instead of
three through the amalgamation of the 'zigouria' with the
'sterpha'. In summer the sheep do not require the same attention that they do in winter; and at the end of July when the
ewes cease to give any considerable quantity of milk a single
shepherd is sufficient for the care of these animals. A family
which would be unable to care for its own animals in winter
and spring, under summer conditions is able to manage on its
own. Whereas the 42 Sarakatsan households which spend the
summer at Neochori form 18 sheep management units of one
kind or another in the winter (including 4 families working as
single households which are not extended families), in the summer when they return to the mountains there are 25 groups, of
which no less than 11 are single households. Indeed, one reason
why Sarakatsani look forward to the summer is that, apart
from the festivities it promises, many families enjoy the release
of attending to their own affairs and their own animals after
the restrictions, tensions, and self-discipline, which inevitably
accompany arrangements in the co-operating 'company'. In
general, only married brothers continue to work together in the
summer when there is no practical necessity to do so.

But whatever the size of a co-operating group, the nature and
method of its operations are the same. The sheep and goats are
divided into flocks in the manner I have already described. It is
generally considered that a flock of more than 250 sheep is not
grazed with ease and efficiency. Therefore if a group has five
or six hundred milking ewes, there will be two or even three
separate flocks in this category. In these instances care is taken
that every family in the stani has some of its animals in each
flock. A flock of milking ewes is tended by two shepherds when
this is possible, and these men are not normally members of the
same family, an arrangement that is partly due to the division
of labour within the family, but which also checks the possibility

of a shepherd showing favouritism to his own animals by guiding them to patches of better pasture. At lambing time each family tries to keep a careful watch in case ewe lambs born to its own sheep are surreptitiously exchanged for unwanted males. A careful awareness of one another and a vigilant concern for family rights govern the attitudes of the partners.

The principle of joint action also covers the various items of income and expenditure which concern the interests of the whole stani. At the cheese-maker's hut the milk is measured and credited to the stani as whole; this is partly a matter of convenience but it also means that all the shepherds have a common interest that the milk yield of the whole stani is as high as possible. Similarly, cotton-cake which supplements the diet of the ewes is bought by the 'company' not the family. The stani is regularly involved in minor law-suits over grazing boundaries, damage to crops, and sometimes there are more serious legal disputes. The fines which have to be paid and the fees for the attendance or advice of lawyers where this is necessary, are met by the stani as a whole; as are the expenses of the tselingas when he makes a journey to the town where the merchants, lawyers, and officials have their offices. Twice a year before the spring and autumn migrations the tselingas sits down with the other heads of family to settle their accounts. After the total expenses of the stani have been agreed, each family pays its share in proportion to the size of its flocks.

The form of association in a 'company' is contractual. Each family has a number of relatively clearly defined and specific obligations to the group. It will not go far beyond these obligations out of feelings of sentiment. Debts, for instance, are seldom allowed to accumulate between families in the same 'company'. Yet in the absence of formal legal sanctions contractual relations depend on a measure of confidence, a sentiment that is possible in this community only between those related by kinship or marriage.

In the table (see appendix I) which indicates the winter dispositions of the Neochori shepherds, two facts emerge about the composition of the winter co-operating groups. In all but one instance the nucleus of the 'company' is a group of brothers or, in one case, two pairs of brothers related as first cousins. A man prefers to co-operate with brothers. The confidence they have in one another is a source of moral and physical strength which supports their prestige in the community. The second observation is that of the other heads of family associated with the brothers who form the nucleus of a 'company', eleven are linked affinally and only seven collaterally. This reflects the bilateral form of the kindred. A man does not co-operate with affines from personal preference; in the absence of brothers he would generally prefer to work and live with cousins, nephews, or uncles. But he must always consider the interests of his children and if a wife's brother or a sister's husband is the member of a strong and influential group of brothers he may attach himself to their stani for the sake of his children, to whom they are closer kinsmen than, for example, his own first cousins.

The tselingas, the leader of the co-operating 'company', holds this position not by reason of particular charismatic qualities, but simply because he is the eldest brother of the sibling group which dominates the stani. It is true that if the eldest son is diffident, lacking in intelligence, or physically deformed, another son will be nominated by the father to succeed him when he retires from the active control of the family's affairs; but this happens only infrequently. If the group of brothers are still living as one extended family the eldest brother is both the executive head of his own family of origin and the tselingas of the co-operating 'company'. After the brothers of the extended family establish separate households, the eldest brother ceases to have any formal domestic jurisdiction over his brothers, but he generally remains as the tselingas of the group because of his greater experience in negotiations with merchants and officials. But although a man becomes a tselingas because of his 'structural' position and not because of personal qualities, he is nevertheless judged against the ideal type leader who above all possesses the quality of cleverness (ἐξυπνάδα). He ought to be mature but not old, and he should have many brothers, a large kindred, influential affines, patrons in high positions, and grazing land. For it is a man with these personal and practical advantages who attracts into his following the families of kinsmen or affines who do not have brothers, cannot agree with them, or whose brothers are not sufficiently wealthy and influential to remain together as the nucleus of a co-operating 'company'.

Membership in a 'company' is in principle based on free association, although in particular cases a man without brothers may be so dependent upon the particular kinsmen who form the dominant nucleus of a 'company', that he has, in fact, little choice. But co-operating 'companies' are relatively stable associations only as long as the problems they help member families to overcome remain problems. They are a loose form of contractual association in which each family jealously guards its domestic autonomy and the right to secede at any time. Power to influence the association's decisions lies with the dominant group of brothers from whom the company takes its name, and it is the desire to escape from the position of dependence on this group which leads the more distantly related families in the association to detach themselves from it in the summer months.

Co-operation between kinsmen and affines has its difficulties. So imperative are the interests of a man's own family that sometimes he begins to suspect even the actions of a close kinsman if he co-operates with him: and he, himself, must sometimes fight against the temptation to defraud a kinsman or an affine. The Sarakatsani say that 'every stani has a pimp' (κάθε στάνη ἔχει τὸ ρουφιάνο της). Ρουφιάνος means a procurer and by extension a man without conscience or manliness. In this context it implies that in each co-operating group the cheese merchant is able to find at least one man who for the favour of more liberal credits is prepared to play the part of informer about the secrets of the group. As a statement of fact this is an exaggeration, but it testifies accurately to the strains and restraints that co-operation between related families involves, strains which are thought to be peculiarly inappropriate in the relations of kinsmen.

# V

# COLLATERAL KINSMEN

## 1. FAVOURS AND OBLIGATIONS

THE Sarakatsani assume that ill-faith, doubt, and suspicion characterize the relations of men who are not kinsmen. In contrast, they think that the values and attitudes which make possible the communion of kinsmen are expressed in the meaning of ἐμπιστοσύνη, faith, trust, confidence; or πίστη, faith, belief. It is, then, not surprising that unrelated men very rarely co-operate in the management of their sheep or in any other venture; except, necessarily, the marriages of their children.

The rights and obligations of kinship are of a general and diffuse kind, not restricted to specific situations. A man is confident that a kinsman will keep a secret. He opens his mind to him freely because he knows he will use discretion in what he should pass on and what he must not. He believes the information that a kinsman gives to him, and he uses it as a basis for action without the fear of a lie or a trap. He is confident that when his own conduct is being evaluated by the community his kinsmen will support his case; and for his part he will not suffer in silence the public criticism of any of his kin. Above all, he feels secure and confident that when he is in difficulty there will be people who care for his interests and will give him assistance. These sentiments of confidence and trust are prescribed and follow from the simple existence of the kin relationship; they do not depend on the history of a gradually developing intimacy.

When a Sarakatsanos receives a favour from another, he must show gratitude. 'One good turn deserves another' (ἡ χάρη θέλει ἀντίχαρη). Even if only between the acceptance of some service and its later repayment, gratitude must for a while act as a makeweight in the balance. Not to show gratitude for help, which has been freely given, is behaviour open to severe public reproach. But to be grateful is to be 'obliged' (ὑποχρεωμένος); and this is an admission of inequality and even of weakness. The rare attempts at co-operation between unrelated persons have invariably ended in accusations and counter accusations that one man has done more for the other who, in return, has not shown the right attitude of a man under obligation. This, in a sense, is true. For neither side can admit to obligation without losing prestige; and both must attempt to claim the superordinate position in a creditor-debtor relationship.

But a man does not feel any embarrassment in asking for help from a kinsman. In these circumstances there is no shame in being under obligation or a debt of gratitude. Irrespective of the state of the balance of favours and counter favours, collateral relatives of the same generation, by reason of their kinship, are conceptually equal since they are descended from a pair of siblings who, before marriage and apart from the chances of age and sex, were socially equivalent persons. A man does not lose prestige through obligation to a kinsman; on the contrary his reputation is increased, for the community pays attention to a person whose kinsmen lend him immediate and effective support. And for the man who gives aid to his kin, the knowledge that men learn of his actions through the gratitude of the kinsman who receives it, is sufficient recompense. For in this way he wins a reputation as a man of honour 'who supports his kinsmen'. If through wealth or influence a man is in a position to act as a general protector of his kindred, not only is he expected to do so, but this, in most cases, is also his wish. There is some altruism here. A man takes pleasure in the company of his kinsman; he finds him on occasion a source of practical advantage, but in particular he holds to him and has confidence in him simply because he is a kinsman. And for these reasons complaints of ingratitude against kinsmen are relatively few.

But although a man is under a moral obligation to help a collateral relative, this assistance is not given unconditionally. The important consideration is that it must not conflict with the interests of the family. This emerges very clearly in situations of physical violence. A man is not expected to accept responsibility for avenging the death of a collateral kinsman. He will give moral support to the family of the victim but he is unlikely to go farther than that. A vengeance killing leads to the arrest of the killer and a prison sentence, which is sometimes followed by self-imposed exile in another district of Greece when there is any fear of counter vengeance. In this way a shepherd's family might lose its protector at least for some years, perhaps for ever. Only in unusual circumstances where a man feels that his honour is very closely identified with the blood of the murdered man is it possible that a cousin, uncle, or nephew may undertake this duty; and there have been no such cases in recent years. In any case such a situation would only arise where the murdered man had no family relative, a brother or even an infant son, who could balance the debt of blood at that time or in the future.

It is quite a different matter when a man is physically attacked in the presence of a kinsman. The latter cannot stand by and do nothing; indeed, it is a personal insult to a man that another should dare to strike his kinsman before his eyes. Fights and brawls are not infrequent; they may happen in coffee-shops when a man is winning too successfully at cards, in a dispute over the boundaries of grazing land, or at a wedding when men drink to excess and see a veiled insult in each word or gesture. Yet these fights seldom lead to a killing. The Sarakatsani are very aware of the consequences of murder and vengeance killing; and even when they seem to be in the grip of ungovernable rage they do not draw a knife unless they see, or sense, that there are witnesses uncommitted by kinship obligation who will prevent them from using it. It is noticeable that in boundary disputes, where two shepherds may sometimes find themselves alone, quarrels are more often decided with iron-hooked shepherds' crooks, capable of ugly but generally not mortal wounds. In a brawl, as distinct from a calculated vengeance killing, a shepherd relies on the active support of a kinsman, for this does no injury to the interests of his family; on the contrary, the family gains honour by action, but loses it by inaction.

We must distinguish between two kinds of favour and service which may be exchanged between collateral kin; and it is, again, the question of responsibility to the family which marks the form of this distinction. In the first instance a man is able to assist his kinsman in a manner which cannot possibly conflict with the interests of his own family or become a charge on its limited resources. Shelter and hospitality, information about the affairs of other people and their gossip, physical support in a brawl, are examples of this kind of assistance. These services are true favours (χάρες) which in a relationship of personal kinship a man is bound to perform. 'We hold to our kindred' (κρατᾶμε

τὸ σόϊ) the Sarakatsani say. But a man's own feelings also prompt
him to give this help. Like the grace of God, which is expressed
by the same word, such favours are generally without motive or
conscious sense of calculation.

There are, however, other forms of assistance and co-operation between collaterals which make some demand on the
material wealth of a kinsman and his family. This is no longer
merely a matter of personal kinship solidarity, since it is the
principle of parental obligation which guides a man in his conduct as trustee of the corporate resources of the family, human
and material, under his control. He is not free to make gifts of
money or animals to a kinsman in difficulties. Yet it is still
possible for the families of these men to help one another in
situations which involve corporately owned resources, providing
that the assistance or co-operation is on a contractual basis of
strict accountability. And this, of course, is only possible because between kinsmen there are normally sentiments of confidence and trust. In this way kinsmen sometimes make modest
money loans, pasture each other's animals for a consideration,
and frequently join in the co-management of their flocks.

The history of the misfortunes of Vasili Arvanitis illustrates
this distinction. In the spring of 1955 his winter pastures were
flooded by the irrigation of adjoining fields and, as often happens
in these conditions, his animals contracted liver-fluke. From a
flock of 105 sheep only 63 survived, an entirely inadequate
number to support a growing family of five children. Vasili has
a first cousin, Spiros Tangas, a more fortunate Sarakatsanos with
450 animals and a small property in the winter pastures near
Preveza. When Spiros learned of the difficulties of his cousin he
at once left home and went by bus to Igoumenitsa, a day's
journey away. There he visited an official of the Ministry of
Agriculture, a friend who had baptized his youngest daughter,
and asked him if he would try to arrange his cousin's application for a considerable loan from the Agricultural Bank. For
such applications are sometimes delayed for many months because of the formalities of proof relating to the cause of the
animals' death. The following day he made another bus journey of some hours to a small town where the Mayor was an
animal dealer with whom he sometimes did business. The
Mayor introduced him to a friend with a few acres of rough

pasture which he was willing to rent to Vasili for the weeks that remained before the Sarakatsani began their journey to the Zagori mountains. Spiros paid him twelve pounds for the use of the pasture and sent a message to Vasili to bring his surviving animals as quickly as possible before they, too, contracted the disease. He also told him to send his wife and children to Spiros' own home, since it would not be worth while constructing new huts for so short a time.

At the time, I suggested to Spiros that he had acted very generously towards Vasili. But he could only shrug his shoulders, not in modesty for this was entirely foreign to his nature, but because he felt that his conduct was only natural and did not call for any explanation. At the same time he made it quite clear that Vasili would have to repay the twelve pounds. He admitted without embarrassment that Vasili would be in great difficulties for many years to come. Nevertheless each family had its own responsibilities, for instance he himself was hoping to set up one of his sons as a shopkeeper in Jannina. He did not expect repayment this year or even next. And anyway, he added, Vasili would not allow him to forget the debt. In fact, later in the summer of the same year when Vasili had received a much reduced sum of money for the sale of his milk, he at once repaid the loan. Spiros' comment to me was simply, 'You see how quickly he paid off the debt. We have trust in our kinsmen.' The time and energy which Spiros gave to the arrangement of his kinsman's affairs, the use of his valuable patronage relationships with a Ministry official and the mayor of a local town, were favours freely given, mere incidents in the personal relations of cousins. But the money, although not a particularly large sum, was part of the wealth of the family and under no circumstance could it be alienated.

## 2. COUSINS

Cousins are the most significant of a person's collateral kinsmen both for purposes of practical co-operation and for simple companionship. This is particularly true of the periods immediately before and after marriage. For these are the years when the individual's social reputation and prestige are judged by the community, and when the problems and difficulties of establishing a family require the practical assistance and moral support of a wide circle of kin. It is entirely consistent with these needs that the collateral extension of the kindred is wider in a person's own generation than in either the first ascendant or descendant generations. As the children of a family approach adult status, a father through the identification of his interests with those of his children, is drawn less into the affairs of his own cousins and becomes more concerned with the cousins of his children's kindred, who from his point of view include affinal relatives as well as the children of his own siblings and first cousins.

The essence of cousinhood, as indeed of all collateral kinship, is that measure of confidence and altruism to which we have referred more than once. Cousins are the children or grand-childen of siblings and the values of cousinship contain the ideal that their affections are like those of brothers and sisters. Cousins are genuinely concerned about each others' successes or misfortunes, hopes and fears. When a man meets a cousin after a long interval of time there is obvious pleasure on both sides. They find a quiet corner away from other people and a conversation begins which, if circumstances allow, may continue for many hours. There is a certain conventional sequence of topics. At first there are detailed inquiries about the health of each member of the two families. This is followed by an exchange of information about sheep and grazing, marriages and match-making in either family or amongst their kinsmen. Afterwards the talk ranges in random fashion over many subjects, the local personalities and gossip of their villages, the latest oppressive measure of government bureaucrats. What is so striking about the private talk of kinsmen is its fluency, freedom, and its mellow modulated tones. It presents a striking contrast with the talk of unrelated Sarakatsani in the forum of the village square or coffee-shop. There, conversation is a contest of wits, cast in a compulsively restrained monosyllabic form, yet accompanied with the striking of assertive attitudes. It is not intended as a means for exchanging information but rather as a form of protagonistic competition.

There are certain kinds of general social intercourse which are possible only between kinsmen, more especially between cousins. For the Sarakatsani, marriage and sexual relations cannot be separated. A girl who loses her honour is in danger of her life at the hands of her own family. The importance of virginity is such that it leads to the complete segregation of the sexes amongst unmarried persons. Only in the family and the kindred is it possible for unmarried persons of opposite sex even to hold conversation. And it will be remembered that generally men do not marry until they are thirty, girls until they are about twenty-five. These two circumstances, a relatively late age of marriage, and the segregation of the sexes except in the family and kindred, inevitably add to the value of an unmarried boy's social relations with his young female cousins; for apart from his own sisters, they are the only unmarried women of his own generation with whom he is allowed to have any contact. A youth is very close to his sister to whom he is bound by categorical obligations, yet his behaviour with her is restrained. With female cousins, on the other hand, he behaves in a familiar manner which includes a good deal of mutual teasing and bodily contact. Particularly among first cousins of opposite sex between the ages of thirteen and sixteen familiarity is expressed in playful wrestling, bottom smacking, and cheek pinching. Generally, teasing between second cousins of opposite sex is a little more restrained; for here one approaches the margin of kinship. The girl is a kinswoman but she is also almost a 'stranger' in terms of kinship distance. The risk, for a boy, of being tempted into some sexual misconduct is inherently greater. Friendship between rather older cousins takes the form of lounging before the hearth, the youth perhaps resting his head on the girl cousin's shoulder while they talk and joke. In this context teasing is a social convention which permits a form of very mild and unacknowledged sexual byplay, yet absolutely prohibits any degree of overt sexuality and is easily rationalized as being 'only a game'. It reconciles the two guises under which a female cousin appears to the youth; first, as the only female company of his own age that he is permitted to enjoy outside his family until he reaches the age of thirty; and secondly, as a kinswoman whose honour he is bound in faith and trust to uphold.

If young kinsmen and kinswomen find in each other the only heterosexual companionship which is permitted outside the family, it is also true in a more general sense that in this community true friendship is only possible between kinsmen. Friends are, necessarily, kinsmen. From this general body of relatives a

man finds perhaps two or three cousins with whom his friendship is particularly intimate; this is a relationship based on sympathy and mutual concern for the other, it is the delight taken
in the company of the other person for the quality of sociability
itself. But these relations of affection and uncalculating trust
tend not to be with cousins with whom a man co-operates, or
has co-operated, in the day-to-day management of the same
flocks. The goodwill of kinsmen is important both in those
situations where purpose, aim, and practical interest are involved,
and for its own sake where pleasure is taken in the quality of a
friendly sympathetic relationship. In both instances a man finds
in his kinsman what lack of trust and antipathy prevents him
from seeking in an unrelated individual. But there is a difference
between a relationship of co-operation and one of sympathetic
friendship. Men who herd their sheep together in the same
'company', are concerned in co-operation between corporate
family groups; the obligations of this co-operative activity are
specific and quasi-contractual, requiring restraint, discipline,
and calculated book-keeping. These are elements at odds with
the free, unrestrained, attitudes of devoted personal friendship
in which obligations are diffuse not specific in character. In
principle one cannot deny a friend what he asks. Therefore,
friendship between kinsmen flourishes better where the demands
put upon it fall into the category of free favours. And this is
more likely to be the case where cousins do not work together.

This last consideration raises the question whether there is
any significant variation in the degree or quality of solidarity
between the various categories of first cousins. Marriage is patrilocal and brothers live for a number of years after their marriage in a united extended family; afterwards they may continue to co-operate as a single sheep management group until
their children are often in late adolescence. Although these
cousins are unlikely to share a relationship of devoted personal
friendship, there is the fact or the memory of common service
to the same flocks and of essentially identified interests. The
possession of the same surname and the value placed upon relationships which are mediated through male kinsmen, are further
factors which encourage a formal preference for cousins who
are father's brother's children. Equally, however, early childhood in a joint household and co-operative labour in early

youth provide enough incidents to nourish any personal aversion which for one reason or another may have arisen between
young cousins. And if brothers quarrel, this, of course, inevitably affects the relations of their children. But a marked coolness between cousins of this class is rare; the Neochori group of
317 Sarakatsani provides only one example.

Relations between men and women who are reciprocally
mother's brother's children and father's sister's children are
almost always close and affectionate. These cousins are the
children of a sister and brother whose relationship before the
sister's marriage was governed by categorical obligations which
concerned the honour of the girl, her brother, and the whole
family. For the sister who arrives at her wedding day with a
reputation in the community for right conduct, a brother has
feelings of deep gratitude and trust which he expresses in his
constant anxious inquiries about her welfare from anyone he
meets who lives near her husband's huts. He is always ready to
help his brother-in-law, however little he may like him personally, in order to make life a little easier for his sister and her
children. And since women spend much time discussing kinsmen and their affairs, the sister's children learn at an early
age about their cousins who are the children of her brother.
But the relations of these cousins are not only a question of sentiment and its extension. Marriage is a contract between two
unrelated families; and despite mutual distrust both groups are
interested to consolidate their alliance. In the early years the
two families of origin of the married pair may find in it a useful
addition to the range of their co-operative relationships. However, the true concern of the husband and his wife's brothers is
that their children shall not lack the support of a strong and
devoted kindred. Their children are reciprocally those cousins
who normally live in different localities and do not co-operate
in sheep management. Between them there ought to be the
kind of trust and sympathy which lead to deep friendship, the
exchange of free favours, and that measure of general moral
support without which a man's reputation cannot survive for
long among the Sarakatsani.

From time to time there are opportunities to strengthen the
affective quality of these relations. For a number of years after
her marriage a woman pays one or possibly two visits a year to

her parents' home and takes her young children with her. These visits which last for five or six days are eagerly looked forward to by the children who find there new playfellows and grandparents, uncles, and aunts far more indulgent than those at their own home. The inevitable frictions and jealousies of communal life do not threaten the cross-cousin relationship in its formative period; on the contrary it grows in an atmosphere of gaiety, holiday, and permissiveness. It is, then, not surprising that in seven cases out of ten a man names a cousin of this category as his most intimate and trusted friend. In later life these cousins are remarkably generous and trusting, and there is a noticeable tendency for cousins related in this way to give small money loans at moments of need or unexpected crisis.

In general, cousins who are related through their mothers' sisters are less likely to have known one another in childhood, and relations in adult life are usually based on the conventional existence of cousinship. Married sisters do not pay one another the kind of formal visit which lasts for a number of days unless their husbands have developed common interests on the basis of their affinal connection. Relations will be more intimate where the two sisters have married men who live in the same summer or winter neighbourhood. The two women will make informal daily visits and their husbands will encourage the children to form close friendships with their cousins. Sometimes a man arranges a marriage between his own cousin and his wife's sister. If the cousin is a father's brother's son, the two sisters may find themselves close neighbours and, perhaps, working in the same co-operating 'company'. Yet even where two young men who are sisters' sons meet for the first time at a wedding or village festival they at once adopt the easy, friendly, and sympathetic attitude towards one another which is typical of the cousin relationship at all times, and equally foreign to the behaviour which must be adopted towards an unrelated person of the same sex and age, even where this unrelated person has been a close neighbour and has shared the same school desk.

The feature of cross-cousin or maternal parallel cousin relationships which distinguishes them from the ties between brothers' sons is that they generally involve physical separation, since sisters in a system of patrilocal marriage must leave the parental home. Men prefer to bring their brides from a distant quarter of the scattered community, both because they seek to establish strategic alliances in neighbourhoods other than their own, and because of the fear of trouble with affines if the young bride is within easy tale-telling distance of her own family. What is decisive in these cousin relationships is whether regular visits are exchanged or whether contact between the cousins must rely on the chance meeting at a wedding or a village festival. On the other hand, where cross-cousins or maternal parallel cousins happen to live in the same neighbourhood, and more especially if they co-operate in sheep management, their relations are of the kind which generally exist between the sons of brothers.

In these distinctions it is not the kind of cousin relationship itself which is strictly relevant (for the norms of kinship behaviour towards cousins are the same whatever the mediating links in the relationship), but whether cousins live near to one another and possibly work together in daily co-operation, or whether they live at a distance and, if so, whether there are regular opportunities for exchanging visits or not. There are, then, two important classes of first cousins; those who live in the same summer neighbourhood and who co-operate or have at some time co-operated in sheep management; and those who live in other neighbourhoods in summer and winter. (The classification is not, of course, exhaustive.) The two classes of cousins give a man and his family different but complementary forms of support.

The attitude of friendly interest and affectionate concern which exists between cousins is also present in a man's relations with his uncles and aunts, nephews and nieces. The differences which have been described between various types of first cousin relationships have their analogues in the ties which exist between uncles, aunts, nephews, and nieces. Uncles who are fathers' brothers are known better than brothers of the mother but they are not always loved better. The wicked uncle, though he is not a common figure, is generally a father's brother with whom the father has quarrelled. The favourite uncle is generally a mother's brother who was excessively indulgent to his nephews and nieces when they came on periodical visits. Aunts who are father's sisters are generally well known but mother's sisters may be seen very seldom.

In general, uncles and aunts, as in our own society, are notoriously indulgent towards their nephews and nieces in their childhood days. Of the father's brothers who may be living for a time in the same extended household, it is the unmarried uncles who are the favourites of the children, dandling them on the knee and buying them sweets; between the married uncles and their young nephews and nieces there is, necessarily, more restraint. Uncles may attempt occasionally to lecture young nephews and nieces but the relationship at this age is essentially one of permissive familiarity. In his adolescence a nephew shows a more formal respect to his uncles who are by this time almost all married men at the height of their powers, yet even now the relationship is nearer to one of easy camaraderie than careful respect. But after his marriage and even for some years before it, the nephew in manner and conversation pays less and less attention to his uncle who is now generally an old man on the brink of retirement if he has not already been forced into it. There is often a touch of impatience in a nephew's attitude to his old uncle; almost, indeed, an air of patronage, though he does not generally show him public disrespect. Affection remains, but an old uncle is of little account in the affairs of the community except occasionally if it is necessary to find a precedent from the past for action in some puzzling situation. For the adult man or woman the practical significance of an uncle or aunt is their function as a mediating link with their children, the cousins of an individual's own age and generation who provide comradeship and support in facing the problems of life in a competitive and hostile community.

### 3. THE EFFECTIVE KINDRED

In many situations formal kinship distance must be the criterion which measures obligation and responsibility, especially where preference has to be given to one kinsman over another. The stani led by Theodoros Ferendinos includes, as well as his married brothers, two cousins; Pericles, a father's brother's son, and Demetrios, a second cousin whose mother and the mother of Theodoros are first cousins. In 1954, when this group could not find sufficient winter grazing, one cousin had to leave the 'company'. Inevitably this was Demetrios, even though he had a very intimate friendship with Theodoros' youngest brother; and despite the fact that Pericles was idle, quarrelsome and inefficient. Similarly, when a man visits another neighbourhood he will always stay at the huts of his first cousin although, on personal grounds, he might prefer to be entertained by a more congenial but more distant kinsman.

These facts are easily understood. A collateral kinship bond is a relationship derived from a pair of siblings. It makes a sensible difference whether this derivation is at one or two removes. And this is so not only on grounds of sentiment but also in relation to the limits of the kindred. The children of first cousins are members of the kindred but the children of second cousins are not kinsmen. The first is a growing relationship, the second is not. A man who is 35 years old will generally know all his first cousins, but sometimes there may be a number of his second cousins whom he has not met personally, although he will always know something about their families and their affairs. Second cousins are on the margin of kinship, people who are nearly 'strangers'. They remain kinsmen who must be guarded and cherished but there is some diminution of responsibility towards them. These facts are illustrated by the different behaviour of first and second cousins which may sometimes be observed at weddings. In the quarrels which flare up on these occasions between unrelated guests, there is always the danger that fighting may become so violent and general that the wedding festivities have to be abandoned; this is a great disgrace for the family which is acting as host. It is noticeable that a bridegroom's first cousins feel it is their responsibility to prevent this both by the swiftness of their intervention, where their own kinship alignments allow this, and by the restraint they hold over their own feelings when they are themselves concerned in some incident. Second cousins on the other hand abandon themselves more easily to considerations of injured dignity and self-regard and, in the rush of blood to their heads, temporarily forget their duties to kinsmen.

Yet despite the general importance of kinship distance as a measure of obligation and solidarity, a quality which is particularly characteristic of the kindred is its flexibility. If a man has interests in some part of the community where he can find only a second cousin, or an uncle who is a cousin of one of his parents, he may yet establish with him a relationship which is closer and more significant than the relationships he has with other kinsmen genealogically less distant but living in places where his affairs do not lead him. Similarly, if a man is forced by circumstances to co-operate in sheep management with a distant uncle or second cousin this transforms a genealogically distant connexion into a close and very significant kinship bond. Naturally, a man normally prefers to co-operate and have intimate friendships with close relatives, but in their absence, or where there is an exceptionally strong personal preference for an individual kinsman who is not closely connected, a distant kinsman is, as it were, 'drawn in' so that what becomes significant is the fact of relationship and not the genealogical distance separating kinsmen. This potential efficiency of any kinship relation is perhaps reflected in the way a man refers to a cousin when he is in his presence. In explaining that a man is a first cousin he will say, 'He is my first cousin', but of his second cousin he will only say 'He is my cousin'. By omitting any reference to the distance of cousinship, the effect is to draw the distant kinsman nearer to the man who is speaking. It might be said that an individual has two kindreds; the first is the 'ideal' kindred in which conflicts of obligation and responsibility to kinsmen are measured by formal kinship distance; the second is the 'effective kindred' in which the frequency and character of kinship intercourse which actually takes place, and the practical needs of a man and his family, are also important considerations.

Genealogical connexion beyond the limits of the kindred is not normally of any significance. Men who are third or fourth cousins may possibly be aware of this fact but in general it does not make them behave towards one another differently than they would if they were unrelated. But if a man possesses wealth or influence in the community so that some advantage is to be gained by claiming relationship with him, then he often finds that his 'effective kindred' extends beyond the conventional range of second cousinship and comes to include third and even fourth cousins. When Sotiri Achnoulas, who unlike most of the Sarakatsani in Zagori has more goats than sheep in his flock, was dismayed at the promulgation of a government order forbidding the pasturage of these animals in certain areas of the

Zagori, he decided to pay a visit to his 'cousin' John, a Sarakat-sanos of wealth and influence. He was confident that John could help him through his influence over the local Member of Parliament. 'He has him in his pocket' (τὸν ἔχει στὴ τσέπη του), he explained. John and Sotiri are third cousins. This otherwise tenuous and formally unrecognized kinship link is 'drawn in' to provide a basis of mutual trust in a relationship which is clearly one of patronage. John, for his part, does not resent the importunate requests of his distant relatives. The ability to bestow patronage is its own reward, for it increases his prestige not only in the community of Sarakatsani but with such personalities as parliamentary candidates who compete for the votes which they believe he commands.

A man's 'effective kindred' may also be considerably more restricted than the conventional limits allow. This happens when a family possesses so little prestige that kinsmen would rather not have any unnecessary association with its members. A case in point is the family of Pistiolis at Skamneli which is desperately poor and although morally upright is almost socially outcast. The genealogical information which the father was able to provide was meagre. He did not even know where most of his first cousins were living, and of second cousins he could name only a few. Over a long period of years he had received very few invitations to the weddings of kinsmen, and although he travelled considerably, earning a pittance by carrying goods on his two pack mules, he was too ashamed to ask for hospitality at a kinsman's home in the places where he knew them to be living; consequently he always slept in the open, a circumstance which encouraged mocking remarks about his shaggy and uncouth appearance.

But besides the flexibility in the range of obligations to collateral kinsmen there are also situations which may lead to their complete abrogation. Trust and mutual confidence is the basis of kin relationship. Quarrels which question these qualities are rare, but where they do occur they are far more serious than the differences which are expected to arise between unrelated men. In the latter instance normal social relations may be resumed after a long period of estrangement, but in the former case, especially where one kinsman has publicly insulted another, confidence is permanently destroyed. The proverb,

'Why is the wound in your eye so deep? Because my kinsman gouged it out' (γιατί'ν'τὸ μάτι σου βαθειὰ βγαλμένο; — γιατί μοῦ τό'βγαλε δικός), expresses precisely this difference.

Between kinsmen who co-operate in a 'company' for the co-management of their flocks it is almost inevitable that from time to time differing interests produce a coolness in their relations. Yet it is remarkable how seldom these frictions develop into the kind of quarrel which causes an irreparable breach. A stern self-control is maintained by these kinsmen on their injured feelings because they know that they depend on each other's assistance in the struggle to survive the hazards, natural and political, which surround them. However, any form of dishonesty in their co-operative handling of the flocks destroys the basis of their association. Recently a cousin who was herding his sheep with a 'company' of married brothers was discovered during the lambing season in the act of trying to attach a number of his kinsmen's newly born ewe lambs to his own ewes, and his own male lambs to the ewes which he had robbed. Inevitably, after such an incident, the trust between these kinsmen was permanently broken.

Incest (αἱμομιξία) represents the most dramatic form of deception that one kinsman can practise on another. Unmarried cousins of opposite sex enjoy an easy, friendly companionship with one another which they are denied with unrelated persons. Very occasionally a youth succumbs to the temptation of sexual experiments with a young kinswoman, an act in which he may destroy both the girl's honour and his own. It seems most unlikely that these affairs, if protracted, can ever remain secret in a community where there are so many questioning eyes. Over a period of ten years I discovered three probable instances, of which one was incest between first cousins. In this case a youth was staying in his uncle's house and there, it seems, seduced the unmarried daughter. The cousin had left his uncle's house before it became apparent that the girl was pregnant, and he naturally denied from a distance that he had had any hand in the matter. The girl for her part claimed that she had been impregnated by divine, not human, means, but little attention was paid to this suggestion. The girl's family did not take any drastic action in the matter beyond disposing of the child when it was born. The girl herself was allowed to live; and in fact, a year or two later was married off to a poor widower who extracted a considerable dowry in consideration of her blemished history. Although the girl had an unmarried brother no action was ever taken against the alleged seducer. The family claimed that it would not be right to kill a first cousin (any more than a brother) whatever the crime committed, and there are those who agree that there was some force in this argument. But there are others who do not hold this view and believe that the family made a virtue of a dishonourable preference. In any case the family emerged from this affair with its honour destroyed. Needless to say, all forms of social intercourse have ceased between the kinsmen concerned. This involved the destruction of the relationship between the brothers who were the heads of the two families. Incest between first cousins is a sin, for the same blood turns in upon itself in the pollution of sexual intercourse. It is something which goes against nature and something also which inevitably wrecks the whole scheme of kinship relations.

Sexual intercourse between second cousins is still described as incest but it cannot be said in quite the same way that it is an act which goes against nature. Second cousins are kinsmen but they are, also, nearly 'strangers'. Men know that in the towns the Church, from time to time, solemnizes marriages between second cousins, and that in two notorious instances in recent years such marriages have even been contracted by Sarakatsani. But so far as premarital sex relations are concerned the choice here lies between calling them incest or fornication. Whichever term is chosen to describe the liaison, it is less an unnatural sin than conduct of the deepest dishonour. As one man put it with ironic scorn, 'It would be better to marry your own sister' (καλλίτερα νὰ στεφανωθῆς τὴν ἀδερφή σου). But although an illicit affair between second cousins is serious enough, for it inevitably destroys the girl's honour and the relationship between the two parents who are first cousins, it does not have quite the same catastrophic consequences for family and kindred relationships as incest between first cousins.

It is clear, then, that where there is a flagrant breach of the norms of kinship, the relationship is annulled. The trust which is the basis of kinship relations is an axiomatic value in Sarakatsan life which is never questioned. From the injured kinsman's point of view there can be no extenuating circumstances which in time, and after long consideration, may provide the offender with an excuse. There is no basis for forgiveness and reconciliation.

The support of kinsmen is also withdrawn sometimes in a manner which does not necessarily imply a permanent rupture of social relations, though it may come to this in the end. I have previously emphasized the importance of the moral support of kinsmen when the community is evaluating a man's conduct. The idea that a man must defend the actions of his kinsmen is expressed in the proverb, Ὁ δικὸς μπορεῖ νὰ πῇ μὰ δὲν μπορεῖ ν'ἀκούσῃ. Literally this means, 'A relation can speak to his kinsman but he cannot listen to something about him', that is to say he can scold a kinsman for his shortcomings in private, but he will not allow others to accuse him in public. This in general is true, but it depends upon the possibility of advancing some reasonable explanation of a kinsman's conduct. Where a man has behaved in a manner clearly at variance with the values of the community a kinsman is forced to abandon him, and even to take some part in condemning his conduct. For if he continues to support his cause his own reputation and that of his family will suffer. By condemning the actions of his kinsmen he expresses in an unequivocal fashion that he supports the values of the community; and he maintains a measure of social distance between himself and his kinsman. In this way he hopes to avoid the taint of association with his conduct and the shame which accompanies it.

The history of Nasios illustrates this process. One afternoon in the summer of 1953 he happened to meet Mitrina Mastoras on the hill-side above his village, and there, after failing to win her willing co-operation, he attempted to take her 'by force' (μὲ τὸ ζόρι); but unsuccessfully according to Mitrina's story. The terrified woman ran down the hill to the huts of her second cousin for, at the time, her own husband was away from home. The cousin at once sent word to the husband who returned immediately. He surprised Nasios, knocked him to the ground, and had already drawn his knife to settle the matter when he was seized from behind by two villagers. In terror Nasios escaped to his home.

Public opinion was unanimous in condemning Nasios. This was not the first time he had attacked women, although on the two previous occasions he had more wisely confined his attentions to gipsy women. His family was in any case poor and of low prestige. There was nothing at all to be said in his favour. He had a number of kinsmen among the Sarakatsani who graze the lands of the same village, and of these the closest was Evangelos Balatsos, a first cousin. Evangelos and the other kinsmen all joined in the universal condemnation of Nasios. During the weeks which followed Evangelos made a point of going each day to the home of Nasios and unnerving him with imaginary accounts of the plots and ambushes which the husband of Mitrina was preparing to lure him to his death. So thorough were his efforts that for the next two months, until the Sarakatsani left for the winter pastures, Nasios was never seen outside his hut in daylight. Evangelos after his daily visits to Nasios made his way to the coffee-shop where he described to an appreciative audience the state of affairs in Nasios's household, how he remained each night, sleepless behind the door with axe in hand, and how his wife was obliged under cover of darkness to remove his faeces from the hut. In this fashion Evangelos took a leading part in the shaming of his kinsman, and saved his own name by denying solidarity with his kinsman and damaging his reputation.

The possibility of losing the moral and practical support of kinsmen, perhaps for ever, is clearly a most powerful sanction of the norms of kinship behaviour and the values of the wider community. If Nasios, a poor man who herded the sheep of villagers, had possessed a substantial flock and had therefore been dependent on the help of kinsmen in a 'company', this estrangement from his kinsmen would have affected him even more seriously than it did. It is also evident that the application of this sanction by the kinsman is itself sanctioned by the threat that a man and his family may lose prestige if he does not temporarily abandon the evil-doer. Since the interests of the family always take precedence over obligations of individual collateral kinship, there is never any doubt that a man will conform. We see, not for the first time, the connexion between prestige values and the isolation of the family; for these values necessarily threaten the solidarity of any personal relationship or social grouping which may conflict with a man's duty to uphold, or promote, the prestige of his family.

## 4. EXPRESSIONS OF SOLIDARITY

The Zagori community of Sarakatsani is geographically dispersed for reasons which are mainly ecological. Patrilocal marriage, suspicion of affines who live near the same village, yet the need for strategic alliances in other parts of Zagori, are factors which lead men to look for brides in a distant neighbourhood. Consequently the kindred of any individual tends to be more or less congruent with the boundaries of the community itself, in the sense that a shepherd generally has at least a few relatives in any quarter of the Zagori. For these reasons the few festive occasions during the year which bring distant kinsmen together are looked forward to with some anticipation. This is so not only for the utilitarian consideration that it is valuable to renew associations with kinsmen whose practical help may be required in the future, but simply for the company of people who value a man and return his affections. It is an aspect of the constant yearning for unity in a society which is, in fact, fragmented by exclusive familial loyalties. It might be said that these occasions when kinsmen meet are important because in the atmosphere of festival excitement the sentiments of kinship solidarity are strengthened and recreated. At weddings, for example, quarrels almost always develop between unrelated guests, and the kinsmen who rush to the aid of their own people are giving a dramatized expression to the ideal of kinship solidarity. But, if it is true that the gathering of dispersed kinsfolk is an occasion for the restatement of kinship values, it is also true that it is the sentiment of kinship which invokes the gathering at all. Thus, although wedding invitations are sent out to all consanguineal and to a large number of affinal relatives, not all of the more distantly related of these persons will attend, and it is always recognized that whether or not an invited kinsman comes to the wedding is an indication of the effective solidarity, or absence of solidarity, between the invited man's family and the family of the groom or bride. Naturally the whole of the kinsman's family cannot attend a wedding together. The demands of shepherding prevent this. But one member at least is expected to go as a representative.

A man, of course, may visit a kinsman at any time; in his huts he will always find shelter and hospitality for the night.

But these visits are unlikely to be merely social and the main purpose of the journey is generally the arrangement of some business. At festivals, on the other hand, kinsmen meet to enjoy one another's company and other considerations are secondary. On the Tuesday after Easter Monday a man often sets off on a journey to a close kinsman living at a distance whom he has not seen during the winter. And after the feast of St. George before the migration to summer pastures there may be a wedding to attend. Later in the year when the Sarakatsani have moved up to the mountain villages of the Zagori there are other opportunities to meet less closely related kinsmen. About the end of July when the impregnated ewes gradually cease to yield milk, there is more leisure for the shepherds to attend the weddings, most of which occur in August and September. Also a number of the villages in the Zagori celebrate in the summer the feast-day of their patron saint. These village feasts (πανηγύρια) last for three days and nights during which there is almost continuous dancing in the village square with much eating and drinking besides. Many Sarakatsani go to these village festivals not only when it is the feast-day of the saint of their own summer village, but also to the celebrations of other villages where they have a kinsman. In the holiday atmosphere they are hospitably welcomed and their company and conversation give pleasure to their hosts. It makes no difference whether visitors are near or distant relatives; the more visitors a family entertains the more its prestige increases. But in addition to these public festivals each Sarakatsan family, or stani, celebrates privately one of the three summer religious festivals which they consider important. These are: the prophet Elias, 20th July, Saint Paraskeve, 26th July, and the Assumption of the All Holy One (The Virgin Mary), 15th August. On these feast-days meat is killed, wine is drunk, and in the larger stanis there is dancing. It is essentially a family celebration but kinsmen, who live in other villages and celebrate a different festival, will come to visit and share in the festivities. These are the various occasions which help to maintain a certain minimal frequency of contact between dispersed kinsmen, although the demands of the sheep prevent any individual shepherd from being present at more than one or perhaps two of these events each year.

But weddings are, undoubtedly, the most significant of these

festivals. An invitation morally obliges a family to send a representative. It is not a question of whether a man can afford the
time and expense to go and enjoy himself for three or four days,
but rather that it is his duty to attend and support the family of
the bride or groom simply because the members of that family
are kinsmen. A man may pay a visit to a kinsman or assist him
in some way out of motives which are in part practical and
ulterior, but he goes to help a kinsman at his wedding without
such utilitarian interest. The kinsman may live in a part of
Zagori or the winter pastures where he is unlikely to be of any
assistance. He may be poor while the wedding guest may be
rich. It might perhaps be argued that a man stands by his kinsmen at their weddings so that in return they will support the
weddings in his own family. For it is true that if a large number
of kinsmen come to a wedding the family gains prestige. But
more important than this outward sanction is the inner concern
for, and interest in, the personal affairs of a kinsman. In this matter
as in the other moral obligations of kinship the Sarakatsani
advance no explanation of why they must act in a particular
way beyond the comment 'That's how we found it and that's
the way we keep it' (ἔτσι τὸ βρήκαμε καὶ ἔτσι τὸ κρατᾶμε). In other
words, in discussing the solidarity of the kindred we are dealing
with self-evident values which appear to a man to be sentiments
innate in every Sarakatsanos.

The wedding customs of the Sarakatsani reflect in many ways
the solidarity of kinsmen. And although it is not my purpose to
give an exhaustive description of these customs it will be relevant to the present discussion if I indicate in a general way how
kinsmen participate in these ceremonies.

The celebrations are held separately by the family of the
bride and the family of the groom at their respective homes. The
only point at which the activities of the two groups intersect is
when the bridegroom arrives on Sunday morning with his
bridal procession of kinsmen (ψίκι) to take away the bride. A
man who is related to both the bride and the groom must be the
guest of only one side. He is not permitted to spend part of the
time with both groups.

Each guest to a wedding brings an offering of food and wine.
This consists of a round of bread (κουλούρα) with symbolical
ornamentations on the crust; a wooden bottle (βουτσέλι) of

wine; and a slaughtered lamb or sheep. For the Sarakatsani a meal is a family communion to which unrelated shepherds are never invited. The wedding-feast is the family meal writ large with the family of the kindred sitting down to eat bread together. For all food is in a generic sense bread. 'Come, let us eat bread', cries the wedding master of ceremonies. As E. S. Drower[1] has said in discussing the symbolism of bread in Mediterranean cultures, 'It is not only the symbol of life. Bread, itself a union of many grains into a single substance, when broken into fragments and divided amongst many, becomes a symbol of life shared, of a society at peace with itself, of a family bound together by a common factor.'

Wine, too, is a life-fluid. It is drunk ritually by the bride and groom during the religious wedding ceremony. From the Saturday till the Tuesday afternoon, when the festivities end, it is drunk to excess by the whole bibulous assembly. A glass of wine must be accompanied by a toast, and every man tries to drink to the health of each of his kinsmen present. Wine is the symbol of blood; and each toast affirms a relationship. 'To your health, John' (Γειά σου Γιάννη). 'To your marriages, boys' (Μωρὲ παιδιὰ στὶς χαρές σας), when drinking with unmarried youths or young men; or simply, 'To your wedding' (στὸ γάμο σου). 'To the marriages of your sons' (στῶν παιδιῶν σας), in a toast to married men. 'A happy old age' (καλὰ γεράματά σας), used in drinking to the old men. And so on.[2]

In the confined space of an arbour covered with thick woollen blankets, between one hundred and two hundred men and boys are gathered. In the centre of the floor space the dancing only stops when the company sits down to eat. Then the plates of roasted meat are devoured almost in silence. Afterwards the dance is on again. Those who are not dancing, sing in accompaniment. The gipsy band beat out strange and exciting rhythms in which the high-pitched clarinet is never silent. In this intense atmosphere with men drinking steadily and shouting their toasts across the heads of the squatting assembly to their kinsmen, any link of kinship makes men like brothers, its absence potential enemies. For it must not be forgotten that although the wedding guests are all related in some fashion to

---

[1] E. S. Drower, *Water into Wine*, London, 1956, p. 44.
[2] See Höeg, op. cit., vol. i, p. 50.

their hosts, they are not necessarily related to one another. Men whose pride is always sensitive become tense with nervous excitement and excess of alcohol. An alleged word or act which is interpreted as insulting, or the memory of a past grievance, may be the occasion of a quarrel; and this, if it is not controlled at once, may end in general violence by mobilizing support for the antagonists along the lines of kinship allegiance. As I have already suggested, these fights give very tangible expression to kinship bonds. But there are, also, less dramatic forms of communion. During the three days and nights of sustained revelry there are occasional breaks of an hour or two when musicians rest or the company observe some item of wedding custom such as the display of the bride's dowry. Then kinsmen sit apart and exchange their news of families and marriages, sheep and politics.

Guests come to a wedding to support their kinsmen. They do this not only by their presence but also by lending practical assistance. Among the men this applies particularly to the first cousins of the bride or groom. These relatives take a hand in preparing the carcasses of the animals for roasting by fixing them on spits. Later they supervise the fires over which the spits are turned and they baste the meat to prevent it from burning. They cut up the whole animal into individual portions. When the meal is ready it is the first cousins who assist the brothers of the family to lay cloths on the ground, pass round forks and spoons and finally hand to each guest his individual portion of meat. After the meal is over it is again first cousins who stand in the middle of the dancing, one with a bottle of ouzo and the other with a plate of cheese or olives to give refreshment to the sweating dancers. These are not considered to be menial tasks; on the contrary, it is a privilege of close kinship to be allowed to assist in this way.

The women hold their sombre, almost melancholy, celebrations apart from the men in a nearby hut where they sing and sometimes dance. Here, again, the close female relatives of the family assist in handing round the food. But of the women guests it is the old grandmothers who play the most important role. Outside in the open-air kitchen they preside over the huge cooking-pots of potatoes, stews, and soups, enlivening their labours with gossip and attended by dogs and children anticipating scraps.

The support of kinsmen for the bride or groom is expressed more specifically in particular points of marriage custom. One of the more important ceremonies is 'The sewing of the wedding standard' (τὸ ῥάψιμο τοῦ φλάμπουρου), which takes place on the Saturday evening after the guests have arrived. For this standard, which flies from the hut of the groom until the marriage has been consummated, is more than a sign that nuptial celebrations are in progress; it is a symbol of marriage itself, the joining of noble youth with virgin maid.[3] In standing with him at this ceremony the company of kinsmen witness their certain knowledge of the bridegroom's nobility and their belief in the bride's virginity. Only the joining of these qualities in a marriage celebrated before God makes possible parenthood with honour. 'Whose is the wedding standard, noble and red? It is the standard of the bridegroom . . .' (Τίνος εἶν' τὸ φλάμπουρο, τ'ἄξιο καὶ τὸ κόκκινο, τοῦ γαμπροῦ εἶν' τὸ φλάμπουρο . . .), they sing. A standard requires a standard-bearer (φλαμπουράρης), and for this coveted position a youth between the ages of sixteen and twenty is chosen. He must not have had experience of sexual intercourse and both his mother and father must be alive. He is almost always a young first cousin or nephew of the groom. On the Saturday night the flag, which nowadays is the national flag of Greece, is sewn by the youth to a pole some six or seven feet in length, at the top of which a small wooden cross is secured. As the boy sews the flag the whole company of kinsmen stand around him in a circle and sing the appropriate wedding song. When the sewing is completed, the boy impales pomegranates or apples, symbols of fertility, on the three points of the small wooden cross and, finally, ties to the flag-pole below the cross a handkerchief and two strands of wool, one coloured red for virility, the other white for purity. The guests now form a dance-ring, the band strikes up, and the standard-bearer leads the dance holding aloft in his right hand the newly sewn standard. He then sets up the flag in the thatch of the groom's hut at the right-hand side of the doorway where it remains until the next morning, when the standard-bearer, mounted on a fine horse, lifts it down from the roof and leads the groom's bridal procession on its journey to the home of the bride.

The groom and his family rely on the support of their kindred

[3] At the weddings of widows or widowers no flag is flown.

to make the bridal procession the spectacular occasion it must appear if their prestige is to be maintained in the community. They give this support by their numbers, their own bearing, and the quality of their horses and the coloured woollen saddle-cloths which are draped over the backs of the animals. For whenever the procession passes through or close to a village both Sarakatsani and villagers line the path, to enjoy the spectacle with critical eyes, and to exchange greetings with the riders. The watchers laugh excitedly and try to draw the riders into an exchange of bawdy quips and jokes, but the horsemen must remain unmoved with upright backs and proud serious faces.

Earlier on the same Sunday morning before the bridal procession sets out on its journey, the bridegroom is prepared for his ordeal. Seated on a chair outside the door of his hut he is attended by a kinsman with the necessary skill, who cuts his hair, shaves his beard, and trims the moustache. This, like the sewing of the standard, is a part of customary wedding ritual. The kinsmen gather about the groom and accompanied by the gipsy band sing about the shaving of the bridegroom. From time to time the singing is interrupted by heated debate between the watching kinsmen and the barber as to the style of the hair cutting, the angle of the moustache, and the effectiveness of the shaving. For they fear the appraisal of strangers on the road and the malicious hopes of the bride's kinsmen that the bridegroom will in some way look ridiculous.

After the barber has completed his task, two or three of the more senior first cousins with a reputation for worldly knowledge go into the hut to supervise the changing of the bridegroom's clothes (ν'ἀλλάξουν τὸ γαμπρό). The Sarakatsani have abandoned the traditional kilt and today the prosaic costume of a bridegroom consists of a white shirt buttoned to the neck without a tie, and a blue suit of manufactured cloth. The cousins help their young kinsman to put on these clothes to which he is not accustomed and they make certain that he does not change his underclothes; for with these an envious man or woman might affect the sexual potency of the groom by sorcery. As a prophylactic against the same peril they place some steel object in the folds of the shirt tails before he puts it on. As he is dressed, almost like a child, they feed him with various pieces of good advice, telling him in detail how he must deport himself that day on the road and later at the home of the bride.

At the home of the bride kinsfolk support her family in a similar manner, particularly in a number of situations where a measure of dramatized hostility is shown to the groom's party when they arrive to take away the bride; but these are episodes which I shall describe in the following chapter. The dressing and adornment of the bride, naturally, is a more elaborate affair than the preparation of the groom. In this, two or three senior married aunts or first cousins generally take a hand, assisted by the more sophisticated village dressmaker who in most cases has been responsible for cutting and sewing the white wedding gown. All through the long night of Saturday the bride sits in her parents' hut. She must not sleep for this would demonstrate an equanimity at odds with the grief she is expected to feel at the thought of leaving her parents and her home on the morrow. Her kinswomen sit closely round her. Two of them hold her hands. From time to time they sing the repetitive, intensely sad, songs that tell of the bride's departure from the only home she has ever known.

\* \* \*

In this chapter I have attempted to give a fuller description of the relations of collateral kin than it was possible to present in chapter three, where I was mainly concerned to describe the formal characteristics of the kindred. I mentioned, then, that various aspects of kindred relations might be seen in terms of an opposition between the solidarity of siblings and the principle of parental obligation, the former being the source of moral solidarity between kinsmen, the latter strongly influencing the isolation of the family group from the collateral kinsmen of its members. The 'free favours' which a man does without thought or calculation for an uncle, cousin, or nephew, are related to kinship solidarity, the qualities of which follow from the notion of an extensive sibling relationship; while calculated co-operation which involves the corporate wealth of family groups is influenced by the particularistic obligations of parenthood. As one might expect, those cousins, father's brother's children, whose families of origin were concerned in co-operative sheep management, are the cousins least likely to form those important links of devoted friendship. Since marriage is patrilocal it is the fathers of these cousins who experienced the various constraints of life in an extended family. These considerations do not generally apply to the other categories of first cousin who normally live in other neighbourhoods. It is among these relatives that a man finds his intimate friends. For these cousins are able to emphasize in their behaviour the altruistic qualities of collateral kinship, particularly in the performance of free favours. Various considerations, then, tend to identify the interests of collateral kinsmen, others to set them apart. We may look at this from another point of view. The fact that for any individual the community is divided into the opposed categories of kinsmen, 'own people', and non-kinsmen, 'strangers', is clearly a factor which unites people who can trust one another against the rest of the world who are not to be trusted. Generally, a man can only co-operate with a kinsman, find a true friend among his cousins, talk to an unmarried girl who is a kinswoman, and so on. However, the members of a man's kindred are not undifferentiated. Some are close kinsmen, others more distant. There is not quite the same measure of responsibility and obligation to a second cousin as there is to a first. Moreover, as children grow up their parents are more concerned with their own descendants and less with collateral kinsmen. But, quite apart from any considerations which relate specifically to the internal structure of the kindred, questions of prestige are always a potential threat to the solidarity of kinsmen. Kinsmen are identified in the thoughts of outsiders and if one man loses prestige, whether it is due to moral error, poverty, or physical deformity, his kinsman suffers with him. In these circumstances his only defence is to withdraw temporarily or permanently from the relationship.

Sarakatsani are fully aware of the fragmented character of their community. They realize that one man's hand is turned against another's. They continually lament the distrust which exists between unrelated men and the element of calculation which must exist even in the relations of kinsmen who co-operate at work. They value their relations with kinsmen who live in other neighbourhoods not only for the various practical reasons we have elaborated, but because of the generally altruistic quality of these relationships. This is an end in itself. It balances the qualities of calculation and restraint which enter into all the other situations of social life, excepting only certain contexts of religious experience. This partly explains the immense pleasure which individuals experience when they take part with their kinsmen in festivals and weddings. There is a sense of release from the restrictions of daily life and local animosities which more articulate shepherds describe by the same phrase that is sometimes used after receiving the Eucharist at Easter, 'A weight has left me', μοὔφυγε ἕνα βάρος.

# VI

## AFFINAL RELATIONS

### 1. BETROTHAL AND ABDUCTION

ALTHOUGH in one respect marriage is a religious sacrament binding together two individuals in the sight of God, it is also a contract between the two families of origin of the man and the girl. In the early years of the marriage a brother's wife or a sister's husband is often referred to in such phrases as, 'She is our bride', or 'We have him as bridegroom'. Similarly, people do not ask whom a man has married, but whose daughter has he taken. Indeed it is only as a contract between two families of origin that a marriage arrangement has immediate significance, for, in effect, there is no real recognition of a new family until the first child is born. And since the prohibition on marriage within the kindred compels the Sarakatsanos to find a bride among families which are not related to him, that is among people who are hostile to himself and his interests, this marriage contract is in the nature of a peace treaty between two previously-opposed social groups.[1]

Despite the contrary testimony of love songs, romantic courtship is impossible. 'The songs tell lies,' the Sarakatsani say. Virtually all marriages are arranged. It would be shameful for a man or girl to express any preference, and they have only to answer the specific question, 'Will you marry this particular man or girl?' It is almost impossible for a girl to refuse the bridegroom of her family's choice if they insist upon it, although it is believed that a good father or brother ought not to force her into a marriage against her will. But it is also said that a daughter should be guided by her parents' or brothers' choice, and in the period of the last twenty years I have discovered evidence of only two cases of 'marriage by force' (παντρειὰ μὲ τὸ ζόρι). It is more difficult for a father or brother to dictate to a potential bridegroom, but here again, in most cases, unless his feelings are very strongly engaged against a particular girl, the weight of family opinion is likely to persuade him to accept their decision. John Myriounis saw a maiden at a wedding

[1] Except in the marginal instance of a marriage between third cousins.

whose fair hair and black eyes captured his heart, but when his father pressed him to marry another not strikingly well-favoured girl, after some resistance he finally agreed, 'so as not to displease' (νὰ μὴ χαλάσω τὸ χατίρι). A marriage is arranged to suit the requirements of the family group, not the individual preference of the youth or maiden.

Since marriage is, from one point of view, a contract between hostile groups, a family which is looking for a bride proceeds with the utmost circumspection, to avoid offending other families with daughters of marriageable age. For this reason they appoint a kinsman or a close affine, generally a senior man with a reputation for skill in these matters, as the marriage negotiator. If the family already have a particular girl in mind, the negotiator will make a tentative approach to a close kinsman of the girl's father from whom he inquires with a great deal of periphrasis, whether he has any knowledge of the family's plans, and how much dowry she is likely to have. The girl's kinsman may undertake to make the inquiries if he does not already know, and report to the negotiator in one or two days' time. If the negotiator has some link of kinship or affinity with both families, he may make a more direct approach to the girl's family.

When the negotiator by one means or another has obtained oblique assurances that the girl's family are willing to consider a marriage proposal, he informs the family of his kinsman. The head of that family now waylays the girl's brother or father in some quiet place, but not at his home. Naturally both are aware why the one has sought out the other. But for a while they pursue a conventional conversation about sheep and weather, until, quite casually, the one remarks that he has a brother or son who is of an age when it is right that he should marry. And then he asks, 'Would you give us the girl so that we may become one house?' (νὰ μᾶς δώσῃς τὴ κοπέλλα νὰ γίνωμε ἕνα σπίτι). At this point he will also mention how many sheep or gold pounds are demanded in addition to the traditional dowry. This too will already be known to the girl's family and is therefore no longer a matter for debate. The other receives the news as if it comes as a complete surprise. He explains that this is not a light matter and therefore he would like to discuss it with his family, and that he will send word to the other's home within eight days. If the negotiator has worked skilfully, there is little chance of the girl's family rejecting the proposal. Within a few days a kinsman of the girl's family arrives at the future bridegroom's homestead, inviting the family to come to the home of the girl's family on the next Sunday to effect the betrothal contract (τὸ σύβιασμα).

It is only in the last ten years that the betrothal ceremony, under the influence of village customs, has developed into a feast where both the families participate. Previously, the father or eldest brother came alone to the girl's house. He was offered Turkish delight and ouzo (κέρασμα), and immediately afterwards the two heads of family exchanged the rings, an act which indicated the formal sealing of the contract. The girl's representative handed over her wedding ring, tied in a white handkerchief, which contained also, rice, red and white wool, and a gold sovereign. In return, he took from the bridegroom's brother, or father, the ring which was to be worn by the groom at the wedding ceremony. Each side kept the other's ring until the day of the marriage as a pledge that the marriage contract would be honoured.

At the modern betrothal feast the exchange of rings is effected in the same manner. But in place of the single representative the whole of the bridegroom's family together with various close kinsmen make the journey on the appointed Sunday to the home of the bride's family where they are entertained with feasting and dancing until the early hours of the Monday morning. There is something inappropriate about this act of commensality between future affines. At the moment of betrothal there are only feelings of suspicion and distrust between the two sides. This is reflected in the unhappy record of betrothal feasts since this village custom was adopted. Brawling between hosts and guests is not infrequent and generally the result of these celebrations is that relations between the two groups deteriorate yet further.

Under the old convention, when the groom's representative arrived to exchange the rings, it was customary to hide away the future bride in the hut of a close kinsman. The ostensible purpose of this manœuvre was to protect the reputation and sensibilities of the maiden from the shame of suffering the gaze of her future father- or brother-in-law. But, also, it was thought to be imprudent to display the girl in case she did not please the groom's representative. Girls marry strictly in accordance with the order of birth and if the eldest unmarried daughter is ugly or unhealthy a family will sometimes try to deceive an inexperienced negotiator into believing that a younger and more personable sister is the next in order to marry. In any event, whether the bride was particularly ill favoured or not, it was considered wise that the groom's people should remain in ignorance of the bride's appearance until the wedding day. And this was the more easily achieved twenty years ago when the Sarakatsani did not live in, or generally close to, the mountain villages. In the modern betrothal feast, the future bride appears only about an hour before the groom's party are due to depart, that is between four and five o'clock in the morning. By this time the rings have been exchanged and there is no way of retreat left open to the bridegroom. The girl appears in the doorway with a tray of Turkish delight and small glasses of ouzo which she offers to each member of the other party in turn, including her future husband. She disappears, to return a quarter of an hour later with cups of coffee which she again offers to the bridegroom and his kinsmen. The groom's kinsmen invariably demand that the girl should appear much earlier in the proceedings before the rings have been exchanged, as indeed she ought to do if the village custom were strictly adhered to. Invariably, the girl's father and brothers refuse the request, and it is often this refusal which is the beginning of the brawling and quarrelling between the two groups. The traditional seclusion of the girl in a relative's hut, the present-day precaution to produce her only when the rings have been exchanged, the practice of trickery and the fear of it, all indicate the quality of the relations which exist between the two sides at the moment they enter into this contract.

The betrothal contract amongst the Sarakatsani is entirely secular and it is an agreement between families rather than individuals. The groom contracts to marry a certain man's daughter whose face he may never have seen rather than a particular person of the opposite sex. If he withdraws from this agreement, not only does he break his pledged word but he damages the girl's reputation in a way which makes it impossible for her to make an honourable marriage in the future. For it will be said that a man would not lightly or without reason change his mind on so serious a matter if he had not discovered some grave moral or physical deficiency in the girl. No man of worth is likely to choose a girl whom another has previously rejected. She can only hope to marry a widower or a poor man from a despised family. Therefore to break an engagement is a violent affront to the honour of all the members of the bride's family, and as such it carries the ultimate sanction of vengeance killing, which the girl's brothers, if they are men of honour, ought to carry through against the person of the bridegroom. It follows that both for the sake of his honour and prestige in the community, and for very life itself, a man is unlikely to break a betrothal contract. On the other hand, a bridegroom, if he finds out between the betrothal and the marriage (a period of between three months to a year) that he is being tricked into marriage with a particularly ugly or unhealthy girl, may consider himself released from his pledge of honour. It is generally in connexion with incurable diseases such as advanced pulmonary tuberculosis that betrothals are sometimes broken off. It cannot, however, be said that the danger of a broken betrothal deters the girl's family from every kind of trickery or concealment when there is the possibility of marrying off an ugly or unhealthy daughter or sister. The disgrace of a girl remaining unmarried is feared more than the bridegroom's reluctance and its possible consequences.

It is mainly to avoid these risks and difficulties that, today, a bridegroom often will not allow the formal approach to be made to a girl's family until he, or a trusted brother, has had an opportunity of secretly appraising the appearance and bearing of a prospective bride. For the same reasons, families with daughters of marriageable age try to display the more attractive girls and prevent their ugly or sick sisters from being seen at wells or in other public places. When a man wants to view a possible bride, he generally goes to stay at a kinsman's home near to the huts of the girl's family. From the women of his kinsman's family he learns of the girl's daily movements and arranges to be near the well or stream when she goes to draw water or wash clothes. He may watch her secretly from behind cover or may saunter casually past and say 'Good day', to which she will not reply. These antics are unnecessary if the man has already had the opportunity to see the girl more naturally at a wedding, a village festival, or perhaps on the road during the two annual migrations between the mountains and the plain. And young men look forward to these occasions as opportunities to assess the virtues of unrelated maidens. But in whatever way a man succeeds in seeing the girl, his purpose must remain secret.

There is no likelihood of a change of mind on the part of the girl's family between betrothal and marriage. Men and youths lead a public life and their virtues and deficiencies are more widely known than those of their sisters and daughters who live and work in privacy close to, or inside, the huts. The action of the girl's family which is most likely to give grave offence to the man and his kinsmen is not the breaking of the betrothal contract, but unwillingness to enter into it at all. Even if the refusal is made through the negotiator, the situation is serious enough, and the reactions of the groom's family depend to some extent on the diplomacy with which the negative answer is given. The usual formula is that the family are not yet ready to marry the girl. She is too young, and she has not yet completed her dowry, or the supplementary dowry asked for is too high, although this last excuse is not often made since no family wishes to plead poverty. In the event of the refusal being made after the brother or father of the man has made a formal request for the girl's hand, the situation is much graver. In any event, the fact that the man wanted the girl, and was refused, is bound to become generally known. If the refusal is made directly and not through the negotiator, it is more obviously an insult. Such direct refusals are, however, rare. What the rejected bridegroom will do depends upon his estimate of the effect of his unsuccessful suit on his own and his family's prestige in the community. If he believes that he has been made to look ridiculous, he may be driven to attempt the only remedy, abduction.

To abduct a girl against her will is a dangerous undertaking. The man, together with one or two trusted kinsmen, mounted on fast horses, waylay the girl when she is collecting wood or water at some distance from her home. Naturally she resists and on this account she is not always handled with gentleness. One wife, who is now happily devoted to her abductor, told me with pride how she was beaten about the head and body and dragged fifty yards by the hair. The captured girl is taken without delay to a prepared hideout in a cave or forest clearing. Here she is held by the bridegroom for three days and three nights. On the fourth day, the man takes the girl to the nearest police post and gives himself up, explaining that he took the girl from her home because he wished to marry her. The police at once send for the father or brother of the girl, and in his presence the police officer asks her if she wishes to marry her abductor or return to her home. She is asked this question three times and gives her answer three times. If she says that she is willing to marry the man they are taken immediately to the church and the service is celebrated. If she elects to return home, she is handed over to her kinsmen while the man is held to await trial on a serious charge which may send him to prison for a number of years. It is remarkable that in the five cases of abduction which I discovered amongst the Zagori Sarakatsani, there is only one instance of the girl choosing to return to her own people. During the days and nights when she is detained by her abductor, the situation is carefully explained to her. If she refuses to marry the man, nobody will believe that after three nights in the wilderness with an ardent lover she is any longer a virgin. In any case, she cannot expect to be sought in marriage except by a man of low prestige or a widower. Secondly, if she goes back to her family, it inevitably obliges one of her brothers to seek vengeance on the abductor when he emerges from prison. And in this case, the brother in turn may lose his life in counter vengeance or, at least, be forced into voluntary exile. Thirdly, she is asked if it is not pleasant, despite the sudden shocks, to be married to a man who is willing to risk his life to take her as his wife. For these reasons, and especially for the first of them, the girl is more likely to say 'Yes' than 'No'.

Abduction, then, is a recognized institution through which, if the normal negotiations between two opposed groups for the arrangement of a marriage break down in a manner detrimental to his social prestige, a man may yet save his reputation and win his bride without necessarily precipitating the two families into acts of reciprocal vengeance. To refuse a bridegroom is to suggest that he is not worthy. The abduction of the girl is a proof of courage and strength which refutes this suggestion and reinstates the man's prestige. The bride's family are extremely angry at the time but their reputation is not unduly damaged; the original assertion of their greater worth, which the refusal to give the girl implied, still carries some of its force and there is considerable material compensation in the fact that no dowry need be handed over.

It is, now, easy to appreciate why much thought and discussion is given to the negotiation of marriages. A marriage is an arrangement between opposed groups which involves important considerations of honour and prestige. Its negotiation is a difficult and delicate operation. The importance of the negotiator in the marriage settlement is that he stands between the two groups and prevents any direct collision which might otherwise prove fatal to the conclusion of an agreement. He is able to present to the girl's kinsmen in a relatively objective and calm manner all the virtues of the prospective bridegroom, and to bargain over the dowry in a disinterested fashion which cannot easily cause offence. If the girl's family decline the proposal, he is able to soften the blow so that it does not inevitably lead to the dangers of an attempted abduction.

The ideal marriage negotiator is a kinsman who is also a kinsman of the intended bride. Such a man serves as a direct bridge between the two unrelated and opposed groups. When the bridegroom's family ask a kinsman to act as negotiator and have not yet decided on a suitable bride, he will first search in his mind for a possible bride from those female kinsmen of his own kindred who are not related to the youth. In this way, it frequently happens that a man takes as his bride the cousin of a cousin. In another direction the negotiator may look among the kinswomen of his own wife or the wives of his brothers and cousins. It is not unusual for two cousins to have as wives, women who are themselves cousins or even sisters. Also, it is possible for a man to marry his third cousin. Such a union has the obvious advantage that the two contracting families are known to one another, but, among some Sarakatsani, there is the uneasy feeling that it is wrong that relations originally founded on the confidence of cousinship should be endangered by the ambivalence of affinal ties of which they are well aware.

In these manœuvres, the object of both the family and their negotiator is to establish a marriage contract with a group in which, by reason of some mediating link of kinship, they can place a measure of trust. Some hostility will still exist between the groups, but there is the hope that it will pass more rapidly from the overt to the latent phase than otherwise is the case. From 121 marriages in recent years, 52 were contracted between families connected by some mediating link of kinship or marriage; nine were marriages between third cousins.

## 2. THE ELEMENT OF HOSTILITY
### MARRIAGE AND THE 'RETURN'

During the months which pass between the betrothal and the day of the marriage, the date of which is fixed at the betrothal, there is no communication between the two groups. If members of the two families or their close relatives meet by chance, they avoid one another. When Machoula Gogolos was approached by a sophisticated cousin of her betrothed after the Easter Sunday church service, she refused to exchange greetings with her, and turning her back, walked away. Each side in an atmosphere of mutual aversion separately attends to its wedding preparations.

The day of the wedding marks an important change in the relations between the two groups. On this day the two sides formally enter into affinal relations (συμπεθεριά), and a daughter leaves her home. The feelings of the girl's family, especially of her parents, are mixed. On the one hand there is relief and self-congratulation that they have succeeded in guarding her reputation unblemished and arranging an honourable marriage. But there is also true grief at the loss of a daughter, a loss which is harder to bear because of their anxiety about how the strangers will use her. It is easy to observe the strained expressions on the faces of the bride's brothers as they watch the groom's people boasting in loud voices and strutting about the homestead. But self-restraint must be exercised in dealings with affines, if only for the sake of the bride. The exchanges between the two groups, when the groom arrives to take away the bride, vary between the openly expressed hostility which sometimes occurs and a formal display of amity which is, in fact, a controlled hostility cloaked with fair words. Midway between these extremes is the ambivalence of certain marriage customs which express the mutual antagonism between the two sides and its limitation within conventional bounds.

When the groom's bridal procession arrives at a point about a quarter of a mile from the bride's home it halts. Five of the younger, braver, and better mounted men (συγχαριάτες) ride on ahead to bear the tidings of the groom's approach to the bride's people. Their object is to ride up to the door of the bride's hut at a full gallop, where they attempt to scatter and terrify the kinsmen of the bride. The aim of the bride's people, on the other hand, is to dismount and thereby ridicule as many of the riders as possible. Traditionally, this was done by firing blank charges at the feet of the oncoming horses, so that they reared in terror and threw their riders. Nowadays, if the bride lives near a village, this method of attack is not attempted because the possession of firearms is illegal, but with the help of barking dogs and the banging of tin cans it is still possible to give the riders an unpleasant reception. Because convention permits this cut and thrust, no offence may be taken, unless it is pursued with an excess of malice. As each man reaches the door of the bride's hut, he claims from an appointed kinsman of the bride the coloured handkerchief which is the prerogative of these riders.

When the entire party of the groom has assembled, they are offered Turkish delight and a glass of ouzo by the bride's family, but this is the limit of the hospitality which is offered. Before the arrival of the groom, the bride's people have prepared a shady picnic site, by spreading blankets on the ground and providing a barrel of fresh water. Thus while the bride's kinsmen eat and dance inside the huts, the groom's party take their midday meal outside under a tree, eating the food they have brought with them. They invariably eat this meal in a mood of impatient ill-humour, with many complaints that the water is tepid and the place unsuitable. By this formal denial of commensality the bride's family express their opposition to those who support the bridegroom.

After the religious betrothal ceremony has been completed, the groom's party are eager to leave. The bride's family, on the contrary, insist that she goes through the lengthy ritual of dancing for the last time with each member of her family.

'She is ours, now', shout the groom's men, which only encourages the other side to delay the departure for another half an hour. These arguments are accepted moves in the game and do not cause permanent offence so long as they remain within the limits of what is conventionally permitted.

Finally, when the bride is prepared to leave, there is some byplay over the acceptance and loading of the bride's dowry. The trunks and sacks in which this is contained are stacked in the doorway of the bride's hut. The young kinsmen of the groom advance to take it, but at this moment a kinsman of the bride jumps astride the first sack and shouts, 'Don't interfere with it. The sack doesn't belong to you. This dowry has great worth' (Μὴ τὸ πειράζῃς, εἶναι ξένο τὸ σακκί. Ἔχουν ἀξία τὰ προικιά). He refuses to get off the sack until the groom's eldest brother pays over some token pieces of money. The groom's kinsmen now drag the bulky sacks and trunks outside, where they begin to load them on to pack mules. This is an awkward operation which gives much enjoyment to the bride's kinsmen who stand round in a close circle mocking at the efforts of the other side to balance and secure the difficult loads.

But fair words are also exchanged. These expressions of amity indicate the readiness of each side to co-operate in establishing the new relationship and in supporting the children of the new family, on the understanding that the other side will also play their part. For the contract which is entered into at the betrothal is not confined to co-operation in the arrangement of the marriage, it also foresees the future obligations which the two families must assume towards the new family group in which both will have a common and balanced interest.

When the groom's party arrives at the bride's house, all the riders, including those unfortunates who may have been thrown from their horses, must exchange conventional greetings which express their common interest in the bridal couple. 'Good health to you, it is well that we have found you! May our bride and groom live long and prosper!' (Γειά σας! Καλῶς σᾶς ηὕραμε! Νὰ μᾶς ζήσουν! Νὰ μᾶς προκόψουν!). And a brother of the groom exchanges the wine and 'bread of the bride' (κουλούρα τῆς νύφης), baked by the women of the groom's family, for the same elements of communion and commensality prepared and presented by the bride's family.

Half an hour later, as they drink the one glass of ouzo which, as we have seen, is the full extent of the hospitality shown to them, the bridegroom's kinsmen sing,

> 'We have not come for food or drink,
> But because we love you,
> We have come to see you.
> I find tables fair and laden,
> And glasses brimming over.
> Three maidens with black eyes serve us.
> Three maidens with the eyebrows of angels.'[2]

They could hardly sing more fairly. Thus during the two or three hours that the parties of the bride and the groom are in contact, marriage custom enjoins the expression of the opposed sentiments of friendship and enmity. It indicates the ambivalent character of the affinal relationship which demands co-operation between previously unrelated and therefore hostile families. Naturally this ambivalence of sentiment is more apparent in the early years, but it never wholly vanishes at any time.

The margin between antagonism permitted and instituted by convention and the display of excessive malice is narrow. Quarrels over the time and precise arrangements of the bride's departure frequently flare up into free violence. In one case, no sooner had the bride progressed some two hundred yards on her journey to the groom's home, than a fierce rain storm broke overhead drenching the bride and her white wedding dress.

---

[2] Δὲν ἤρθαμαν γιὰ φαΐ γιὰ πιΐ
ροϊδούλα, ροϊδούλα.
Μεῖς σᾶς ἀγαπήσαμαν,
ροϊδούλα, ροϊδούλα,
ροϊδούλα, χαμαϊδούλα,
κι'ἤρθαμαν νὰ σᾶς δοῦμε.
βρίσκω τραπέζια νόμορφα
ροϊδούλα, ροϊδούλα,
ροϊδούλα, χαμαϊδούλα,
γυαλιὰ παραγιομάτα.
Τρεῖς μαυρομάτες μᾶς κερνᾶν,
ροϊδούλα, ροϊδούλα,
ροϊδούλα, χαμαιδούλα,
κι τρεῖς ἀγγελαφρύδες.

Her relatives, leaping to their horses, rode after the cavalcade insisting that the bride return and take shelter. The groom's kinsmen angrily refused to halt, pointing out that if a bride retraces her steps or even looks round upon the house she has left, it brings ill luck upon her new home. Refusing to be drawn into further argument, they rode on. The enraged kinsmen of the bride dismounted, and blaspheming against the sisters and mothers of their future affines, sent them away to a fusillade of rifle shots over their heads and stones aimed at their bodies.

However, the separate celebration of the wedding feast, each family in its own home, the denial of commensality, and the mutual display of antagonism institutionalized in wedding custom, are the last occasions on which the two families are permitted to bear witness openly to the aspect of mutual opposition in their relationship. Before the eldest brother of the bridegroom leaves the bride's house, he is offered a glass of ouzo by the bride's father or brother who says, 'We shall wait for you'. This refers to the customary visit or 'return' (ἐπιστροφή), which is made by the bride and groom and the latter's close relatives to the former home of the bride, generally on the second Sunday after the wedding. Meat is killed, quantities of wine are bought, and there is feasting and dancing through the night.

The 'return' is an important occasion. By this time, the new marriage relationship has been established both by the secular contract of betrothal between the two families and by the joining of the two individuals in the religious sacrament of marriage. In the first words of the service which refer to the bride and groom, the priest says, 'Let us pray to the Lord for his servants (X., Y.) who are now joining the one with the other for the common life of marriage.' The two individuals are now a social unity, a man-and-wife (ἀνδρόγυνο). It is not possible to help the one and not help the other, or withdraw support from one without withdrawing support from the other. Thus, the behaviour of both families at the 'return' is necessarily oriented towards co-operation and forced goodwill.

At first conversation between the two families is stilted and formal, and restricted to neutral topics such as weather and taxes. The bride and groom, under the eyes of their respective affines, sit silent and constrained. But as the evening wears on, the wine and the dance produce a mellowing effect on the assembly; the groom begins to smile, and even the bride, with the merest flutter of her lips, tries to follow the singing.

One effect of this reunion of the bride with her people is to establish the interest of the bride's family in the new family which will be formed at the birth of the first child. The knowledge that the unborn children of the married pair will be affiliated equally to both their maternal and paternal relatives forces both sets of affines to act towards each other in a calculatingly friendly manner. However, this attitude is dictated not only by their common interest in the new family, but for reasons of prestige. Other people are uncharitably amused when a family is having in-law trouble (πιάστηκαν οἱ συμπέθεροι). In general both sets of affines try hard to conciliate one another and it follows that the attitudes of affines act as a strong sanction on a spouse in his or her actions within the marriage relationship. Similarly, in a wider sense, the attitude of one set of affines is a sanction for the correct conduct of the other set.

But what is undoubtedly uppermost in the minds of the bride's kinsmen at the 'return', is an anxiety to find out how the girl has been treated in general and in particular a certain malicious hope that perhaps the bridegroom has encountered some sexual difficulty. Conversely, the object of the groom's people is to deny the bride the opportunity to transmit this kind of information. A sister or brother's wife of the bridegroom is always a member of the groom's party; she sits close to the bride, and attends her every movement so far as good manners will allow. However, the young wife generally succeeds in whispering a few of the desired details into the ear of her mother or a sister; and every Sarakatsan woman is a mistress of the art of conveying meaning with her eyes.

In the morning the affines say farewell. No sooner have the echoes of the piously uttered sentiments of goodwill died away than each side indulges in a critical appraisal of what was said and done by the other side at the 'return'. The bride's family, in particular, may have some very interesting material to discuss whether it is fact or simply conjecture. Invariably the criticism is very unfriendly and reveals the hostility of the affinal relationship, a hostility, however, which must no longer be openly expressed.

Betrothal, marriage, and the 'return' are the three stages in which affinal relations are fully established. The betrothal is the formal contract between the two hostile groups after which there is a period of separation while the two sides, like two opposed camps of war, prepare for the marriage. At the marriage the emphasis is still upon the distance which separates the two groups. Each family surrounded by its own kinsmen and affines celebrates the occasion apart. The two sides make contact only at the point where the groom comes to take away the bride. And this confrontation, although it is marked, as we have seen, by the expression of friendship as well as antagonism, is essentially characterized as a warlike descent.[3] The martial array of the groom's procession, the standard-bearer, the charge of the leading riders to the door of the bride's hut, and the deployment of the bride's supporters to repel this attack, all contribute to form this dramatic impression. After the marriage, until they meet generally two weeks later at the 'return', the two sides adjust themselves to the realities of a new situation. The groom's family try to help the bride overcome her loneliness and despair, while the bride's family, in a sense the defeated party, are anxious and sensitive about the treatment of the bride at her new home. The two groups, despite the inevitable undercurrents of animosity and suspicion, meet at the 'return' fully conscious of the necessity and the advantages of future co-operation.

### 3. THE OBLIGATIONS OF AFFINES

The recognition of affinal relationships is even more flexible than the recognition of cognatic kinship. Affinal relationship may be claimed not only with the elementary family of origin of a person's spouse, or the elementary family of origin of the wife or husband of any member in a person's kindred, but also with the entire kindred of the marriage partner. Consequently a man may, if it suits his convenience, describe himself as an affine of the second cousin of the spouse of his second cousin. Generally, however, a man limits his use of the term affine to the kindreds of his own wife, and of the marriage partners of his brothers and sisters, and to only the elementary families

---

[3] Cf. Chatzimichalis, op. cit., vol i, Part A, p. ϱοε'.

of origin of the marriage partners of his collateral kinsmen. There are also two quasi-affinal relationships which must be mentioned; that of co-bride (συννυφάδα), which is the link between a man's wife and the wife of his brother; and similarly that of co-bridegroom (μπατζανάκης), which describes the relationship of two men who are married to sisters.

The importance of the principle of parental obligation is once more apparent when we ask which are the significant affinal relationships. These are, in fact, the relationships between an individual and those affines who are, or will be, parents of the first cousins of his (or her) own children; more specifically relationships with the husbands or wives of siblings, and with the siblings of the individual's own marriage partner. Whatever a man's personal feelings may be, for the sake of his children he is almost compelled to co-operate with these affines. A brother tries hard to win the goodwill of his sister's husband. He is anxious that she should receive good treatment among the strangers to whom he and his family have given her. And it is noticeable that in the early years of marriage while the bride is still unsure of her position in the new family, her brothers often do more favours and good turns for the husband and his family than they receive in return.

But from the point of view of the husband, too, this is the critical affinal relation. So long as his dealings with the siblings and parents of his wife remain friendly his children are assured of adequate kinship support. In the early years of marriage, the nostalgia of the wife for her family of origin and her old home is not easily appeased. The physical separation of affines does not make visits to her parents very easy, and in any case, as we have seen, her husband and his brothers are not pleased if communication is too frequent. In practice, most young brides manage to visit their homes about twice a year. It is an accepted custom that young brides accompanied by their husbands set out on the Tuesday after Easter to visit the bride's home for five or six days. In the early years, these occasions may be something of an ordeal for the bridegroom. He must show a careful and studied respect towards his father-in-law and mother-in-law (πεθερός, πεθερά). Even with the brother or sister of his wife (κουνιάδος, κουνιάδα) he cannot relax, but must appear at all times severe and grave.

For their part, the family of the bride both for her sake and the sake of her children try very hard to please the 'bridegroom'. 'The father-in-law must entertain the bridegroom and keep him content' (ὁ πεθερὸς πρέπει νὰ εὐχαριστήσῃ καὶ φιλοξενήσῃ τὸ γαμπρό), they say. When the bridegroom comes on a visit meat is always killed, an honour which is not automatically accorded to a blood kinsman however close. After the passage of some years and the establishment of the new family, relations between the husband and his wife's family of origin become less tense and formal, and if the bridegroom is an honourable man, his father- and brothers-in-law may eventually trust him with some of their secrets. Yet even after the passage of years, close affinal relatives of the same generation must behave in a dignified and restrained manner in each other's presence. The easy familiarity between cousins of both sexes finds no parallel in the case of affinal relations. Affines do not laugh and joke together.

We need not discuss again the position of the bride in her husband's extended family of origin; something has already been said about this in chapter four. The brothers and sisters of the married pair may see one another from time to time. The husband, or a young unmarried brother of the husband, always escorts the wife when she goes to her home to see her parents, and one of the wife's brothers brings her back to her husband's home at the end of her visit. On these and other chance occasions, some at least of the members of the two families of origin come to know one another. But these relations never become easy and familiar. The link between co-parents-in-law (συμπέθεροι)[4] is formal. At the time of the marriage of their children, the fathers have already retired or are on the point of doing so, and since affines generally do not live in the same village, and the parents-in-law do not visit each other's homes, social contact between them is minimal.

In general, effective co-operation between affines does not usually occur beyond the limits of the two elementary families of origin of a married pair. The significance of affinal relations beyond this range is negative, that is to say a man avoids giving offence to or dealing deceitfully with such people. But even

[4] As we have seen, συμπέθεροι is also used in a wider sense to mean affines in general.

within this narrow circle affinal relationships which do not mediate links of cousinship in the first descendant generation are vulnerable to stress and friction. In particular a man's relations with the brothers of his brother's wife are easily beset with resentment and jealousies. Inevitably one brother sometimes makes a more successful marriage than another, whether this be judged in terms of dowry, the social standing of the bride's family, or her physical beauty. Furthermore, marriage and the birth of his children end a man's categorical obligations to his own siblings; and at the same time he must give particular consideration to his relations with the close kinsmen of his wife. These are events which must lead to a growing distance between the members of a sibling group. A man feels free to show more enmity to affines related through his brother's wife, persons who stand for the weakening of kinship ties in his family of origin and his kindred, than to affines related through his own wife who represent co-operative endeavour in the support of his own descendants.

An example of difficulties between affines occurred in the extended family of Theodoros Ferendinos, whose affairs were discussed in some detail in chapter four. The second brother, Demetrios, married the sister of George Balatsos. During the village elections, in 1955, an agreement was made between the heads of all the Sarakatsan households to cast their votes in unanimous support of the opposition party which had secretly promised a reduction in pasturage dues. This agreement became known to the other side. The President of the village by an astute combination of bribery and threats persuaded Balatsos and another influential family head secretly to ignore the agreement and vote for his own group. In the event, the President retained office by a margin of five votes. The defection of the Balatsos family from the original agreement did not, however, remain a secret. When Theodoros Ferendinos met George Balatsos in a street in Jannina a week after the election, bitter words passed between the two men. From that day, although the two families lived in the same village, the members of the two groups avoided meeting or talking to one another. Demetrios and his wife, however, were exceptions. Without mentioning the fact Demetrios paid a number of visits to his affines whose huts lay only some 300 yards away. Theodoros and his other brothers were able effectively to express their hostility towards the Balatsos group for their faithless behaviour. But Demetrios, because they were the family of his wife and the close maternal kin of his two young children, felt that in some way he must maintain these relations. For some months this fact was a source of considerable annoyance to his brothers, who inside the family circle and in the absences of his wife ridiculed his attitude of compromise. Fortunately he is an easy-tempered man and accepted these rebukes in silence. But an element of strain was introduced into the relations of the brothers which in other families might have led to blows and the permanent severance of relations. A man must try to hold a balance between his attachment to his siblings which derives from the bonds of mutual identification in his family of origin and his relations of contractual co-operation with the kinsmen of his wife. This is not always easy.

It is this 'balance', in relation to parents' categorical duties to their children, which leads to the emancipation of the elementary family from both the families of origin of the two parents. In describing life in the extended family we saw how the control of the husband's family over his bride suddenly weakens after the birth of her first child; how the brothers of the husband no longer give the bride peremptory orders in his presence; how they must never interfere with her handling of her children and so on.

There is a corresponding degree of independence from any influence of the wife's family of origin; but in this instance it is established immediately on the day of marriage. When a bride goes to see her parents, she is not permitted for the four or five days of her visit to do any work. As an honoured guest she sits by the hearth, and to occupy her hands, while she gossips, she spins wool. But it must be her own wool especially transported in a small sack by her husband for this purpose. She is not permitted to spin her mother's wool even in a situation where the family is under pressure to finish the dowry of a younger sister.

Moreover, when a father or brother has given his daughter or sister in marriage, he is quite powerless to interfere directly if the husband maltreats her. Chronic wife-beating is rare, but where it does occur, the wife's family can only help her by indirect pressures, such as the withdrawal of moral and practical support from the husband or, if his conduct is not widely known, the threat to ridicule him in public. But these, it may be added, are powerful sanctions.

The content of co-operation between affines is not significantly different from the kind of assistance given and received by cognatic kinsmen. Since affines generally live in a different neighbourhood, it happens not infrequently that a wife's brother acts as negotiator in arranging a marriage for a younger brother of his sister's husband. The fact that he is willing to perform this service is in itself a recommendation of the prospective bridegroom's family. It is also because they generally live in different neighbourhoods that a man sometimes turns to a close affine when he is in difficulty over the pasturing of his animals. When Apostolis Zygos had a few acres of grazing land in excess of his winter grazing needs, he rented them to the husband of his brother's daughter for a sum somewhat lower than an offer made to him by an unrelated neighbour. The neighbour was hard-pressed for grass and later showed his resentment, it is alleged, by stealing two of Zygos' lambs. The niece's husband brought a hundred of his sheep from his own winter grazing, forty miles away, and employed a local village boy to assist one of his brothers in watching them. Thus, affinal ties, like relations within the kindred, although they often involve physical separation, generally take precedence over the more tenuous obligations of being a good neighbour.

Another example of help given to an affine illustrates the variable character of this assistance. In the territory of certain of the eastern villages of Zagori the Sarakatsani do not live in or close to the village but build their encampments, each stani separately, some miles away and close to their grazing land. Alec Katris lives three miles from the village of Laista. His small ten-year-old daughter Chrysanthe cannot make this long journey to school each day unaccompanied. And since Alec has no kinsman or affine who lives close to Laista, he sends his daughter for the summer term to live with the family of the brother of his sister's husband who lives at Skamneli, a neighbouring village, where she attends the school. There is no money payment for the girl's board but at the beginning of the term the father sends a generously large sack of flour to his relatives. And when he heard that his affine was in need of some timber to repair the rafters of his house, Alec at once despatched, as a free gift, a mule load of sawn planks of which he happened to possess a small store. The difference between the help given to a kinsman and the co-operative assistance lent to an affine is that in the latter instance there is no such thing as a 'free favour'. Had Alec Katris been able to send his little daughter to live with a cousin or some other kinsman, he would have made a contribution in flour to cover the expense of her presence in the kinsman's family, but it would not have been necessary to make a counter gift of a load of valuable timber. The 'trouble' as opposed to the 'expense' of having the child in the home would have been a 'free favour', making no demands upon the family's corporately owned resources. But where a man does a personal service for an affine, some return favour is always awaited. In these relations the element of contract is always present, and a certain competitive attitude as to which set of affines fulfils its obligations with the greater punctilio.

The fate of a man who lives as a son-in-law in the home of his wife's parents is the extreme example of how affines are always expected to claim their pound of flesh. This arrangement is made only in a case where a man has daughters but no sons. After the elder daughters have been married off in the normal manner, the youngest girl marries a man who 'goes as bride-groom' (πάει γαμπρός) into the home of his wife. As his contri-bution to the establishment of the new elementary family, he brings with him his share of the flock in his own family of origin, an amount of wealth which corresponds in function to the woman's dowry in the normal marriage. Materially, the bridegroom may do very well out of this transaction, since eventually he becomes the trustee of the whole of his father-in-law's flock. Yet it is difficult to find a man from a family of good standing and moderate wealth to take this step. Particularly in the earlier years a man loses his self-respect and manliness in a situation where he is at the beck and call of his wife's parents, who feel entitled, without embarrassment, to exploit his labour in return for the eventual inheritance of the wife's patrimony; this in most cases greatly exceeds the value of an ordinary dowry. Yet the Sarakatsani say of such a bridegroom that his fate is 'worse than that of a skinned fox' (χειρότερα ἀπὸ τὴν γδαρμένη ἀλεποῦ).

A man never entirely trusts his affines. Yet precisely because of the co-operative compact which has been established and their equal concern for children who will claim both sets of affines as blood kinsmen, close affinal relatives must give positive proof of seeming to trust one another. A man will sometimes entrust his unmarried sister to the care of a sister's husband or a sister's husband's brother. When Patra Achnoulas went to Athens to see an eye specialist, her sister's husband, who also had business in the capital, accompanied her. It is reasoned correctly that only a mentally deranged person would act dishonourably in such a situation since his punishment at the hands of the community would be ostracism. Yet such is the suspicious attitude adopted towards affines that the Sarakatsani have many stories, no doubt spurious in the main, about illicit sexual intercourse between a bridegroom and his wife's sister; although it is true that these cautionary tales generally involve villagers or gipsies and not Sarakatsani. The true incidence of such affairs amongst the Sarakatsani themselves is probably very low; I could discover only one case, and that did not occur in recent years. If we speak generally of breaches of trust, it may be said that where these occur between kinsmen they produce a feeling of horror akin to the reaction to treason in our own society; but where the breach of trust is between affines the shock rather prompts a degree of criticism that, affines being what they are, a man did not take more care.

## 4. SOME STRUCTURAL IMPLICATIONS

The marriage contract which establishes affinal relations between two previously unrelated families is unique and may not be repeated. For instance, two brothers may not marry two sisters, although they are permitted to marry women related as first cousins. Like the prohibition on marriage in the kindred this reinforces the tendency towards the isolation of the family from collateral kinsmen. The suggestion that if the first marriage were successful it might be a good thing for two brothers to be married to two sisters is met with shocked incredulity. 'They have made one blood. They must search elsewhere,' the Sarakatsani say. The restriction on the marriage of close affines, associated with the prohibition on marriage in the kindred, forces those who are searching for prospective brides always to look outside the circle of well established relationships.

Indeed this examination of affinal relationships has largely turned on the various correlates of the prohibition on marriage in the kindred. We have seen that a man must marry a person who, in effect, was formerly an enemy, and that the element of hostility never entirely vanishes from the affinal relationship although a common interest in the children of a marriage produces and sanctions a degree of co-operation between affines. The marriage prohibitions symbolize and divide off a category of social relations based on trust. Those people with whom marriage is permitted are, on the other hand, suspect. The prohibitions clearly set apart non-kinsmen; 'strangers', from kinsmen, 'own people', and the two opposed behaviour patterns which are proper to each of these categories of relations. Affinal connexions compose a third interstitial category of social relations with persons previously strangers to whom a man is related through the contract of marriage of himself or a kinsman. In the opposition between kin and non-kin they tend to be assimilated to the latter category when the practical consideration is one of trust or confidence, and to the former when it is a question of the possibility of co-operation.

The marriage prohibitions prevent alliances in the kindred which would in some degree reverse the process of isolation from collateral kinsmen. They also force each family to regard un-related families as potential affines. In this analysis of Sarakat-san kinship the importance of prestige values has been con-stantly emphasized. If men of standing will not marry the daughters of a family or give their own in marriage to its sons, the prestige of this family must inevitably fall. The kind of marriage a man or woman makes is an index of prestige and at the same time is a very important element in the future reputation of the new family they are establishing. Therefore marriage prohibitions while they contribute inevitably to the relative isolation of a man from his collateral kin, not only have the consequence that marriages establish co-operative re-lationships between previously opposed family groups, but they are also an important incidental factor in support of the community's values; because, if men do not conform to these, they and their close kinsmen will not make honourable marriages. What sets men apart in one set of circumstances, tends to unite them in another.

The characteristic ambivalence of affinal relations has analogous consequences in terms of the spatial distribution of kinsmen. The Sarakatsani do not approve of marriages between families who live in the same village neighbourhood. For instance, the marriage of Demetrios Ferendinos to the sister of George Balatsos is the only case in his summer village. It is significant that this alliance provides us with an example of friction between affines. The Sarakatsani tell one that 'affines quarrel easily' (πιάνονται εὔκολα οἱ συμπέθεροι). It is particularly dangerous if the bride is able to run to her parents and brothers with tales of ill-treatment, and gossip about what goes on inside her husband's family. Not only is it safer to keep affines at a distance, but in another neighbourhood they may sometimes be of practical use. Marriages which are arranged between families in different neighbourhoods tend to produce individual kindreds which are dispersed and whose geographical 'boundaries' are roughly congruent with the boundaries of the community itself. A man through his scattered kindred and affinal relations participates vicariously in the life of the community of the Zagori Sarakatsani. If he has a kinsman or affine in a distant neighbourhood, he is interested in its local affairs, for these affect his relative whose interests are a matter of sympathetic concern to him and in certain circumstances may affect his own prestige. Therefore distrust of affines leads to the practice of taking a bride from another, preferably a distant, neighbourhood; this is one factor in the wide dispersion of individual kindreds in the community; and, in turn, this dispersion of recognized kinship ties increases the individual's consciousness of participation and membership in the total community.

These, then, are instances where marriage regulations or conventional attitudes about affines lead to a certain distance, between kinsmen in the first instance, between affines in the second, but in their further consequences encourage a wider synthesis; in the one case, in terms of conformity to the values of the community and the constant proliferation, through marriages, of new relationships between opposed families; and in the other, a moral participation in the affairs of the different local segments of the geographically dispersed community. In both cases these considerations depend ultimately on the simple fact that 'kinsmen' and 'strangers' represent opposed but complementary categories of persons.

\*    \*    \*

This completes the discussion of the general characteristics of Sarakatsan kinship and marriage. Naturally the consequent system of personal relations has various implications beyond the field of kinship behaviour. Here I will indicate only one of these, but one that is peculiarly characteristic of Greek society and will continue to concern us in the chapters that follow.

As we have seen, the community from the viewpoint of each individual is divided into kinsmen and non-kinsmen, 'own people' and 'strangers'. The division is unequivocal; kinsmen inspire loyalty and obligation, strangers distrust and moral indifference. Yet within the category of kinsmen itself the only stable solidary group is the family. Plainly, the nature of the physical and social environment is such that it forces this small group, however it may value the ideal of autarky, to cultivate both intensively and extensively the support of kinsmen and affines. But for reasons inherent in the structure of the kindred, which it has been my purpose in this and the three preceding chapters to analyse, that support is contingent upon a kinsman's prior commitments to his own family. Thus the family emerges as a social isolate in two associated respects. In the first case, families unrelated by kinship admit virtually no moral obligation towards one another; in the second, families related by kinship nevertheless owe only conditional services. In a community where social relations are marked by such radical discontinuities it follows that the primary values are necessarily particularistic. The mutual opposition of family groups is expressed through the concept of honour with its connotations of exclusiveness, not the morality of universal values such as honesty or fair dealing. And Christian virtues such as humility, meekness, and self-effacement suggest only weakness; whereas strength is simulated better by the heroic attitudes of self-assertion, pride, and even arrogance. Strength, individual prepotence, is what each man needs to be an effective protagonist for his family, and the protector of its public reputation and honour against the calumnies of those who are also its judges.

# VII

## THE FAMILY: A SYSTEM OF ROLES

### 1. HUSBAND AND WIFE

THE elementary family contains a number of different relationships and it will be convenient to say something about each of these in turn, always bearing in mind that these constituent relationships do not exist *in vacuo* but are mutually affected by each other and their position in the total complex of family relations of which they are part. There is some difficulty in writing about relations familiar in our own society. We are describing shades of difference and emphasis in relationships which are common to European society. But the importance of the elementary family group in the Sarakatsan community is so considerable that its constituent relationships merit attention.

One source of strength in the Sarakatsan marriage relationship is its complementary form. A man only participates fully in the community as the head of a household and the father of sons. Similarly, a woman realizes herself in marriage and motherhood. Only as the mother of adult sons does she, to a degree, emancipate herself from male domination. To remain unmarried is failure and the admission of some grave moral or physical deficiency. Both the man and the woman, therefore, become mature social personalities in marriage directed to parenthood. And from a marriage that has been physically consummated there is no escape except in death.

The roles of husband and wife are complementary, and generally restrict each partner to a particular sphere of activity. The role of the husband is representative and protective. His work lies with the sheep, their management, and the disposal of their produce. He alone handles money, negotiates with officials, and takes definite decisions about the marriage alliances of his children. He also is the protector of his wife from rape and insult, and when she is sick he brings her medical and spiritual assistance.

The wife's role is domestic and expressive. Her activities centre in and around the huts where she cooks, spins, weaves, and cares for her children. Her role is expressive in that she is a symbol of the mutual love and acceptance which bind the different members of the family to one another. The shepherd husband is often away from his home for days and nights, and if the weather is bad he spends much of this time soaked to the skin and shivering. In these depressing conditions he thinks and talks about little else than dry clothes, hot food, and the fire he will sit by when he returns to his hut. The hearth with its fire situated in the centre of the circular hut and tended by the wife or mother is, in fact and in symbol, the centre of Sarakatsan family life; it gives physical warmth and protection against the spiritual forces of evil. The husband is dependent on his wife for the simple but to him very important attentions which he associates with its light and warmth. In return he seldom interferes in what concerns the work and duties of his wife. In a contingent sense, she is independent in her own sphere of action.

But, ultimately, the authority of the husband over the wife is absolute. A wife must show respect (σεβασμός) to her husband before strangers at all times. If they have to walk together in the village or the town, the wife follows some two or three yards behind him. When visitors are entertained in her hut, the wife never sits and eats with her husband and the guests, but stands erect and motionless ready to attend to the needs of the squatting men. Even in the extended family household husband and wife do not eat together. The men eat first, the women of the household afterwards. No portion of a cooked dish (προσφάϊ) is set aside for the women, who must satisfy themselves with whatever is left by the men; this is often very little. The act of eating together implies sharing equally in what is placed upon the one common dish from which the Sarakatsani customarily eat. It indicates in that particular context, a certain equality between those who partake. Only sometimes in the intimacy of the elementary family may the husband, wife, and children sit and eat together. For in this most private situation, the relationship of mutual identification between the members of the elementary family makes them, for that moment, equals in the communion of their common meal.

Indeed, there is a marked difference between the public and private behaviour of a man and his wife towards each other.

Publicly a husband addresses his wife in a stern severe voice. Requests are commands, barked out in sharp phrases. It is important for a man's self-regard (ἐγωϊσμός) that other men should see that he is master in his own house. In public the wife is meek and modest, silent and submissive. She does not smile at him or laugh with him before strangers. But in the seclusion of the hut matters are otherwise. She abandons the mask of expressionless humility and discusses with her husband all the affairs of the family, putting forward her own suggestions in a respectful but fearless fashion. Yet even here respect is implicit and a wife must never use tones of mockery or abuse towards her husband.

Obedience to her husband is a moral imperative for the wife. She will not be excused by public opinion, however badly she may have been treated by the man. She cannot refuse to co-habit with him sexually. Conversely, the act of disobedience by which she damages her husband most severely is adultery. In adultery she makes her husband a cuckold (κερατᾶς), one who wears a horn. 'She puts horns on him' (τοῦ βάζει κέρατα), it is said. The implication that the cuckold wears a horn may be an ironical allusion to the sexual potency which his wife's action suggests he does not possess.[1] Adultery attacks the moral integrity and honour of the family and makes a laughing-stock of its leader and head. Thus, Sarakatsani always insist that if a husband surprises the guilty parties in the act, he must first kill his wife and then her seducer. The axiomatic acceptance of family obligations, the uncompromising character of the sanction, and the extreme difficulty of conducting such a liaison secretly, are all factors which contribute to the extremely low incidence of adultery. Indeed, since 1950, there appears to have been only one clear and unambiguous case of discovered adultery.

The disobedience of the wife in the sense of flatly refusing to do the spoken bidding of her husband is also rare. This situation or the mutual irritation which arises over the 'trivia' of com-munal living results in the wife receiving a beating with a stick. The Sarakatsani of both sexes accept the right of a husband to strike a disobedient or erring wife. It is also true, however, that men who are continually beating their wives (and certain men

---

[1] Cf. Pitt-Rivers, op. cit., p. 116; and Onians, op. cit., p. 243.

in the community have this reputation) are held in considerable contempt.

The story is told of a shepherd who habitually beat his wife before leaving his hut to go to the sheep. One morning he was some distance on his way when he remembered that he had forgotten to beat his wife. He at once returned to his home where he found the woman working at her loom. 'Get up,' he shouted to her, 'so that I can give you your beating' (Σήκω, μωρή, νὰ σὲ δείρω). At these words, his little son, only four years old, flung himself on his father and tried to wound him with a knife. Whether or not this cautionary tale has any foundation of truth, its moral is clear enough. The unjust and over-frequent use of physical force by the husband destroys the moral unity not only of the marriage relationship but of the elementary family itself.

The wife submits herself completely to her husband because she accepts her position as part of a natural and inevitable order. Her sex is part of her fate. The physical strain of domestic labour under harsh conditions is immense. It is rare to find a wife after four or five years of marriage who retains the least hint of her former comeliness. 'When you are married you are enslaved because God wills it so' (παντρεύτηκες, σκλαβώθηκες, γιατ'ὁ Θεὸς τὸ θέλει), the women chant. But the wife's acceptance of subordination and physical hardship is also made tolerable partly by her relative independence in her own domain, and more particularly by a consciousness of the significance of her position as wife and mother in the family, a position which relative to that of her husband increases in importance with the passage of the years. Therefore, a wife accepts her husband's authority, shows respect and esteems him, if he proves himself able to protect her children and herself and if he uses his power over his family with a measure of justice. The husband reciprocally approves of his wife if she cares for her children with love and faces her physical labours without showing herself to be that most feared type of female, a quarrelsome grumbler (γκρινιάρα).

The striking complementarity of the roles of the marriage partners (and therefore their mutual dependence), and the unquestioning acceptance of the husband's authority by the wife, partly explain the impressive strength of Sarakatsan marriages. But in the Sarakatsan family the obligations of the parents towards their children transcend all other considerations. It is their duty to bring them up in an honourable and integral family group. Divorce is not possible. Consequently the marriage bond, if for no other reason than its position within the total complex of family relations, is an indestructible tie. The husband and wife, through their categorical obligations to their children, are compelled to an almost complete identification of interests.

## 2. PARENTS AND CHILDREN

Children from the day of their birth are the centre of attention and interest in the family. The needs of the infant take priority over all others. Since the family generally lives in a single hut without internal partitions, the adults must make many concessions. The new-born child sleeps tightly swaddled in a wooden rocking cradle which is enveloped from end to end in a blanket, so that he lies in a kind of dark airless tent. Mothers are fearful of the effects of cold air and evil spirits, and even at the height of summer a fire is kept burning day and night inside the hut to the discomfiture of the adults. If the child is a light sleeper, nobody is allowed to talk. For the first forty days after the birth, the hut or house after dusk is like a city under siege, with windows boarded, the door barred, and salt and incense at strategic points such as the threshold and window cracks to repel any invasion of the Devil. The child is the single concern, and its condition almost the only topic of conversation.

From its earliest days the infant receives attention from all the members of the family. The grandmother nurses it while her daughter-in-law moves about her many tasks. When he returns from the sheep the father at once turns to his child and plays with it. The grandfather, the uncles, and the unmarried aunts, are always bending over the cradle to smile at it, and young siblings, ignoring the child's resentment, plant enormous kisses on its face. This intense attitude of love and concern for the child on the part of all the members of the extended family does not change as the child grows up.

By the age of four, a child has differentiated in an elementary fashion the various roles of different individuals in the extended family. He has distinguished between the attitudes of his kinsmen who love him and unrelated adults who simply ignore him. He is clear about the difference between 'our sheep' around which he skips and smiles, and 'strange sheep' at the sight of which he screws his face into a comical grimace of resentment. About this age, when his spirit of adventure takes him beyond the protection of his own huts, he is almost certain to meet with some unpleasant treatment at the hands of older unrelated children. In these ways the child quickly comes to associate membership in his own family and kindred as synonymous with love and acceptance, and non-membership with hostility. Later experience in adolescence and adult life gives him no cause to change these early established attitudes.

During these first four years the child suffers only the minimum of discipline, almost exclusively at the hands of the mother and sometimes the grandmother. Weaning is a gradual process and most children take some milk until they are two years old, and occasionally for a year longer. Training in cleanliness is a simple matter. They are not punished for fouling the hut until they are walking strongly; generally, by the age of two a number of sudden evictions from the hut when they have misbehaved, and the ridicule of their siblings and cousins, have persuaded most children to walk outside. In other matters the child does very much as he likes. He is continually assured by his adult kinsmen that he is admirable and remarkable and his father, in particular, is consistently loving and indulgent. But from about the age of two or two and a half years a mother in her attempts to reduce her child to a minimum of discipline begins to refer to the father as an authority figure. 'Your father will beat you,' she sometimes says in desperation when her own authority fails. The child of three or four years knows quite well that this is most unlikely to happen, but by the time he is four years old he recognizes that the father is the leader of the family and a person in authority. He observes his mother's deference and the disciplinary action which a father sometimes exerts on his elder siblings.

The general picture of the first four years of a child's life is one of extreme permissiveness on the part of both parents. The mother is a source of physical care, comfort, and love, but also of some discipline. The father appears as benign and indulgent, but in the last year of this period he begins to be recognized by the child as the family leader, although he is not yet actively exercising his authority.

From the age of four until they go to school for their compulsory primary education, at an age of between six and a half and seven years, children remain for the most part in their mother's care. But they begin now to identify themselves with the parent of their own sex. Little girls of four or five follow their mothers about pretending to spin thread from a distaff or to help them in their work; or they play amongst themselves at being mothers, with dolls improvised out of pieces of stick and rags. Boys of five and six are given miniature shepherd crooks with which they solemnly help their fathers and uncles to control the sheep when they are mustered near the huts. They begin, too, to join in the play of their elder brothers and cousins where they learn to throw and wrestle. A small boy always loses but if he shows spirit he is approved of, and his father pats his head and tells him he is a 'tough lad' (γερὸ παιδί). The father remains indulgent but there is now a suggestion that his easy permissive attitude is contingent on the child learning more grown-up ways of behaviour.

In his seventh year the child begins to attend school. In the case of both sexes this marks a degree of enforced emancipation from the constant care and supervision of the mother, an emancipation which is greater in the case of the boy than the girl. This introduces a new element of strain into his life. The child now for the first time plays a representative role for his family *vis-à-vis* the outside world. The other children will know from which family he comes, they will tell their own parents what he did or did not do, the schoolmaster will sit in the coffee-shop and tell his audience that the child of John Carvounis is clever or dull. Not only is the child's new role representative but it involves responsibility since his success or failure in public behaviour reflects in some degree on all the other members of his family, particularly his parents.

As their six years of schooling advance, children become progressively more aware that the loving indulgence of their father is conditional on their living up to the standards which are expected of a child of their particular sex and age, especially in behaviour outside the family. The affection of Sarakatsan children for their fathers is remarkable; and the positive sanction of the warmth of the father's reciprocal affection is correspondingly strong. The mother, on the other hand, remains the source of unconditional love, care, and support. When Lambrine, who is twelve years old, returned home with a note from the schoolmaster which said that on account of her constant inattention and consequent backwardness he intended to keep her in the same grade for another year, her father, Theodoros, harangued her bitterly in the courtyard of his house in front of an audience of half a dozen siblings and cousins. The crying child turned to her mother who silently comforted her while the father continued his merciless criticism. It is significant on these occasions that the mother does not disagree with the father's strictness, nor does the father complain at the mother because she is comforting such a shameless child. It seems clear that their roles are complementary; the father acts as an agent of discipline and instruction through whom the child learns that he must hold his own against other children of the same age and sex and that in his behaviour he has a responsibility towards the whole family; the mother, while she does not deny that the child has done wrong, assures him that he is still wanted and accepted within the family circle.

However, very little direct instruction in correct behaviour is received by children through solemn lectures from the father or the mother in the form of 'You must do this, you must not do that.' Children of all ages are tolerated on almost all family occasions and no topic of discussion is considered unfit for their ears. They hear their elders interminably discussing and criticizing the behaviour of adults and children in other unrelated families. Rape, adultery, the quarrels of brothers, public disrespect to a father, the whole gamut of lapses from social virtue is brought indirectly to their attention. Furthermore, the child of ten or eleven is allowed to make his own contributions to such discussions which are listened to with attention if they are not always accepted as correct. During a discussion in one family about the shamelessness of villagers, the young son of eleven years old was able to give some interesting evidence about how he was sitting in a cherry tree when a villager began to seduce his sister-in-law immediately beneath. Out of his shame at the thought of witnessing such an act, he shook the tree violently so that the guilty pair hurriedly made off. There was a general murmur of approval. 'You did well,' was the verdict of his uncle, the senior man present. In this way, the young child learns at an early age how people in various roles and at various ages ought to behave in any particular situation. He discovers that an infringement of these norms of conduct reflects upon the reputation of the individual, but also upon the general prestige of those with whom he is closely connected. He learns what is right and what is wrong very largely in terms of a responsibility related to the loyalty he owes as a member of a group which loves and accepts him; in terms, that is, of identification rather than of authority. The school years, then, are a time for the learning of new skills and attitudes, and a new role as a representative of the family in a wider world. It is a period of trial and error during which the child is constantly encouraged by the love and support of all the members of the family and other kinsmen. The importance of success is continually stressed, but occasional failure is still not an irretrievable catastrophe.

Children leave school when they are about thirteen years old. Between the ages of thirteen and sixteen girls work under the instruction of the mother, and attempt all the usual tasks that fall within the general domestic duties of a woman. If she has a number of older sisters still unmarried she has an easy life, but in any case a mother with a view to her daughter's marriage prospects is careful not to overtax her physical strength. These years are perhaps the most care-free of a girl's life. Her beauty is not yet blemished by hard physical labour; she goes to many weddings and spends much of her time spinning, knitting, and sewing, in the company of other related girls of about the same age.

But from the age of seventeen until she marries, a period of seven to thirteen years, a girl's deportment inside and outside the family changes considerably. She must now behave as a maiden of virtue who is acutely sensitive to shame (ντροπαλή). No longer may she show her feelings in an uninhibited way, and in her conversation and her movements a careful self-control is demanded. Her relations with her father now become less familiar. Since she left school at thirteen, a certain barrier has already arisen between them, and from that age she is expected in front of strangers to show him respect by standing when he sits and helping her mother to wait on her father and his guests. By the time a girl is seventeen there is a noticeable neutrality of tone in her conversation with her father. She is careful to avoid any reference to sexual matters or the possibility of her marriage. They are both conscious of the categorical obligations they owe to one another and the severe penalties which sanction their fulfilment. If a father does not arrange an honourable and successful marriage for his daughter, his reputation in the community is diminished. If a daughter does not preserve her virginity and her reputation for virginity, she faces death possibly; or, should she avoid this fate, she must certainly endure dishonour and a dishonourable marriage to a widower or a poor man of ill repute. Although between puberty and marriage a daughter receives almost all her instructions from her mother, her father, to whom she is subordinate both by reason of sex and generation, remains the ultimate source of authority.

*　　*　　*

At thirteen, when a boy leaves school, he generally begins his working life as a goatherd. He comes at once under the direction of his father who in his role of leader and co-ordinator of the family labour group exerts a stronger authority over the boy than he has yet experienced in his relations with his father. A son is now careful to show his father respect. Occasional lapses in correct behaviour towards a father are not taken too seriously while a boy is still at school. He is, then, still a child and is in an obvious sense under the power and instruction of his father and the school teacher. He cannot, however rebellious his nature, become independent at this stage. The boy leaves school at an age which coincides approximately with the onset of puberty and at the same time he becomes a full and responsible working member of the family under his father's leadership. He still offers no threat to his father's position as leader, yet his sexual maturity and the responsibilities of his new status in the family foreshadow the inevitable retirement of the father shortly after the marriage of his eldest son. The firm authority exerted by the father at this stage, and the required attitude of respect from the son, serve to dissuade the latter from any attempt at precocious self-assertion. And it protects a man from the ridicule of his equals; for if a youth answers his father's remarks or instructions in a rude or argumentative fashion, other men smile with satisfaction and say that already 'the boy is acting as family head' (τὸ παιδὶ κάνει τὸν τσέλιγγα).

The respect of the son is a general attitude which accepts the authority of the father as right and legitimate. A son shows his respect for his father by carrying out conscientiously the instructions he is given. If he is under the age of twenty, he does not smoke or drink ouzo in his father's presence. Similarly, he does not swear or make coarse remarks or jokes about sexual matters before his father. If a youth is sitting in the village coffee-shop when his father enters, he unobtrusively gets up and leaves. Drinking, smoking, and playing cards in the coffee-shop are the social activities of those equal in status, and are therefore incompatible with the respect owed by a son to his father. After a young man returns from his military service, when he is about twenty-three years of age, he will begin to drink and smoke with his father at home, a step which he generally takes at the express invitation of the father. The son no longer has occasion to leave the coffee-shop, but this is because a father knowing his son to be there stays at home or, in a large village, goes to another shop; the son, similarly, avoids giving embarrassment and showing disrespect to the father by entering the shop if he knows he is there. If the son is in the shop, the father understands that it is unfair to expect him to leave. After his return from military service, the young man becomes a member of the 'pallikari' group[2] of fully adult but unmarried men of the community. When he is not with the sheep, he is expected to show himself in the forum of the coffee-shop, to give periodic proof of certain outward signs of his manliness by drinking, smoking, arguing, and by general self-assertion. He cannot do these things in front of his father, without diminishing his father's honour and his own prestige.

The idea of an adolescent or adult son striking his father is

---

[2] Nowadays this consists of the young unmarried men who have completed their military service, that is of unmarried men between the ages of 23 and 30. The ideal type παλληκάρι is the hero warrior unencumbered with family responsibilities.

almost unthinkable. Only slightly less serious is swearing at or insulting a father. Both are acts of insolent and wanton violence. Of one son, not a Sarakatsanos, who publicly struck his father, the Sarakatsani said, 'He has the devil in him' (ἔχει τὸ διάβολο μέσα του), in a sense which was not intended as metaphorical. It was indeed the only way of explaining the youth's behaviour. To swear at a father at any time, but especially in public, shows the contempt of the son for his father. If he had been a good father with the moral authority of a good father, it is held that such an incident could scarcely have occurred. A son, it is pointed out, takes after his father particularly in his moral constitution, and thus both the outraged parent and the guilty son are dishonoured through the action of the son. To curse or strike a father is, also, a grave sin (ἁμαρτία), for it is an act which upsets a part of the absolute order in life instituted and sanctioned by God. The misfortunes of a person guilty of such acts are always considered to be punishments from God.

The relationship of a father and a son in late adolescence or early manhood is one of delicate balance. The son continues to accept the authority of the father and to show him respect, but this acceptance by the son is now to a degree contingent on his father respecting the growing maturity of his son's social personality. Violence, whether it comes from father or son, destroys the moral basis of the relationship and the mutual esteem which ought to exist between them. During the last five or six years before the eldest son marries, there may be many differences of opinion between an ageing father and his young sons. That these very seldom occasion a show of public as distinct from private disrespect to a father, and almost never develop into quarrels with physical violence, is undoubtedly due to the consciousness of a responsibility felt by both father and son to the total family group, in which through common membership and common loyalties their interests are identified.

In chapter four I have already said something about the transfer of executive power from the father to his eldest son. It will be remembered that the eldest son, impatient to be recognized in the community as a family head, cannot be expected to wait beyond his thirtieth or thirty-first birthday before taking a wife, and that after the birth of his first child, he expects to take over control of the family's affairs. The sanction for these arrangements is public opinion. However reluctant a man may be to hand over the reins to his son, he knows that he will lose less personal prestige by moving into retirement than by attempting to hold power against the conventions of customary usage. He is also aware that any temporizing over this problem will lead to the kind of friction with his son that is unlikely to remain private and may result in a further loss of prestige for the whole family.

There are two other circumstances which may help to persuade a father to cede his position at the customary time. Grazing land in summer for a herd of three hundred sheep and goats represents a considerable area of mountainous country. The journey from the huts of the family near the village to the farthest limits of the summer grazing is very often a walk of two or three hours, climbing steeply the whole way along difficult rock-strewn paths generally no wider than a rabbit's track. Such a journey two or three times a week for a man in his early sixties, which is the age a father is likely to have reached when his own son approaches the age of marriage, is a severe physical strain. But if the family head is not physically able to see for himself the condition of the grass and the state of his animals, his shepherd sons cease to treat his instructions or criticisms with any seriousness, and in respect to animal management virtually arrange matters for themselves. From this point it is a short step to question the father's authority in other matters. Physical or mental feebleness of the father is invariably the explanation of a son assuming control of family affairs at an early age.

The second circumstance has to do with the relation of the family to the outside world. With few exceptions the shepherds who are today over sixty years of age are illiterate. Under modern conditions these men are at an obvious disadvantage in understanding the content of government agricultural regulations and in filling up the increasing number of printed forms. Unlike their more sophisticated and literate sons, men of this age group do not understand the ways of minor officials. 'They don't know how to go about things in the offices' (δὲν ξέρουν τὰ γραφεῖα), their sons explain. In part, the prestige of letters is attributable to the idea that they are the necessary weapons for a successful resistance or adaption to bureaucratic administration. It is easy to understand that if the head of the family must be constantly asking his young son to read, explain, and advise on all written documents, he finds it difficult to maintain his authority until his son has reached the customary age of marriage. Significantly, the sack in which the business papers and account books are kept has become in recent years a symbol of the authority of the head of family, who alone has the right to open it.

In the majority of cases, however, these two circumstances, although they may cause difficulties, do not force or even allow a father to hand over executive control much earlier than custom demands. If, for example, a father of fifty-nine hands over the control of family affairs to a son of twenty-six, he will undoubtedly be considered a man of weak character even where it is known that he suffers some physical disability. He must, for reasons of personal and family prestige, attempt to assert and exercise his authority. Sons are not unaware of the father's position and difficulties. During the last years of a father's exercise of power a degree of rivalry between a father and his sons is always present, but because fathers and sons, together, accept responsibility for the prestige of the family, they guard most carefully against any public expression of their differences.

After the eldest son assumes control, the father continues to do such work as he is capable of. It is generally a task of his own selection and the senior son is careful to avoid giving direct instructions of any kind to his father. There are always a few sick sheep or late lambs which need to be grazed close to the huts, and occasionally he will spend a day with one of the flocks to relieve a son. In some families with many sons, where there is no essential task for the old father to perform, he will create some activity to occupy his time. The old father of John Charisis daily saddles and exercises a favourite horse. When visitors ask where the old father is, his sons reply with affectionate but patronizing smiles that he is out with his horse again. The visitors join in the laughter at the old man's expense and the sons do not take offence, for this is a general attitude to old people in the community. They are respected if they have led honourable lives, yet in relation to present preoccupations they are unimportant. The old father always expresses his views

about current problems but, as with the opinions of women
and children, they are gently ignored. Yet even after a father's
retirement a son continues to owe filial respect to him as long
as this does not interfere with his full control of the extended
family's affairs. A father must give his consent to the arrangement of a daughter's or son's marriage if this is made after his
retirement. And at the celebration of a wedding he always
acts as the formal head of the family. Any exhibition of arrogance by a son who tries to deny his father the centre of the
stage on this occasion is severely condemned. Vestiges of the
relations of authority and respect, which previously bound
father and son in the elementary family, always remain; but
in his declining years an old man's relations with his son are
more characteristically marked by their common concern for
the grandchildren to whom the grandfather is devoted.

* * *

We must now retrace our steps to make some comment on
the relation between mother and son after the boy has left
school at the age of thirteen. It is noticeable that a boy during
the last two years at school begins to resent his mother's acts
of protective care and love. After he has left school this attempt
to behave in a completely masculine manner becomes more
evident. He no longer suffers his mother's caresses. If he
returns from his herding duties cold and wet, he pointedly
ignores the dry clothes which his solicitous mother puts ready
for him. Particularly between the ages of thirteen and sixteen,
he is given to outbursts of rudeness towards his mother and his
sisters. By this abruptness to the women of his family he hopes
to give a further demonstration of his growing manliness.
Mothers are amused and also a little proud as they observe
these antics of their young sons. They understand their feelings
and approve of them.

From the time that a son becomes fully adult his attitude
towards his mother becomes less strained and there is a
recognition of his deep attachment to her. When Sarakatsani
talk about their mothers, they very often mention the original
physical connexion; for this appears to them to be an important
element in the moral solidarity between mother and son. One
cannot abandon an old mother because 'she brought me into

the world' (μὲ ἔφερε στὸ κόσμο). With the physical connexion between mother and son, goes a recognition of the overwhelming pain of childbirth, and the passive courage which is necessary to resist it. Women work until the last moment. Some Sarakatsani tell how their mothers were out gathering herbs or firewood when the pains began. They point out the tree or stone that marks the place of their birth. They tell how the mother assisted by a companion, or in some cases entirely alone, having cut the cord and buried the afterbirth, then loaded up the new child and the bundle of firewood and returned to the hut.

The attachment of the son to his mother draws strength from his own childhood memories and from the accepted qualities any Sarakatsan mother is presumed to possess. There is the long suckling period. He remembers how his mother was always the provider of food and unconditional love; how she made a phylactery and secured it under his shirt to protect him from the attacks of the Devil. He remembers her distracted care for him in sickness and her divination to find the evil eye that was the cause of it.

The status of a mother of married sons is considerable in the extended family. I remarked earlier that the wife/mother plays an expressive role. What she expresses is the integrity and solidarity of the group. The brothers explain their attachment to one another with reference to the fact that they were born from the same mother. The mother acts as the diplomat and peacemaker between the dissident wives. Despite the ambivalence of attitude between mother and daughter-in-law, wives work amicably enough under the instructions of their husband's mother. They do not work amicably under the wife of the eldest brother and it is noticeable that extended families, where the mother of the brothers is dead, do not survive long. In such cases there is lacking a social personality that symbolizes and mediates the mutual attachment of the various elementary families within the extended group. Thus, married sons in an extended family come once more to respect their mother's authority in her own particular sphere as mistress of the extended household. The senior brother who is head of the household punctiliously consults her about all decisions that affect the family, whether they are strictly concerned with her domestic affairs or not. Sitting for most of the day at the hearth with her various grandchildren around her, the mother becomes the physical and moral centre of the extended family, while the father, if he is still alive, is now a genial nonentity.

\*    \*    \*

Parenthood brings to a man or woman joy and pride, but also anxiety. It is often said, 'Children bring worries' (ἔχουν στενοχώριες τὰ παιδιά). The quality of this worry which besets Sarakatsan parents is nicely reflected in the literal meaning of στενοχώρια, a narrowness of space or insufficiency of room. It is both the desire to do more for children and the lack of means which prevents this, and the relative helplessness of a parent in the face of the various physical and spiritual dangers which surround a child.

Sons and daughters, for their part, recognize that 'bringing up a child has many troubles and cares', and this is an important element in the belief that a father or mother, even in extreme senility, cannot be repudiated. The obligation to support aged parents is absolutely binding on children. But just as the regard of a father for his children was conditional upon their conduct, so in his old age the affection and respect he receives from his children is qualified by their judgement of him as a good or bad parent. On the other hand, a mother's love is always unconditional: and equally so are the attitudes of care and devotion to her in the last years of her life. She toils without thought of self. A mother 'sacrifices herself for her children', it is often said. In return she has an absolute right to be mistress of the extended family household of her married sons; and after the separation of the brothers she has a further right to the services of the wife of her youngest son.

Parents and children not only have categorical obligations towards each other but they are morally identified. The responsibility for the wrongdoing of a child is in part referred back to his parents. In general, evil children must have been born of evil parents and, vice versa, wicked parents beget wicked offspring. In illustration of this idea that children share the moral virtues and weaknesses of their parents, Sarakatsani explain that 'The apple will fall under the apple tree' (τὸ μῆλο ἀπὸ κάτ' ἀπ' τὴ μηλιὰ θὰ πέσῃ). It is thought that God often punishes a man in his children, a belief which finds expression in another proverb, 'The sins of parents torment the children' (ἁμαρτίες γονέων παιδεύουν τέκνα).[3] Clearly the inherent inequity of this idea is rationalized in the belief that the moral defects of parents pass down to their children. If misfortune falls on an innocent and blameless child, it is argued that in time the child would in any case have followed the evil example of its parents and thus merits the prophylactic wrath of God.

The relationship between a mother and her children takes its general character from the close physical and psychical dependence of the childhood years and the memory of this in later life. A mother is so closely identified with her child that even her thoughts may affect its welfare. When the nine-year-old son of Demetrios Carvounis went to Athens to sit a scholarship examination, success in which would have placed him in a school three hundred miles from his home, his mother in tears and distress admitted openly that she did not want him to go. People said that in the face of this attitude the child, however brilliant, could not possibly succeed. It follows that there is no defence against a mother's curse.

The intimacy of the relationship is antithetical to any very strong element of authority. Whatever ability a mother possesses to make a child of any age conform to her wishes, is the result of a response to her free and unquestioning love and acceptance. Unmotivated love (ἀγάπη) is the true basis of the bond between a woman and her children. Whereas the relationship of the father with his children is characterized, ideally at least, by respect (σεβασμός); but in this there is the hint of the external sanction of the father's power, and the child's fear of it. Both these attitudes of love and respect are represented to some degree in the relations of children towards either parent. But a Sarakatsanos would use the word ἀγάπη more readily in connexion with his father than he would σεβασμός towards his mother. Kin bound by ἀγάπη are in a relationship sanctioned by a moral sense of duty. In this sense the verb, ἀγαπῶ, in modern Greek, is opposed in some contexts to ἐρωτεύομαι which is used only to express the free unreasoning libido of sexual love.

[3] Not a demotic proverb but often quoted by the Sarakatsani.

The close intimacy between a mother and her children finds a different expression according to the sex of the child. A mother with her daughters is on terms almost of camaraderie as together they tackle the heavy domestic responsibilities of their sex. Between mother and son, because of the opposition of their sexes, there is some abruptness, especially during those years when the son is trying compulsively to behave in a masculine manner. But their relationship is none the less close, unconditional acceptance of her son and his deeds by the mother, protective concern on the part of the son for his mother. To take in vain the name of a man's mother is to offer him the worst possible insult. The bond between mother and son is indestructible. She gave him life; in him she fulfils herself and transcends the moral inferiority of her sex. Although a mother is more in the company of her daughters, it is the sons who are closest to her heart. They are her pride and the significant achievement of her life.

I have said that the mother plays a role expressive of the solidarity of the family. A Sarakatsanos sometimes says that 'The mother is the heart of the family'. Any kind of breach in the physical unity of the family distracts and worries her. After the first few years of her marriage, a wife shows less eagerness to pay visits to the family of her birth. She begins to fret and agitate to return after only one or two days' absence from her home, particularly if she has not brought all her children with her. For the first days after a daughter's marriage or a son's departure on military service a mother is inconsolable. Squatting by the hearth and rocking back and forth on her haunches, she maintains a continuous low moaning broken only by bouts of deep sobbing. It is the wife or mother who is the leading mourner at the death of a husband, son, or daughter. For the twenty-four hours which intervene between death and burial, she does not leave her position at the right of the head of the corpse. During this time she is the chief singer of dirges (μοιρολόγια) in which she recites the golden qualities of the dead man or woman. But for the most part, she expresses her grief in simple and terrifying screams of lamentation (σκούζει), while she and the other women beat their breasts and tear at their hair and cheeks (μαδιοῦνται). For a son a mother remains in full mourning for five years whereas a father does not continue beyond the second year. Each morning at dawn, each evening at dusk, during these long years she sings her dirges and lamentations again. Even when the period of mourning is completed, she will never again dance at a festival, or sing a ballad, during the remaining years of her life.

If the role of the mother expresses the solidarity of the family, its honour and integrity largely depend on her virtue. A mother who is thought to have lost her virginity before marriage or, afterwards, to have been guilty of adultery, or even an apparent inclination towards it, infects her children with the taint of her dishonour, and however closely these children may conform to right ways of behaviour, they cannot retrieve the reputation of their family.

Although the honour of a woman is so intimately connected with the disciplining of her sexual activity as to be almost synonymous with it, any lapse from social rectitude also affects her honour; for it is argued that if she fails in the one respect, she is very likely to fail in other and more critical situations concerned with her sexual virtue. The wife of Costas Pistiolis is a woman who cannot restrain her laughter. It is held against her that 'she always jokes and never talks with seriousness'. This is an attitude unbecoming to a married woman of modesty with children and responsibilities, for it betrays a lack of self-discipline. Her family is, in any case, poor and despised. She ought to be conscious of so many worries that laughter should be impossible for her. It is insulting to suggest to a young man that he might consider marrying the daughter of this family. The girl, Chrysanthe, is acknowledged to be modest, comely, and hard-working. But it is pointed out that, although there is no positive evidence of sexual misconduct on the part of the mother, her uncontrolled and unwomanly behaviour makes the possibility of this not unlikely. And despite the seeming virtue of the girl Chrysanthe, the fact that she is the daughter of such a woman leads a man to await with some confidence the time when serious moral faults in her character will be discovered. Thus, upon the honour of the mother depends the honour of her children in a sense which logically precedes the mutual responsibility which members of a family in their conduct bear at all times for the reputation of the family. A brother can take some action to cleanse the dishonour of a sister, either against the sister herself or her seducer, but a son is unable to do anything to wash away the stain of his mother's dishonour.

The role of the father in the elementary family is concerned with leadership and representation of the group to the outside world. The management of the flock, the handling of money, and the arrangement of matches, fall within his sphere of activity and upon his successful manipulation of these affairs depend his own prestige and that of his family and its descendants. For these reasons a father must be an 'able[4] protector' (ἱκανὸς προστάτης). He must at least be able to provide his family with food, clothing, and shelter. A man who fails in this duty forfeits any respect in the eyes of the community; he is heedless of his obligations, depraved, lost (χαμένος). But to be accepted as an 'able protector' demands more than this. A man must be a skilful shepherd and a shrewd bargainer, possess friends in the right places, and be of sufficient wealth to sustain honourably his family responsibilities. Above all, he requires the quality of manliness (ἀνδρισμός), to guard the honour of the family from rape or insult, and by his general behaviour in public to uphold the prestige of the group.

The father's duty of protection is balanced by his right to a position of authority. This is legitimate by reason of social convention, and is sanctioned by public opinion and in the early years by the simple fact of power. Children acknowledge the father's authority by their attitude of careful respect. And from this position the father is able to discipline them into accepting important social values, and to co-ordinate their various activities in the family's labour force. But the attitude of respect towards a father also prevents any precocious assertion of authority by a son which would damage his father's reputation, and place father and son in open competition. The fact that all economic resources are owned corporately by family groups presents a problem for the method of succession to wealth and status in the community, a problem which inevitably causes difficulties between members of proximate generations in the same family. We have seen that by the time a son is approaching the age of thirty less deference

---

[4] I translate ἱκανός as able or capable, but it also indicates 'One who suffices, one who is able to provide', specific meanings which are significant in the present context.

is shown to a father in private, but that public disrespect is carefully avoided. Friction between father and son is lessened by the definition in customary usage, within narrow limits, of the age at which a son may expect to marry and hold executive authority. In the case of an unmarried daughter, on the other hand, the authority of a father is always more complete since a daughter by reason both of sex and generation is subordinate even to a father of advanced years.

We have already remarked how a father imposes scarcely any discipline on a child who is less than four years of age. It is difficult to describe the confusion and noise created by young children in a Sarakatsan hut. If a father is asked why he bears this with such patience, and would not a little discipline, even perhaps an occasional beating, benefit the child, he generally replies that the child has no developed sense of judgement to distinguish between right and wrong, and that to beat a child of this age will only destroy his love for his father, with the unhappy consequence that a son may not treat his father with consideration in his old age.

After the age of four, whatever his fears as to his treatment in later life, a father's love for his child inevitably becomes increasingly conditional upon the child's behaviour; for it is the duty of the father to guide, by his approval and disapproval, the child's first attempts to represent his family in the outside world. And it may be suggested that the love of a four-year-old Sarakatsan child for his father, which makes an immediate impression on the observer, on the one hand is related to the period of extreme permissiveness in the child's early years, and on the other is a lever by which early steps in its moral education are in part accomplished. According to its age and sex, a child must assimilate certain lessons of conventional politeness, show a constant loyalty to his family, and display a proud and combative front before unrelated children of his own sex and age. Already at this early age the importance of pride and prestige weighs upon the small boy or girl. Yet these values of personal and family prestige, which it is the duty of the father to foster and approve in his son or daughter, foreshadow his own abdication from power at some future time.

From the moment that a son is subjected to the direct authority of his father after he leaves school, a strong element of contingency and reciprocity enters into the relationship. A son must give his father respect, be an efficient worker, and above all else show that he is a courageous protagonist of his family. The love and esteem of the father depend on his performance in these matters. By the time a son has returned from his military service, the conditional element in the relationship is increasingly on the side of the son, who avoids showing public disrespect to his father and continues to accept his authority on the understanding that the father, for his part, respects his son's maturing social personality. After the retirement of the father, the sons in the extended family are under an absolute obligation to care for the old man, but the degree of their concern for his comfort may vary according to the past history of their relations. The conditional character of the affection of the father for a daughter is even more pronounced. If the girl's reputation for virtue remains unblemished, she receives his favour; if it does not, she may suffer the ultimate sanction of death at the hands of her own father. In turn, the attitude of a married daughter to her father is contingent on whether he has given her to a good husband of an honourable family. The daughter of a rich and powerful family, forced against her will to marry her second cousin, swore to her father as she left her home that she would never set foot in it again. Such a case of a complete breach of trust and mutual esteem between father and daughter is rare; but there are also women who harbour resentment against their fathers because, as they allege, they were given to indifferent husbands in order to avoid the payment of a substantial dowry.

### 3. SIBLINGS

The idea of 'one blood' which they share in their common filiation to the same parents is the value that underlies the impressive solidarity of siblings in the elementary family and their almost complete identification of interests. In the eyes of outsiders siblings are morally identified. Whatever, for good or ill, is suffered or achieved by one sibling is held to affect the other siblings to an almost equivalent degree. An insult to any member of the group is felt with the same resentment by all the brothers and sisters. If the brothers are adult, the Sarakatsani believe that an unmarried brother is the right and appropriate person to redress the wrongs of rape and homicide. The solidarity of siblings is also passive, in the sense that the loss of prestige suffered by an individual on account of his evil or dishonourable acts equally affects his siblings. Therefore, the individual is responsible to his brothers and sisters for whatever he says or does. Only in the context of a vengeance killing do siblings generally escape the liabilities of passive solidarity; for the brother of a homicide is not generally considered to be a legitimate surrogate as an object of vengeance for the victim's family.

The emotional identification of siblings has its origin in the common experiences of early childhood. As children they sleep under the same blanket and eat from the same bowl. Older siblings look after the younger ones and protect them from the bullying of other children. There is an unthinking trust and loyalty. It is rarely possible to persuade an unmarried sibling to pass even a mildly adverse comment about a brother or sister. Usually personal secrets are not entrusted to anybody but a sibling of the same sex. Sisters discuss their fears and hopes of marriage, a subject which it would be shameful to mention even to their mother. Brothers share each other's anxieties about personal animosities and imagined insults.

The sympathy and emotional identification of sisters emerge with poignancy on the day of a girl's marriage. The unmarried sisters whom the bride leaves behind display a grief which in its public aspect is certainly conventionally expected, but for some days after the wedding they seem even within the privacy of the family hut to be stunned by the loss of their sister's accustomed presence. Sisters sense the dread and apprehension which the bride herself feels when she leaves the protective circle of her family to be given into the care of strangers. The violent shock of the sexual assault is also in their thoughts.

Unmarried brothers work together in service to the family flock. They are conscious that the physical survival of the family as well as its prestige depend in the last resort on the animals. This common dependence and service to the flock is another ground for their close identification. They do not work (as is the case in the co-operation of cousins or married brothers with separate households) with one eye on their partner to make sure that he is not shirking his share of the work. The mutual identification of brothers tolerates some variation in individual skill, strength, and energy, and a man does not complain although it may be clear that he contributes more to the total effort than his brother. For if in this fellowship my brother is as myself, a strict sense of calculation and reciprocity is out of place. Brothers practise a simple communism in respect of the small amounts of pocket-money which they receive from a father or elder brother. If a brother wants a shilling so that he can go to the coffee-shop, another brother will at once give it to him without question, or thought of repayment. Brothers borrow goat-hair capes, shepherds' crooks, water-bottles and articles of clothing indiscriminately from one another without asking permission and without causing offence.

But it will not be imagined that the relations of brothers and sisters always proceed smoothly according to the preferred pattern of solidarity based on mutual identification, understanding, and support. Precisely because siblings are conceived by one another and by outsiders as occupying in many respects similar status roles, their performances may be compared and evaluated, and the resulting rivalry may lead to envy, and at a further remove, to open enmity. The danger of such competition to the solidarity of the family is particularly acute in a community where social relations outside the family are largely regulated by the struggle for prestige. If a brother sees the possibility of winning the applause of outsiders, although it may be at his brother's expense, he may be very tempted to take the opportunity. The danger is greatest in situations where individual skills or qualities, for instance abilities as a shepherd or as a dancer, the proof of courage or the possession of a fine physique, may become the basis for judging differences between brothers. And outsiders delight in making and voicing such judgements because they appreciate the strains they may cause. In other situations, there may be a desire to escape the effects of public disapproval for the action of a sibling even though this involves disloyalty. 'Hang my brother, I am too busy' (κρεμάστε τὸν ἀδερφό μου, ἐγὼ δὲν ἀδειάζω) is a proverb which expresses this idea with a certain astringency.

The effective sanction against such behaviour is simply the knowledge that while a quarrel between brothers which is not known and talked about outside the family generally allows some hope of reconciliation, a quarrel that follows on the public humiliation of a brother very often leads to a permanent estrangement. Such an estrangement seriously affects the prestige of all the members of the family and destroys the solidarity of a group on which unmarried brothers and, in the early years of marriage, married brothers are almost wholly dependent.

But rivalry between brothers is also inhibited in two other ways; by the dogma of the equality of siblings of the same sex; and by the fiction of the specialization of technical roles.

It is a truism that equals are rivals. Rivalry, here, is an attempt to upset the pattern of equality which then provokes in others reciprocal attempts to reassert once more the original relation of equality. However, in so far as there exists a precise equality in rights and duties between siblings of the same sex, and to the extent that other members of the family refuse to discriminate between brothers or sisters, the possibility of disruptive rivalry is checked. All unmarried siblings of the same sex have exactly equivalent rights and duties. Brothers are equally committed to the duties of vengeance in the defence of family honour; they are similarly entitled to an exactly equal patrimony. Sisters have the same rights to adequate dowries with which honourable marriages may be arranged for them. In lesser matters, too, the equality of brothers implies the notion of equal shares. A ten-year-old boy returning home from a cherry-picking expedition with bulging pockets at once spread out his loot and divided the fruit with scrupulous care between his two younger brothers, himself, and a sister. Lacking a single cherry to make four equivalent heaps, he gave the fractionally smaller portion to the sister.

It is significant that a parent will never admit to liking one of his children in preference to another. He will agree that, of course, sons are more important than daughters, but he is quick to add that they are all his children and that to show any discrimination would be sinful. Practice confirms this assertion. One child is often clearly more gifted or attractive than another, yet parents take great care to give the same affection to all their children. Adult Sarakatsani act with a conscious self-discipline in these matters since they are well aware of the dangerous consequences of envy (ζήλεια). 'There is not enough room in the pen for the envious sheep' (τὸ ζηλιάρικο ἀρνὶ μὲς τὸ μαντρὶ δὲ χωράει), it is said.

A person's position in the birth order of the sibling group is part of his fate; therefore it is considered right that siblings of the same sex should marry strictly in order of seniority. There are no exceptions to this rule. It removes from the sphere of competition a matter which, in the case of brothers, is intimately connected with status and prestige. Similarly, it is normally the eldest brother who becomes head of the family after the retirement of the father. Thus, the question of succession to this position does not provoke rivalry between brothers. Only rarely does a younger brother take the position of leadership in preference to a senior brother who may be temperamentally unsuited to the position of responsibility. But, in general, authority is an element foreign to the relations of siblings of the same sex. The position of family head, when it is held by a brother, is treated as merely one of a number of specialized tasks which different brothers must undertake. Important decisions are, in fact, arrived at through a consensus of opinion.

Rivalry between brothers is also discouraged by the specialization of technical roles.[5] Shepherding in the Zagori country demands skill, resource and, sometimes, daring. His success or failure in this activity considerably affects the prestige of the Sarakatsanos. But within the family the fiction is maintained with considerable vehemence that each brother is a specialist at his own task. In the family of Theodoros it is said that Theodoros, the head of the family, has a certain ability as an efficient negotiator with the outside world; Demetrios is a specialist cheese-maker and muleteer; only Eleutherios knows certain high places in the winter pastures where the sterile ewes will thrive and recover their fertility; Vasili is a specialist in fattening up the lambs and young sheep; and Aristoteles is said to have some intuitive facility for the management of the milking ewes. It is a fact, however, that all the brothers are quite capable of undertaking any task of animal husbandry

---

[5] An early statement of the idea that competitive pressures are eased by qualitative differentiation of roles is perhaps to be found in E. Durkheim, *The Division of Labour in Society*, translated by Simpson, Glencoe Illinois, 1949, p. 266.

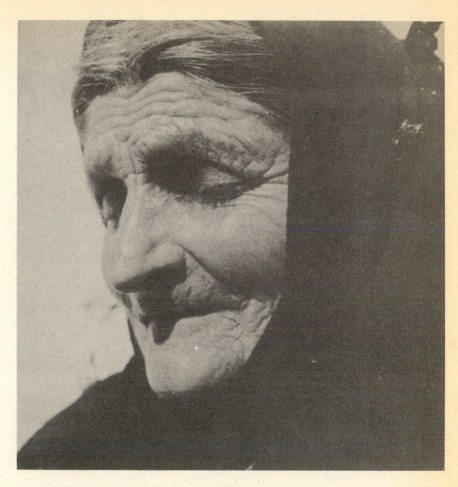

3. Sarakatsan Grandmother

and that this does occur in various emergencies without any apparent loss of efficiency. But the important point is that the belief is firmly held that each is better than anybody else in his own department; and for the well-being of the family, each department is essential. On the other hand, where brothers are found alongside one another in the performance of the same task, rivalry is almost always present. If brothers are milking a flock of ewes there is invariably an argument about who has drawn off the most milk. Similarly, at the spring shearing the speed and efficiency of the cutting is a matter for competition and debate. Such rivalry is generally acted out as a form of play, yet it causes sufficient sullenness and passing bad-temper to indicate the importance of the differentiation of technical roles which has been described.

Although the Sarakatsani insist upon the mutual devotion of brothers they recognize that brothers do sometimes quarrel seriously. Such a development strikes at the unity of the family and threatens the horror of fratricide. 'When two brothers quarrel, two madmen rejoice' (Δυὸ ἀδέρφια μάλλωναν καὶ δυὸ τρελλοὶ χαίρονταν), as a proverb expresses it. But the consequences of a serious quarrel between brothers partly depend on the stage of development reached by the family. Quarrels between adolescent brothers are quickly extinguished by the father's authority, and in differences between unmarried but adult brothers the pressure of elder brothers and parents is generally sufficient to bring the contestants to reason. It is possible for an adult unmarried son to claim his share of the sheep and leave the family, but one man and a hundred sheep do not, in this community, form a viable economic and domestic unit. Even a married pair do not. To some degree, brothers are dependent on one another for many years, often, indeed, until their own sons are in late adolescence. It is said that if brothers quarrel today, tomorrow they will be talking again because, 'The one has need of the other'. 'Blood' (αἷμα), and 'necessity' (ἀνάγκη), provide the motivation and the sanction for fraternal solidarity.

Quarrels between married brothers with separate households are more likely to lead to a break in relations, particularly if some of their children have finished school. The factor of importance, then, is whether the quarrel took place in public with mutual insult. If it did, it is very likely to end all forms of co-operation. But if the parents of the brothers are still alive, even a quarrel of these dimensions may sometimes be healed.

The ties between unmarried sisters are particularly close. If dishonour attaches to one sister, it infects them all. Together, passively and modestly, they await with anxiety for some stranger to ask for their hand, an event which is both dreaded and desired. Unlike the brothers who separate to carry out their different work, the sisters are constantly in one another's company and are often working together at the same task. Their relationship differs from that of brothers in the absence of any considerable rivalry. While brothers stand in the public gaze, sisters are closeted within the privacy of domestic life. The reputation of a girl does not depend upon positive self-assertion, but rather on the passive preservation of her virginal condition. She succeeds in this through the closest possible association with her sisters; their physical inseparability is her chief defence against the slander of enemies. Differences in physical beauty may cause some jealousy but these are facts which cannot be altered and, since sisters in any case marry strictly in order of seniority, competition to snare a husband does not exist. The absence of competitive attitudes between sisters means that any elaborate fiction of differentiated roles is unnecessary, and sisters work happily and amicably at the same task without any serious comparison of productivity or skill. [6]

The ties between brother and sister are also close. Here again, from the viewpoint of the outsider, brothers and sisters are identified as children of the same parents; the short-comings of a sister reflect upon the brother, and vice versa. But the difference of sex introduces into the relationship an important element of complementarity. The brother is the guardian of his sister from rape and insult and he must avenge any violation of her person or character. If his father has retired, it is the duty of the eldest brother, with his father's consent and guidance, to arrange for his sister an honourable marriage. And the youngest brother in a sibling group must remain unmarried until all the

[6] Young sisters or cousins sometimes compete to see who can spin more quickly than the other. And they mark a cross on the forehead of the loser with a piece of charcoal. But these are games played in an atmosphere of great hilarity and goodwill.

sisters have been settled. On the other hand, the honour of the family which affects so intimately the prestige of the brothers, is largely in the keeping of the sister. Her honour is their honour. Later, through her marriage, she provides her brother with new affinal relationships of co-operation; he, in turn, is able to influence her husband to treat her well. Brother and sister are interdependent.

Since the female sex is subordinate to the male sex, the unmarried sister is always under the authority of her brothers. There are no conventional forms of respect between brother and sister but the latter obeys the instructions of an older or adult brother without debate. A brother watches over his sister's conduct and criticizes her freely when he thinks her public behaviour is unseemly. This disciplinary care begins at an early age. Ten-year-old Nausicaa was discovered one day by her young brother Charilaos, who is only six years old, when she was performing for my benefit a very comic imitation of how old men dance at weddings. Pink with the shame of it and with tears streaming down his face, he vainly tried to stop her mimicry.

After puberty, a certain formality enters into the relationship. Physical contact is avoided and there is little teasing. Conversation about family interests is easy and natural, but is more restrained in regard to personal matters. This is, no doubt, a conventional attitude which helps to maintain the neutral character of a relationship which exists between members of opposite sexes. But it seems also to be not inconsistent with the gravity of the categorical obligations which bind so closely a brother with his sister.

### 4. INTERRELATIONS

In all societies, the biological differentiae of sex and age provide criteria for the ordering of social relations in the family, although the emphasis on each factor and their mode of combination is peculiar to the particular society.

As one might expect, difference in age or generation is an equivocal criterion for the ordering of family roles in a community where the importance of competitive values is so pronounced. Persons of different sex have complementary functions and they do not compete. Naturally, difference of age and generation provides a basis for the authority of the parents during the childhood and adolescence of their sons and daughters, an authority which is sanctioned both by social convention and the simple fact of power. But as the children of a family approach adult status, we have seen that parental authority becomes less assured, especially in father-son relations where the son's continued acceptance of his father's authority becomes increasingly conditional upon the father's tact in his attitude towards his son; and in the relationship between the mother and her adolescent son, where differences of sex and generation do not reinforce one another as is the case in the relationship between father and daughter.

The diminished authority of the father is the inevitable outcome of his sons' assumption of adult status which, in this community, is incompatible with subordination. Marriage completes the process by which a son asserts his individuality and after the establishment of his own family, his categorical obligations are centred in his family of marriage and not in his family of origin.

On the other hand, difference of sex provides the basis for a radical separation of male and female roles in the family, which is not confined to a clearly marked division of labour, but involves, also, more general sex-linked values which influence behaviour and attitudes. The activity of female roles is essentially confined to the house and they require passive, co-operative, and self-disciplined attitudes. Masculine roles are concerned with the management of the flocks and the representation of the family in the community. Since this wider participation is realized in terms of strife and rivalry, male roles demand extreme self-assertion in situations outside the family. Male and female spheres of action are mutually exclusive but they are also complementary. We have noted the complementary solidarity and mutual dependence which exist in the relationships between husband/father and wife/mother, father and daughter, mother and son, brother and sister. Further, the female sex is subordinate to the male sex. In adult relationships involving persons of opposite sex, the female owes obedience, the male protection to the other person. Only in the case of the relation between a mother and her adult married son does a woman in some degree escape the dominion of the male.

Not only are the various relationships between roles of opposite sex based upon a complementarity of function, but the whole complex of relationships between the two parents and the children of both sexes is similarly structured. No doubt the same statement might be made about parental roles in many societies. This is a matter of degree. But I believe that the very clear definition of the complementarity of the parental roles in the Sarakatsan family is related to two significant features of this community.

The first of these features is the relative isolation of the members of an elementary family from their collateral kin and the opposition of the family to all other unrelated families. A consequence of this is that almost all the individual's categorical obligations fall within the one small group; where also he finds the only source of unconditional security and support to which he is able to turn. Hence the relations between the mother and the other members of the Sarakatsan family group, of whose solidarity she is the material and symbolic focus, possess a particular intensity and unconditional quality. I have illustrated a number of ways in which the mother represents the solidarity of the family and the security to be found within its circle; in the valuation of the physiological connexion between mother and child; in the ideal of the mother as the unselfish and self-sacrificing giver of protective care. We have remarked the absence of strong authority in a relationship of intimacy, and the sexual virtue of the mother as the symbol of the family's honour and moral solidarity.

The second characteristic feature of the community that concerns the parental roles is the importance of prestige values. In the first four years such mild discipline as the child suffers originates from the mother; the father and all other members of the family are loving and indulgent. After the age of four the father's authority is gradually established and the very strong affection of the child for the father which grew up during the first four years of permissive behaviour is used by the father to encourage the child to more adult ways of behaviour and to a sense of responsibility to the family group. The mother is now the more permissive of the two parents. As we saw in the case of young Lambrine, however harsh and angry the father becomes the mother remains compassionate and unchanged. Thus after the child's first four years there is virtually a reversal of roles between mother and father. And this occurs precisely at the point in time when the child begins to play a representative role outside the family. The behaviour of the child now becomes a legitimate object for criticism by outsiders and the reputation of the whole group is at stake. Therefore the authority of the leader of the family is invoked to sanction the correct pattern of behaviour; pride, loyalty, and fearlessness in a boy, sexual modesty and obedience in a girl. But the father achieves this purpose more often by the withdrawal of his affection and the encouragement of feelings of shame, than by direct physical punishment.

During the period of adolescence (13–21 years of age approximately) the son or daughter must show a careful respect to the father and there is less familiarity. In the case of a daughter this is related to her sexual maturity and the need to discipline her actions; in the case of the son it prevents his premature self-assertion and protects the prestige of the father against the ridicule of outsiders. On the other hand, while a son's relations with his father are stable at this time, he goes through a period of some abruptness towards his mother in his efforts to prove his manliness.

As a son reaches the threshold of full manhood (23 years of age) the importance of his prestige ranking within the 'pallikari' age group becomes incompatible with undue deference to any senior person, even his father. This is reflected by an argumentative attitude in the private life of the family circle, and publicly by a measure of avoidance which makes it possible for a son not to show disrespect to his father without, however, showing positive deference. But this period of latent competition with the father, also, sees the son renewing a firm attachment to his mother.

After his retirement the opinion of the father counts for little except in questions concerning the marriages of his children and as a commentator on morality. Yet by identifying himself with his sons and daughters through an intense interest in his grandchildren he finds consolation.

On the other hand, the status of the mother (so long as she is not physically or mentally feeble) increases with age. As a mother of honourably married sons and daughters she has transcended the inferiority of her sex and becomes the focus of her sons' co-operation within the extended family, or later in a group of autonomous households. Only she is able successfully to mediate and contain the conflicting loyalties of married brothers.

It is clear that the various difficulties between parents and children are all related in some degree to the necessary involvement of the individual and his family in the community's system of prestige values. When the child begins to play a representative role outside the family the father has to educate and discipline it in a way that puts a considerable strain on a small boy or girl. An adolescent son in adopting the prescribed attitudes of manliness becomes abrupt to his mother. The adult 'pallikari' is particularly sensitive to his public reputation for honour and self-assertion, and it is this that bedevils his relations with his father. Thus the peculiarly clear-cut complementarity of the parental roles has to do with the fact that when the relation of a child (particularly a son) to one of his parents is strained, the relation to the other parent is one of positive attachment and identification.

In this complex of family roles and relationships the ties between parents and children represent the core of the system. The categorical obligations of parents towards their children are the values underlying the isolation of the family. They are values which in the popular mind are supported by their reference to a divine model, to the unmotivated love of God, to the patient devotion of the Mother of Christ. But sons and daughters must also be educated to conformity with the system of values of the wider community which makes demands even on small children; requires self-discipline and self-assertion in youths; and places young men and their fathers in competitive opposition while the former advance to adult status and independence. Throughout this process of development the moral solidarity of the family must remain unbroken. And this, in effect, is the achievement of the complementary structure of the two parental roles and their reciprocals.

It seems that there are three important contexts in which the stability of family relations may be threatened by conflict from within. In the first case, the integrity and solidarity of the family is destroyed when a female member willingly compromises her sexual honour. Secondly, there is the danger of competitive differences between a father who has not yet retired and his adult but unmarried sons. Thirdly, the rivalry inherent in the relations of brothers is a continuing threat to the solidarity of the family. It grows in inverse proportion to the degree of authority which the father is able to exert, and to the extent that brothers are dependent on one another for co-operative assistance. In each of these instances, we have already reviewed particular sanctions and institutionalized arrangements which generally help to prevent altogether, or to keep within tolerable limits, these types of disruptive behaviour. But in each of these instances, there is also the positive sanction of the mutual identification of interests and the responsibility of all members of the family for the actions of other members, attitudes which follow from a common opposition to all those persons who are not members of the family. And it is to the consideration of the solidarity of corporate family groups, which is a consequence of their mutual hostility, that we turn in the following pages.

# VIII

## THE FAMILY AS A CORPORATE GROUP

### 1. THE SOLIDARITY OF THE FAMILY

THE Sarakatsan family is a corporate group. The property of the family is owned in common. It holds exclusive rights over the productive powers of all its members and the reproductive capacities of its women. And in principle all its members are held to be responsible for the action of any other member. It is true that, in effect, it ceases to exist when the married brothers divide the joint household some 40 years after the marriage which originally brought the family into being. But during this period its members think of it as a permanent entity, and in so far as they consider the future separation of brothers' households they see it at this time as merely a modification of their corporate existence which will be extended in their continued association.

The solidarity of the corporate family is symbolized in the idea of blood (αἷμα). In marriage a man and woman mix their different blood to produce 'one blood' which is the blood of their children. One says of a child, 'he is my blood', (εἶναι αἷμα μου). Relationships in the family are a participation in this common blood. It provides the reason and the sanction within the individual's conscience for the fulfilment of those exigent and uncompromising duties of family membership. The relevance of blood to intelligence and moral character, and their inheritance, is an idea with a long history.[1] But for the Sarakatsani, the blood which children inherit not only represents, but it 'is' the physical and moral attributes that form their social personalities. If a man is not of honourable lineage his blood does not 'take fire' at an insult; and when he is faced with sudden danger 'his blood is cut' (κόπηκε τὸ αἷμα του). These are not metaphorical usages. The blood centred in the heart is both the medium and the agent of emotional thought and feeling. Thus blood is intimately related to courage. And it is a matter of common observation that as a man loses blood,

---

[1] Onians, op. cit., pp. 48, 121.

he loses strength. Since courage and physical strength are particularly the qualities that men require in order to defend the reputation of their families, it becomes clear why, for the Sarakatsani, the honour of the family is literally the honour of its blood.

The solidarity of the family group restricts the expression of purely individual feelings, opinions, and personality. This is reflected in the way that individual members are normally described by reference to the father, who until the marriage of his eldest son holds the chief authority. After her marriage a woman is never again addressed by her baptismal name except when she visits the home of her birth. She takes instead the christian name of her husband to which the suffix '-ina' is added; for instance, Periclina (see p. 70, above). In this way there is expressed not only the severance of a woman from her family of origin and her subordination to the authority of her husband, but also the absolute quality of their union. Similarly children of both sexes are known by their own christian name followed by the name of their father in the genitive case, for instance 'John the son of George'. In the eyes of its own members and the outside world, the family is a unity.

Whether we regard Sarakatsan marriage as a solemn contract between two opposed groups, or as a religious sacrament establishing the union of a youth with a maiden, it is certainly a transaction which transcends individual interests and desires. Just as the partners must be spotless (nobility in the boy, virginity in the girl), if the relationships which result from their union are to approach and participate in the qualities and nature of the divine model, so it is clear that either divorce or illegitimacy is incompatible with these values. To be born and to grow up in a complete and legitimate family is a minimal requirement for the honourable establishment of children.

In fact, divorce is permitted in Greece by the Orthodox Church on a number of grounds including adultery. Among the Sarakatsani I discovered only two instances of divorce; but in neither case had the marriage been consummated. In one instance, the father of the bridegroom advised his son not to have intercourse with the bride because she was coughing and expectorating blood. The Sarakatsani are apprehensive of tuberculosis, and after eight days during which the girl's condition did not improve, she was returned to her father with the dowry. In the second instance, the bride discovered after the wedding ceremony that the bridegroom had a cleft palate. She succeeded in evading the embraces of her husband by feigning sickness and escaped in the night to her father's home. But once the blood of a woman's virginity has been dedicated to her marriage and the honour of her unborn children, the marriage bond is indestructible except in death.

Ideally a girl who has a premarital love affair should be killed. However, there have been cases where either the father or the brother had not the courage to do it, or was persuaded by the girl that she was raped rather than seduced. But where the fate of the mother may hang in the balance, that of the illegitimate child is never in doubt. It cannot be allowed to live in the community, a testimony to the dishonour of the girl's family. It is placed on a mule-path where it may perhaps be found by others and delivered to an orphanage before it dies. No trace of pity is felt for the infant, for it is a thing without honour and therefore scarcely to be considered human at all. In this community an individual cannot exist simply *qua* individual, he can only be taken account of and evaluated in relation to his family membership; and this implies membership within the group of a wedded pair and their legitimate offspring. To harbour in the family a bastard, only one of whose parents belonged to the group, would be a contradiction in terms. It seems clear that the impossibility of divorce and the destruction of illegitimate children are, in different ways, indices of the solidarity and exclusiveness of the corporate family group.

The property of the family is owned corporately. Although the father and, later, the elder brother administer it, it is never, in Sarakatsan thought, the individual 'dominion' of the head of the family. When the elder brother takes the place of his father, he does not succeed to an estate but only to an office. Speaking of the Indian Joint Family, Vinogradoff[2] suggests that the material goods belonging to it are regarded as a common stock of wealth providing means for the subsistence of its members. This applies equally to the Sarakatsan family. Of the sheep it is said, 'They guard us, they allow us to live' (μᾶς φυλᾶν,

[2] Sir Paul Vinogradoff, *Outlines of Historical Jurisprudence*, Oxford, 1920, vol. i, p. 265.

μᾶς ζοῦν). Every member of the family has a right to draw on this common stock according to the needs of his status and situation. From it are drawn the dowries of the daughters, which sometimes exceed in value the patrimony of a brother. It is the family flock which must support the expenses of a son's higher education, or the cost of medical treatment in emergencies.

As we have observed in chapter four, no partition of the family property ought to occur before all the daughters have been married with dowries which represent their share of the commonwealth. Thereafter each son has a right to one share in the flock and any other property which the family may own. One further share is reserved for the support of the two parents if they are still alive when the joint property is divided, and this property passes with them into the family of the youngest son in which by custom they spend the last days of their life. If only one parent is alive at the time of partition, only a half share is retained for his or her support. When the old people eventually die, their sheep remain with the flock of the youngest son. This is not regarded as a form of ultimogeniture any more than the succession of the eldest brother to the office of family head is considered to be primogeniture. The additional wealth which passes to the youngest brother is thought to be only a just compensation for the support of the aged parents which, although it is a sacred duty, is also in their declining years of mental and physical feebleness a considerable burden. The right of a son to a share in the flock of the corporate family may be implemented at any time after he reaches adult age, which today is judged to be his twenty-second or twenty-third year, on his return from military service. In practice, he will not claim this share until he is married and the father of children, yet if he should quarrel with his father or brothers and decide to leave the family before this time, or if he is driven out, he is entitled to his share of the family wealth. Normally, however bitter the quarrel, a son may not be disinherited. A father may drive his son out of the house but not out of his inheritance; unless he is guilty of some ultimate crime such as incest or fratricide.

We can see from these facts that in principle the father and his sons, by virtue of their common membership in the corporate family, stand as equals in relation to the common flock and the common property. Strictly speaking, the son does not inherit property from his father; rather the father and the son both have claims on the corporate property which they exercise when they leave the group or when the group is dissolved. Through their dowries, the daughters also have parallel claims, and should a daughter remain unmarried she too will receive something, a half share, with which, like her parents, she passes into the family of her youngest brother. The partition of the corporate property and the single household does not come about so much as the result of individuals claiming individual rights, as through the redeployment of the resources of one corporate family group to endow and accommodate the needs of a number of new corporate families which, in part, are sprung from it. That this process of growth cannot be contained within the framework of a single corporation with continuity through time, is a consequence of the bilateral kinship system.

The authority of the head of the family group is limited in a number of ways. In the early years, before the maturity of his children, the authority of the father is unquestioned, but in the administration of family affairs his position, even then, is that of trustee rather than master and owner. A father who squanders the wealth of his family through gambling or inattention to his duties is despised. If the community discovers that he punishes his wife and children too harshly, or without reason, he will lose prestige. In the later years of the family's development when the father holds his authority over adult sons and daughters, and *a fortiori* during the period when the elder brother presides over an extended family group, the head of the family increasingly exercises an authority which is based on a process of collective decision and unanimity. During these years, for instance, the family head does not buy or sell stock or other property without consulting his sons or brothers. Through discussion, in which everybody participates, a collective viewpoint about conduct and action emerges, and the family is prepared to continue a debate for many hours until unanimity is reached. As opinion begins to harden, the remaining dissenters give way out of loyalty, if not from conviction. So tightly drawn to one another in the mutual identification of their interests and affections are the members of the family that they cannot tolerate a permanent minority opinion. To dissent is a kind of treason. In a qualified sense, it may be said that authority over the affairs of the corporate family, in the later years of its existence, is corporately exercised. In practice, there are naturally many matters in which the head of the family through his experience in bargaining and negotiation has more expert judgement; and here the family will be guided by his recommendations. But, similarly, he in turn will take the advice of his sons or brothers when difficulties arise over the grazing and condition of the animals.

No outside person or group has the right to interfere in the internal affairs of a family. The family has an unfettered jurisdiction over its own concerns. Public opinion exerts an immense moral pressure on a family, if the conduct of its members falls appreciably short of the ideals of family life; but it has no means of legitimately and forcibly restraining an unrepentant father or brother. One day, together with a Sarakatsan friend, I was passing the home of a man from whose courtyard we heard a confusion of shouts and cries. Looking carefully over the high wall, we saw the father lashing his thirteen-year-old daughter with a leather belt; it seemed that the girl's only fault was that she was too frail to lift and secure some heavy sacks on to a waiting mule. My friend's fury was evident. Sarakatsani cannot tolerate any form of cruelty to children. Yet he insisted that he could not interfere with the father's action even if he were on the point of killing her. But, lifting a heavy stone, he tossed it over the wall. The man, realizing that somebody had been watching him, at once ceased his blows on the child.

Within this autonomous family group there is a certain equivalence of rights and obligations between the members. It must be said, however, that this abstraction and separation of rights and obligations only emerges somewhat artificially in our analysis. Because of their very diffuseness it would not normally occur to an individual to balance his rights and privileges against those of another member of the family. There is no conscious accountancy in this solidarity. In general terms everybody has the right to expect material, moral and affective support from the family, as well as assistance in the event of physical assault. We have already stressed that a person will never admit to an outsider that a member of his family is worthy of moral blame in any dispute. We shall discuss again the right to moral support, as well as the right to protection from physical assault, when we consider the concept of family honour. As to the right to material support, this has been dealt with in the discussion of family property. It remains, therefore, to examine a person's right to affective support.

It is only within the privacy and secrecy of the family hut that a man or woman is able to relax, to laugh, to give affection and receive it. The burden of public life is a heavy one. Outside his house a man must be severe and proud. He must strut about like some turkey-cock as if his affairs were matters of abnormal consequence. He must on no account show his emotions unless it be an unrestrained anger at some actual or imagined slight. Publicly, he treats his wife and daughters with disdain, barking at them orders in harsh staccato phrases. An unmarried girl or a wife must walk slowly with measured tread and downcast gaze. Only inside the hut is it possible to abandon these conventional attitudes. After the evening meal, an act of communion to which only a visiting kinsman will be admitted, the whole family, men, women and children, sit or lie around the hearth in no fixed order, laughing, gossiping and asking riddles. The centrally-positioned hearth, around which the family gathers, seems to symbolize a common fellowship rather than a hierarchy of relations. Despite a measure of conventional restraint in certain relationships, especially that between father and daughter, the general tone of the family in assembly is one of the utmost intimacy, solidarity and identification. Trust between brothers is proclaimed in the action of a younger brother who leans his head against the shoulder of his older brother's wife. It is an atmosphere of easy camaraderie and undemonstrative affection, which is impossible with unrelated persons in any situation, and possible for the members of a family only when they are shielded from the public gaze.

A person also has obligations to the family which gives this protection and support. The most general of these obligations is an attitude of loyalty and reciprocal support towards the other members of the family who must be sustained morally and physically in all situations without any consideration of the consequences. A sequel to the affair of the man who beat his daughter which we have just described illustrates the strength of this loyalty. This girl was a regular visitor to our hut. On the first visit after her ordeal, some expression of sympathy was made. The girl's composure was visibly upset, tears came to her eyes and her lips trembled, but she would not discuss the incident and even refused to comprehend what we were talking about. Whatever maltreatment the individual may receive in the family, he remains loyal in the face of outsiders. And indeed there is no alternative, for the individual cannot abandon or change his family, or live outside its limits.

Secrecy about the family and its affairs is a measure of loyalty and of the internal cohesion of the group. The Sarakatsani are, in fact, extremely secretive. As a matter of policy and habit they never give accurate answers to questions about numbers of sheep possessed or quantities of milk sold. The answers to taxing authorities are diminished, and to other persons, when the purpose is to impress, responses to the same questions are inflated beyond credible limits. The marriage aspirations and negotiations of sons and daughters are guarded secrets. Information about private family life is denied to all unrelated persons; and with reason, because people are always seeking to find or fabricate incidents of intimate family life to destroy the reputations of others. But secrecy goes beyond the point of mere discretion and becomes an end in itself. A Sarakatsanos declines to give almost any personal information to a non-kinsman, even where it could not remotely damage the family's interests or prestige. One housewife will not disclose to another what she is cooking for the evening meal. Two shepherds leading mules meet on a path and pause for ten minutes to deny each other the simple pleasure of knowing where each has come from, what he is carrying, and where he is going. The questions are as pertinent as the answers are evasive. Children are drilled into these attitudes from their early years. Asked by another adult Sarakatsanos or villager who his father is, a child replies with an air of false innocence, 'And you do not know me?' Secrecy erects a barrier around the members of the family and their intimate relations. The family secrets, whether they have significant content or not, are relevant, simply because they represent something which is denied to other people who are not members of the group.

But the obligation that Sarakatsani must not on any account fail to fulfil is the defence of family honour. Honour (τιμή) is directly concerned in a limited range of situations; typically these emerge after physical assault or verbal insult, or following a sexual assault on the women of a family, or their own misconduct. Whether or not honour is lost depends essentially upon two qualities in the moral characters of its members; the manliness (ἀνδρισμός) of the men, and the sexual shame (ντροπή) of the women. Objectively, therefore, honour is an aspect of the integrity and social worth of the family as this is judged by the community; subjectively it represents the moral solidarity of the family, an ideal circle that must be defended against any violation by outsiders.

Honour is concerned with strength or prepotency rather than justice. The most direct blow to the strength of another family is simply to kill one of its men. His blood pours out and with it go life, consciousness, and strength. Sarakatsani believe that in some way a killer absorbs the strength from the blood of the man he slays. 'I shall drink your blood' (θὰ σοῦ πιῶ τὸ αἷμα), is a phrase that threatens murder. Given the connexion between strength and honour, it follows that the family of the killer validates its claim to honour, except in circumstances where the motive of the killing is itself dishonourable; such motives of dishonour include sexual lust but not theft. On the other hand, the family of the victim must remain inferior until one of its members 'takes out the blood' (βγάλη τὸ αἷμα) from the violator himself, or until he is at least driven into exile. One avenger bathed his hands in the blood of the original killer and returned to show his mother 'the blood of her son'. With certain qualifications that will concern us in a later chapter, all Sarakatsani are born with honour. But it is constantly threatened; and its conservation is, in effect, a struggle to maintain an ideal equality. When a life or the virtue of a woman has been taken away, something equivalent must be taken back if the family is not to fall for ever from grace and social reputation.

The family of the victim, then, have this duty of active solidarity[3] 'to take out the blood' of their kinsman from the

[3] The useful distinction between active and passive solidarity is borrowed from Glotz. See Gustave Glotz, *La Solidarité de la famille dans le droit criminel en Grèce*, Paris, 1904, Chapter 6.

person of his violator. On the other hand, the family of the original killer do not have to suffer the consequences of passive solidarity; a brother, father, or son of the killer is not generally an object of vengeance. But despite the absence of passive solidarity in vengeance killing, the ideal course of a vendetta is still visualized as terminating in the mutual extinction of the two families. As we shall see, this is most unlikely to occur in practice. It is generally to a brother or son, more especially the former, that the duty of vengeance killing for murder falls. A father is seldom involved, for women and children are inviolate, and only in the case of the killing of an only son without issue will he be left as the one possible avenger. Normally, an unmarried brother avenges a brother, a son his father, when the latter has no unmarried brother.

During the period 1945–55 it seems that only two successful killings have occurred amongst the Sarakatsani that were specifically vengeance for a previous murder, although for the same period I have details of varying completeness concerning seven other killings for various causes (other than the hostilities of the 1947–9 civil war). One reason for the low incidence of vengeance killing is that the killer is generally removed or removes himself from the scene of action immediately after the event. Today, the Greek police are well organized and omnipresent. Generally, killings occur either as the result of boundary disputes or questions of honour, so that the identity of a killer is widely known. He is quickly arrested and finds asylum in prison. When he is released from prison some five to ten years later, his kinsmen will advise him whether the victim has a brother or son able to revenge him, and depending on the nature of this advice the killer will either return to the community or move to another district of the Epirus or to Thessaly. Therefore, in most cases, the absence of passive solidarity in blood vengeance and the removal of the killer to prison and later to voluntary exile prevents the execution of vengeance. Exile is clearly not so honourable an outcome as a vengeance killing for the victim's family, but it strikes some kind of rough balance between the two groups. It relieves the avenger of the need to spend a number of years in prison, followed possibly by exile. The killer himself is believed to suffer considerably in his exile, distant from the support of his family and kinsmen. And it is the reputation for manliness of the victim's group which has driven him there.

But if all the dead man's brothers are married, he is unlikely to be avenged. A married brother's obligations to his own family take precedence. If he were to kill the murderer he would be removed to prison, and afterwards would face exile or possible counter-vengeance. In either event his family would be deprived of its head at a time when the sons were almost certainly still children or adolescents. Yet the consciences of married men with an unavenged brother are never altogether easy. If the dead man has a son, however young, they feel less troubled. For this son will be expected to revenge his father before he marries. However, by the time the son is mature enough to act, the killer is probably an old man and removed from the public scene. In this situation a son tends to put off the execution of his duty in the hope that the murderer will soon die naturally without his assistance.

If the dead man has an unmarried brother, ideally the latter may not marry until the murderer has been killed or driven into exile. But if the dead man has also a son, even though it is still in the cradle, he will probably take a wife; particularly if the killer has a long sentence to serve. If the dead man has no son, an unmarried brother will certainly wait until the murderer emerges from prison, but if the latter does not then return to the community the brother will probably consider himself free to marry a year or two afterwards.

Yet despite the dearth of reciprocal vengeance killings, the idea of this obligation is very real, and it remains a potent sanction against light-hearted killings in a community with a taste for violence. Of five Sarakatsan murderers released from prison in recent years, three moved to other parts of Greece, and the two who returned to the community only did so because their victims had left no ready avenger on the scene.

The details of a vengeance killing which occurred in 1950 illustrate some aspects of the problem. During the civil war of 1947–9 the Sarakatsani were unable to reach their summer grazing in the mountains and remained in the plains of Thesprotia under conditions of extreme heat and absence of grass. There was a boundary dispute between the extended family group of Achnoulas and a 'company' of families led by

John Stratos. Accused of stealing the grass of the other group, a young shepherd of the Achnoulas family insulted a brother of John Stratos, who struck him with his crook. Both families heard the shouts and rushed to the aid of their kinsmen. In the scuffle that followed the old father of John Stratos was wounded by the knife of one of his own sons which had fallen to the ground and was then picked up by one of the Achnoulas brothers. He died from the wound. The fight was so confused, with six men grappling in a body, that the Stratos family never discovered which Achnoulas brother killed the old man. Nor did the police. After a lengthy inquiry, nobody was charged with the killing since much of the evidence appeared to suggest that it had been accidental. The Achnoulas family felt reasonably secure from direct attack because of the anonymity of the killer and nothing happened for nine months, until one day George Achnoulas, drunkenly quarrelling at a wedding, told an adversary to take care, hinting darkly that he was not afraid of spilling blood since it would not be the first time. The Stratos family, informed of this incident, necessarily accepted the evidence as sufficient, and an unmarried brother, Charalambos, waited in ambush for George and shot him dead as he walked along a path.

What we are faced with in these seeming evasions, or half evasions, of a duty which is declared to be sacred, is generally not any real weakness in the solidarity of the family of origin, but the conflict of roles between the duty of the brother or son on the one hand, and, on the other, the obligations of a father to his own family, or the right of a brother or son to marry and found his own elementary family at about the age of thirty. This conflict is, of course, related to the bilateral form of the kindred and the isolated corporate family which is associated with it. It places an inherent limit on vendetta. Clearly, a community fragmented into family commonwealths, where the individual's categorical rights and obligations are contained exclusively in this small group, where the help a man can claim from his collateral kin is severely limited, and where a family to exist in any real sense must have at least one adult male to support and lead it, is peculiarly ill contrived to prosecute blood vengeance.

It is, then, not inconsistent with these considerations that the

Sarakatsani have no notions about the blood or spirit of an unavenged victim turning upon the kinsmen who have failed in their duties. For this would be an uncomfortable belief to accommodate where successful vengeance killing is contingent on a number of circumstances. This is interesting because, as we have already seen, blood is the material medium of kinship and its values. In other related contexts Sarakatsani clearly believe that blood has mysterious and intelligent powers. A horse standing outside a house when its master was murdered 'dropped dead from the blood' (ἔσκασε ἀπὸ τὸ αἷμα). A shepherd who killed a woman 'was seized by the blood' (τὸν ἔπιασε τὸ αἷμα). He was paralysed before his victim until the husband returned to kill him. For this was an evil and unnatural deed where supernatural sanctions rightly operated. Sarakatsani will even say that the avenging brother's blood gives him the courage to reclaim 'his own blood' from the killer. But suggestions that a dead man might be personally angry and dangerous if he is not avenged are met with amused and pragmatic disbelief. If care is taken over a man's burial so that the Devil cannot use him as a 'βρυκόλακας' (phantom), a dead man is simply dead. Vengeance, then, is a duty owed to the honour of the family and not to the memory of a particular individual. And honour depends on the strength, confidence, and self-regard of living men, not on any mysterious or spiritual powers.

The problems which the duty of vengeance killing presents to a family sometimes have an element of paradox. For in prosecuting vengeance and defending its honour a family almost inevitably deprives itself of one of its men. This may represent a dangerous weakening of its strength; and strength, it may be remembered, is the basis of honour. In the very act of defending one's honour one may in fact be jeopardizing it. The violator is always in mortal danger immediately after the deed, when grief and humiliation are fresh. But if he survives the first two years unscathed the victim's family begin to consider the situation in a more calculating and unemotional fashion. It then becomes a question rather of whether there are reasonable grounds, of the kind we have discussed, for 'not' prosecuting vengeance. This depends entirely on how the community views their predicament. If all the brothers of the victim are married when the killer returns from prison, the consensus of opinion is likely to be favourable to a policy of inaction but mutual avoidance. There is, inevitably, some loss of prestige but this may be the lesser of two evils. But mutual avoidance (which is possible in this dispersed community) is essential. If the killer were to appear before the victim's brothers on a public occasion, such as a wedding or a festival, the humiliating confrontation would force the brothers to kill him or forfeit their honour. Generally, both sides have strong motives to keep out of each other's way. In the case of the vengeance killing between the Achnoulas and Stratos families, after some months the Stratos family may have felt relief that they did not know the identity of the killer. But the incident at the wedding was generally interpreted as a display of public boasting by George Achnoulas, and this made retaliation almost inevitable.

The loss of a life in a killing is seen as a loss of blood, and for this outrage the violator ought to pay with his own blood. We have shown that there is no passive solidarity in vengeance killing; a man does not generally suffer for a killing committed by his brother. This is a convention which plainly restricts the possible extensions of a vengeance killing and prevents a number of families from losing their 'protectors'. It is the analogue of those qualifications of active solidarity that we have already discussed. However, this does not detract from the importance of active and passive solidarity in other situations nor the significance of the shedding of the common blood. This is very evident in fights which do not involve homicide.

An evenly contested fight in which no blood is spilled is an episode complete in itself; a fight of similar character and proportions in which one side physically loses blood but the other does not, inevitably provokes its own sequel in the attempt at some later time to draw blood from the opponent. But a man does not himself revenge the outrage which has been committed on him. This is the task of a brother or son. Also, the object of vengeance need not be the original opponent; any male member of this man's family is appropriate. In a typical dispute over the boundaries of grazing areas, Aristoteles was cut about the head by the other shepherd's crook. Some weeks later, Christos, the brother of Aristoteles, found himself at a wedding feast opposite the brother of the man who had recently quarrelled with his own brother. In his own words, 'I suddenly saw him there, drinking and putting on airs. I remembered that his brother Vasili drew blood from my brother. I could not stand it.' The consequences for the other man was a head wound from a broken bottle before the two men were parted and expelled from the wedding. It has to be remembered that fights and brawls in which individuals have the duty of both active and passive solidarity are relatively frequent, but that killings are rare.

The second category of affairs of honour concerns the sexual conduct of women. The family has exclusive rights over the sexual capacities of its women, and in this respect women always remain *in loco filiae*. Here we are concerned not only with external attack as in the spilling of blood, but also, sometimes, with treason from within when a daughter or sister betrays her virginity or when a wife voluntarily commits adultery. The will of a woman is vulnerable and her sensuality is evil. She is the weak link in the chain. For this very reason her sexual purity is an appropriate symbol of the family's honour. Its destruction, although itself a dishonourable act, in some way places the destroyer and his family in a position of superiority; for they have demonstrated that the woman is willing to abandon sacred loyalties for the gratification of her sensual feelings by a stranger. In these circumstances vengeance becomes primarily an act of purification. A father (or brother) must first destroy his daughter (or sister) and only afterwards turn his attention to the lover. Similarly, a husband ought first to kill a wife taken in adultery and then the paramour.

If it seems surprising that such violence may occur in a group whose jural and affective solidarity I have been at some pains to stress, this nevertheless seems to be a characteristic of small groups whose solidarity is very intense. In the mutual identification of one member with another, there is no flexibility to contain widely divergent interests. We have seen that brothers, if they cannot reach unanimous decisions, must part company. Similarly, the association of family members demands absolute loyalty; the treachery of one member disrupts the group in such a way that this member's very presence is a denial of the qualities and attitudes on which the harmony of its internal relations depends. The objectionable element must, therefore, be excised. This is the only way in which the family honour can be reinstated. And the father[4] or brother who accomplishes this terrible work wins a grudging respect in the general community.

Families do not always find at once the moral strength to take the only honourable action. In an affair between two second cousins in 1955 near a village on Mitsikeli, the girl's brothers first tried unsuccessfully to kill her lover. The girl then ran away to the man's home; no doubt as much through fear of her family as out of devotion to her lover. In another case, which occurred in 1944, the lover of an unmarried girl escaped from the neighbourhood after one unsuccessful attempt to shoot him. Although the girl's association with the man had been notorious, no action was at first taken against her, but over a period of six months the family suffered acutely from public sneers and scorn until, quite suddenly, the girl disappeared. The nature of her fate was never satisfactorily explained.

The most recent instance of the vengeance of a family on a daughter occurred in 1948 when a Sarakatsanos wintering his sheep near the Gulf of Arta discovered that his daughter was conducting an affair with a villager, who had seduced her with false promises of marriage. At the time, there was no other Sarakatsan family in the immediate neighbourhood, so that there seemed to be some possibility of hushing up the matter; but the girl discovered that she was pregnant, and the man refused to marry her.[5] The father took the girl to a secluded place, shot her with a pistol, and disposed of her body by rowing out into the gulf and sinking it with weights attached. Later, he killed the villager and dealt with his body in the same way. This case is often cited as the right solution to problems of this kind.

In cases where a girl is raped or a wife is similarly violated, or where at least the community accepts this presentation of the matter, the action is one of straightforward vengeance. The natural avenger is the brother for a sister and a husband for a wife. Such an attempt will certainly be made where an avenger is available, and it will be recalled that in the case of unmarried girls one of the brothers does not marry until all the sisters are

[4] It seems to be the opinion that the father who begot the girl is a more appropriate executioner than the brother.

[5] Marriage is not an honourable solution to a premarital affair unless, as is most unlikely, the liaison is known only to the two families, and not to the community.

established in marriage, an arrangement which expressly provides them with this avenger. Consequently, in cases where an act of vengeance concerns the sexual honour of a sister or a wife, there is little chance of it not being executed through default of a ready avenger.

A question of honour is also involved when a man breaks the contract of betrothal. The girl's brother ought to kill him. Here the attack on the girl and her family is not a physical assault upon her virginity, but the suggestion that in this or some other respect she is not worthy of marriage. And the knowledge that the breaking of the contract involves an obligation of vengeance only establishes more strongly in the minds of other members of the community the suspicion that there must exist some serious fault in the girl. I know of only two instances of broken betrothals over a period of ten years and significantly both these cases were arrangements between Sarakatsan girls and village men. Marriages between Sarakatsani are only arranged after exhaustive inquiry and considerable debate; mistakes are thus unlikely. In the first of these two cases, the former bridegroom fled to Athens after he had lost the top of a finger in an unsuccessful attempt on his life; in the second case, the father of the unhappy girl had no adult son, and was glad enough to have the additional excuse that the man lived some considerable distance away. He was loud in his threats, but in the event he did nothing; and people were quick to point out that this was exactly the kind of conduct one might have expected from this particular individual.

Between the two categories of 'affairs of honour' which I have described there is one important difference. In the first category, a killing demands a counter killing, and in theory, at least, this process may continue until all the adult male members of the two families have exterminated one another. The first killing which initiates the affair is not itself a random or indiscriminate act. It happens generally as the reply to an insult or as the consequence of a boundary dispute or some other quarrel. A man does not intend to kill in these situations, but accidents happen. The rough balance which in most cases, as we have seen, is struck between the two sides, satisfies neither group. The community remains relatively indifferent to questions of 'right' and gives its preference to the side which shows the greater manliness. In the second category, however, where an affair concerns the sexual honour of a woman, the community strongly upholds the 'right', in an ethical sense, of a family to kill a man who has assaulted one of its women. For this act is evil and dishonourable. An avenger in an affair of the second category does not generally go into exile, since his life is to a degree protected by public opinion. Where a balance is struck between the two groups in affairs of family honour, it is inherently less stable in cases of the first category than in those of the second. And this appears in the fact that two families, between whom there is a killing and an exile, are extremely careful to avoid meeting in circumstances where their presence may represent an affront to one another. Mutual avoidance is a means of preventing the disturbance of a precarious equilibrium. It appears, then, that the processes of vengeance provide through exile a sanction against killing, and through vengeance killing a sanction against breaches of the code of sexual behaviour.

When a man is killed or a woman is assaulted something, a life or honour, is taken away, not merely from the violated individual, but more importantly from his family. One group has committed a wanton and hostile act upon the other, and between the two groups a debt of honour now exists. Something has been taken, something equivalent must be taken back. Until some kind of a balance is re-established, the victim's family is in the eyes of the community inferior to the group of the violator, even where the act of outrage, as in the case of sexual assault, is in itself evil.

It is a peculiarity of 'affairs of honour' that they consist of at least two events between which some interval of time elapses. The first is the violation of family honour which is generally an outrage on one particular member; the second is the act of vengeance which is similarly performed, in most cases, by one member only. In both instances the individual as victim or avenger represents his family. If the honour of the individual and the honour of the family are analytically separable, in action they are one. And if the execution of vengeance brings a measure of personal glory to the individual, at the same time it is also an act which is essentially altruistic.

The longer the interval of time between the two events the

less effective is the response. To some extent this is so even where the reasons for delay are physical: for instance, the killer is in prison, or the avenger is not yet adult. But it is said that if an affront to honour remained unanswered over a period of years after an adult unmarried avenger was available and the killer physically present in the community, then the quality of the dishonour ascribed to the family would be such that an eventual vengeance killing would not reinstate the reputation of the victim's family. For, on grounds of damaging conjectures about the personal motives for this delay, other families would be able to continue asserting the relative integrity of their own honour by denying it to the family of the victim. The case is hypothetical since there has been no instance of this kind in recent years, but it is indicative of Sarakatsan thinking on this matter.

The defence of family honour is at once an indication of family solidarity and a process which recreates it. The honour of the family, the solidarity of this group, and the mutual responsibility of its members, are correlated notions. It is true that passive solidarity does not extend to questions of vengeance where a life is demanded, but in other respects it is complete. A man may suffer physical assault for the offence of his father, brother, or son. Further, if one member of a family acts dishonourably, all the other members of the family lose honour in the eyes of the community. If a man is killed or a sister's betrothal is broken, and the family remains inactive, all its members are equally dishonoured. Since all are responsible for the actions of any one, every member is accountable to every other member. All the members of the family necessarily form a single solidary group for the protection of their common honour.

## 2. HOSTILITY BETWEEN UNRELATED FAMILIES

In the preceding chapters we have seen that for each individual this community is divided into the two opposite but complementary categories of kinsmen and strangers; trust marking relations in the one category, distrust in the other. Distrust prevents co-operation between shepherds who are not kinsmen or affines, and the four or five men that are necessary to manage a flock are either father and sons or a co-operative 'company' of kinsmen and relatives by marriage. Moreover, the produce of the flock is sold to persons outside the community. No Sarakatsanos who remains a member of the community acts as a trader or shopkeeper. Indeed, unrelated families are only dependent on one another in two significant ways, for marriage partners and social reputation. In both instances this form of dependence helps to breed hostility and suspicion, which is all the more intense since there are no other forms of social or economic co-operation. Perhaps, too, the dispersed character of the community, and the fact that for most of the time shepherds are bound to the care of their animals, allow attitudes of intense hostility without giving too frequent opportunities for its physical expression.

The hostility that exists between unrelated families is encouraged by the belief that their interests are mutually destructive. There is the story that after he had created the other countries, God had a few stones and rocks left in his sack. He threw these over his shoulder and they became the land of Greece. It is believed that there are not enough resources and wealth to satisfy the needs of everybody, and that therefore the success and prosperity of other families is necessarily a threat to the very existence of one's own. It follows that a man must rejoice when another suffers misfortune and 'falls in the mud' (πέφτει στὴ λάσπη). For the Sarakatsani, these beliefs have an immediate relevance. If the village President allots one man an area of good summer grass, another must receive an area of indifferent grazing. Again, in the winter, pasture is scarce, and every family that has successfully negotiated for its requirements of winter grass leaves less for the others. Whether it is a question of material assets or social prestige the Sarakatsani see life as a kind of seesaw. If one family goes up in the world the others must necessarily come down.

The hostility between unrelated families is intimately related to the nature of rights and obligations inside the elementary family. These have a diffuse character; that is to say, a man is obliged to support his brothers, sisters, parents, or children in every situation and circumstance unless this assistance conflicts with other and higher obligations. But not only do all a man's significant interests fall within the limits of the family, but in most contexts loyalty to the family is the supreme social value. Moreover, there is no social group in this community which through common membership can commit him to any duty towards persons with whom he is not related by kinship or marriage. Indeed, any relationship with an unrelated person would be regarded by other members of the family as a form of betrayal. For a man's energies and affections belong to his family and his relatives, and to nobody else. This explains why personal friendship with an unrelated person, based simply on liking and sympathy, is impossible. There is devoted friendship between cousins, but even here we have seen that such an association is immediately sacrificed if any friction develops between the two families. The solidarity of the family resides in its exclusiveness and opposition to those who do not belong. And any relationship between one of its members and an outsider, which is not shared by the others, necessarily weakens it.

The mutual distrust of unrelated families emerges very clearly on those rare occasions when for some specific purpose they are forced into co-operation. During the summer a hut is established high in the mountains above the village so that the various shepherds who have sold their milk to a particular merchant are able to deliver it twice a day to his agents who at once turn it into cheese. Towards the end of July these operations come to an end, and it is then the responsibility of those selling their milk to the merchant to carry down to the village on their mules the machinery, utensils, and the mass of accumulated cheeses. The cheese-maker and his assistant calculate from their books the total quantity of milk which each family has delivered during the whole summer, and in proportion to these quantities each family is allotted so many mule-loads of cheeses and equipment, which it is their duty to transport as far as the village. But the assessment of these loads by the cheesemaker is not accepted without many amendments and bitter wrangling. The cream separator for instance is a heavy, awkward thing to load on a mule. Who is to say what the equivalent in cheeses or smaller pieces of equipment may be? Each family is determined not to be outmanœuvred by the others into performing any service which can possibly be avoided, and no trust is placed by anybody in the impartiality of the cheesemaker. It sometimes happens that the family which has sold the largest quantity of milk has only one mule, while another group with only a small flock possesses three or four pack animals. But this never leads to a comradely offer of assistance which might finish the task in a single mule train. A man with a single animal may have to struggle three or four times in the day up and down to the village while the man with three or four mules sits and watches as his animals graze in idleness.

All social relations between unrelated persons are pervaded by this attitude of distrust. We may recall how sometimes in marriage negotiations the girl's family try to conceal her short-comings and attempt by implication to suggest that a more attractive younger sister is the prospective bride. A man and his family distrust unrelated people because they expect to be ex-ploited and tricked by them. They admit that they themselves would act in a similar manner. They say that a man must pro-tect his family, and to do this in the world as he finds it some cunning and some lies are necessary.

Before 1937, the mutual hostility of unrelated families found an institutionalized form of expression in the custom of 'animal theft' (ζωοκλοπή), more especially of sheep. Although the severity of the penalties introduced by the government of Metaxas effectively stifled this activity almost overnight, most of the heads of families are old enough to remember the alarms and excitements of sheep theft. The desire to steal is still privately expressed (and occasionally indulged in) and the qualities of courage and intelligence which were necessary in these adventures are still the ideal attributes of the hero and 'pallikari'. As we shall see, theft of another sort has now re-placed it. But one cannot doubt that but for the pressure of the State law sheep theft would still be a vigorous institution.

The more general form of sheep theft was the small-scale expedition undertaken by a lone individual or in company with one or two trusted kinsmen. The object was to steal one or two sheep from the flock of an unrelated man, transport the animals with speed to the huts of the families involved where the sheep were at once killed, roasted, and eaten, as a precaution against the discovery of incriminating evidence. Sheep were never stolen from kinsmen or affines and generally not from other flocks in the immediate vicinity. This precaution was taken not from any neighbourly spirit, but because it was realized that, if two neigh-bouring groups engaged in a sequence of theft and counter-theft, shepherding would soon become impossible, and the strength of both flocks would rapidly be reduced to vanishing point. The evidence suggests that small-scale theft was not generally found among those families using the grazing lands of the same village, but was concentrated on the flocks within the territory of immediately neighbouring villages, that is to say in an area some 5–10 miles distant from the homesteads of the thieves. But at this distance an expedition became a planned undertaking requiring the absence of shepherds for perhaps two days and nights from their own sheep, a circumstance which significantly limited the frequency of these raids. It is extremely difficult to assess what was the frequency, but it seems unlikely that the average family enjoyed this sport more often than four or five times in a summer.

The Sarakatsani justify animal theft on the grounds that before 1937 a man could not provide his family with enough food without stolen meat. It was, therefore, an honourable undertaking. Moreover, since other men stole your animals, both interest and honour demanded retaliation. The older men are lyrical about the satisfaction of eating a stolen sheep by moonlight. A man only kills his own animals for meat at important social and religious celebrations, and then with reluctance. The stolen sheep was a luxury, a luxury at the enemy's expense.

After these expeditions, a shepherd was torn between the precaution of secrecy and the desire to win renown for the daring and cleverness of his exploits. He would openly boast about the number of sheep he had recently lifted, but would not generally reveal their original owner. The latter, however, on his own account or through the reports of kinsmen, formed certain shrewd suspicions. In any event, whether he suspected the identity of the thief or not, he had to take some retaliatory action on somebody since otherwise he would not only become a laughing-stock, but a prey to other thieves sensing an easy victim. The best defence against theft was swift retaliation with interest. Even where a man was sure of the thief's identity, his retaliation against the flock of the stani of which the thief was a member might not fall on a sheep or sheep which belonged to the original thief. Therefore, in either instance, an original act of sheep theft might lead to a series of thefts not necessarily confined to the original participants.

There existed also a more ambitious form of sheep theft, which was less often attempted, partly because of the considerable danger and partly because it made even greater demands on the time and energy of the thieves than the variety already described. Three or four kinsmen, travelling swiftly from their homes, arrived at the victims' grazing land about dusk. As soon as it grew dark, they cut out fifty or so sheep and, using a carefully prospected route, drove the animals through the hours of darkness to a secluded river bed or forest clearing, which was distant both from the thieves' own home and the home of the victim. From this place of relative security, the animals were delivered in batches to some Jannina livestock merchant for slaughter; the latter would ask no questions, but also paid a price less than the market rate. Sometimes the ear-signs on the animals were carefully altered and the animals were added, some to the flocks of the thieves, and others to those of kinsmen who lived at a distance from the victim. Care was taken to arrange a wide distribution of the animals so that the chances of recognition were less than if the animals remained together in a single body. For reasons analogous to those already given for the avoidance of small-scale sheep theft on the flocks of immediate neighbours, these more ambitious operations were carried out at even greater distance from the homes of the raiders, generally at the farthest limit of the community some 15–20 miles distant, or on the flocks of Koutsovlachs beyond the community boundary. Fear of massive retaliation also prevented men from boasting about this kind of exploit, at least until some years after the event. Secrecy was essential. Nevertheless, the prestige motive was not altogether lacking from these thefts, since wealth, either in money or in sheep, was an important element in the prestige standing of a family.

Before 1937 it seems possible to distinguish, in very broad outline, three areas and modes of hostility. Towards unrelated families, within a radius of some five miles from a family's own sheep, hostility was expressed in attitude rather than act. There existed constant distrust and suspicion, but an avoidance of provocation. In the second area, stretching beyond the first to a distance of ten miles and often somewhat farther, hostility found expression in the small-scale theft of sheep; the frequency of these acts, however, was limited by considerations of time and

4. Stani in Winter

distance and perhaps a certain moderation sanctioned by the fear of too many reprisals. In the third and farthest area of the community, any individual family only rarely, and possibly never, undertook hostile raiding operations on an ambitious scale; here again the frequency of these acts was limited by considerations of time and distance, and more certainly by the fear of retaliation. According to the distance which separated unrelated families, there was a certain inverse relation between the frequency of hostile contact and the severity of its manner of expression.

The vigorous measures of Metaxas ended extensive sheep theft. But today hostility still finds a parallel form of expression. Since 1937 the sheep population of the Zagori has considerably increased, with the result that the lands of most of the summer villages are over-grazed; it is now the constant anxiety of each group that its animals may not find enough grass to mate effectively and resist disease, let alone return a good milk yield. At the beginning of each summer, the President of the village allots to each family or 'company' grazing land in proportion to the size of each flock. If the number of Sarakatsan sheep entitled to graze on the land of the village increases, there is less grass for each sheep. In a very obvious sense the size and condition of a family's flock are threatened by the sheep of other families, and the grass they eat. It is now too dangerous to steal the sheep, but it is possible to steal the grass. During the summer heat, sheep are grazed at night; the technique of grass stealing is to pasture sheep just over the boundary dividing a man's own land from that of his immediate neighbour, but never so deeply into his territory that he cannot retreat rapidly at the approach of the other shepherd or the agricultural guard. It is the duty of this official to summon all offenders before the local agricultural court, where fines, generally of the order of two or three pounds, are levied. It is very doubtful if the value of the grass taken in the course of the trespassing is equivalent to the fines which are paid, even if the fact is ignored that a neighbour is almost certainly making similar raids in the opposite direction. The Sarakatsani are well aware of these facts, but they feel that inactivity would be weakness and would be so interpreted by the neighbouring groups. It is the consciousness and certainty of the hostile intent of other families threatening the group from without which drives it to reciprocal action. There is no missing the intense satisfaction expressed by shepherds after a successful night's grazing on another's grass. Such acts define the exclusiveness and prepotency of a family group against other family groups and the world in general.

Under present-day conditions the distinction between different ways of showing enmity towards immediate neighbours and more distantly situated families is not so immediately clear, but nevertheless exists. In its relations with another family group using the grazing land of the same village, a family maintains a measure of restraint it would not be concerned to show in chance encounters with families which live at a distance. We have shown how a grass thief is careful never to stray too far across the boundary of his neighbour. He does not boast about these exploits, and if accused would deny that he was aware he had crossed the line. Similarly, the victim, unless he accidentally comes upon the thief red-handed, is unlikely to make wild or insulting accusations which transform an affair of limited hostility into a 'question of honour'. A man whose grass is being raided merely retaliates upon the thief, if he is not already doing so.

But a family has hostile relations of grass-stealing with only its immediate grazing neighbours. And since the summer pastures are reallotted each year a man is unlikely to have the same neighbours two years in succession. Therefore, over the years these hostilities are diffused, as it were, throughout the local gathering of families. In general, shepherds who must live in or close to the same village express hostility in their attitudes rather than in their actions. An almost aggressive secrecy, the cloistered care of unmarried girls, the pleasure taken in the misfortunes of others and the fear of the evil eye, the slanderous vilification of all unrelated people and their motives, are indicative of these attitudes. On the other hand, people are punctilious in their formal greetings when they meet. Women exchange careful and guarded conversation at the well, probing for information and avoiding the need to give it; but with civility. And their men drink in the coffee-shop and play cards with self-assertion but apparent *bonhomie*—yet always on guard for a possible slight, and always with a mental picture of who is for them, and who against, in the immediate vicinity.

During the spring and autumn migrations between the mountains and the plains, many thousands of sheep move along the main road from Jannina to the coastal area around and south of Igoumenitsa. On these occasions, men and their sheep who normally live at a distance find themselves head to tail on the same stretch of road, jostling one another for the meagre stretches of roadside grass, blocking one another's passage on the road, or travelling in the pall of dust raised by the flock in front. In these circumstances, families give a very free rein to their hostility, fights are frequent and sheep theft at night is one of the excitements of the road to which young men look forward. But if on these occasions a man finds himself immediately behind a flock with which he may share a boundary during the coming six months, he moves off the road and waits for half an hour until distance or another flock places a barrier between future neighbours. However, it would be wrong to interpret the relative restraint shown in relations with neighbouring families as reflecting any measure of co-operation. But shepherds and their sheep are peculiarly vulnerable to attack, and it is a structural imperative of such a community that hostility between groups living in close proximity be controlled, if only through their fear of mutual destruction.

Hostility is a kind of relationship, and providing it is limited in such a way that it cannot succeed in its ultimate aim, that is the annihilation of the adversary, it may represent an important element in the pattern of social relations of a community. This is the case among the Sarakatsani where the opportunities for the expression of open hostility are limited by the constant demands of the flocks on the shepherds' attention, and the circumstance that the shepherds and their animals are physically dispersed. Obviously the ability of one man to get at another is always an important factor in a relationship of hostility. But these behaviours are also controlled, partially at any rate, in the competitive forms through which they are acted out. And it is perhaps not unprofitable to consider theft in the general context of competitive gift exchange. The victim, both from honour and self-interest, is obliged to commit a counter-theft. Like the return gift in other societies, the return theft amongst the Sarakatsani should ideally be greater than the original theft. Like a series of prestations and counter-prestations, in theory a series of thefts never ends, for after each reciprocal act an amount of debt remains.

The sheep are part of the family corporation, they are its source of life and wealth, and a family's prestige and pride are closely bound up with the size and condition of its flock. Each sheep and its eccentricities are individually known. The theft of a sheep from a family removes something more than a material object, it takes away also a spiritual value. Thus before 1937 the theft and counter-theft of sheep provided 'a pattern of spiritual bonds between things which are to some extent part of persons.'[6] The modern practice of stealing grass, although its effects are less direct, may be viewed in a similar way. Whereas gift exchange in other societies achieves a measure of co-opera-tion between differentiated groups, amongst the Sarakatsani the reciprocal exchange of theft relates one family group to another in a nexus of debt, while at the same time it denies the need, or the possibility, of co-operation and stresses the mutual exclusiveness and opposition of unrelated families.

\*    \*    \*

The analysis of family roles in the previous chapter revealed that the solidarity of the family was vulnerable in certain impor-tant respects. These were the loss of sexual honour by a woman of the family, and competition between father and son or between brothers. In the first part of this chapter I have dis-cussed certain values and institutions which support the intense solidarity of the Sarakatsan family and are in various ways sanc-tions against the potentially deviant attitudes described in the analysis of family roles; for instance, there were ideas about blood, divorce, illegitimacy, secrecy; and institutions of cor-porate property and family honour. In the final section of this chapter certain beliefs about the inevitable opposition and hostility of unrelated families have been examined as well as some institutions through which they are expressed. And this reciprocal exchange of hostility represents a further sanction that encourages the identification of the interests and affections of family members in opposition to all who do not belong.

[6] Marcel Mauss, *The Gift*, translated by Ian Cunnison, London, 1954, p. 11.

# IX

# PATRONAGE

## 1. COMMUNITY

THE Sarakatsani of Zagori are profoundly conscious of their
identity as a community in relation to villagers or towns-
people. Hostility to villagers is not only a question of a
conflict of interests but also a difference of values. The Sarakatsani believe that if the material conditions of their life are indeed regrettable, yet the moral life of their community upholds
Greek traditional values which villagers, especially in Zagori,
have debased and betrayed. Specifically they claim that the
men may be cursed or the women seduced with little fear of
provoking the reaction expected of honourable men. These
claims are spiced with illustrations. The classic instance is the
case of the postman who surprised another villager in the act
of intercourse with his wife. He took no action, however, except
to observe that this did not seem to him to be the conduct of a
good neighbour. Other tales inform of homosexual practices
with gipsies, and of ugly widows and unmarried spinsters who
satisfy their lusts with dogs. The evidence is rather more convincing for the accusation that they are mean and inhospitable.
The common purpose of these allegations is, simply, to deny that
the villagers of Zagori have honour. The men are lacking in
manliness, courage, and generosity: the women are shameless
and given to sexual lust. Criticism is sharpened by the knowledge that the shepherds themselves are despised by the villagers
as people unfit to live in civilized society, physically unclean
barbarians who put their trust in violence and self-help rather
than the processes of law.

In these attitudes two ideal types are opposed. For the villagers
of Zagori, actions must be judged against the image of the
clever, astute, educated merchant and patriot who may travel
abroad but continues to support the village by his benefactions.
His activities, however, require an orderly social environment,
a respect for the minimum of law and order, an absence of
physical violence, and (although this would not be admitted) it
required in the past a qualified understanding with the Turkish

master. In contrast the Sarakatsan model is the anarchic pallikari hero whose ideal is personal freedom and aggressive pride,
the patriot of the klephtic ballads, trussed with bandoliers,
physically hard and morally self-disciplined. By implication
such men are shepherds, not villagers; the latter, whether they
live by agriculture or not, are despised as 'bent men' (σκυμμένοι
ἄνθρωποι), men who servilely dig in the earth.

The community is a closed group: individuals are members
because they were born into it. On the other hand, some people
leave it through marriage to villagers; and through education
or wealth where these lead to a change in occupation or the
material conditions of living. In one respect, then, the Sarakatsani of Zagori are an occupational group sharing a homogeneous
style of life: in another, a community practising preferential
endogamy. For probably not more than 5 per cent of all
Sarakatsan marriages are to persons outside the community.
Significantly such marriages meet with some disapproval; and
even where a man who has taken a village wife continues to live
from his flocks, he is no longer considered to be a full member
of the community without some qualification.

The Sarakatsani of Zagori, while they have this clear sense
of their solidarity in opposition to the villagers, are nevertheless
a widely dispersed community in which the only group able
to act together on the basis of local community, rather than
kinship ties, is the local gathering of shepherds who in summer
live on the grazing lands of the same village. This gathering of
families has little group consciousness and no formal organization. There are various reasons for this. A family may sometimes
have ties of kinship and marriage with as many as half the
families in the local gathering, but never with all. Distrust
between unrelated families does not prevent the momentary up-
surge of feelings of identification against villagers, but it completely cripples the co-operation that is necessary for systematic
opposition. In difficulties men turn for practical help to kinsmen
and affines, not to unrelated neighbours. A further reason is that
the local group is dissolved in the autumn when each co-
operating group moves down to its winter pastures which are
seldom in the same neighbourhood. Since a family has one set
of Sarakatsan neighbours in the summer and generally an entirely different set in the winter, the feeling emerges that there

is something impermanent, almost fortuitous, about the local neighbourhood whether in summer or winter.[1] At the same time the significance and solidarity of the total Sarakatsan community is emphasized. The expression, 'we, the Sarakatsani of Zagori' is common; but 'we, the Sarakatsani of Tsepelevo' (or any other village), is heard less frequently.

Yet it is in the local neighbourhood that hostility between Sarakatsani and Zagori villagers is actively expressed. Property rights are jealously guarded, and in the absence of fencing it is inevitable that Sarakatsan sheep and mules are discovered in the crops or gardens of villagers. They trespass regularly and deliberately on certain areas of grassland reserved for the cutting of hay on which the villagers rely to feed their livestock during the winter months. The shepherds also attempt to defraud the village treasury by concealing some of their sheep when the flock is numbered each spring. For their part the Sarakatsani resent the fines they must pay in the agricultural court for the depredations committed by their animals. They believe, too, that they are cheated in the allotment of watering time by the villager who regulates the irrigation of village vegetable gardens. There are quarrels over the regulations for the grazing and watering of mules, which favour the villagers. There is trouble over the use of springs for washing clothes and over the refusal of the Sarakatsani to use earth-closets. Indeed, there is trouble between the two groups at every point of contact between them. Since their rights are entrenched by the decrees passed in the village council and because the executive administration of village affairs is necessarily in the hands of villagers who are in residence all the year, the villagers are almost always in a legally secure position in differences with Sarakatsani. It follows that the villager appeals to the law which happens to favour his interests, the Sarakatsanos more often turns to self-help and violence. Justice is not a question of the impartial administration of existing law, although this, too, may be lacking in the view of the Sarakatsani. If the law does not allow a man to protect the interests and dignity of his family, then it does not represent justice.

[1] In this connexion it is worth remarking that before the Sarakatsani became village citizens in 1938 a family, or stani, did not necessarily go to the same grazing village in Zagori each year.

Although the individual family receives from the local gathering of Sarakatsani no practical support in its difficulties with the villagers, there may be expressions of moral support. In the coffee-shop where the Sarakatsan heads of family gather to drink, play cards, argue, and discuss the village news, a man who has had a quarrel with a villager, or difficulties with the village council, will be asked what happened. He may not tell his audience all the facts, or the truth, but he will tell them something of the matter, careful always to present his own actions and arguments so that they appear honourable and vigorous. The villagers in the case he will condemn as unjust, cowardly, and as men who do not love honour. Such a recital is a formal statement of the moral solidarity of the whole Sarakatsan community against those who molest it and its way of life. Every Sarakatsanos present supports without reservation the condemnation of villagers. 'Eh, what a "poustis"[2] that man is.' They all agree. Many, of course, will have unspoken reservations as to the part played by the narrator. Yet in regard to the actions of the villagers in the dispute, the solidarity of feeling is complete. Often at the end of the discussion, just as a hymn sometimes closes a religious service, somebody will start to sing a wild klephtic ballad in which the whole assembly join their voices.

Parallel to this conflict of interests and values is the social exclusiveness practised by each community towards the other. Sarakatsani do not generally invite villagers to their homes at weddings or festivals unless they are patrons or the godparents of their children. Nor do the villagers receive the Sarakatsani in their houses unless there is some particular relationship. At the festival of the village patron Saint, the reluctance of the master of ceremonies to allow shepherds to lead the traditional ring dance may be interpreted by the Sarakatsani as an attempt to humiliate them publicly. Each year it provokes in some villages violent incidents. In this context men forget the absence of relationship and stand together with the help of visiting kinsmen from other villages in defence of the honour of the whole Sarakatsan community against the villagers of Zagori who attempt to ridicule and belittle their way of life.

[2] A ποῦστης is the passive partner in a homosexual relationship.

On the other hand, any attempt to organize systematic co-operation between the families of the community faces almost insuperable obstacles. An 'Association of Nomad Pastoralists' was formed in 1950 to represent the interests of the community to the government and other agencies. But enthusiasm waned rapidly as soon as it was realized that it could not miraculously improve the situation without the moral and financial support of its members over a number of years. The members are almost exclusively Sarakatsani but significantly the salaried executive secretary is a villager; first, because no shepherd possesses the legal expertise to negotiate with officials; secondly, because, although few shepherds trust the secretary, it would be even more distasteful to discuss one's problems with another Sarakat-sanos. Here we touch on the difficulty which faces any attempt at community organization beyond the competence of the co-operating 'company'. It necessarily involves the acceptance of some executive authority. But for reasons of pride and distrust a Sarakatsanos cannot surrender any fraction of the sovereignty of his family.

As we have seen, this does not mean that the community has no sense of its solidarity and opposition to villagers. On the contrary, when the honour of the community is publicly attacked, unrelated men will stand together in its defence. To do nothing would be to betray their manhood in one another's eyes. This is a relationship of identification. But the conflict of practical interests between Sarakatsani and the villagers, the merchants, or the government, is a different form of threat. And although these problems are similar in kind for all, the problems of one family are generally separated in time and space from those of another. When a man's own interests are not immediately endangered, he is secretly pleased about the misfortunes of other men who are not kinsmen or affines. To face these difficulties as a united community would require co-operative relationships between non-kinsmen. Since these are not possible, we must now consider how, in fact, each family attempts to protect itself from the external threats to its security and prosperity.

## 2. SPIRITUAL KINSHIP

In his struggle to protect his family and live his own way of life the Sarakatsanos must come to terms with various persons and groups in the village, the town, and the State, which have the power to threaten his interests. The officers and merchants with whom he must deal have a common quality that they stand outside the community's field of values. In the absence of strongly held universal values concerning the obligations of a man towards general humanity they feel free to exploit, or at least not to help, another person from whom they are divided by the absence of common ties of kinship, community, or class. If they have power, they see no reason why they should discipline themselves in its use towards a person from whom they are morally isolated.

To protect himself the Sarakatsanos tries to establish some kind of link which will transform an otherwise impersonal confrontation into a personal relation; that is, he attempts to draw the individual whose goodwill he wishes to influence into an institutionalized relationship which may exist across the frontiers of community and involves the person's self-esteem and to some extent the sanction of public opinion, so that he must discipline himself in the extent and manner in which he exercises his power. The most effective means of achieving these ends is the form of spiritual kinship between the bridegroom and his wedding sponsor (κουμπάρος). After the birth of a child this changes into the even more significant relation between the natural parent and the spiritual parent.

The duties of the wedding sponsor begin on the day of the wedding, throughout which he supports the bridegroom by his close presence both in the secular marriage custom and feasting, and at the religious services of betrothal and marriage. He stands at the right hand of the groom and it is his privilege to exchange three times the crowns of the bride and bridegroom. By his public sponsorship of the marriage he declares that it is an honourable union and that the partners are persons worthy to receive the sacrament of marriage; on the spiritual plane he becomes responsible for them. The relationship (κουμπαριά) which is established between the groom and his sponsor (and for which there seems to be no adequate modern English translation) does not end with the ceremony. It looks forward to the birth of children which is the explicit purpose of the marriage. It is the right and the duty of the wedding sponsor to stand for these children at their baptism, and consequently to enter a twofold relationship of godfather-godchild and spiritual parent-natural parent.

The sacrament of Baptism, which is immediately followed in the Eastern rite by the sacrament of Holy Chrism or Confirmation, is the spiritual foundation of these social relationships. In the two sacraments the Holy Spirit purifies and recreates the nature of the child, uniting it to the body of Christ and bestowing Spirit upon it. The rite of Baptism marks the acceptance of a soul into the Church, it makes possible the remission of future sins and it releases the individual from the weight of original sin. In the rite of Holy Chrism the Holy Spirit descends upon the person of the newly-baptized. In a simple fashion these things are well understood by the Sarakatsani. If a child dies unbaptized its soul 'goes into the air and is lost'. They think that men require the grace which is initially conferred by the Holy Spirit through these sacraments both to realize the inherent nobility of their manhood (identifying a condition of honour with a state of grace), and for the more pragmatic reason that if the barrier of sin between a man and God is too considerable he will not be able to protect his family against the many forms of catastrophe which threaten it.

In these critical sacraments the child needs a spiritual guardian to stand and answer for him. Since they are related to the child through the act of generation the natural parents are unable to assume this role and, perhaps, for the same reason, they are not present at the ceremony. The godfather (νουνός) receives the child from a member of the family at the door of the church. The service begins with an exorcism of the Devil and the evil spirits of error, wickedness, idolatry, covetousness, lying, and uncleanness, in which the godfather indicates the child's renunciation of Evil, blowing and spitting three times to effect this rejection. The rite of Baptism then begins. The water is blessed in a long prayer and the priest intercedes that the person may put off the old man which is corrupt through deceitful lusts and put on the new man after the image of Him that made him, that he may eventually be a partaker in His resurrection. Olive oil is blessed, the surface of the water is signed with it and the child is anointed with the oil of gladness in the Name of the Father, the Son, and the Holy Ghost. The priest then baptizes the child by a threefold total immersion. The

sacrament of Holy Chrism follows at once. In this rite the child
is anointed with chrism, a consecrated unguent of many in-
gredients, on the forehead, eyes, nostrils, lips, ears, breast,
hands, and feet; each time the priest says, 'The seal of the Gift
of the Holy Spirit. Amen.' During the service the godfather
holds the child.

At the beginning of the service the priest asks the godfather
the name of the child. Although a father may give some hint of
his preference, it is recognized that it is the absolute prerogative
of the godfather to name the child. Generally, he follows tradition by naming the child after one of its grandparents or perhaps after the saint on whose day the Baptism occurs. As soon
as the name is known small children rush from the church to
the home of the parents to give the news and to be rewarded
with small coins or sugared sweets. In the child's home there is
always some anxiety until this information is received, for a
person's first name is in some peculiar way an important aspect
of his individual personality; and it links him, also, to a particular saint to whom he will turn for protection.

At the end of the service those who have attended return with
the godfather to the child's home where they offer their wishes
for long life and prosperity. The godfather hands back the child
to the mother and tells her, 'I return the child to you in this
life; but I shall ask it back from you in the next. Protect it well
from fire, water, and all evil.'

There are certain exchanges of gifts between spiritual kinsmen. The wedding sponsor makes a not inconsiderable outlay
at a wedding. He must give the bride a dress, and a gift of
money when he takes his leave at the end of the celebrations;
he must provide the wedding crowns, the candles, and sugared
almonds, as well as his share of bread, meat, and wine; he must
tip the band generously when the bride, the bridegroom, and his
close relatives are leading the dance; and he is responsible for
the offering to the priest. The sum of these expenses is unlikely
to be less than ten pounds. In return the bride gives the sponsor
the choicest blanket from her dowry. Later, as the godfather,
he is expected to give his godchild a complete set of clothing, a
gift which is generally offered when the child is one or two years
old. It must be reciprocated by the child's family at the next
Easter with the gift of a lamb with fleece dyed red, a round of

bread, and a new shirt. Each Easter the godfather must send to his godchild a candle to take to church for the service on Easter Saturday, and a red egg. At Easter, the relationship between the godchild and the spiritual parent takes a fresh strength and emphasis when men with repentant hearts are renewing their state of grace, a condition which is made possible for each individual through Baptism.

Bridegroom and wedding sponsor, or natural father and spiritual father, address one another reciprocally as κουμπάρε; the godchild addresses his spiritual father as νουνέ. The very use of these terms of address carries with them an implied pattern of conduct, of duties, and privileges. The quality of the relationship between the natural parent and the spiritual parent is recognized in the prohibition on marriage between members of the two elementary families of marriage of the co-parents. Sexual relations between these persons are incestuous. The joint responsibility of the co-parents for the spiritual condition of the child, not only in their relations to the child but more particularly in their behaviour to one another, is the strength of the relationship. For if the natural or spiritual father of the child employs any sharp or dishonourable practice against the other, 'he destroys the oil' with which the child was anointed and, consequently, his right relation to God. Therefore such actions are wanton and sinful. This heavy responsibility of the natural and spiritual co-parents is consistent with the more significant ritual role that is played by the sponsor-godparent at the Baptism in comparison with his duties at the marriage ceremony. In the latter rite he sponsors a responsible adult, in the former he stands in the place of a small child who cannot answer for himself.

The natural father and the spiritual father must have confidence in one another; they must never quarrel, or gossip about one another's affairs. It is argued that kinsmen by blood are not chosen, consequently it is inevitable that a man will quarrel with some of them. But the duties of spiritual kinship are entered into freely and for this reason spiritual kinsmen ought never to allow any difference of interest to threaten their relationship. Behind this belief are two considerations. The relationship is concerned with critical religious sacraments, therefore the appropriate behaviour pattern ought to follow the ideal of Christian fellowship. On the other hand, it is a relation with a person generally not connected by kinship or marriage. It is therefore, despite the ritual sanction it contains, an inherently fragile bond which can only be sustained through the meticulous disciplining of attitudes and feelings on both sides. Two people formerly unrelated are drawn into a relationship of exacting ethical standards in which their mutual esteem and respect are profoundly committed.

Just as the gift of God's grace which is implied in the rite of Baptism is a free gift, a gift without motive, and one which expects no reciprocity, so it is held that a godfather ought not to refuse any reasonable request of his godchild. In practice a godchild has little to do with his godfather, to whom, however, he must show a formal respect more punctilious than the respect he observes to his natural parents. While the ritual relation between the godfather and his godchild is more important than that between bridegroom and sponsor, the social relationship between the natural parent and the spiritual parent, persons of the same generation with common or complementary interests, is more important than that between the spiritual father and his godchild. Nevertheless, when a man seeks a favour from the godfather of his child, he asks for this help implicitly, or explicitly, in the name of the child; for it is understood that he has the right to make this request because of the ritual relation which exists between his child and its spiritual father. It follows that, in an important sense, the social relationship between the natural and the spiritual parent is dependent on the ritual link between godfather and godchild.

The wedding sponsor, in theory, has the right to baptize all the children of the marriage. The Sarakatsanos, however, seldom wastes these opportunities by allowing a single godfather to baptize all his sons. When the second son is born he tactfully asks the godfather of his first son if he would mind surrendering his right on this occasion because X has asked him if he might have that honour. He may add that as X is an important man he fears to give him offence. This, of course, is not true but the lie serves its purpose. In this way a man may establish almost as many links of spiritual kinship as he has children. If the first child is a girl, the sponsor baptizes her but normally he must also become the godfather of the first son when he is born. However, if two or three girls are born in succession, he may be asked to waive his right before the birth of the next child in case he is bringing bad luck by having an 'unlucky hand' (κακορίζικο χέρι).

A man may sometimes ask a father if he can baptize his child, and it is agreed that ideally this is the correct procedure. However, since the prospective godfather is more often a person of higher social status or prestige, it is generally the father of the child who takes the initiative in establishing the relationship. It is not easy for a person to refuse to 'baptize' a child, but a man who is forced somewhat unwillingly into the relationship does not generally become a useful or co-operative spiritual kinsman. Yet the advantages of the relationship do not all lie on the one side. A man who has 'baptized' many children has many clients who are in some measure morally bound to support him whether with votes, commercial custom, or in some other way. A man with many dependants wins prestige amongst his equals. And to stand as godfather is in itself a good thing, an action pleasing to God.

Considerably more than half the spiritual kinship relations of the Sarakatsani are with persons outside the community. The occupations of these persons are various. They include cheese merchants, animal dealers, village Presidents, members of village councils, village shopkeepers, other prominent villagers with influence, transport lorry owners, veterinary experts, lawyers, Members of Parliament, grammar school teachers, tailors, and others. They have one quality in common that they all are able in different ways to help or hinder the families who wish to establish a link of spiritual kinship with them.

Spiritual kinship is not the only means of introducing an element of moral commitment into a relationship with a person outside the community, but it is the most effective. The ritual sanction 'locks' the relationship. An accusation of ingratitude may easily break well established relations of friendship of the kind that are based on the exchange of complementary favours, but it cannot destroy a connexion of spiritual kinship, nor is it a justification for retaliation against the other partner whatever the provocation. Although there are godparents who do not alter their course of conduct after entering the relationship, this is rare. Public opinion and a man's religious and social conscience put some restraint on him. Naturally, merchants and others are well aware of the motives behind the naïve manœuvres of the Sarakatsani. But, as we have already said, they also gain various advantages. They do not, except in the unusual case of a very rich or powerful individual, become lavish patrons. Few of them give away anything for nothing. But they become helpful rather than hostile, they will exert their influence for their spiritual kinsmen and in doing so they themselves win prestige. A shared system of values regulates their mutual behaviour in which friendship and trust replace hostility and suspicion.

### 3. VILLAGE FRIENDSHIP AND PATRONAGE

In the villages authority rests in the hands of a council of five members. From its own number it elects a President and Vice-President while the choice of the council itself is the result of local elections which are held every four years. In these, all adult villagers of both sexes, and those shepherd families who possess citizenship rights in the village, are entitled to vote.

For electoral purposes any person may form a party providing he can present to the electorate a card with the names of seven candidates. In practice village elections seldom produce more than two parties, those who support the President in power because they are his friends, and those who want a change because they are not his friends. These parties are essentially personal followings, not corporate associations, and there is not necessarily any direct alignment with the parties of national politics. The citizens vote by handing in the party card of their choice with four crosses against those of the seven candidates who are preferred. The party which polls the greater number of cards wins the election. The four candidates of the successful party who record the largest aggregates of personal votes become members of the council. The person amongst the candidates of the defeated party or parties who claims the largest number of personal votes is also elected to the council as the representative of the defeated minority's interests. The five members of the new council then proceed to elect two of their number as President and Vice-President. These men hold office for two years, at the end of which period their authority may either be confirmed for the remaining two years of the council's term of office, or they may be replaced by the election of new officers.

The powers of this council are wide. By a simple majority vote it may institute any local by-law it pleases, providing this does not conflict with the letter or spirit of national legislation. Within statutory limits, it determines the local grazing charges to be levied on the flocks of pastoralists. And it draws up its own budget of future communal expenditure. These privileges are balanced by the discretionary power of veto over budgetary and taxation decisions which is possessed by the Nomarch, who is the provincial administrator appointed by the central Government.

The day-to-day administration of village affairs is the task of the President, who receives an allowance in compensation for the time he spends on community affairs. He is assisted in this work by a permanent salaried village secretary who keeps the registers up to date, deals with correspondence, and draws up a variety of returns which are required by different Government Ministries. Indeed, both these village officials act, not infrequently, for the central Government in matters of routine administration, instruction, and in the collection of information. Although in the decisions of the council the President's vote, of itself, carries no greater weight than that of any other member, his control over the administration of parochial affairs and his intimate relations with the Government bureaucracy, whether he is acting as a negotiator representing the interests of the villagers, or as an agent of the bureaucracy, give him in fact substantially greater power than other members of his council.

For these reasons it is generally with the President that the Sarakatsani must negotiate their affairs. In a number of important matters he has the power to affect their interests collectively or individually. In the first place, the council decides the scale of grazing charges. The village is permitted by law to charge, for summer grazing, up to two shillings a head for the first 150 animals and up to four shillings for the remainder of the flock. It may, however, charge less.[3] And it is noticeable that in those villages where the shepherd families are in a politically strategic position grazing charges tend to be lower than in other villages where this is not the case. Threepence or sixpence a head difference in a grazing charge does not represent a very

---

[3] The minimum charge is $4\frac{1}{2}d.$ a head.

large sum of money, but to men who are already deeply in debt to merchants or shopkeepers, it has significance. For them, debt implies a form of dependence which is a measure of weakness.

The Sarakatsani say that if a village President and council enforce all local laws without allowing some flexibility, it becomes impossible for a shepherd family to live. If, on the other hand, the President is willing to grant them various favours (ρουσφέτια, εὐκολίες), which take into consideration the effect of the law on personal circumstances, their position may be, at least, not entirely hopeless. In practice, all Presidents with Sarakatsani on their citizenship rolls relax certain regulations for the shepherd families which support them. The political skill of a President, even an implacable opponent of the shepherds, is that he grants just a sufficient number of favours to a few Sarakatsan families to detach them from the ranks of the opposition at the time of the elections.

It is the President who decides each spring which area of the village grazing land shall be allotted to each family or co-operating 'company' of shepherds. At Skamneli, for instance, there are three main areas, Goura, Tsoumako, and Gyphto-kambos. Goura has the best grass, Gyphtokambos the worst. It is the customary arrangement that each family goes to a different area each year. Yet within each general area different sections are of different quality so that friends may still be rewarded and enemies punished in a way that touches them very closely through the milk yield and the condition of their animals.

The President is often able to influence the actions of the village agricultural guard and forester. Both these officials, although they belong to a Government service, are dependent in various ways on the goodwill of the President, and if he is displeased with their work it is relatively easy to have them exchanged. By regulation, if an agricultural guard discovers a trespass on village land, or the forester finds animals grazing in forbidden areas, they must issue a summons against the shepherd in charge of the offending animals. But if the President is able to have a word with the guard or forester before he writes the details of the case in his report book, and if no third person is present, he may be able to persuade him to ignore the matter.

The President has more direct control over the man who is employed by the village to regulate the flow of water to the village vegetable gardens. He is able to arrange matters so that a fair share of water is given to, or withheld from, a Sarakatsan family.

For a number of purposes the Sarakatsani require the signature of the President on forms, certificates, or passes. He may be able to cause considerable trouble to a shepherd through delay, or by finding technical irregularities in his documents. These powers of the President are particularly feared. Although some of the leaders of co-operating 'companies' of families are extremely able and alert men, the ordinary Sarakatsan head of family is completely bewildered by documents, printed forms, and regulations, most of which are written in an official language which he only half comprehends. A Sarakatsanos with a large family and only 60 sheep lost six of his animals through disease in the summer of 1955. He came to the village office to ask the President to sign a form for a loan from the Agricultural Bank to replace the dead animals. At the time he was in considerable difficulties, his family was short of flour, and on account of his poverty, small flock, and deep indebtedness, his cheese merchant would make no further advances of credit. There was no doubt about the authenticity of his claim. The agricultural guard had made a report that the animals belonged to this man and that they had the unmistakable symptoms of liver fluke. After ignoring the man's presence in the office for about three-quarters of an hour, the President suddenly pointed to one of the many conditional clauses in the regulations printed in small type. 'You understand that yours is a difficult case. It is only five days since you arrived here from the plains and this clause says that confirmation of the details of the case must be signed by the President of the village where the disease was contracted. Obviously they became sick in the plains or on the road; anyway, not here. Perhaps you must return to Philippiada to have this signed. However, I shall write to the Ministry of Agriculture in Jannina and we shall see.' The man haltingly explained his difficulties, referring to the plight of his family. The President spread his hands and smiled benignly, 'You know that I always try to help you tent-dwellers (σκηνίτες) but in this case,' putting his thumb on the offending clause, 'what

can I do?' After the man had left the office the President explained that he would sign the form in a few days. He was a
man who loved honour, he added, but it was necessary that
the men who had voted against him in the recent election should
learn that their interests lay in supporting him and not that
communist cuckold (a reference to the leader of the opposition
party).

The Agricultural Bank has been mentioned. Each year, the
shepherd applies to the bank for an annual loan, the application form for which must carry the President's signature as a
guarantee that the information given by the shepherd is
accurate. Long-term loans are also available from this bank to
assist families which have lost their stock through disease. In
these cases, the shepherd must produce evidence that the animals
in fact died of a particular disease, and were not sold, or given
away as dowry. In addition, the application must be approved
by the local officer of the Ministry of Agriculture; and this
support will be hard to win if the village President has characterized the shepherd as spendthrift or inefficient.

Twice a year when the Sarakatsani leave the mountains, or
the plains, the local village President must sign a clearance
certificate which confirms that all their grazing charges have
been paid. This is required by the police before they will issue
the pass without which a family cannot move its flocks to another
district. These moneys are not paid directly to the village council but into a treasury in Jannina, whose official collector arrives
in the village some three weeks before the flocks are normally
moved to their winter pastures in the plains. If, as frequently
happens, a Sarakatsanos is unable to pay his dues, the collector
may send a demand notice to the police, and if this is not met
when it is presented, the shepherd is arrested. But in many
cases the President intervenes and persuades the treasury to
allow the defaulter six months' grace until he returns in the
spring.

A man requires the President's signature on his identity card.
He requires it when he applies for an allotment of free timber
from village forest land for the repair of his house, and on other
documents which it would be tedious to enumerate. In all these
situations the President may be the helper who makes all things
easy, or a deliberate and successful obstructionist.

There are other ways, less legal, in which the President may sometimes help Sarakatsan friends. When the sheep are mustered for counting each spring on their arrival at the village, it is relatively easy for the President to arrange that the total of animals is underestimated so that perhaps 350 instead of 400 is entered in the records for taxation purposes. Similarly, when milk, meat or wool are sold to a merchant a tax of 2 per cent is levied on the value of the sale. For a friend the President may mark down the price actually paid over for animals or the products they yield. With the connivance of the President and the schoolteacher, a family which is short of labour may sometimes take a child from school before the full term of its compulsory education is completed. It is also possible for the President to do some things to a Sarakatsanos which are strictly against law or custom, because the man may be frightened that if he takes the case to the courts, or the Nomarch, he may suffer worse injustices in the long run. After Theodoros voted against the President in the elections, his sheep were sent for the second year in succession to the worst area of village grazing land. Theodoros could have appealed to the Nomarch but decided it was more politic to settle his differences with the President by more indirect methods.

The strength of the President's position is apparent. In their efforts to come to terms with his authority and influence, the Sarakatsani attempt to draw him into some form of personal relationship that will introduce a moral element of mutual consideration. Three methods are in general practice: spiritual kinship, friendship, and gifts. The first of these has been discussed. The second possibility is that the Sarakatsanos may be able to align himself as the 'friend' (φίλος) and political supporter of the President, if he will accept him.

Here a brief digression is necessary to consider the nature of friendship in Zagori villages.[4] Between villagers ties of friendship relate persons who are, in principle, equals. All villagers, without discrimination, possess the same legal rights in the local polity. If a man is also honourable in his conduct, a good neighbour, and legitimately born of Zagori parents, he is entitled in the social life of the village to be treated with a degree

[4] Friendship in Epirote villages appears to be very similar to the parallel institution in Andalusia. Cf. Pitt-Rivers, op. cit., chapter 7.

of consideration that represents a recognition of his social personality. Persons who are equal in these respects must show some concern for each other's social sensibilities by avoiding public rudeness and by a careful and courteous exchange of greetings when they meet.

Friendship begins where one man accepts a favour (χάρη) from another. The person who gives the favour will assert that he expects no return; it would be insulting to suggest that his act of friendship had a motivation. It is, however, the very altruism of the act, whether this is simulated or not, which demands a counter favour. Default destroys the friendship and provokes accusations of ingratitude. Although liking and sympathy are alleged to be the premises on which friendship between village equals is based, it would be more true to say that villagers who are able to do each other reciprocal favours sometimes discover from this experience confidence in one another. From these beginnings there may grow a relationship of intimacy and warmth. But in essence friendship of this kind remains a contractual relation, a form of co-operation in which services of various kinds are exchanged and accounted.

The network of friendships of the President or of other influential villagers becomes in reality a system of patronage. Accountancy is then more difficult because the patron is able to do more material favours for his client than the latter is able to return. But although the character of the relationship is now, in effect, asymmetrical, patron and client, because they are interacting in the context of village community relations where all true villagers are in principle equals, they continue to treat one another as if they were equals in the situation of their friendship as well. Both patron and client claim publicly that the other 'is my friend'. The patron says that he helps his client simply because it pleases him to help those of his friends who are in difficulties. The client explains that he is the friend of the patron, not simply because he receives benefits from him, but because he is a good man. In short, their friendship exists within the field of village values where behaviour is evaluated against the ideals of independence and love of honour.

In the Sarakatsan community the situation is different. There is no co-operation between unrelated families and no established political authority in the shepherd community which might lead to relations of political friendship. A relationship which has many of the aspects of patronage exists between the dominant family and the other associated families in a co-operating 'company', but these connexions are based on the values of kinship, not friendship. When a Sarakatsanos says 'I have him as a friend', he generally means that he has established a relation of mutual advantage with a person outside the community who in most cases is in the superordinate position of patron. The use of the word 'friend' by the Sarakatsanos is not here encumbered with any theory of equality or disinterested motives. The fact that in terms of power he is the weaker partner in the majority of his relations of friendship is recognized by the Sarakatsanos but does not immediately concern his pride since these people stand outside his community. On the contrary, the more effective relationships of this kind that a man possesses, the greater his prestige in the community since it proves him to be an able protector of his family and his flocks.

It is by no means certain that a President will accept any Sarakatsanos as his political client. What the President has to offer will be clear enough from the earlier description of the ways in which he can help or hinder. The chief service the shepherd is able to pledge in return is his vote and those of his family and associated kinsmen. But to accept a man as a client commits the patron to protection instead of exploitation, and to that extent it is a restriction on the free exercise of his power. A President generally prefers to assume these obligations only to Sarakatsani with some influence. Naturally, more humble families have vicarious access to his patronage through their influential kinsmen, but the intermediate link which separates them from the President's beneficence makes it less likely that their affairs will be settled with the same despatch and satisfaction.

The extent to which a President needs to enter these commitments depends, of course, on the balance of the political groupings in his village. In one village the President commanded about three quarters of the village vote, but by his generally uncompromising hostility he had driven the Sarakatsani into the arms of the small opposition party. A month before the election it appeared that he had no Sarakatsan supporters and that his cause was lost. Conveniently the election was held in November, after the Sarakatsani had departed to the plains eighty miles away. The opposition party chartered a lorry to transport, as they had calculated it, an adequate number of Sarakatsan voters to assure their victory. But, in the event, the President skilfully contrived a narrow majority by making secret agreements with two shepherd families. The five members of these families who returned from the plains, ironically enough in the lorry chartered by the opposition, were sufficient to give the President victory and a new term of office.

After the election the two families received a number of favours. In the spring the sheep of one family were short-counted by sixty and the flock of the other, which by right of the customary rotation of grazing areas ought to have gone to an area of indifferent grazing, spent a more profitable summer on the village's best grassland. In the face of the unusual solidarity of the local Sarakatsan group at the time of the election, the action of the two dissident families was described as treacherous. They were branded as 'The President's men', with an overtone of meaning which implied that they were puppets dancing at the command of the master, capable even of betraying their own people. Yet as passions cooled and the months passed, evaluations changed perceptibly. At first the members of these families were unequivocally 'traitors', but later they were considered merely 'cunning' (by no means an entirely pejorative judgement), and eventually one sometimes heard grudging admissions of their 'cleverness'. For it is recognized that each family is free to seek its own protection and the political friends who can provide it. Indeed, Sarakatsani believe that in the nature of the situation favours and concessions are to be won only by some, not all families. It is, therefore, the duty of each head of family to scheme and intrigue for his own security. Only in the case of a breach of faith between kinsmen is an accusation of treachery seriously considered.

But the friendship which a Sarakatsanos achieves with a village President, or indeed with any other influential person, involves more than the exchange of specific material favours; it establishes, also, an asymmetrical relation of sociability which enhances the prestige of both men. A Sarakatsanos who has friendship with the President boldly sits down with him at the same table when he enters the coffee-shop. The President offers him a drink, he stands him a drink in return. Meeting him in the village square, the shepherd stops to talk for a few minutes about this and that. Were they not patron and client, a curt 'Good day' from each side would be the extent of their social intercourse. However, it is not a relationship of equals. The shepherd belongs not only to a different community, but to a qualitatively inferior one. While the President will say of a villager who is similarly his client that this man is his friend, he will not say this of a shepherd. If an explanation in his presence is necessary, he may say, 'George is a good lad, I help him', but behind his back he will simply say, 'He is my man'. Yet, although they are his social inferiors, the President gains prestige by being seen publicly with his shepherd clients. If he drinks with other villagers who are his supporters, this is no cause for comment. He merely keeps company with those who are his social equals and natural companions. When he drinks with four or five shepherds it draws attention to his possession of power, to his ability to hold men who do not waste their time drinking with ordinary villagers whom as a class of persons they detest and despise. The Sarakatsanos accepts his position of inferiority in the relationship because he must. He does not, as most villagers would, address the President by his Christian name; but he is not subservient in his manner. He speaks to him courteously as 'President'. When another person of importance comes to speak to the President, and it is clear that he is dismissed, he moves to another table, or with a 'Good health, President', to which the latter replies, he leaves the shop. These are the conventional terms on which these unequal friendships are founded. What is important to the Sarakatsanos in these situations is that other shepherds who do not possess this valued link should see and envy him.

In asymmetrical friendship relations, since it is assumed that the patron has more favours to offer than the client can return, or that reciprocal favours are so dissimilar in quality that accountancy is difficult, there is often greater stability than in friendships between equals, which are very frequently bedevilled by accusations of ingratitude. Yet, even here, there are many complaints, the patron asserting that the client should be more vocal in his gratitude, the client complaining that the patron does very little in relation to the client's worth and needs, and the services he has rendered. In short, the patron wants more honour, the client more benefits.

The third widely practised method of placating or influencing the President is to present him with a gift of cheese, butter, or meat. Some families do this each spring as a matter of general policy without having in mind any particular favour. They hope that the gift may moderate his general attitude towards them in the coming months. More often, families wait until they face some specific difficulty. A gift of cheese or some other produce is delivered to the President's home and then, perhaps two days later, the gift-giver walks into the village office and makes his request. The President may be helpful or he may not. The assumptions of the giver and the recipient of the gift are not necessarily the same. The giver hopes that the gift will arouse some sense of obligation in the receiver. But the latter, if he chooses to feel that the gift was forced on him against his will, may decide that he is not obliged to feel grateful. If he intends not to grant the favour, the refusal is never direct. The many difficulties which stand in the way are elaborated at very great length. He explains that he will see what can be done, he will write to a friend in Jannina, he wants to help. In fact he will do nothing; and the original gift is not returned.

A gift is frequently offered to the President by a Sarakatsanos when he meets with legal troubles. Stratos and a number of his kinsmen were using 20 mules to transport wooden planks from a saw-mill to the road below the village where the wood was loaded on to lorries. The area for the grazing of Sarakatsan mules and horses is an hour's climb above the village and this was very inconvenient for Stratos and the other muleteers. They chanced their luck and grazed their animals at night in the little-frequented village orchards close to their loading-point. On the thirty-ninth night of their operations they were discovered by the agricultural guard who from his examination of the length of the grass and some damage to young apple trees was confident of a very successful case. Stratos was not able to claim that the President was his friend, but since he was a law-abiding careful man his relations with the President had been generally good. He begged for his assistance, explaining the extreme difficulty the group would have suffered if each night

the mules had had to be released so far from the scene of operations. He managed also to mention that he would like to help
the President in the current rebuilding of his house. It so happened that he had two loads of timber which he did not require.
The next day, the President saw the agricultural guard and
warned him that, in his opinion, it would only be reasonable to
take into consideration the one night when he had actually seen
the mules. For the rest, who could say? There had been high
winds recently which often damaged trees, and he added that
he had noticed one of the agricultural guard's own goats straying one evening in the direction of the orchards. Accordingly,
the President received his wood, Stratos and his kinsmen escaped
with a small fine, and the agricultural guard's dream of a
triumphant case came to nothing.

Two points must be stressed about this method of influencing
the President. Gifts must be presented with finesse. A man of
honour is not to be crudely bought by social inferiors if he does
not wish to lose prestige in the community. The shepherd must
give the lamb, butter, or cheese to the President as if it were
merely an expression of friendly respect, and in no way tied to
the favour he is about to request. Secondly, whether in relation
to these gifts of produce, or to other perquisites of his office, the
limited dishonesty and corruptibility of a President is not dishonourable. 'He eats money' (τρώει παράδες), others say with
envy. But they concede that this is the right of his office. His
allowance is not large, he too must live, he also has a family to
support. If a favour, even where it is entirely legal, involves
trouble beyond the ordinary routine duties of his office, why
should he weary himself for a man to whom he is not related in
any way, unless that man by a gift, or in some other way,
demonstrates the esteem in which he holds him.

We have now discussed in the order of their effectiveness
three ways in which the Sarakatsani attempt to influence the
President of their summer village—spiritual kinship, friendship,
and gifts. In principle, spiritual kinship binds a President to
help the shepherd in all situations. Ideally it is a diffuse relation,
there is nothing reasonable that cannot be requested, and the
right to expect this assistance is sanctioned by the ritual link
between godfather and godchild. Friendship of the kind established between a village President and a Sarakatsanos, is a

patron-client relationship of some stability over time, and the
range of favours which may be demanded is almost as extensive
as that between spiritual kinsmen, but the atmosphere of calculation is more pronounced. Confidence which is ritually sanctioned in spiritual kinship is more easily destroyed in the relations of patron and client. Gifts given by a shepherd to the
President generally have a specific object in view and each gift
is effective for only a short period of time if, indeed, it is effective
at all.

The President is not the only man with power or influence in
a village; the other members of the council, the schoolmaster,
the priest, other villagers of wealth or reputation may have
these qualities in varying degree. When the President is particularly severe towards them, the shepherds attempt, by the
same methods we have just considered, to attach themselves to
other persons in the village who are known to have influence
on the council, or personally over the President himself.

When the sheep of Theodoros were despatched by the President to the poorest area of grazing for the second year because
of his active opposition during the elections, Theodoros did not
appeal to the Nomarch against this injustice. He went instead
to Vlachopoulos. Vlachopoulos is the Vice-President of the
village, and the President's closest friend. He also owns the
older of the two village coffee-shops which is the one more
generally patronized by the Sarakatsani both for social gather-
ings and for the many small purchases which they make. After
the bitter feelings aroused by the autumn elections there was a
spontaneous boycott of the Vlachopoulos shop by the Sarakatsani and at the time when Theodoros approached him two or
three weeks after the shepherds had returned to the summer
pasture, only a few Sarakatsan men were to be seen drinking in
the old shop. For a week Theodoros assiduously made small
purchases in the shop. Finding Vlachopoulos alone one day, he
took the next step by remarking that he was not a man to dwell
on old scores and that he thought his return to the shop proved
this point. It seemed, however, that the President was still
governed by his rage and spite. This was surely unjust, and he
asked Vlachopoulos if he would not intercede with the President
on his behalf. Vlachopoulos agreed to do this. It is a fair assumption that he was especially pleased to see Theodoros who leads

a substantial co-operating 'company' and has many other kinsmen in the local group of shepherds. It was very probable that
if Theodoros returned to his shop to drink, as well as to buy,
the boycott would be over. This proved to be the case. Vlachopoulos persuaded the President to rearrange the grazing areas,
and after a week or two of further delay to impress upon
Theodoros the misguided nature of his opposition in the previous autumn, the President eventually effected the necessary
changes.

A Zagori village and the local group of Sarakatsani that is
linked to it through rights of citizenship, form a network of
friendship relations, some of which are symmetrical and others
of the patron-client variety. This network enables a man in
many situations to obtain a measure of satisfaction from a
person with whom he is in direct opposition. He achieves this
by indirect pressure because he is a client, or friend, of the
friend of his enemy. Villagers and shepherds are careful to
maintain friendship links with opposed political factions and
personages whenever this is possible. The implication is that
there are often inherent limits on the way in which the President
or other influential villagers may use their power against most
individuals, since, very probably, in any particular act of
victimization they are attacking the friend, or client, of one of
their own friends. Only very poor villagers, or Sarakatsani with
small flocks who are not attached to the co-operating 'company'
of more powerful kinsmen, may be treated unjustly without en-
countering some responding pressure through the system of
friendships; for these persons, having little to offer in return,
may not have patrons. But in other cases to ignore the pressures
received through the system of friendships may endanger important relationships on which a man's influence and prestige
largely depend. It is not suggested, however, that a man with
strategically aligned friendships is secure from all injustice. On
the contrary, Theodoros suffered a considerable financial loss
until his friendship with Vlachopoulos rescued him from further
punishment.

In the Zagori villages, as in the Sarakatsan community, a
dominant feature of the social system is the isolation of the
family and its struggle against other families, whether in terms
of the possibility of bare subsistence or of social prestige. The

more important social obligations are particular to the individual's family, and these stand in direct conflict with the weaker and more general responsibilities of good neighbourliness. The notion of service to the community (εὐεργεσία) exists, and is honoured. But the service takes a form which honours the individual, his family and the community in equal degree as, for instance, in the foundation of a church or school. Such services are never anonymous. The idea of service to fellow citizens of the same community exists also, but it remains an ideal value which is not realized in a society where familial obligations have an absolute priority. The President and councillors of the village are firstly heads of households and only secondly public servants. A President does not feel under the same moral obligation, even within the sphere of his formal duties, to help equally a close kinsman, a spiritual kinsman, a friend, and a man to whom he is linked only by common citizenship. It is suggested that in this absence, for the most part, of universally applicable values the system of village friendship and patronage in fact achieves a distribution of various facilities which, although it is never equitable, guards most families, even those of the hardpressed Sarakatsani of Zagori, against complete exclusion. The system of friendship and patronage achieves this, not by upholding any general rights of citizenship, but, in a sense paradoxically, by an appeal to the individual and family interests of a person in authority. For without friends a man loses all power, influence, and social prestige.

## 4. LAWYERS AND GOVERNMENT OFFICIALS

The Sarakatsani not only need to come to terms with the village authorities, they must also adapt themselves to the laws and regulations of the State, and attempt in their own interests to influence the administration of Government regulations so far as these affect their own affairs. This involves relations with civil servants at various levels in the hierarchy.

Some State regulations are administered through the structure of village authority which has been examined. In other instances the impact of State administration is direct. In the Zagori, as in other local districts, an agricultural officer of the Ministry of Agriculture has an office in the capital village of the district. Such matters as loans from the Agricultural Bank, permission to burn off grass, appeals against the various restrictions on grazing in forest areas, advice about animal disease, and free distribution of sprays to combat insect pests fall within this official's competence. But in these and other questions a shepherd is often referred to the provincial office at Jannina, or in winter at Igoumenitsa, Arta, and Preveza. The Greek police, a paramilitary organization, have a central station under the command of a captain in the capital village of each local district, but sections of police are also stationed in outlying areas of the district, each section serving three or four villages. It frequently happens that Sarakatsani are late in the payment of their grazing dues. Although these are assessed by the village, they are paid to the public treasury in the provincial centre. When the police are informed by the treasury that a payment has not been made, they must attempt to serve a demand notice. If payment is again withheld, the debtor is taken under escort to the public treasury and, if he is still unable to pay, from there to prison. But the circumstance that these demands for payment must be served on one individual in person, and not merely to his home or a member of his family, results in a perpetual pantomime of hide-and-seek between police and heads of shepherd families. This causes irritation and bad feeling on both sides. It is a common experience to find a man secreted under a blanket in the darker corner of a kinsman's hut when it is known that police are in the village.

Sarakatsani are sometimes involved in difficulties with the military authorities over conscription. A family with only one son, a physically handicapped father, and without sufficient resources to hire a shepherd, may submit a case for the postponement or abbreviation of the son's term of military service before a committee of appeal. This committee, however, is not thought to be very liberal in its decisions.

The Sarakatsani face the jurisdiction of the State in their frequent adventures in courts of law.[5] The laws that concern the Sarakatsani in their daily life do not generally favour them. The interests of shepherds tend to be opposed to those of peasants or townsmen. For instance, there are many civil suits between owners of private properties and Sarakatsani who claim

[5] I am not considering here the many cases of animal trespass which are heard in local agricultural courts.

a disputed right of protected lease for their grazing. And, some-times, shepherds are plaintiffs in cases challenging the decisions of a village administration. The regulations of village life differ from the conventions of semi-nomads. And their adherence to the traditional code of honour necessarily conflicts with the laws of a modern State. They distrust legal procedures because their pleas are frequently unsuccessful and in many instances they regress into acts of violence which two generations ago would have been the general response to the interference of outside authority. Often a certain *naïveté* or simple ignorance about what is legal, and what is not, leads them into trouble. It is rare for a head of family not to be involved in some capa-city in at least one suit each year. In 1955 George Carvounis, who was not exceptional in this respect, acted as a principal in two cases, one civil, one criminal. In the first he was sued for violent assault and defamation of character by a village woman, whom he had rough handled when she attempted to pull down a wall which she alleged had been set up by Carvounis on her land. In the second case he was charged with forgery, having found it innocently convenient to sign a document with the name of another member of his co-operating 'company'.

But the critical point of contact between the Sarakatsanos and the bureaucrat is in the situation where his winter grazing is in danger. Then, the leader of a stani must attempt to in-fluence the highest State officials in the Epirus if he is to face, with confidence, the threat of exclusion from his winter pastures.

Gifts and money bribes are freely offered in making ap-proaches to a minor State servant. Gifts of produce are generally made to the agricultural officer; for, even if he is not a native of the district, he becomes a member of the local village com-munity where he occupies a respectable position in the system of village friendship; moreover, since he has some pretensions to education and culture it might be insulting to offer money. Gifts of produce are also preferred in dealing with a local police sergeant. Not all policemen are venal and it is a serious offence to offer bribes of money to a member of this force. Money bribes are often effective in preventing agricultural and forest guards from reporting the trespasses of animals, if the offence has not been observed by a third party. These guards belong, generally, to poor families of low prestige, and in the Zagori they are often villagers of gipsy origin. Such persons are despised by the Sarakatsani, and they themselves are generally prepared to accept money bribes without the least embarrassment.

To conduct business with minor public servants in the administrative offices at Jannina, Sarakatsani use small bribes. Often at the doorways of these buildings there is a desk staffed by two or three ushers. These men examine with a brusque lack of sympathy the forms which the shepherd has in his hand, or they demand to know his business, if only to ignore his explanation. He may wish to see a particular official to whom he has been recommended. He believes that a gratuity of five to ten shillings is essential if he is to find the right man. If he wishes to submit an application form in the general office of the same building, he hands it over the counter to the clerk with the equivalent of a ten shilling note on the underside. The shepherd hopes that this will at least ensure that the form is filed; and perhaps nearer the top than the bottom of the pile. Here, the relationship between the shepherd and the junior official is temporary and anonymous. The reputation of the man of higher status, in the eyes of the man in the lower position, is not at stake. The bribe is small, not necessarily effective, and it is not discussed. It is passed secretly. And this saves each clerk from losing the esteem of his colleagues who are themselves engaged in the same practice.

But in affairs of great importance, which must reach the desk of senior officials, the shepherd leader generally feels unable to conduct his own affairs. It is difficult, in any case, for a humble shepherd to penetrate to the offices of senior officials. If he does reach this point, his rough clothes and awkward manners, alternating between obsequiousness and effrontery, make progress difficult. Sarakatsani say, with good reason, that in offices nobody pays the least attention to a man without a collar and tie. And they have little confidence in their own forensic abilities in this kind of situation. As one Sarakatsanos said of himself and his people, 'Shepherds hesitate. If I can make five points in a conversation, he (the official) can return twenty.'

Moreover, even the director of an office does not conduct business privately. His secretary and aides have desks in the same room. By the public transaction of affairs, and the display

of his power, he emphasizes his status before the eyes of his
subordinates and stresses their dependence on himself. To listen
patiently to the incoherent ramblings of a Sarakatsanos, the
name of whose very profession, shepherd (βλάχος), is a synonym
for stupidity, much less to take trouble and thought over assisting him, would be to lose prestige and betray the status of his
position, the validation of which lies in pride, not humility.
Generally such officials are curt, rude, and unhelpful, or to in-
dulge their attendants, use the shepherd for a show of witty
mockery. Direct bribery is out of the question in the absence of
secrecy, and it is also dangerous, since the corruptibility of
officials grows less certain as the hierarchy is ascended.

Where he cannot reach or influence a high State official, the
shepherd turns to his patron or, if he is a man without influence,
to the patron of a more powerful kinsman. The patron may be
a man of any profession with political influence in Jannina, a
doctor, engineer, or merchant; but most frequently he is a
lawyer. The lawyer in Greek rural society is not only the man
who gives legal advice and attends a client in court, but he
also acts as an intermediary between the peasant or shepherd
and the State authorities. He acts in the general role of a professional 'fixer'.

Some of the difficulties which arise between the State and the
Sarakatsan community have their origin in the necessarily
general character of government legislation. Perhaps it is decided to protect the nation's forests. A law is passed which
forbids the grazing of goats in forested areas. Incorporated within the general law are a number of conditional clauses relating
to the definition of various kinds of forest, the priority for their
protection, and the question of hardship to pastoralists which
may lead to a relaxation of the restrictions in certain circumstances and in certain categories of forest. But the law-making
assembly cannot legislate for all possible local contingencies.
The administration and interpretation of the law lie in the
hands of the public servants.

However, within the public service there exists a certain
inertia and reluctance to delegate power. A senior official defines the unequivocal superiority of his status in the hierarchy
by forcing his junior officers to refer to himself every case which
involves the initiative of judgement and decision. In this manner

he attaches junior officials to his own will since they cannot move without his approval, and he enhances his prestige because he is seen to be indispensable. At the same time, he secures his power and nourishes his self-regard. But the convergence of so many cases awaiting decision upon a limited number of senior officials in Jannina and Athens who cannot personally know the detailed circumstances of a case except through the exiguous details set out on printed forms, creates interminable delays and inhibits the equitable administration of government laws and regulations. In the Epirus, where many villagers and shepherds live on the margin of bare subsistence, these limitations of administration might prove disastrous for many families, were they not able to put their affairs into the hands of a lawyer or some other patron. For if, in the example we have chosen, a man cannot graze his goats in the one area where he has the right to do this, he must sell the animals which provide him with his living. The lawyer is able to bring a case to the direct notice of a senior official, to frame it to the best advantage; and sometimes, if he has considerable influence, to gain concessions for his client which are not strictly within the relevant law's terms of reference.

The significance of the lawyer's position is his ability to face in two directions. Because of the prestige and status of a successful lawyer in Greek society he may be able in a provincial town to number amongst his friends, judges, army officers, doctors, the Nomarch, and other senior officials of the Government bureaucracy. With these men he sits and drinks at the tables of the town's more fashionable coffee-shops and in the lounge of the best hotel. As a member of this professional *élite* he is able to recommend the affairs of his clients to the attention of various friends who may be able to help. They give this help because of their friendship for the lawyer; they are relatively indifferent to the worth of the client and the justice of his case. In return, a lawyer is able during local and national elections to promise the political support of his clients. He also assists his friends by legal advice in their own affairs and in the affairs of their kinsmen many of whom, often, are themselves villagers.

The Sarakatsani because of their many political difficulties and disabilities are critical assessors of the personal abilities of different lawyers. The profession is over-crowded and there is a wide range of choice. It is essential for the Sarakatsanos that his lawyer has influential affiliations with the leading political parties. It is not fortuitous that the Jannina lawyer with the largest Sarakatsan following in 1955 happened to be the secretary of the Epirus branch of the Government party. But the secretary to the Liberal party also has many clients. Although he supports an opposition party, Government servants do not lightly refuse his requests for they are anxious to avoid questions and 'revelations' in Parliament, and to secure some form of reinsurance against the day when the Government changes.

In general, it is to the advantage of both the lawyer and the Sarakatsan family head to make their association a personal relationship with diffuse mutual obligations. The lawyer becomes obliged to act as a general protector of the shepherd in all his affairs, the shepherd as a good client must show esteem and respect and give his patron the political support on which his power depends. It is not unusual for lawyers to become the godparents of their clients' children. Clients, whether or not they possess ties of spiritual kinship, cultivate the goodwill of their lawyer by periodic gifts of cheese and butter, and sometimes at Easter a lamb is presented. The nearer the relation between a Sarakatsanos and his lawyer approaches that of a patron and client friendship the more nominal the professional charges of the lawyer for legal services become. But in the nature of things it is easier for the leader of a substantial co-operating 'company' to establish an enduring friendship with his lawyer and to persuade him to win important concessions. He has more followers and more votes to offer. The lawyer does not lose prestige by attending to the affairs of simple men. This is his professional duty, and the more clients who throng his office and call out greetings to him as he walks along the street, the more political power he has, the more friends amongst the body of the provincial *élite*, and the more social prestige.

It would be tedious to present in detail examples of the many successful interventions by lawyer patrons. An over-zealous policeman in one village who made a speciality of arresting Sarakatsani for alleged disturbances of the peace was removed by the influence of a lawyer patron to a post in Mitylene. Another instance is the abbreviation of the military service of Christos Balatsos, an only son, whose family was handicapped by poverty and a father disabled by pleurisy. In this case the lawyer was a friend of the chairman of the appeal committee.

In the many court cases in which Sarakatsani figure the lawyers play a more strictly professional role. But there may still be scope on occasion for informal action, especially in civil suits which are heard before the bench without a jury. In a case concerning a disputed right of protected lease which threatened a Sarakatsanos with the loss of his winter pasture, the man in desperation asked his lawyer to approach the judge with a gift of £25. The lawyer took the money and the case was won. Without exception, villagers and shepherds assumed that at least half this money found its way into the judge's pocket. Villagers and shepherds have a simple faith that anybody, if he is approached in the right way and with the right sum, may be bought. In fact, there is no evidence that judges may be bribed. It may happen rarely. It probably happens more often that a lawyer friend is able to mention in conversation to a judge some aspect of a case which comes before him. And it certainly happens frequently that Sarakatsani put money into the hands of their lawyers which they believe will be used to bribe a judge or a senior government official, but which remains, in fact, in the lawyer's pocket.

Yet there is no doubt about the genuine assistance the lawyer gives to the shepherd in his critical fight to retain his rights of winter grazing. For instance, in the example already mentioned in chapter four, a considerable 'company' of families that winter their sheep in Thesprotia were able to counter the refusal of the villagers to rent them grazing land by presenting their case, through the influence of two powerful lawyer patrons, directly to the Governor-General of the Epirus. The lawyers pleaded that humanly and politically it was impossible to allow eighty men, women, and children, and two thousand sheep, to walk the roads. As individuals moving in the same social *élite*, they were able to present an argument immediately suggesting that the Governor-General's reputation for honour, and his political interests, were in danger.

The Member of Parliament for a provincial district plays in Athens a role very similar to that of the lawyer in the provincial centre. More members of the Greek Parliament belong to the legal profession than to any other. It is partly by possessing many clients, and many friends with clients, that a man is successful in national elections.

Since decisions of importance are rarely made by junior officials it frequently happens that a man must take action in Athens if he is to find a favourable solution to his problems. The friend or client of a Member may ask him to use his influence in the office of the Ministry which is handling his case. When the Member visits his constituency his political friends and clients of all social standings come to wait on him in his office, or to drink with him in the coffee-shops. On these occasions he carries a notebook in which he writes down the details of the favours he is asked to arrange.

We see that the Sarakatsanos in facing the hierarchy of Government confronts persons of higher social status who share with him no bond of kinship or community. As a rule only nationality and common humanity link them together. In Greek society this is not an adequate basis for the acceptance of social obligations other than the common duty to defend the nation against its external enemies. The indifference or hostility of very junior officials may be bought off. It is a simple *ad hoc* commercial transaction between persons almost entirely isolated from one another in terms of social relations or morality. But the indifference of senior officials cannot be directly countered with bribes, nor is it easy because of the social distance which separates them for a shepherd to approach successfully a senior official. These circumstances are also related to the public arrangement of business by senior Government servants and the need to assert their status and maintain their prestige before their colleagues and immediate subordinates.

The system of lawyer patronage, which is an extension of the more strictly legal practice of the lawyer, makes it possible for the affairs of villagers and shepherds to receive attention at that level of the administrative hierarchy where decision and execution are possible. A shepherd and a senior official are not directly linked to each other by social obligation or morality. A Government servant sees no reason why he should assist some illiterate shepherd and many reasons why he should not, such as loss of prestige before his professional colleagues. But the lawyer, as the intermediary who stands between them, is related by obligations of patronage to the first, and the duties of friendship to the second. In this manner the shepherd, because he is useful and necessary to his patron through the power and prestige which his political allegiance and social attentions confer on him, is never entirely powerless to resist those administrative actions of Government which threaten his way of life. The system of patronage introduces a flexibility into administrative machinery whose workings are very often directed by persons remote from the people whose fortunes they are affecting.

## 5. MERCHANTS

A further system of relationships, which cross the boundaries of the community and relate it to the world outside, results from the shepherds' need to market the produce of their flocks.

They must sell this produce to provide the money required for the flour used in their bread, for the payment of their grazing dues, and for the growing list of luxuries which since 1938 through close observation of village life they have discovered to be essential to a family's self-esteem. These luxuries are for the most part articles of manufactured clothing, cotton summer dresses for the girls at school, European as against traditional shoes for men and women, tailored shirts for the men. Ten years ago the homespun cloth for men's jackets was cut by the women; it is now sent to a professional tailor. Pieces of cheap earthenware crockery and glassware begin to replace the heavy pewter plates and drinking mugs. There is increasing pressure to conform to village standards in these matters and each year more money is spent on the clothes and other things that have become prestige symbols. Each year, as the available winter grazing tends to decrease in area, its cost rises. While twenty years ago the whole community ate the yellow maize bread, today almost all the families make their bread from a more expensive brown flour which is largely wheaten in content. Only a few very poor families continue to eat yellow bread, and for this economy they suffer much ridicule. On all counts, the minimum money income required by a family to live in a style that will secure its prestige has greatly increased.

In the memory of living people the community has always exchanged some of its produce for money, and like many other pastoral and agricultural communities elsewhere it has always lived on credit for part of the year, paying off the greater part of its debt in the early summer when it has reaped the harvest of milk, meat, and wool. The last twenty years, and especially the years since the war, have seen a new situation in which the shepherds have sold an increasing proportion of their annual produce, have themselves spent more money (not solely on the needs of physical subsistence), and have become, generally speaking, deeply and permanently indebted to merchants.

Only three of the 42 Sarakatsan households at Neochori have assets, which suggest that each summer they are virtually clear of debt. Speaking very generally, for these details are hard to collect and even harder to check, the average weight of debt carried by each elementary family is about £100. Only when a family of man, wife, and small children, has at least 200 sheep is there generally the possibility of it being relatively free of debt. But it is impossible to express the matter in a simple numerical statement, much depends on the price a family is forced to pay for its winter grazing. This may vary between such wide limits as half a crown and ten shillings per head of stock.

The need of the many semi-nomad pastoralists in the Epirus, not only Sarakatsani, to find a market for their produce is the merchant's opportunity. The most valuable of these products is the milk of the ewes. The constituent families of co-operating 'companies' of shepherds are generally so deeply in debt that they are discouraged from the further heavy borrowings which would be necessary for the rent or purchase of equipment to turn their own milk into marketable cheese. And since there are no large urban populations in the Epirus, the large quantities of butter, cheese, and meat must find their principal outlet in the Athenian market; but for the distribution of their products in the metropolitan area the shepherds have neither the facilities nor the knowledge.

The ewe gives substantial quantities of milk for six or seven months in the year, between the time when it drops its lamb in January and the establishment of its pregnancy once more in July or August. The spring milk is sold in the winter pastures between 1st of February and the 20th of May. After the ten-day migration to the summer pastures the milk is again sold in the Zagori between the 1st of June and a date within a few days of the end of July. The milk which is taken during the move into the mountains, before the 1st of February, and after the last week in July, is made into a rough cheese and stored for the use of the family.

In each area where a merchant collects milk he establishes a cheese-maker (μπάτζος) with an assistant. These men are paid and fed by the merchant, who also provides the necessary equipment, the cream separator, cauldrons, cheese boards, and rings. The shepherds who bring their milk to the cheese-making hut (μπατζαρειό) are responsible for its construction and for supplying it with water and firewood. It is not economical for a cheese-making station to serve less than 1,000 ewes, and the upper limit beyond which the quantities of milk become too great for a single cheese-maker to handle may be set at about 2,500 sheep. The spring milk is three times greater in quantity than the summer milk[6] and the more important merchants concentrate their main activities and have their headquarters in the winter pastures, but they also buy some summer milk in the various districts of the Pindus mountains of which the Zagori is one.

Before 1945 the cheese merchants in winter or summer were small *entrepreneurs* seldom controlling more than two or three cheese-making stations. Between 1944 and 1949 currency inflation and Communist insurrections ruined many of these men. Only the stronger and abler merchants survived. The financially strong merchant was able to steal the custom of his weaker competitors by offering more substantial credits at a time when the shepherds needed a larger cash income than formerly, but were also slipping farther into debt. Today in the winter pastures there are a number of merchants with five or six stations but few with less. The situation in the winter pastures, especially in Thesprotia, is dominated by the merchant 'X' who controls 45 stations drawing on the milk production of 50,000 ewes. He also has a wholesale agency in Athens through which his butter and cheese have a secure market outlet to the metropolitan consumer.

The establishment of a cheese station requires, in the first

[6] Winter milk production varies considerably. One stani produced 38 okes per ewe in 1945 and as little as 13½ okes per ewe in 1954. Generally for the period 1950–5, milk production in winter has varied between 20 and 24 okes per ewe. Summer production is more stable at 7 to 9 per ewe. An oke of milk is equivalent to 2·35 pints.

place, a capital outlay of some £85 for the equipment, of which the most expensive item is the cream separator. Working capital for a spring station includes the wages of the cheese-maker and his assistant at 12s. 6d. and 6s. 3d. a day respectively, the cost of their food, and large quantities of salt for treating the cheeses. Altogether it amounts to about £125. The normal advances on the milk represent between one-third and one-half of its value and involve the issuing of credits for some £500. Working capital and the money for these credits is borrowed by the merchant from banks and private individuals. The bigger merchants store a substantial part of the cheese and butter which they make in the spring and summer and bring it forward on the metropolitan market in the later months of the year when milk products are scarcer and their prices higher. The money which is borrowed to give the August milk advances to the shepherds is secured against the cheeses in store. But the rate of interest on all these loans is unlikely to be much less than 10 per cent. In general, a merchant expects to make a gross profit of about 3d.–4½d. on every 'oke' of milk which he handles. Since the pastoralist receives about 1s. 1½d. for every 'oke' of milk which he sells, it cannot be said that he suffers from an outrageous exploitation. This is not the result of the merchant's benevolence. He is caught between two limits, the highest price which consumers in distant places can be persuaded to pay for milk products and the marginal price to shepherds which will just make it possible for them to live and maintain their flocks. For if the flocks vanish, so will the cheese merchants. The margin between these two limits is not wide. The prosperity of the individual merchant depends on his cornering a very substantial supply of milk and aiding the shepherds who sell it to him to maintain that level of production or even increase it. By the extension of interest-free credits, which in fact are seldom entirely repaid, he binds the interests of the shepherd to his own and assists him to maintain his way of life in the face of increasing difficulties. But the extension of credit also enables the Sarakatsanos to assume a style of life which goes beyond the absolute needs of subsistence. The Sarakatsanos has achieved this at the expense of the merchant but also at the cost of binding himself even more firmly to the merchant's will. That it pays a merchant of the stature of 'X' cannot be doubted. By sustaining a burden of debt and advance payments of perhaps £20,000 he makes an annual net profit on the spring milk alone of about £8,000.

The Sarakatsan financial year (see Appendix III) begins and ends in August, when the shepherd takes the advance for his winter milk, which represents between one-third and one-half of the value of the estimated winter yield of milk. A man with 200 ewes would receive about £100. With some of this money he is able to complete his payments for summer grazing. This he is normally bound to do before the police will allow him to move his sheep towards the plains in the autumn. He hopes to leave the Zagori village in October with perhaps one-third of this advance still in his pocket to tide his family over their general living expenses in the early winter months. During the winter months there is a constant struggle between the shepherd and the merchant for further loans. The original advance is generally almost exhausted by Christmas, especially if cotton-cake has been bought to supplement the diet of the pregnant ewes. The merchant tries to stave off further requests for additional advances since he does not want to carry an unnecessary weight of debt beyond the amount that is necessary to hold the shepherd as a client. He keeps the shepherd physically alive by granting him credit in the form of flour. In this way he checks luxury spending by the shepherd at his expense and makes, on paper at least, a small profit for himself by selling on credit flour of questionable quality at a slightly inflated price. The shepherd and his family exist as best they can, running up small debts with the shopkeepers in the winter villages and towns who themselves compete for his trade by offering credit which they hope will make him a permanent customer. Eventually some crisis occurs. He must have money to engage a lawyer in a court case, or money to pay a doctor or to bribe an official. He goes to the cheese merchant and explains the situation. The latter, if he is astute, knows the critical moment when he must slacken the reins; a further *ad hoc* advance is given.

Some weeks before Easter the financial outlook may improve. There may be fifty or more male lambs to sell at about thirty shillings each. Later, after Easter, the sheep are shorn and, if there are no daughters for whose dowry blankets and cloth must be woven, some wool will be sold. A shepherd tries to keep these transactions secret from his cheese merchant but generally with only partial success. In April the shepherds hurry to meet the summer cheese merchants, conclude their agreements, and take an advance on their summer milk which for 200 ewes will be about £30. But this spate of spring revenue is often quickly dissipated in paying the heavy costs of winter pasturage, possibly of more legal wrangles, and sometimes of an Easter wedding. The celebration of Easter also brings its expenses. New shirts and shoes are bought for the family, cloth is sent to the tailors to be made up into new jackets and trousers. For if the family attends the Easter church service in old clothes it loses prestige. Also it is believed that at the service on Easter Saturday night each person ought to wear something that is new, to honour the resurrection of Christ.

About the middle of May the heads of shepherd families visit the merchant to agree with him the statement of their accounts. Money advances and the value of the flour issued are balanced against the value of the milk delivered to the cheese-making station. In an average year the result is generally a small profit or loss for the shepherd of perhaps £10 which is added to, or subtracted from, the total debt owed to the merchant. But in bad years when the grass has been poor, or many ewes have not produced lambs, the loss may be more substantial and this the merchant must bear if he does not want to force his client into selling his stock. If the shepherd is in difficulties, he may seek a further loan before leaving the plains. When the merchant grants this favour, the shepherd must accept a slightly lower price for his milk in the coming winter, about a farthing an 'oke' less than whatever proves to be the ruling rate for the next season.

When the shepherd arrives in his summer village in Zagori, he will generally have some money in his pocket. He immediately pays off the greater part but not all of the debt which in most cases he left behind in the village shop the previous autumn. This may amount to £20–£30 in some instances. Having paid off part of this debt he is in a better position to ask for credit later in the summer when he may again become short of cash. In the same way he will pay off some of his debts to winter shopkeepers when he first reaches the plains in the autumn.

At the end of July the shepherd takes the balance of his

summer milk money, if he has not already been granted a second advance. It is not usual for summer cheese merchants to carry the debts of the shepherds who sell milk to them beyond some very small amount such as £10.

In August the shepherd's financial cycle ends and begins again with the taking of the first advance on the winter milk. Here we must mention the loans which are available to the shepherd from the Agricultural Bank. Each pastoralist is entitled to a loan renewable every six months. Up to fifteen shillings for each milking ewe may be advanced at a rate of 6 per cent per annum. But it is a regulation that between the period 1st of July to the 1st of October the loan must be repaid in full with interest, for a period of twenty days. The shepherd therefore repays this loan with the money of his August milk advance. For the statutory period the principal remains in the bank, after which the shepherd takes it out again.

On all counts it is evident that the activities of the winter cheese merchant support the structure of credit on which the shepherd lives. The many advances which he gives to the shepherd make possible a continuous state of indebtedness to the bank and to the shops. Clearly an important element in the relationship between the cheese merchant and the shepherd is the overwhelming economic power of the merchant and the corresponding weakness of the shepherd. The ultimate sanction is the threat to claim repayment of the debt by taking the shepherd to law and obtaining a court order for the distraint of his sheep. In theory, it is always open to a shepherd to leave a merchant with whom he has quarrelled by selling his milk to another merchant who will then lend him the money to cancel his debt with his creditor. By the repayment of his debt he severs the relationship and escapes from his bondage. But in practice this is not often possible. In the first place, unless he can carry with him a number of other shepherds so that he is able to offer the milk of at least 1,000 ewes, he will not induce another cheese merchant to open a station in an area where he is not already established. Secondly, if he is attempting to leave a powerful merchant, his debt may be of the order of £100 or more, and a smaller merchant is unlikely to be able to sustain long-term loans on this scale. The whole technique of a merchant such as 'X' is to draw the shepherd into an amount of debt from which it will be virtually impossible for him to escape.

Powerful cheese merchants have political as well as economic power. A shepherd who quarrels with 'X' is likely to meet with trouble in his dealings with Government authorities. Smaller merchants are also afraid of 'X'. It is said that some years ago a cheese station which was established by another merchant in an area lying within 'X''s sphere of influence was mysteriously burned down in the night and that the police showed no interest in making any investigations. In 1951, in a village of Thesprotia, another merchant by offering a slightly higher price succeeded in claiming the custom of three stanis which in the previous year had sold their milk to 'X', who already had a station in the neighbourhood. The latter showed no immediate hostility to his competitor. Indeed, the next winter he suggested that they should co-operate to manage one station since this would make for economies on both sides. The other man agreed and 'X' undertook to find a cheese-maker. It is claimed that this man, on 'X''s instructions, systematically allowed the cheeses to deteriorate by not treating them with sufficient salt. For 'X' the total destruction of these cheeses was an insignificant loss; for the smaller merchant it was a disaster. Whether or not these allegations are true, the important fact is that he is believed to be ready and able to deal with difficult shepherds and competing merchants in this uncompromising fashion.

In the hope of introducing some measure of restraint into the merchant's exercise of economic power over himself, and of diverting its use from his exploitation to his own protection, the shepherd tries to draw the merchant into a relationship of patronage. In most instances, however, the latter is only willing to adopt this role in a restricted sense. When clients come to consult a merchant in his office the social atmosphere is one of cordiality and equality. Glasses of 'ouzo' are not long in appearing. When differences arise in the discussion of business there are appeals to 'friendship' from both sides, and statements such as 'You cannot believe that I should wish to deceive you', are frequently made. But these attitudes may be the fiction rather than the reality of patronage. For patronage assumes a measure of protective concern over all the client's affairs. In most cases a merchant prefers to restrict his role of protector to certain specific contexts, that is to saving a shepherd from eviction from his pastures and from the need to sell his stock because of his indebtedness to others. If a merchant has a firm hold over a man through the nexus of debt he does not want to assume unnecessary obligations which may limit the range and flexibility of his economic operations. Cheese merchants who are sometimes forced unwillingly into becoming godfathers to Sarakatsan children do not always make very satisfactory spiritual kinsmen. On the other hand, in certain cases where an influential Sarakatsan family is clear, or nearly clear, of debt a merchant may be very willing to enter into the diffuse obligations of friendship if this will enable him to hold it to his custom. There is a difference between the relationships which a shepherd establishes with his lawyer and his cheese merchant. The lawyer gives advice and support to a client over the whole range of his affairs; the more complete his patronage, the more obligated the client and the greater the lawyer's power over him. The merchant's interests in the shepherd are more specifically economic; his economic success depends upon a certain flexibility in his commitments so that, for example, he may wish to make smaller advances and grant fewer long-term credits when interest rates are abnormally high. This seems to be an example of a general difference between political and economic power; the former has a particularist and affective quality, the latter is characterized by its relative generality and impersonality.

But the relation of merchant and shepherd can never be merely specific to the act of purchase or without some affective content as in simple market exchanges. The merchant carries a dead weight of debt; this he can only recover by a legal action which would deprive the shepherd of the animals on which depend the family's physical subsistence and its social prestige. Both sides realize that the existence of the debt, whatever may have been the motives which encouraged it, has meant the possibility of the family continuing to live honourably in their traditional way of life. By the mere fact of having done a good thing, even if without that purpose, the merchant is morally obliged not to undo it. It is a remarkable fact that since 1945 the merchant 'X' appears to have called in only one debt by recourse to the law.

The Sarakatsanos does not deny the obligation to his merchant. Two heads of family went so far as to say that they would feel ashamed to leave, without just cause, a merchant who had supported them not only with credits but also, sometimes, with his political influence. But their feelings of obligation are ambivalent. In other contexts hostility is expressed. It is alleged that the merchant shamelessly exploits the shepherd and that all his actions are moved by entirely selfish motives. 'He, too, has a burn on his bottom' (ἔχει καὶ αὐτὸς τὸ κωλοκάψιμό του), that is, he, too, has his own troubles and interests.

Through the cheese merchant the Sarakatsanos is able to dispose of the most valuable part of the produce of his flock and to obtain the money he needs to pay for the pasturage of his animals and the needs of his family which are related to prestige as well as to bare subsistence. The system of credits provides the shepherd with the means to survive years when natural or political difficulties would otherwise force him to sell part of the flock to meet his commitments. It has also made it possible for the shepherds in recent years to raise slightly their material standard of living.

The growth of debts has brought a certain stability and particularism to relations between merchants and shepherds. Debt provides a basis for a permanent balance of expectations between the two parties despite the asymmetrical character of the relationship. The merchant is assured of the supply of milk which is essential for his prosperity, the shepherd is relatively assured of credit and political support when his grazing rights are threatened. The powerful merchant's ability to support a wide system of credit brings him prestige and the right to move amongst the provincial *élite*; the credit which he gives to the shepherd provides the necessary material basis of the latter's social prestige in his own community. Debts maintain these relationships. They produce in creditors some sense of obligation coupled with a determination not to allow the relationship to become an affective and diffuse bond of patronage, in debtors a mixed attitude of gratefulness for the support and protection they receive and enmity because they cannot escape.

## 6. CONCLUSION

It is evident that the form and function of patronage connexions are immediately related to the moral solidarity and isolation of the family, and to the reciprocal hostility and distrust that exist between families unrelated by kinship or marriage. In general, there are few circumstances where his own wishes, or public opinion, allow a Sarakatsanos to honour an obligation outside the family at the expense of an obligation within it. Moreover, with the assistance of some kinsmen or affines the economy of each family is generally self-sufficient, and working co-operation between unrelated men is seldom necessary or, indeed, practicable. Families, within the community, compete for social prestige in terms of values which underline the particularist obligations to the family honour. A man's work, affections, and moral obligations are almost exclusively contained within the one small group. The commitment of energy, physical resources, or deep affection to an unrelated person is a kind of betrayal. For these reasons men do not associate, even within the community, on the basis of any universal principle of fair dealing. Nepotism is an obligation not a moral fault; and honour is opposed to the canon of honesty.

Inhibitions against self-seeking conduct are yet more tenuous in the relations of men who do not share the common bonds of community. The Sarakatsanos expects to be exploited by the merchant and ignored by the government official. The bureaucrat or merchant not only stands outside the local community, he is divided from the villager or shepherd by his status as a member of the urban middle class. The shepherd is aware of the ill-concealed contempt of the 'civilized man' (ὁ πολιτισμένος) for country people and their ways; he knows of the official's meagre and insufficient salary, and something of his competitive struggle to win prestige symbols (houses, clothes, cars, radios) which validate the nuances of family status within this urban middle class. He does not believe in the existence of any ethic of professional bureaucratic service to the community. 'They are all "eaters"' (φαγάδες), he says in sweeping condemnation. It is thought that few officials will exert themselves over the affairs of a man of lower social status unless he is offered some inducement. And generally it is believed that concessions and facilities are seldom to be won on a broad front for the whole community but only as exceptional dispensations to favoured families. In these circumstances men consider it useless to conduct their business with the State on the grounds of their general rights as citizens.

As I have already said, from his side a Government official sees no reason why he should assist some illiterate shepherd or villager and many reasons why he should not, such as loss of prestige before his professional colleagues. Like the villager or shepherd he has the same primary and categorical obligation towards his own family and its status. He also owes a loyalty to his service and his colleagues; but this is shown by marking the distance between those who rule and those who are ruled, by the display of arrogance, not service.

There are other, less personal, reasons for the distrust between the bureaucrat and the villager or shepherd. One half of Greece is a society of small village communities dependent on agriculture or pastoralism. To administer and physically control these many discrete communities, and the small towns which serve them, the central Government in Athens has erected a complex and costly bureaucratic organization which links, in the formal sense, the simple village community to the central body which governs and legislates for the nation. This is not a structure which has developed even in part from the villages themselves; it is an organization which has been imposed from above by the Government. Moreover, Greece is not, by European standards, a rich country. For the greater part of her national history taxation has been almost wholly absorbed in paying for the luxury of maintaining the panoply of a modern state with its full quota of Ministries and portfolios and in supporting substantial armed forces. Under these conditions, the State (τὸ κράτος) and its agencies must always appear to the villager or shepherd as a body from which he is excluded, something threatening and hostile, which takes away from the family and returns nothing. It stands, therefore, in opposition to the nation (τὸ ἔθνος), the community of Hellenism for which every Greek feels a deep and natural devotion.

Each family in a village, or in a shepherd community, therefore attempts to establish an exclusive and particular relationship with persons in power. As we have seen, decision or initiative is seldom possible at the lower levels of the Government service because of the reluctance of an official to delegate power. To reach that level at which his affairs can be effectively dealt with, he tries to discover a patron, generally a lawyer, who in return for a man's political allegiance, places his case before a friend in the right place. The lawyer, or other patron, bridges the gulf of hostility and indifference created by the absence of relationship and the difference in status. And he introduces some flexibility into the rigid and uncomprehending administration of village life by a centralized bureaucracy.

In effect, patronage converts impersonal and ephemeral connexions into permanent and personal relationships; for in Greek society it is, generally, only in established personal relationships, of which the archetypal forms are found in the family, that any considerable element of moral obligation exists. The initial motive is utilitarian, protection and assistance on the side of the client, political power and social prestige on the part of the patron. But when such a relationship endures for any length of time it takes on a strong moral quality. The patron feels obliged to assist and take a general interest in all the client's affairs, and in doing so he is able both to sense his superiority and approve his own compassionate generosity. The client is conscious of a duty to support his patron politically without undue concern about his protector's party allegiance, and to give free expression to his feelings of gratitude and indebtedness.

The role of patron is to give benefits; that of the client is to honour the patron by accepting dependence. In a society where the concept of honour is intimately connected with notions of individual strength and prepotence, to abdicate one's independence, even to a person of power who is not a member of the community, is an act of renunciation of some significance. The patron in accepting the dependence of his client, who thus admits, implicitly, the inferiority of his status, himself recognizes moral obligations towards the client. The dependence of the client draws attention to the power of his patron, while the protection of the patron suggests that the client is a man of some standing and respectability in his own community. The first consideration protects the patron from the accusation of weakness or foolishness which he would otherwise face if he casually assisted a man of lower status with whom he had no particular relations of kinship, friendship, or patronage: the second represents for the client honourable grounds for the admission of an inferior status which in other circumstances would betray the honour of his community and his own manliness. The social reputations of the two men are now linked. If a patron cannot effectively protect his clients his prestige is diminished; and in his own community the client, too, suffers for the incapacity of his patron, since the potential of his strength from this source is seen to be less than was supposed. But when the protection is effective, both patron and client gain prestige from the relationship. The colleagues of the patron envy him the power which his control of a body of clients assures for him, other families in the client's community envy him his cleverness in winning powerful patrons. But the Sarakatsan client will not share with others the vicarious influence which patronage brings him, unless they are kinsmen or affines. For he believes that if he shares his advantage, he loses it. And this is a further reason why relationships across the boundaries of the community with persons of influence are exclusive and particular connexions established by the individual family.

We see that while the organization of administration stretches down, as it were, from the central Government towards the village community but loses power and the ability to take decisions the farther it extends from its point of origin, the structure of the system of patronage, which is based on social relationships between clients seeking for a man with the ability and friendship connexions to protect them and a patron who accepts these duties in return for political allegiance, grows upwards and through lawyers, other persons of influence, and Members of Parliament, is linked to the legislative assembly. Thus the organization of government and the structure of patronage are parallel hierarchies. At any particular level the two hierarchies are related through ties of friendship. The shepherd or villager is excluded from the Government hierarchy, but through the structure of patronage he may be able vicariously to submit his case before a senior official in the public service.

Patronage is the means through which the local community is linked to the wider national society. And it is significant that the group which seeks this connexion is the individual family and not the community. This is clearly the case amongst the Sarakatsani, but even villagers do not co-operate in seeking Government favour except where the interests of the whole village as such are attacked. If the President of a village is able to help a village friend by his influence in the town, he does so in the role of friend or patron, not as President and leader of the village. And in personal affairs a villager or shepherd may often go directly to his patron[7] in the town. The importance of this is that the community is integrated piecemeal with the wider society along lines of personal obligation and not through membership of a large corporate group capable of attempting an infinitely stronger resistance to the authority of the State.

More generally, patronage links persons of different social status introducing into their social relations a common area of shared values which would otherwise not exist. In the context of the Zagori village it links the shepherds to the more important villagers, enabling the former to come to terms with the villagers' hostile attitude and the latter to mobilize the voting power of the shepherds in their own support. Since different shepherd families support different village personalities, it ensures that the latter continue to hold office and power even in villages where shepherds considerably outnumber villagers on the electoral roll.

Similarly, the patron-client relation between the lawyer and the villager or shepherd relates members of local village and shepherd communities to the professional classes in the small towns and larger provincial centres. It gives political power and prestige to the patron. It brings prestige to the client also but above all it means that he is never entirely helpless in the face of the impersonal indifference of Government action which threatens the precarious balance of his economy. Patronage relations produce a certain equity in the distribution of facilities and privileges and place some check on the victimizing of individuals. It achieves this by relating the universal franchise to the personal, social, and political aspirations of individuals competing for power and honour; or to put it more briefly, by relating natural rights to personal prestige.

Finally, the bond of debt and the qualified patronage of the merchant and the town shopkeeper brings the shepherd into a permanent association with some of the leaders of town

[7] In the case of a villager the 'protector' is very often a kinsman. See Ernestine Friedl, 'The Role of Kinship in the Transmission of National Culture to Rural Villages in Mainland Greece', *American Anthropologist*, 1959, vol. lxi, pp. 30–38.

commerce. It provides the merchant with an assured source for his raw material and the shopkeeper with a stable clientele. It gives the shepherd vicarious access to the metropolitan market and to the credit facilities of the national banking system. Without these facilities it is fair to say that he could not continue to lead his traditional way of life.

# X

## THE VALUES OF PRESTIGE[1]

### 1. THE HIERARCHY

A CONSIDERATION of the bilateral kindred and the marriage prohibitions associated with it has shown that the only relatively enduring kin group in the Sarakatsan system of kinship and marriage is the elementary family. I have placed considerable emphasis on the concentration of most of the individual's significant obligations within this group; and these normally take precedence over any other moral commitments. It is a feature of evident importance that the community is fragmented into about six hundred of these exclusive corporate family groups.

Within the community these families are jurally autonomous. It is true that they must often co-operate with kinsmen or affines in the management of their sheep. And in particular though rare circumstances when the honour of the community is in question, men who are unrelated may stand together against villagers and others. Nevertheless, in none of these situations is the sovereignty of the family compromised. Moreover, unrelated families see their different interests as being in fundamental and inevitable opposition. We have already examined various attitudes and institutions through which this mutual hostility is expressed, for instance attitudes of intense secrecy and distrust, and institutions of sheep-theft and mutual trespass. Hostility directed outwards is, of course, the counterpart of the immensely strong jural and affective solidarity of the family. And both are conditions consistent with the system

---

[1] In some respects there are obvious parallels with Homeric society, and I have benefited by the work of Sir Maurice Bowra, *Tradition and Design in the Iliad*, Oxford, 1930; Bruno Snell, *The Discovery of the Mind*, translated by Rosenmeyer, Oxford, 1953; M. I. Finley, *The World of Odysseus*, London, 1956; and Arthur W. H. Adkins, *Merit and Responsibility*, Oxford, 1960.

Anybody considering the values of a Mediterranean culture is under an obligation to J. A. Pitt-Rivers, *People of the Sierra*, London, 1954. Bichr Farès, *L'Honneur chez les Arabes avant L'Islam*, Paris, 1932, is an interesting attempt to discuss a somewhat similar system of values on strict principles of Durkheimian sociology.

of patronage that links each family individually to the wider structure of Greek society.

But, clearly, there is a limit to the amount of openly expressed hostility that this community is able to tolerate. Shepherds and their sheep are vulnerable, and in practice prudence discourages the free expression of hostility. The reciprocal trespass practised by shepherds who share a common grazing boundary is generally confined to areas from which there is a secure line of retreat; and in grazing disputes shepherds are careful to fight with weapons which may cause unpleasant wounds but are unlikely to kill. Wanton murders are discouraged through the removal of the killer by imprisonment, voluntary exile, or vengeance. By whatever agency this may occur, the family is too small a group to afford the loss of a man, and only an imperative obligation of honour justifies such a risk.

But this relatively limited display of active hostility is not in balance with the unequivocal character of the oppositions between families unrelated by kinship or marriage. These find a more extended and satisfactory expression in competitive behaviour and values which have been mentioned so frequently. The sociological importance of competition[2] is precisely that it represents a kind of opposition which is often indirect. In this instance protagonists compete for social prestige, that is for something which in material form none of them possesses. Where the prize has this intangible quality, direct attack may be irrelevant. Indeed, since social prestige requires the favourable response of the community to a man's qualities and actions after these have been evaluated in terms of the accepted system of values, it depends overwhelmingly on the opinions of enemies. To oppose successfully other unrelated families in terms of prestige, men must compete to the limit in their adherence to these values. They do this without causing one another obvious material harm; and the more they oppose one another in this way, the more they affirm their support of a particular system of values and beliefs. In this context competition for social prestige, while it clearly encourages that family particularism of which it is itself a symptom, nevertheless gives to this competitive complex a certain unity and coherence through a common system of values. These are, as it were, the rules of the game.

[2] Georg Simmel, *Conflict*, translated by Wolff, Glencoe, Illinois, 1955, p. 57.

It may be agreed (and, in general, correctly) that in a system where a number of groups compete for prestige, a strong group, if it is denied the social recognition it expects, may in frustration turn from competitive action to direct violence and attempt to establish its superiority by force; or it may attempt other forms of direct opposition, perhaps through the use of economic power. But in relation to the Sarakatsan community the family is small and weak. Its inability to make alliances outside the kindreds of its members and their affinal connexions, and the physical dispersion of the Sarakatsani which restricts the activities of any family to only a small area of the total community, are other factors which would tend to prevent a family group and its allies from dominating the remainder of the community; even if we leave aside the certainty of State intervention if violence were used or threatened. Economic or political control of the community by one family and its allies is equally unlikely. Unrelated families do not co-operate to market their produce and consequently there are no co-operative institutions whose officers might manœuvre themselves into positions of economic dominance. Similarly, the community has no institutions of local government which the members of a family and its kinsmen might infiltrate in the attempt to establish a form of political control. The pathetic showing of the Association of Nomad Pastoralists illustrates the concern of all families to prevent the delegation of any effective representative power to others. Each family faces the total community in a condition of dependence. The position it is able to occupy in public life, the quality of the marriage alliances it establishes, depend entirely on its social prestige, that is, they depend on the favourable response of enemies; or more accurately, on the inability of enemies effectively to denigrate a family's reputation.

Prestige (γόητρο) and 'name' concern the Sarakatsani in every context of public action. 'Better to lose your eye than your name', runs the common proverb. This intense competition of families to maintain their prestige against the permanent threat of denigration, and the continual evaluation of other people's conduct, which is fed by an insatiate and hostile curiosity, result in a certain hierarchical ordering of Sarakatsan family groups. In the local gathering of families which share the pastures of the same summer village the hierarchy of prestige is based upon a fairly precise knowledge of the genealogy, wealth, moral character, and conduct of each family; but, in the wider ordering of social reputations in the total community, elements of prejudice and speculation play a greater part.

In either case, there is more general agreement about the ordering of families at the two extremes, which define the hierarchy, than in its middle reaches. A number of families with the surname of Tsoumanis by their wealth and descent from a few dominating personalities of the past three generations are generally recognized to be the leading families of the community; these are the families of 'first lineage'. And certain of the families who bear such names as Tangas, Myriounis, and Ferendinos might be associated with them. On the other hand, families with the names of Sultanos or Pistiolis are assigned by general opinion to the lowest grade of social reputation; for them, indeed, social prestige does not properly exist. For the most part these families are economically poor and their genealogies lack any mark of distinction.

The positions at either end of the hierachy are not only more clearly defined, they also possess a fixity that is absent elsewhere. A family with the surname Pistiolis possesses large flocks yet it remains a family of the 'lowest lineage'. Its daughters are virtuous but their hands have not yet been sought in marriage even by men of indifferent social standing. However closely such families may live in the spirit of the community's values others do not give them the just recognition of their merits, so that certain of their number lose heart and are no longer concerned to act honourably; for in their case virtue is not its own reward. And the evidence of this reaction supports the original evaluation of the community.

If it is scarcely possible for such a family to gain prestige, it is at least difficult for the leading families of the community to lose theirs. There are few instances where a member of a family of the highest lineage has failed in a 'question of honour'. If a man is naturally timid he finds it all the more difficult to resist the immense moral pressure of family and community to act as he is expected to act. At the same time membership of a leading family in itself protects the individual from gratuitous slights. It is true that if a family of wealth and high lineage loses its sheep through disease its reputation must fall, but in the living memory of its past greatness it will retain a position of some distinction. On the other hand, if their reputations for wealth and honour are untouched, men of these families may often commit breaches of social convention which leave little permanent mark on their prestige. One tselingas of the 'first lineage' married his daughter to her second cousin, a marriage permitted by the Church but not by the customs of the community, yet after the first shock of his action had passed, his position in the community was essentially unchanged.

The families which fall between these two extremes represent the greater part of the community, perhaps four-fifths of its number. In their case, it is difficult to determine any order of ranking that is objective since these families show few differences in wealth, courage, and honour. Yet this level of equality is not merely a residual category between the two extremes. However subjectively it may be assessed, each family believes in a particular and detailed ordering of prestige in which it must continually struggle to maintain its position. Always action of one kind must be taken, action of another kind avoided, 'so that you do not throw down your prestige' (νὰ μὴ ῥίξῃς τὸ γόητρο κάτω). It is precisely among these families of equivalent prestige that rivalry is greatest. For here doubt and insecurity are considerable, and this is reflected in the display of ostentatious pride, a touchy sense of honour, and a compulsive attempt to conform to accepted standards of conduct. The very intensity of this competition supports the stability of the ranking order at either extreme. Other families in the community have a common interest in refusing to accept any claims of increased wealth or virtue put forward by families of the lowest prestige. In this way they confirm their higher ranking. Similarly they unite to deny the pretension of any of their own number to be a family of 'the first lineage', or to establish other grades of differentiation, since this would lead to a relative lowering of their own positions.

In radical form, then, the hierarchy of prestige, considered objectively, has only three ranks: there are those who are first and those who are last, in either case they are few in number. The majority are in the interstitial category from which pride and their common interest against further differentiation prevent any of their number from moving in an upward direction. There is always the possibility of falling to the category of those who are last, but the absence of any great differences in wealth, and the value given to the struggle to protect personal and family honour, hold the majority of families to an unwilling recognition of their equality in prestige, which is seldom admitted in speech but is less precarious than it seems.

## 2. HONOUR

The social reputation, whether of a man or a family, is a composition of various elements, analytically separable in description but with greater difficulty in life. Among these it is convenient to begin with a consideration of the concept of honour (τιμή) since this is fundamental to any assessment of prestige. Indeed, it is doubtful if prestige may be said to exist in its absence.

The translation of this concept by the English word 'honour' is useful if it is remembered that the analogy is only approximate. In modern Greek usage τιμή is conferred as a sign of the recognition of the excellence or worth of a person. It becomes the respect or esteem owed to certain persons, for example, to the heroes of the Revolution. From the point of view of the receiver it is whatever raises him up in the eyes of another and gives him reason for pride. In other contexts it may indicate certain qualities or conditions on which the reputation of an individual, or a group, is dependent. More specifically, it refers to the sexual virtue of a woman. It also describes the monetary price, or value, of an object or service. The last instance points to the common element in these various contextual uses. Τιμή expresses the idea of worth, whether this is an economic value in a market, or social worth evaluated in a complex of competing groups and individuals. Most Sarakatsani would understand this range of use, but they restrict their own employment of this word to the three last instances.

Among the Sarakatsani the concept refers particularly to the honour of the individual and the family, these two points of reference rarely leading to any conflict of loyalties since the solidarity of the elementary family is so complete. The situations in which this honour is typically violated or betrayed have already been examined: homicide, the drawing of blood, verbal insult, seduction, rape, and broken betrothal.

Honour, then, is a condition of integrity, of being 'untouched' by this kind of attack, insult, or betrayal. The integrity of a family and its equality (at least) of status is recognized when others take care not to give offence in these particular ways. If they do gratuitously commit an outrage against a family, they make it clear that they consider its social existence of no account. In that case, whether the violation is accidental or not, the outraged family must answer at once, and with violence, if its reputation is to survive.

But honour is not only to be considered in terms of the various external situations where it may be lost. The intrinsic principles of honour refer to two sex-linked qualities that distinguish the ideal moral characters of men and women: these are the manliness (ἀνδρισμός) of men, and the sexual shame (ντροπή) of women. With the exception only of persons of the lowest lineage, all Sarakatsani are assumed to possess these qualities 'by nature', although in the fallen condition of this world a reputation for manliness or shame is easily lost. In this sense it is not difficult for a man to move in a direction opposite to the true inclinations of his nature. One aspect of honour, then, is a struggle of self-discipline over cowardice and sensuality, flaws of animal nature that continually threaten to limit the natural nobility of man.

In general, the qualities of manliness are obvious and familiar. 'To be a man' the individual must show himself to be courageous and fearless. He must be strong in body and spirit. But there is also a nuance of meaning peculiar to a community where values are agonistic and social reputation is frequently at risk. In these circumstances a man must have boundless self-confidence in his own powers. Where few men owe him more than conditional support, and the great majority none at all, he must rely on himself. Manliness implies not only the condition of being courageous but the ability of a man to do something efficient and effective about the problems and dangers which surround him. For in this complex of values results count for almost everything and intentions for very little.

The physical characteristics of manliness are important. A man must be βαρβᾶτος, that is, well endowed with testicles and the strength that is drawn from them. The word also describes a certain ruthless ability in any form of endeavour. Here again we see the 'efficient' aspect of manliness. But βαρβᾶτος is in no sense a moral term, and in other contexts it may describe the dishonourable conduct of a man who rapes a woman or bullies weaker men. The manliness that is related to honour requires this physical basis, yet it must discipline animal strength and passions to its own ideal ends.

The quality required of women in relation to honour is shame (ντροπή), particularly sexual shame. Subjectively the woman's sexual shame is not simply a fear of external sanctions; it is an instinctive revulsion from sexual activity, an attempt in dress, movement, and attitude, to disguise the fact that she possesses the physical attributes of her sex. Maidens must be virgins, and even married women must remain virginal in thought and expression. But honour is always something imputed by others. In these matters the individual woman can never retreat within her own conscience. Her honour depends upon the reputation which the community is willing to concede, not upon the evidence of facts in any case difficult to determine. Therefore she protects her honour most effectively by conforming in every outward aspect of her deportment to a code of sexual shame. The woman who succeeds in this is τίμια and τιμημένη, honourable and honoured; but, if she fails, she is ἀδιάντροπη, shameless, and σκύλλα, a bitch, a woman without restraint, whose behaviour is compounded of the reflexes of her animal instincts. She becomes 'used' (μεταχειρισμένη), if only on the lips of men, and therefore 'lost' (χαμένη).

The sexual shame of women is no doubt related to the ambivalent attitude of the Sarakatsani towards sexual relations even in marriage. But it is also consistent with the importance of legitimacy as the essential qualification for membership in the family group. The sexual, reproductive, and working capacities of women belong exclusively to their families; and there is no more certain way of defiling the honour of another family than by seducing one of its women, particularly since mixed attitudes of awe and shame surround the sexual act and the reproductive life process. There is double cause for shame. Something of intimate spiritual value is rifled and desecrated by a stranger while at the same time the moral blame for this loss is generally ascribed by the community to the sensuality of the woman and, by extension, to the moral weakness of her kinsmen.

This kind of shame is a quality that is thought to descend in the female line from mother to daughter, but its loss always implicates the honour of the men of the family, reflecting on the manliness of the husband, and, more generally, on the whole social personality of brothers and, particularly, sons. The woman is soiled, λερωμένη, and blackened, μουντζουρωμένη; and she marks with her dishonour all those who are close to her through kinship or marriage. Essentially, sexual shame is felt to be an inborn moral characteristic, part of a woman's personality. Conventional deportment requires training of course; but however thorough her education the true character of a naturally shameless woman is certain to emerge, for fundamentally sexual shame is a question of heredity. If it becomes known that a young maiden has been struck by her father or brother because of some immodesty, people laugh and ask rhetorically what good do they imagine this will do since the fault proceeds from her mother.

Clearly manliness and shame are complementary qualities in relation to honour. The manliness of the men in any family protects the sexual honour of its women from external insult or outrage. The women must have shame if the manliness of the men is not to be dishonoured. We saw in an earlier chapter how the dishonour of a mother cannot be remedied by the sons. It is true that when a man kills a daughter who has lost her honour he wins the grudging respect of the community; yet, at the same time, the dishonour of the family is never entirely forgotten. Even when the rape of a sister has been avenged, a measure of dishonour remains, the dishonour of the girl's failure to preserve her virginity. The reputation for manliness of the men of the family is a deterrent against external outrage, but it cannot entirely repair the damage if such an attack against its women proves successful. It is, then, not surprising that the worst insult that can be aimed at a man is to use the name of his sister, or mother, in an unpleasant sexual context.

Honour considered as the possession by men and women of these qualities is the attempt to relate existence to certain archetypal patterns of behaviour. Female values are referred to the ideal conduct of the Mother of God: modesty, virginal attitudes, and selfless love. Male values appear in different exemplars. Christ is the ideal of continence and selfless sacrifice even of life for those to whom one is committed: the horsed and warlike saints George and Demetrius present the pattern of assertive courage, physical, spiritual, and invulnerable. Nearer to the realities of a shepherd's life, these two aspects of ideal manliness meet in the legendary image of the klephtic hero, a man who so refined his powers of courage and continence that he partly transcended the limitations of the material world. Bullets could not find their mark on Katsandonis. Shepherds in Zagori know the place where he leaped his horse a hundred paces across a chasm. Such heroes are both prepotent and efficient. Whatever the odds, these men always defeat their enemy, except in the final contest when only the pre-ordained moment of fate and the presence of Charon succeed in taking away life. The last struggle of the hero, although hopeless, is heroic, a final flourish of his essentially human worth in the face of fate. But, in the end, honour wins over death and the hero lives on in the songs that commemorate his fame.

Men and women, then, struggle to attain these ideal modes of being and conduct. Where they fall too far short in the effort of identification honour is lost. As I have said earlier, honour and the two sex-linked values of manliness and shame, which are associated with it, are qualities that, in principle, the majority of families are presumed to possess. It is the natural birthright of most Sarakatsani to be manly and of their sisters to have shame. Therefore, in the sense that τιμή is used by the Sarakatsani, it is difficult to talk of competition to win more honour than another man or another family. Honour is something which most families are presumed to have, but which they may very easily lose if they do not guard it with all their resources of courage and self-discipline. There is, rather, a constant struggle to maintain an ideal state of equality in honour between most individuals and families. And since the downfall of one family validates and in some sense improves the status of other families, men attempt by every means of allusive gossip and criticism of conduct to deny each other their pretensions to honour.

Even in the most favourable circumstances loss of honour is unlikely to be entirely remedied within the living memory of those who know of the affair. A man whose family has lost its honour cannot in any real sense be said to possess prestige at all. People say of a man who has allowed his father's slayer to remain undisturbed in the same neighbourhood, 'We don't even say "good morning" to him'. In fact this is not true. People do greet him, but formally and without enthusiasm. He is occasionally seen in the coffee-shop, but he sits in a corner and little attention is paid to him. He is tolerated but his prestige is negative. Loss of honour does not mean direct social ostracism. The sanction is more subtle; it implies the withdrawal of full recognition or response.

Although honour is an essential prerequisite of prestige it is not itself entirely independent of it. Families which on quite different grounds, such as poverty, have no prestige and are classed generally as 'lost' families (χαμένες οἰκογένειες), are denied the imputation of honour even though no positive accusation of dishonour can be pointed against them. Quite small incidents, which are not in themselves exactly questions of honour, are seized upon by the community to show prospectively that such a family, if it were faced by the duty of defending its honour, would be found wanting. The family of Costas Pistiolis is very poor. In the Sarakatsan view there must always be something morally wrong with a very poor man, and given their system of values this is not difficult to understand. A poor man is dependent on others for employment, or favours, if his family is to survive. He is not in a position to insist upon an equality in honour which, in any case, the community will not allow him. One day I saw a youth pelting the little son of Costas with pieces of dung in his father's presence. Costas, however, could do nothing since the youth's father was an influential member of the co-operating group which only tolerated with difficulty the presence of the Pistiolis family among its number. Another witness of the little scene swore and told me that you could copulate with this man's daughter and he would stand by and hold your coat.

Any attack made on the family's honour demands an immediate response. Failure to respond fatally damages the prestige of the outraged group and all its members. Without honour prestige is not possible. But also for those families, which on other grounds have no prestige, honour itself is already lost.

### 3. THE HONOURABLE MAN: POSITIVE IDEALS

The number of roles which the individual is required or able to assume in this community is limited, and some description of these has already been given in earlier chapters. Whether or not the individual fulfils the more general expectations of his various roles is a further consideration in the assessment of his prestige. Therefore, in this section I shall discuss certain values and qualities which are associated with the different complexes of roles that are appropriate for men and women at various stages of life. These are related to honour and the concepts of manliness and shame but are not always entirely consistent with them.

Together with age, the division of the sexes is the significant discriminating factor in the system of social roles. The two opposed but complementary categories of persons that result from this division provide both a division of labour and a pattern of moral virtues and faults.

The division of labour is unambiguous but not rigid. Some tasks which are normally performed by one sex are carried out by persons of the other sex in an emergency. This does not provoke criticism except where the reversal of roles becomes an established feature of a family's working arrangements. A family which day after day sends a twelve-year-old daughter to herd goats will certainly lose prestige. There are, however, a number of tasks which are never attempted by the other sex. For example, women never milk sheep or use a shepherd's crook; men almost never milk goats. Although men will lift heavy objects to secure them to a mule, they never carry burdens on their backs. However sick or feeble his wife or daughter a man will never help her with the intolerable burden of heavy water barrels. These tasks have become diacritical symbols of the two sexes; and to ignore them is to deny that one possesses the essential qualities of one's sex, manliness or shame.

As we have seen in earlier chapters, companionship and co-operation between people of opposite sex is possible only within the family and the kindred. Outside these limits the sexes (except in the case of the very old and the very young) are rigidly segregated, and the categorical opposition is evident. For in this context women are always a potential threat to the honour of men whether the latter are kinsmen or strangers. Thus unrelated persons of opposite sex seldom speak except to exchange a curt and conventional 'good day' if they meet on a narrow path. Although a man calls out a greeting to an unmarried girl, she keeps her eyes on the ground and never replies. At weddings unrelated persons of opposite sex, even though they are members of the same kindred of the bride or the groom, may not speak to one another. On these occasions the two sexes hold their feasting and dancing separately. In recent years at village festivals unrelated Sarakatsani of both sexes sometimes dance in the same ring but a woman is always flanked on both sides by men to whom she is related.

Within the group of related families which co-operate in the management of sheep, there are occasions when this opposition is expressed in accepted attitudes of sexual solidarity. If a number of women are working together on a common task such as the building of a hut, a group of men with nothing better to occupy their time will stand about smoking while they freely criticize their women's craftsmanship, and even revile them for their more general faults of ugliness and cunning. From time to time one of the more senior women will attempt some reply. 'Men', she calls out, 'are lazy good-for-nothings who do nothing but talk.' These exchanges begin in tones of banter but sometimes, in the later stages, they find sharp edges. In family life a favourite topic of evening conversation is a debate on the relative contributions and sacrifices which are made by the men and the women of the family for its well-being and security. This kind of talk is good-humoured but serves to draw out and emphasize what is expected of male and female roles.

Women face a hard and merciless routine of work and suffering. *Camaraderie* and the consciousness of a common fate help them to face it. This aspect of the solidarity of women is often expressed in the frequent discussion among those related by kinship or marriage of their common subjection to men in sexual activity. There is a great deal of bawdy reference to the male sex organs, and women constantly speak of their dislike of sexual intercourse and the absence of physical pleasure they find in it. A bride, during the last days before her wedding, is kept company by those unmarried kinswomen who live close at hand. They help her in the last feverish preparations of her dowry. The girls sympathize with the bride, but say that they will never leave their homes to submit themselves to a strange man. The bride applauds their decision, and says that she will secrete a knife upon her person and that when the bridegroom comes to her she will castrate him.

Unrelated men, when they are gathered together, criticize women in a general way. Wives, it is often said contemptuously, need two things, copulation and beating. But men are not given to obscenity except in oaths, and they do not discuss the intimacies of sexual relations, since these concern their manliness in a very literal sense; moreover, any discussion of a woman's sexual qualities diminishes her honour.

The opposition of the two sexes is also reflected in a pattern of sex-linked attributes which are antithetical but complementary. Men are courageous, austere, possess manliness and pride, but lack patience. Women are fearful, lacking in resolution but have greater depths of love; they are sensitive to shame, modest and patient. However, the masculine values transcend this opposition and provide the ideal virtues of the total community. Men must never in any circumstances be too modest or sensitive to shame. But when their family is threatened with violence and outrage, even women will find a pride and courage of heroic quality, and for this they will be honoured.

If the female sex is opposed to the male sex, it is also inferior. The Sarakatsani believe that man is a being created by God for the highest and the noblest purposes. Since the Fall there has been a legacy of sin in his constitution yet all in all he remains noble. The flaws in the human condition are envy and sexuality, for these are the thoughts and desires that particularly have the power to turn men's thoughts away from God and from the struggle to draw closer to Him. Manliness has a physiological basis but it only becomes a true manliness when it is disciplined and spiritualized. Sexual intercourse, then, is not an unmixed good. It is something which is 'unseemly' or 'out of alignment' (ἀνάποδο). In some way it pollutes (μαγαρίζει). After sleeping with his wife a shepherd ought to wash his hands before milking sheep. A ewe is a 'sacred thing' (ἱερὸ πρᾶμα), and παρμάρα, a disease which attacks the udder of the sheep, is often attributed to the omission of this precaution. Another illustration of this idea of pollution is the prohibition of sexual intercourse on the eve, or the day, of an important religious festival. Sexual activity is necessary in that it produces children, who are God's children, but evil in that some sensuality is unavoidable. It must be performed in the utmost secrecy, without speech, and the woman must remain motionless and passive. It is thought shameful for a husband to gaze on his wife's body.

In this situation, where man is noble (as indeed he must be in a system of values that puts stress upon the concept of honour), but where certain aspects of his propagation are matters for shame, the discomfort of inconsistency is avoided in a kind of sexual dualism. If man is nearly all nobility, a natural predisposition to evil (κακία) is the most striking feature of the female character. She is above all cunning, especially in the sense that her cunning involves the corruption of another, that is the man. She is a constant threat to his honour. Πονηρός, cunning, is typically the adjective which also describes the Devil, and the Sarakatsani believe that the Devil has a hold over women who are his peculiar emissaries dispatched to provoke men's hearts with sexual passions. Thus the whole burden of the shame of sexual relations is shifted on to the female sex. Since her powers of sexual attraction are of this supernatural order, man, in general, is unable to resist them. It is simply the quality in a woman of being a woman which inflames the man. She may lure him to disaster without even a glance or a gesture. Once he advances on her she has not the strength to resist him. In the Sarakatsan view, the power of woman's sexuality, the weakness of her will, and the physical strength of a man, are the important factors involved in sexual activity. It is for these reasons that the individual woman is expected by her kinsmen to have 'shame', in the sense that in speech, gesture, attitude, and dress, she must, as far as possible, cloak the existence of this sexuality. For the same reasons the family watches over its women with the greatest care; especially in the case of an unmarried girl anxious eyes follow her if she must go to the well or collect firewood unaccompanied.

These beliefs about the sexes are accepted by the women as

well as the men. They admit that they do not possess the intelligence of men. But they take a certain perverse and compensatory pride in their reputation for cunning and the ability to deceive their men 'forty times each day'. They agree that women are weak, and that the fault in cases of seduction or adultery lies mainly with the girl or the wife. Therefore they accept it as right that, in the first place, retribution should fall on the woman. In customary behaviour this social and moral inferiority is expressed in a number of ways. Women walk behind their men when they are together in public and show them respect. In church the women huddle at the back or line the left-hand wall. Women agree that they are inferior to men in every way, and they continually bemoan their fate that they were not born into the other sex.

Nevertheless, through the possession of shame it is always open to a woman to discipline and redeem her sexuality. The inclinations of her nature, whether conscious or not, make this difficult; but it is the prerequisite of honour. Virginity is a quality which provokes the deepest respect and a sense almost of awe. But the moral dualism of the sexes is finally transcended through the paradox that from women are born the noble sons who will protect the honour of the race. And, as the mother of adult sons whose reputation for manliness is untouched, and as a woman now past the period of her active sexuality, she has almost overcome the moral disabilities of her sex.

\* \* \*

This opposition of the sexes provides the frame for contrasted ideal types of social personality for men and women at each of the three stages of adult life.

For the unmarried but adult shepherds, the boys (τὰ παιδιά), the pallikaria (τὰ παλληκάρια), physical perfection is an important ideal attribute. A youth ought to be tall, slim, agile, and tough. Ideally, at least, a pallikari is never short in stature. A certain regularity and openness of feature is desirable but without any hint of effeminate fineness. Swarthy complexions and narrowly set eyes are deplored. Any kind of physical deformity is fatal to the reputation of a young shepherd.

But moral qualities are also demanded of the young shepherd, especially courage and strength of purpose. If in addition to these qualities he also possesses the necessary physical attributes a young Sarakatsanos can fairly claim to be λεβέντης καὶ παλληκάρι. The first of these terms is perhaps the more composite, describing a youth who is handsome, manly, narrow-hipped, and nimble; such a youth will distinguish himself at a wedding by his upright carriage, restrained manner towards his elders, and his agility in the dance. Παλληκάρι is rather the hero warrior with physical strength and assertive courage who is prepared to die, if necessary, for the honour of his family or his country. Caution must always be foreign to his nature.

It is also said that the young shepherd is free and independent. This does not indicate a freedom from social obligation that permits the indulgence of individual fancy. On the contrary, it means an independence from the cares and duties of a married head of family that frees the young unmarried man to give all his thoughts to the defence and vindication of personal and family honour. A head of family must consider what will happen to his wife and children if through involvement in some affair of honour he is killed or thrown into prison.

Since it is only in the years before he assumes the practical responsibilities of parenthood that a man is both innocent of the sexuality of woman and free to model his actions without compromise according to the ideal pattern of honour, these years of youthful manhood (τὰ νιᾶτα) represent for the Sarakatsani a time of perfected manliness when a man reaches as high a point of moral refinement as the human condition will normally allow. Speaking of his youngest unmarried brother Elias, Demetrios Carvounis explained that he, as leader of his family in a world where the majority of men are without love of honour, was forced from time to time to acts which his conscience did not approve. One day it might be necessary for him to go into court, place his hand on the Holy Bible, and swear falsely to save a member of his family, or his stani, from a crippling fine. Another day he must forgo his natural pride and obsequiously seek the aid of some Government servant. Deceit and lies are always needed in his work. On the other hand Elias was every day with the sheep on the high ridges in the clean mountain air, alone or with a single trusted comrade. Evil could not touch Elias in the same way.

He was simple and innocent (ἁπλὸς καὶ ἀθῶος); not simple in the meaning of an absence of intelligence but in a simple singleness of purpose; and innocent in the sense of freedom from guilt or the need to use guile. Such young men, Demetrios added, since they do not know women, are παστρικοί, that is, clean and pure. Male virginity is the ideal. And continence is thought to confer a certain invulnerability on those who face dangers, especially the danger of bullets in war or brigandage. Of sex relations in marriage Aristoteles, a young man of 28, who in every way conforms in conduct and person to the ideal pallikari pattern, was able to say before other men that he was ashamed even to think of them. Sex, sin, and death are related; similarly virginity, continence, and life. The Sarakatsani anticipate marriage with joy, but also with regret. The founding of a family is wholly good, yet marriage, sex relations, and children, inevitably foreshadow death. The pallikari, not the head of family, is the ideal of manhood.

It is during these years of early manhood that the community begins seriously to take stock of a man. His marriage will be the means of linking two families in affinal alliance, and the assessment of his manliness is one factor which, in part, determines how other people will treat his family. When he is twenty or twenty-one years old and shortly before he goes on military service, he will grow a moustache, and his father, or brother, will buy him a broad-bladed dagger. These are the outward symbols of his assumption of the status of manhood and of his pretension to be a pallikari.

The community will gradually form an opinion of his prowess as a shepherd, his fearlessness on the high ridges, his devotion to a sick or injured sheep, and his skill in grazing. It is difficult to say how this opinion is formed, since unrelated shepherds seldom work together. Possibly the estimate is sometimes inaccurate. But the critical moment in the development of the young shepherd's reputation is his first quarrel. Quarrels are necessarily public. They may occur in the coffee-shop, the village square, or most frequently on a grazing boundary where a curse or stone aimed at one of his straying sheep by another shepherd is an insult which inevitably requires a violent response. In any case some account of the event becomes public property. If the quarrel occurs before unrelated bystanders, the community may obtain a reasonably factual account of the fight. If it is not witnessed by an impartial audience, the contestant with the fewer marks of injury and the greater number of persuasive kinsmen wins the day. It is the critical nature of these first important tests of his manliness that makes the self-regard (ἐγωϊσμός) of the young shepherd so extremely sensitive. It is not only the reality of an obvious insult which provokes him to action, but even the finest of allusions on which it is possible to place some unflattering construction. To direct the slightest public mockery (κορόϊδευμα) against a young shepherd challenges him to fight. It may be possible to recover from an early failure of nerve and conduct, but a series of failures is fatal to a man's reputation. The more clearly his weakness is exposed the more often he risks open ridicule, and only the careful protection of brothers and kinsmen will save him from complete social obloquy. In fact there are few failures. Few physically weak children survive, and from an early age sons learn the meaning of their personal responsibility for the pride and honour of the family.

Sudden death stands close to the Sarakatsani and they are continually aware of its presence. 'He is behind our ear' (τὸν ἔχουμε στὸ ριζάφτι),[3] they say. Many children die in their early years, childbirth is dangerous, shepherds miss their footing on high ridges or fall into swollen rivers. But the tragic quality of the death situation is most evident when the pallikari dies for honour. For the young man will lose the perfection of his manliness if he will not on the instant give up his life in the cause of honour. If men must lead their lives according to a pattern of exemplary actions which express a system of agonistic values, the meaning of existence is the freedom to struggle to realize a certain mode of being and honour which, in the case of the pallikari, the Sarakatsani believe to be as near perfection as the determinations of the human condition will allow. Death extinguishes life, and the ability to compete in terms of pride and significance in social life at the very moment when the pallikari is most fit to compete. Death also removes an individual who was closely bound to family and kin; this is part of the tragedy expressed in the funeral dirge. But if death destroys the individual in the pallikari it leaves untouched his 'persona',

[3] Cf. Chatzimichalis, op. cit., vol. i, Part A, p. ροη'.

that part of his personality which, shed of individual traits and circumstances, relates him to the ideal type of manliness that he has realized in dying for his honour. Dishonour can no longer threaten the dead pallikari. He is free. And it is in their certain knowledge of this that the women of his family will sing in their dirge not only of their grief, but also of their pride.

After marriage the pallikari becomes the head of family. Now the essential ability demanded of him is that he should be an able protector of his family and his flock. Cleverness (ἐξυπνάδα) is the quality which he must possesss. It implies a quickness of mind and a degree of foresight. Such a man is not caught asleep or off his guard. It implies also the skill to plot with guile and craft. This appreciation of cleverness is evident in many stories and anecdotes which are told and retold around the fire after the evening meal. There is the tale of the shepherd who had scarcely returned to his huts with a stolen lamb when he saw a detachment of police approaching along the path. At once he threw the animal into a baby's cradle, covered it with a blanket, and ordered his wife to undo her blouse and give it the breast.

Lambros, the leader of a substantial co-operating 'company', has a reputation for craftiness. In 1937, in the winter pastures, he shared a grazing boundary with a family of Albanian Muslims who owned a property of 250 acres. Foreseeing that at some time in the future these Albanians might be expelled from Greece, Lambros filed a statement with the court of First Instance to the effect that he had held a lease of protected rights over this property since 1929. At the time there was no reason for the clerk to verify Lambros's statement, since any attempt to implement a false statement would have been repudiated with ease by the owners; and Lambros would have faced a serious charge of perjury. Lambros's foresight was justified in 1944 when the Muslims fled from Thesprotia. He was now able to produce his document and in a few weeks he was duly confirmed in his rights of protected lease over a property which in fact he had never previously occupied. It is this kind of subtlety that wins for a man the reputation for cleverness.

It is conceded that a head of household must continually use lies. Lies are not the same as purposeful cleverness, although they are obviously involved in it. But men lie as a matter of habit and principle to deny other people information. And it is one way of expressing their mutual hostility. A head of family who was sincere (εἰλικρινής), or without cunning words (ντόμπρος), would be considered foolish and neglectful of his duty.

This is not to say that the Sarakatsani fail to understand the virtues of truth and sincerity; indeed, relations between kinsmen, or between man and God, are based upon them. But between unrelated men the narrow limits of the human condition, particularly envy and poverty, prescribe opposite and meaner values. The essentially 'fallen' character of these relationships is implicit in linguistic usage. Κακός,[4] bad or evil, is sometimes used to indicate a skilful man, especially in operations where cleverness or cunning is required. Πονηρός, which means cunning in the sense of the worker-out of evil, is very frequently used to describe a man like Lambros whose cleverness has to be grudgingly admitted and admired by other men. And, on the other hand, καλός, good, in contexts of character description often refers to a man who is merely weak and irresolute.

But the truly clever man does not give the impression that he is a threat to other men. Except where the interests of his family are critically at stake, he is careful to appear as honourable and well-intentioned towards unrelated men. There are, however, men who practise a small kind of cunning in all their actions. These persons are described as cunning in a sense that is wholly bad. Μάγκας, which means a cunning untrustworthy person, a bearer of mean and untrue scandals, is a word often applied to this kind of man. In the Sarakatsan imagination such a man is small, bent, thin featured, and with narrow close set eyes. The cunning of these men is not the intelligent cleverness of a Lambros, rather it resembles the sexual cunning of women. Both corrupt. The latter corrupts the nobility of men, the former society in general. Cleverness and cunning are legitimate and praiseworthy where their object is the protection or advancement of family interests, but not beyond these limits, or for their own sake.

The heads of families whenever they are free from shepherding

[4] Cf. Höeg, op. cit., vol. 2, p. 168.

duties gather in the village square or the coffee-shop. On this public stage the chief representatives of the families of part of the total community appear, and by their attitude and bearing and the recognition and response they accord to one another they confirm or deny the ideal equality of one family with another. This equality is only maintained by a constant effort of self-assertion. A family head must strut about as if his affairs are of the greatest consequence. His expression is expected to be severe and proud. Modesty in these circumstances is no virtue but a sign of weakness. Ideally, the claims and assertions of other men must be at least equalled, and preferably surpassed. Yet care must be taken not to make a boast which can be proved to be empty. The boaster whose bluff has been called is despised. Conversation has a sharp, monosyllabic, contrapuntal quality. It is concerned with self-assertion, not with communication or the exchange of information. On these occasions a man must on no account sit quietly in a corner unspeaking (ἀμίλητος). To withdraw is to admit defeat. Card games often supplement the drinking and the conversation. Although they are games of chance rather than skill, they are acted out with great seriousness. As each man plays his card, this is struck down on to the table with the full force of his open hand. Quarrels are frequent if one man wins too handsomely and makes facetious or boasting remarks to the losers.

Yet a man ought to combine with this competitive behaviour a generally sociable attitude. The essence of being one of a company (παρέα) is equal sharing. Each man in his turn is expected to buy a round of drinks for the others. Any hint of meanness is enough to brand a man as tight-fisted (σφιχτός), a very serious charge. On the other hand, the man who moves to the other extreme, who spends lavishly and indiscriminately on entertaining others, or gambles recklessly at cards, is also condemned. Such people are known as wasteful spenders (σπάταλοι), without any sense of responsibility towards their families.

Caution, moderation, and self-restraint are the qualities demanded of the family head if he is to be a successful steward of his dependants' interests. We have already seen that in questions of honour the head of the family is unable to hazard himself as freely as his unmarried brother. For similar reasons the self-regard of the head of family is not so sensitive as that of the unmarried man. The man whose quick anger before marriage was approved as showing the spirit of the pallikari, is condemned as irrationally violent (ζουρλός) if, after his marriage, he draws a knife at the least imagined provocation. The underlying self-restraint of the head of the family, and the fact that the more volatile unmarried shepherds are isolated each with his own flock for the greater part of the year, contribute to a relative degree of peace and order in Sarakatsan communal life.

The family head must be able to cut a figure at a wedding or a village festival. At a feast he ought to be able to drink continuously without becoming either stupefied or aggressive. To fall asleep even after long hours of dancing, feasting, and drinking, is a mark of weakness. A repertoire of songs, and a proud upright bearing in the dance, are necessary for a man's social prestige. Similarly his clothes and appearance on these occasions are important. A man like Costas Pistiolis with his unkempt appearance, clothes fouled with dirt, and his inability to sing or dance, is a figure of mockery at the very few weddings he attends. Graceless (ἀχάριστος), and unnatural (ἀφύσικος), is the verdict passed on this wretched man.

Finally, the degree of dependence on, or independence of, others is a factor which differentiates the prestige of heads of family. To be a tselingas, or a member of the dominant sibling group of a co-operative association of families, carries the greatest prestige. The dependence of a man without brothers on more distant kinsmen is by no means dishonourable, but it is clearly a situation of less prestige. But the family head who is forced to watch the sheep of another unrelated Sarakatsanos, or a villager, for a wage (ρόγα) forfeits any pretension to social reputation. It suggests that he is so poor that he cannot live from his flock without the money supplement of the wage, or that he has no relatives with substantial flocks with whom he might co-operate, or that he is not acceptable to them. Customarily a shepherd's wage is paid only partly in money, the balance being given in kind, grain, and a pair of shoes for every six months of service. The galling feature of becoming a wage shepherd is the fact of dependence on an unrelated man and the sense of being a kept man.

After a man retires from the active arrangement of affairs, which he hands over to his eldest son, he is referred to as the 'old man'. He is now expected to become a man who is dignified but quiet (ἥσυχος). He ought to be quiet in the very literal sense that he does not attempt to cross the authority of his son when the latter makes a decision or issues an order. Quarrels between father and son detract from the dignity and prestige of both individuals. But the old man ought also to acquire an inward quietness of spirit, which follows from his release from the worries and cares of leadership and the knowledge that he has reached old age with his reputation for honour untouched. For this reason he ought no longer to possess a sensitive self-regard. For good, or ill, the record of his life will have established his social reputation. Now he ought only to be provoked by extreme insults. Such insults will in any case be judged as wanton and dishonourable, and will rebound on the reputations of those who level them. Normally there is no shame in delivering insults, only in receiving them. But a man of worth does not revile or pick quarrels with women, children, or old men. These categories of persons are inviolable. On the other hand, old men are expected to accept with dignity and good humour the mild affectionate mockery which is directed at them by their juniors.

But, although an old man is expected not to interfere in the practical arrangement of everyday affairs, he is listened to with respect in moments of moral crisis. He has passed beyond both the excessive bravadoes of the pallikari, and the cautious calculation of the family head. It is felt that the old man, now near to death, sees the ultimate values in a situation of moral conflict with a clearer eye than do his sons and men of their generation.

For women there are also three stages of adult life. The first of these is the category of unmarried girls between the age of sixteen and such time as they are sought in marriage, generally when they are about twenty-five or twenty-six years old.

It follows from what has already been said about the relations between the sexes, that the critical quality demanded of the maiden is shame. Just as the freedom from parental responsibilities permits the young man to live according to the values of the pallikari, so the fact that she is not yet a wife and mother allows the maiden to cultivate her shame which lies in her seclusion from the outside world and the denial of her sexuality. This is scarcely possible for a married woman. Not only must she submit to her husband's sexual embraces but her practical duties take her to some extent into the world outside her huts.

The maiden's cultivation of her shame demands that her clothes hide her femininity. Her hair is hidden under a black cotton scarf. A girl who by artifice or accident allows her scarf to become frequently undone gains an evil reputation. The only concession to the display of the hair is that girls grow their hair long, plaited into pigtails. The length of these pigtails, often artificially increased, is a point of pride and beauty. Thick, black, homespun blouses and woollen cardigans are buttoned to the neck and the wrists. The breasts are not supported and the shapeless bodice of the blouse effectively prevents the least hint of a provocative contour. A black woollen skirt is worn to the ankles. Generally as many as three thick underskirts are also worn under this. The general impression of the whole costume is one of shapelessness. The shame which is felt at the exposure of the body, even when no other person is present, means that undergarments are not changed for long periods and the body between the neck and the ankles is never washed. In contrast the hair is washed at least once a week, and the face, hands, and feet once or twice each day.

After she reaches the age of sixteen or seventeen a maiden must discipline her movements. No movement even in domestic labour must be hurried. She ought to walk with a slow and deliberate step. In the dance she must not lift her feet more than an inch or two from the ground. A girl who is seen running risks ridicule and a reputation for shamelessness. If, by evil chance, she were to fall backwards 'with her legs in the air' (ἀνάσκελα) she would virtually lose her honour. A girl should be proud but in a sense different from male pride. Thus she ought to be tall with an upright carriage, but with a gaze which is downcast, not level, and an expressive attitude which is directed inwards, not outwards.

A maiden ought to be secluded, as far as this is possible, from the gaze of the outside world. Not only does this guard her name against slander but, if she is unhealthy or ugly, it may help in deceiving possible suitors. But seclusion is also an element in the cultivation of sexual shame which is essentially hiding and turning inwards thought and facial expression which otherwise become a threat to her own honour and that of others. It is this knowledge of the powers of her sexuality that causes her, out of shame, to lower her eyes and withhold a greeting when she meets a man on a narrow path. It is often through the eyes that a woman lures a man to disaster. The attraction need not be consciously exercised. In keeping with these ideas unmarried girls over sixteen years of age go only twice a year to church to communicate, at Easter and at the feast of the Assumption. They are never guests at weddings which occur outside the immediate neighbourhood and they do not dance in public at village festivals. A girl in this age grade is never sent to draw water at the well or to collect firewood when a brother's wife is available. Ideally, she ought to spend most of her time preparing her dowry and weaving cloth at the wooden loom. Such tasks keep her out of the public gaze. If a girl is seen too often abroad it is soon suggested that she is being shown off to catch a husband. And in Sarakatsan thought it is shameful for a girl either personally, or through her family, to seek a man in marriage, or in any way to attempt to provoke his desire.

Necessarily, the married woman and mother is not able to have as much shame as the maiden. She cannot remain secluded. From time to time she must leave the protective circle of the huts to fetch water and firewood, milk goats, and rescue her vagrant children. But this is not the same thing as saying that she may ever act in a shameless fashion. Her clothes must be as modest as the unmarried girl's and her physical movements, if they need not be as subdued, must still be carefully controlled. A careful constraint is the quality she must display in her public appearances. The Greek word σωφροσύνη, prudence in the sense of an inner control of feeling and action, although I have never heard it used by Sarakatsani, seems to express exactly what is required of the married woman in this respect. Self-discipline is necessary precisely because she is allowed to move about more freely and with less supervision. She must appear modest (σεμνή) and serious in disposition (σοβαρή). It may be remembered how the unrestrained joking of the wife

5. Sarakatsan Shepherd

of Pistiolis provoked the criticism of other families. Women must never show emotion in public except where it is conventionally expected, as at a death. A married daughter meeting her father for the first time after a serious abdominal operation from which he had not been expected to recover, merely said in a matter of fact voice 'How are you, father?' A husband does not kiss his wife publicly even in farewell. Sarakatsan women must never shout in public to each other or their husbands as do the village women. In childbirth extreme fortitude is expected. The woman is given a blanket to bite so that she may not scream; and to guard against the possibility of outsiders hearing her groans the other women laugh and talk and, if necessary, beat tin cans. In general, any lack of self-restraint in conventional behaviour suggests that a woman may also be without self-control in respect to her sexual virtue.

There is no need to elaborate again the behaviour expected of a married woman in her roles within the family, qualities such as devotion, humility, and a readiness to co-operate with other women in the group. Physical strength and robustness, rather than fragile beauty, are the physical characters admired in a wife and mother. Without strength the woman is unlikely to survive for long the immense strain of her labours. Health is a question of deep concern for all Sarakatsani but especially for the married woman. To be sick is inexcusable, unless it is an illness that is easily diagnosed and rapidly curable.

As we have seen in an earlier chapter, the woman, especially the mother, expresses the moral solidarity of the family. Women become terrified when they see their men involved in a fight, moaning aloud in their anxiety and continually crossing themselves. But they are also quick to point the path of duty when men hesitate. The scorn of a wife, mother, or sister, is normally more than most men are able to tolerate. When a man has failed to act honourably a portion of the blame falls to the women of the family who are said to lack the courage to shame their men into the right course of action.

But it is in her family that the community chiefly judges the married woman. She must have sons, but one daughter is also desirable. Her own virtues and deficiences will appear in her children, and upon the manliness of her sons and the shame of her daughters her reputation is dependent, just as the honour of the children is itself contingent on the sexual virtue of their mother.

The final stage of a woman's life is the period between the marriage of her eldest son and her death. She now gains a new freedom both from the authority of her husband, who retires about this time, and from the restrictions of social convention. She goes freely into shops to make small purchases for the family and may stop to pass the time of day with unrelated men she meets. With a young bride to do the heavy work about the hut she at last finds a respite from constant drudgery, and her sons treat her with a new-found respect as the mistress of the extended family. Such an old woman should have a kind heart and treat the wives of her sons with firmness but justice. She is their moral guide and practical adviser, to whom they turn in difficulty or doubt. At childbirth she is the midwife who delivers their children and gives them comfort and courage.

The reputation of an old woman is already formed on the basis of her behaviour in earlier life. If she has passed through her life without any questioning of her virtues, if she has sons who are manly, and if she has a kindly personality, the community probably approves of her. When she is above sixty years of age, or if her husband is dead, the sexuality of woman is considered to be spent and she is said to have a 'clean soul' (καθαρὴ ψυχή). Such a woman draws the water and kneads the bread which is taken to church at Easter. In these respects the prestige of some old women is considerable.

But old women are also feared. Knowledge of magic techniques and remedial procedures for the evil eye are attributed to them; and their curses are believed to be efficient *ex opere operato*. Where old women have a good name they use these skills in a socially approved manner to protect their families from spiritual dangers. But certain old women have a reputation for the evil and aggressive use of these powers. In these cases there are often allegations of dishonour in earlier life. A woman who surrenders to lust loses her soul to the Devil and remains his familiar. Envy is often the motive ascribed to her. Typically she is the woman accused of magically impairing a bridegroom's potency because he did not seek the hand of her own daughter. The attribution of envy often rests on valid grounds, for such women come, in the main, from families of low prestige and little material prosperity where difficulties in arranging honourable marriages are almost inevitable.

This completes the description of ideal types. Men and women struggle to identify themselves with the ideal type personality that is appropriate to their sex and time of life. And if a man lives in conformity with these normative expectations of social conduct, he is described as τίμιος, honourable. Clearly τίμιος, honourable, is a word with considerably wider reference and less specificity than τιμή, honour, since it covers a range of qualities whose applicability is relative to the age and sex of the person described as honourable; while, on the other hand, the values associated with τιμή remain always unchanged. If the head of a family fails to avenge the breaking of his daughter's betrothal because there is no adult son, it may be argued that as an 'honourable' man his inaction is due to his concern to protect his family. But if circumstances of age and family commitments excuse to a degree the loss of honour, nevertheless honour is lost. Opposition of the two concepts 'honour' and 'honourable' is not frequent but, when it does occur, the former is always the significant standard where prestige is concerned.

## 4. THE HONOURABLE MAN: NEGATIVE RESTRICTIONS

If the man who is τίμιος, honourable, must attempt to achieve a pattern of ideal conduct, there are also certain negative restrictions on action which he must accept. That these restrictions concern, in almost every case, conduct that wantonly threatens the integrity of the family life is not remarkable when we remember on the one hand the spiritual and material significance of the Sarakatsan family group, and on the other the distrust, hostility, and competition which mark the relations between families that are not related through kinship or marriage.

Scandal which falsely questions the virtue of a maiden is believed to be particularly wicked. It may be easily achieved by only a few allusive remarks, whose author probably succeeds in remaining anonymous. For this reason, perhaps, it is strongly believed that God will punish those who spread lying scandals.

Sometimes, however, the identity of a scandalmonger becomes known. John went to another village to catch a glimpse of the daughter of George Carvounis whom he was considering as a possible bride for his younger brother Demetrios. In the coffee-shop he casually mentioned the girl's name to Michael Goulas who, perhaps guessing the direction of the visitor's interest, told him that the girl was round-shouldered and absent-minded. At first John accepted this statement and without further delay returned to his home: but later he was persuaded by the marriage negotiator that he had been deceived, and after a further visit the marriage contract was eventually arranged. Goulas is relatively prosperous but already had a reputation for meanness and taciturnity. Even before this incident he was an infrequent visitor to the coffee-shop where he was careful to avoid any large gathering in whose company he might have to spend money. Meanness, envy, and unsociability form a pattern of qualities related in Sarakatsan thinking to evil and dishonour. The unsociable man is so because he has something to hide, he hides what he lacks, and what he lacks makes him envious of others. Meanness follows naturally upon envy. Had the poison of his scandal been effective, the crime of Goulas would probably never have become known. In the event, he was condemned and avoided by those who accepted John's version of the incident, and people did not hesitate to describe him as a man without honour (ἄτιμος).

It follows that an honourable man, when he covertly glimpses a prospective bride, is careful never to disclose, except to trusted kinsmen, the true purpose of his visit. For if he decides not to ask for the girl's hand, and this fact becomes public knowledge, people will wonder what flaw he sees in the girl's character and qualities. More generally, it is evil to spread any false scandal which may provoke insult, and response to insult, between other men, and may lead to killings and orphans.

The hut or house is inviolable. No stranger may invade it without an invitation. Similarly, whatever takes place within the sanctuary of its walls is private and sacred to the members of the family. This understanding makes possible the warmth, affection, and easy intercourse of family life secluded from the public gaze. It is a sin, and a source of the greatest shame, if a man is caught with his ear to the wall of his neighbour's house or hut. It is, nevertheless, true that people are insatiably curious about the details of domestic life and relations in other families. The condemnation of eavesdropping, although ideally it points to the recognition of the right of family privacy, in practice merely places a negative sanction on one particularly blatant method of obtaining information about other people's affairs.

Men are not honourable who, possessing great physical strength, use it to tyrannize others. They are men who without cause or restraint attack others with insults, using their mothers' or sisters' names in offensive sexual contexts or uttering other provocative blasphemies. Such a man, it is believed, purposely stages an incident to humiliate another who must either lose honour by not responding, or suffer a physical beating. It is accepted that, in most instances, to insult another is neither avoidable nor dishonourable. A sheep strays across a boundary, another shepherd stones it, its owner insults him, blows are exchanged. This sequence of events is to be expected in a community where the interests of different families conflict and each man must maintain his self-regard and the honour of the family. But wanton and unprovoked outrage is evil.

There are, also, categories of persons whom it is always dishonourable for a man to assault: women, old men, young boys, and children, persons weaker than himself. A man who interferes with women, or picks a quarrel with an old man or a young boy, quickly loses his social reputation. It sometimes occurs that, when grazing land is disputed, a family will send its sheep under the guard of a young shepherd boy into the disputed area, knowing that the other shepherd will not improve his case with the community, the villagers, or the police, if he strikes the youth. However, this is a dangerous tactic since, if the young shepherd is struck, honour demands retaliation.

There is one other category of persons that a man must not exploit, the very poor. Whereas a Sarakatsanos will not hesitate to trick or deceive other men, it is not honourable to take advantage of a very poor man with only twenty or thirty animals, particularly if he has a young family. It is the very fact of his dependence on the generosity and forbearance of those of greater power and prestige that morally prevents them from exploiting him. In the face of the implicit admission of his failure in life they cannot press home their advantage. Since he has failed to provide adequately for his children, others must assume a responsibility not to make their humiliating condition worse. If men oppress the very poor of their own community, there is an element of hubris in their conduct that respects neither God nor the family which is His institution.

In general, where the interests and honour of a family are not affected, every effort ought to be made to avoid giving needless affronts to others. When people pass in hailing distance, conventional greetings must be carefully exchanged. When he is asked for some information which he does not wish to give, or when he is requested to do something which he does not wish to do, a man ought not to reply with a curt negative; rather he should answer in the one case with polite and elaborate evasions, and in the other with a declaration of his willingness to help, balanced by a list of insurmountable difficulties which, nevertheless, he will struggle to overcome. Within the limit of his pride a man ought always to appear sociable and concerned. These prescriptions are not entirely prudential. There is a consciousness of common humanity. Competitive hostilities prevent men from expressing this feeling except in the marginal areas of social life; but to ignore it entirely is not only socially dangerous, but it denies the essential nobility and generosity of man and provokes the anger of God.

The community, then, places certain bounds on the expression of hostility. They are not very onerous limitations, but clearly there may often exist doubt, in the evaluation of a man's conduct, as to whether he has overstepped the limit of permissible hostility and, thus, has lost his reputation for acting as an honourable man. Inevitably the duty to further family interests, and the limitation on the expression of hostility, conflict in certain circumstances.

Ideally, it is maintained, a man ought to go beyond the negative prescriptions contained in the notion of the honourable man; he ought also to be positively concerned about the interests and honour of an unrelated man, he ought to be φιλότιμος, caring for, or loving, his honour. That is to say he ought to be so intensely concerned about the nobility of his own conduct that he takes into account how his actions affect the honour and prestige of others. It is still an essentially self-regarding attitude, but the acute concern about the purity of his own motives spills over into an incidental concern for others. Such a man, it is said, will resist the approaches of a woman even where she clearly wishes to be seduced, and where there is no danger of discovery. He never uses lies or deceit to trick another man, or takes advantage of a situation to make another look foolish. A Sarakatsanos when defending his conduct will often say, 'I am a man who loves honour'. But others will not accept this estimate of self. Φιλότιμος is an epithet never attributed by one Sarakatsanos to another unrelated shepherd, because they believe that the responsibilities which each individual owes to the family group absolutely preclude his acting in this manner. On the other hand, it is not infrequently used to characterize a patron whose protection is effective; for here interests are complementary, not opposed, and in the particular context of the patron-client relationship it is possible for a man of power to appear to be acting in this way towards his client. And, in a condescending sense, it is possible for a patron to admit the same quality in his client.

\* \* \*

Three concepts, 'honour' (τιμή), 'honourable' (τίμιος), and 'loving honour' (φιλότιμος), have now been considered in their relation to the community's evaluation of a man's conduct and its implicit recognition of his prestige. Although τίμιος and φιλότιμος indicate, in different degrees, some concern about other men, all three are essentially self-regarding terms. In each case it is a question of a man attempting to realize a particular ideal pattern of conduct. What interests him is the success of this quest, not the effect of his actions on others.

The quality of being honourable has this in common with honour, that most men are assumed to have it. It is not something which must be competed for, but something which must not be lost. Although there is certainly the need constantly to re-achieve standards of conduct, the emphasis is on the fact that most Sarakatsani have honour, and are honourable, but that individuals, to a greater or less degree, may stray from the path of normative virtue and lose their prestige.

Both the concepts of honour and of the honourable man

assume, ideally, a community in which all families are equal in their possession of honour, and all men are equal in the honourable discharge of the duties associated with their social roles. Although a Sarakatsanos seldom explicity attributes prestige to another, and struggles always to find some failings in another's character when he discusses him, yet by the recognition that he gives another in public life, by the way he shares conversation and drinking companionship, he may implicity admit him to a position of equality. A man may also talk or drink with a person he considers to be of inferior prestige, but there are fine nuances of attitude which make this difference between them very clear. If this evaluation of prestige is acceptable to the general community the man who is treated as an inferior will receive no public backing if he chooses to interpret this treatment as a slight, and reacts to it violently.

The flagrant breaking of social norms leads to the withdrawal of recognition and response, that is to a definitive loss of prestige. After it became known that Goulas had falsely denigrated the daughter of George Carvounis he appeared even more infrequently in public, an admission of his shame and humiliation. When he did enter the coffee-shop people greeted him unenthusiastically, if an exchange of greetings was unavoidable; but nobody engaged him in conversation, or bought him a drink. His presence was tolerated, but he was tacitly expelled from the intimacies of social life. He was no longer an equal in honour.

Conformity is the chief defence against denigration where people believe that the hostile criticism of others protects in some way their own reputation. Moreover the precision of this criticism is considerable since the social roles which a man or woman assumes at any period of life are few in number, and their implications are perfectly understood both by the protagonists and those who observe them. Yet it would be too simple a judgement to think that the concepts of honour and the honourable man depend only on the external sanctions of competition or mutual hostility. For the Sarakatsani believe that these ideals and values, which breathe meaning, purpose, and value into their lives, require no justification or sanction. They are a way of life, not a code of interdictions.

But even social conformity does not necessarily protect

reputations. Honour and prestige depend, also, on other factors besides the possession, or apparent possession, of personal qualities. We turn now to a discussion of these other factors.

## 5. THE MATERIAL ELEMENTS IN PRESTIGE

The elements of prestige we now discuss differ from those that have just been described in that they emphasize, not the ideal equality of honourable men, but the inevitable inequalities which differentiate families in terms of numbers and wealth and certain other criteria. Whereas the concepts of honour and the honourable man are purely social facts, the elements of prestige we are about to examine are clearly not; they involve demographic and ecological factors, and chance.

### (A) NUMBERS

῎Ογκος means mass and, by extension, social influence. The Sarakatsani often use the word to refer to the numerical strength of the family, particularly the number of sons or brothers. It is noticeable that in folk-songs and folk-tales the pallikari is typically one of five brothers, or more. The ideal type hero is never an only son. To have many sons is the crowning pride of a man's life, and conversely, sterility, and to a less degree a family of girls, is a mark of failure.

That a strong and united group of brothers supports a family's reputation is wholly understandable. They are able effectively to guard its interests by physical force, they are not necessarily dependent on others for co-operation in the management of their flocks and, until the extended family is divided, there is at least one unmarried brother prepared to revenge its honour. Other men think twice before they offend a shepherd with four or five brothers.

At the other extreme, the man without brothers, or the father without sons, is weak. A man without a brother may be killed with less fear of revenge than is generally probable, a girl without a brother runs a greater risk of insult or a broken marriage contract than do other unmarried women. For in these circumstances the only person under any formal obligation to retaliate is the father, a man of advancing years who is isolated in his family without the active support of other men, and fearful that he may leave his dependants without a protector. But although the predicament of a man in this position is appreciated by other Sarakatsani, it scarcely mitigates the loss of prestige. If a man has no adult son to protect his daughter's virtue, the fault is his. For weakness is despised. In itself it tends to diminish the prestige of a family even before it has led to dishonour. And men who are isolated without brothers or sons are noticeably less proud, less confident, and in some cases are, by Sarakatsan standards, pathetically diffident and nervous—overt personality traits which I have not observed in men born into large sibling groups with a number of brothers.

## (B) WEALTH

Tò βιό is the property owned by a family, particularly its flocks of sheep and goats, the mules and horses. Although money invested in other objects of prestige such as village houses is important, animals in a pastoral community are the significant form of wealth and a critical element in social reputation.

Today there are few families that own more than five hundred sheep and goats. A household with more than 150 animals holds a respectable position in the community, one with 80 to 120 animals is on the brink of poverty, while a group with less than 40 animals is despicably poor. Yet the question of wealth is not quite so simple as this arithmetical scale might suggest. The Myriounis extended family of five brothers have 476 animals. Only the flocks of two other families in the Neochori local group exceed theirs in size. So long as they remain a single family with this large flock and five adult men to serve and protect it, the family is clearly, in this respect, a group of high prestige among the Neochori shepherds and indeed in the total community. But when the family is forced to divide into a group of autonomous families, each brother will possess only 80–90 sheep and goats; it may, therefore, seem that at a single stroke they will fall from one end of the wealth-prestige scale to the other. In fact, however, so long as the families of a group of brothers hold together in a co-operative association, folding their sheep together in a single flock (although with different ear-signs), they continue to derive some prestige from the aggregate number of their animals. Still it will now be said, for instance, that Theodoros has only 80 sheep and goats of his own, but four children to provide for. As soon as people begin to calculate in this manner, the inadequacy of his personal wealth emerges, and to some extent his prestige falls. Men with no brothers who are forced to join the 'company' of a cousin or an affine gain some prestige and cover from the size of the co-operating group of which they form a part, but the size of their own flock is always very precisely appreciated by outsiders. The worst situation is that of the family head with only a few animals who is forced to become a wage shepherd to an unrelated man, since in this case poverty associated with dependence on a stranger destroys prestige.

Taken together, numbers and wealth are the necessary material foundation for high family prestige. They imply the independence of the family within the community, both economically in the sense that the group is viable (and possibly free of debt), and technically in that it has enough manpower to manage its flocks unaided. It suggests that the family will possess powerful patrons outside the community and that in the competition for winter pastures it will be in a better position to rent grazing land. A village generally prefers to let an area of reasonable size, and to negotiate with a prosperous group able to provide a steady and profitable flow of bribes and presents.

Also, it is the family of wealth and numbers, with powerful patrons and sufficient winter grazing, that draws to itself a number of less fortunate kinsmen. The dependence and support of these men make the protecting family the nucleus of a co-operative association, extending yet further its strength, influence, and prestige. It attracts many passing visits from other kinsmen. Men do not often visit kinsmen of low prestige, since such association only draws attention to a relationship which is best forgotten: on the other hand, they take every opportunity to pay a call on a kinsman of position and repute, to cultivate a relationship that is a source of possible support in future misfortune and, of itself, brings a measure of vicarious prestige.

Men like Pistiolis, who are at the lowest level of the community hierarchy of prestige, seldom receive a visitor from one year's end to another. Indeed, the number of visitors that a family receives is generally a reliable index of its reputation. It is always known in the neighbourhood when a family has had guests (μουσαφίρηδες); their quality, relationship, and the possible reasons for their visit are debated in detail by the other families. Comment is often caustic, but the very interest which is aroused is a recognition of the importance of the event. If a family of numbers and wealth entertains a patron from the town, this is a triumph which it enjoys to the full. Meat is killed and wine is bought. Largesse is demanded of the family which entertains many guests. And in some mysterious way neighbouring families discover the measure of generosity, or meanness, which a host has shown to his visitors; and criticism, encouraged by envy, will not spare him. In hospitality (φιλοξενία), a virtue in which the Sarakatsani believe they are naturally pre-eminent, there is always a strong element of competition.

## (c) LINEAGE[5]

Νταμάρι, lineage, refers to the quality of the kindred relationships which a man inherits from both his father and mother; and the importance of this for prestige has already been discussed in chapter three. If he possesses the surname of one of the leading families, or is directly descended, preferably in the male line, from a famous tselingas of the last century, this also is a significant element in a man's reputation. It might appear to indicate that for the highest and the lowest families, at least, reputation of lineage is patrilineally inherited. There is, indeed, a bias in favour of relationships traced through the father (particularly agnatic relationships) in the evaluation of νταμάρι in all families, and this is certainly accentuated at either extreme of the hierarchy of prestige, where certain family names are associated with the idea of high or low reputation, but the inheritance of νταμάρι remains fundamentally bilateral. In general, as we shall see in a discussion of marriage, men are careful to marry their sons or daughters into families of equal reputation. Where a member of a leading family takes a bride of markedly lower lineage, the community withdraws from the new family the recognition of the prestige associated with the husband's surname by the simple procedure of refusing to call

[5] Lineage, here, does not, of course, refer to a unilineal descent group but to the quality of pedigree through all lines of descent.

him by this name, and substituting some nickname, or patronymic.

But the prestige of lineage depends itself on the attributes of wealth and numbers which have already been examined. It does not help a poor man to claim that his great-grandfather was a famous tselingas with two thousand sheep. It is true that a father, or grandfather, who had the necessary wealth to support the nobility of his line is a saving grace for those who have lost their flocks, but it is a small one. The children of a leading family whose wealth has vanished suffer the same fate as the children of a family whose father, although from a family of the 'first lineage', has married beneath himself, that is they literally 'lose' their name, the surname of the father. Lineage refers to prestige in the past, while the essence of competition in this community is concerned with influence in the present. Therefore, a 'name', without the means to support it, is not recognized.

This, in practice, is the mechanism that restricts the number of families that can successfully claim to be of 'first lineage'. Not all the collateral relatives of a leading family are recognized as equivalent in prestige, for without numbers and wealth they cannot aspire to this. And it is inherently unlikely that they will all possess these advantages. There are two important limiting factors. With the rule of equal inheritance between brothers, the size of the group of brothers which is necessary to build and protect wealth and prestige, itself is the cause, in the next generation, of the fragmentation of this wealth. The second factor is disease. Twenty years ago sheep-pox, and today liver-fluke, are diseases capable of decimating a flock within a short time. However honourable a man, the loss of his flocks must diminish his own prestige to some degree, and that of his children more seriously.

(D) MARRIAGES

Τὸ συμπεθεριό is the affinal relationship between two previously unrelated families. It is in the early days of summer that the families of men who wish to take wives in the following year begin to consider the question of finding suitable affines and, during these weeks, the gossip of the community is much concerned with news and speculation about matchmaking.

The problem of choosing a bride or accepting a bridegroom involves a consideration of the other family's total prestige, the personal qualities of the candidate bride or bridegroom, and the question of dowry. The prestige that a family will derive from the marriage depends on these three interrelated factors. For severely practical reasons a man may value certain elements of the prestige of the family into which he is trying to marry, more highly than others. He may seek an affinal connexion with a family possessing abundant pastures, or a group with a number of brothers, if he himself has none and proposes to co-operate with them. A family rich in stock is sought when the object is to extract a large dowry. Nevertheless, whichever of these, or other motives, is in the forefront of a man's mind, he will not leave out of account, if he has any self-regard, the reputation of the girl's family for honour and honourable conduct.

A man will not normally marry into a family he considers to be of lower prestige. He often attempts to take a wife from a family of somewhat higher prestige than his own, and such is the haunting fear of a daughter remaining unmarried that her family will sometimes allow a daughter without striking attractions to marry a man from a somewhat inferior family. This is so especially in a case where a man has two or three daughters. For in the case where the girl's lineage is distinctly superior to the bridegroom's, the bride's family is unlikely to pay any considerable sum in money or sheep in addition to the traditional dowry.

But, in other cases, the gradual introduction since 1945 of a system of dowry that includes the transfer of sheep and money (dowry-wealth) as well as the traditional blankets, furnishings, and clothes, may work against the slightly hypergamous trend that was previously a feature of some marriages in the community. To take a substantial amount of dowry-wealth is, now, a point of prestige in itself, and also in the sense that it increases the total wealth of the bridegroom's family. Thus it happens, more frequently than in earlier years, that a man will take a girl from a family considered to be of a somewhat lower prestige, if this short-coming is balanced by the advantage and prestige of 50 or 60 sheep.

A large amount of dowry-wealth in sheep or money serves as

a makeweight that balances various shortcomings in the bride whether these refer to the prestige ranking of her family, or to some personal inadequacy, or both. The virtuous daughter of Leonidas Gogolos was the victim of a road accident when she was a small girl. She walks with a limp, and her leg, below the knee, is pitifully thin and ugly with scar tissue. But it is generally believed that she will not remain unmarried if her father is willing to give her to a man of undistinguished family together with a dowry of 50 sheep.

In some instances brides are taken without dowry-wealth. Necessarily, marriages between poor families are generally contracted without dowry-wealth. And it sometimes happens that a family of wealth, when it takes a girl from a less affluent group, may, with a gesture of pride, waive the question of dowry-wealth. Pride, however, may also work in the opposite direction. A family of the 'first lineage' was asked for dowry-wealth of fifty sheep by a suitor of good repute. To show his wealth, to make plain the superiority of his family, and to place the groom under obligation to him, the father of the girl gave a hundred.

It is always said in general discussions of the matter that a girl who loses her honour, if she is not killed by her father, will never marry. The few cases of such women in the community do not support this statement. The wife of George Raftis was the daughter of a family of high repute. It is alleged that when she was a young woman she was seduced by a member of a wealthy and powerful Tsoumanis family which pastured its sheep on the land of the same summer village. The family did not dare to attack this powerful group, nor did they have the necessary resolve to execute the girl. Although the girl's family was of respectable lineage and some wealth, the loss of her honour and the inactivity of its men utterly destroyed its reputation. But finally, at the age of 39, the woman was sought in marriage by Raftis, a poor man of no standing, a wage shepherd with a handful of sheep whose wife had died leaving him with two young daughters.

Marriage to a widower is always a possibility for women whose eligibility for marriage is in some way anomalous. There is little prestige in marrying a widower, and the fathers of respectable families do not normally entertain the idea of marrying their virgin daughters to widowers. Thus widowers, in the main, are the means by which non-virgins, 'used women', whether they be honourable widows or dishonoured maidens, are fitted into the community institutions of family and marriage. Naturally, the dishonoured amongst their number tend to marry the widowers of lower prestige, and sometimes bachelors who are of poor family or with some physical imperfection. A widower takes a dishonoured woman as a second wife when her remaining childbearing years are few, and he takes care not to make her pregnant. In effect, she is little more than a domestic slave caring for the children of another woman. But any marriage, almost, is better than the shame of 'remaining'. I have only one well documented case of a healthy woman who did not marry, but the deep fear of this fate is nevertheless very real, and often expressed.

## (E) THE DISPLAY OF PRIDE

Περηφάνια, pride, is a sentiment that a man is entitled to feel if he possesses the elements of prestige. But in the present context we are considering a number of situations where men and their families are expected, or are permitted, to give certain expressive demonstrations of pride.

The importance of constant self-assertion if a man is to hold his own in the coffee-shop oratory and boasting has already been mentioned. This is the necessary minimum for social reputation. But a successful display of pride demands something more. Here, the etymology of the word ὑπερήφανος, proud, is relevant.[6] From ὑπέρ and φαίνομαι it is one who shows himself above his fellows. In displaying pride a man must behave in such a way as to show that he believes himself to be superior to other persons. It requires a suggestion of presumptuousness, a subtle air of arrogance, that suggests a man is dominating the gathering, and yet does not proceed as far as an insult or open challenge to others. It is an important element in prestige, but clearly it is also largely derivative from it. A poor man of inferior lineage or low prestige cannot give himself these airs without provoking ridicule.

Not only attitudes, actions, and persons are described as

[6] Cf. Archbishop Trench, *Synonyms of the New Testament*, London, 1871, p.96.

'having pride', but also things. A shepherd's crook with a carved wooden handle is the privilege of respected heads of family. It has pride. A tselingas of high lineage trains a horse as a μπινέκι, an animal that will trot with the foreleg and hindleg moving together. Mounted on such a beast his pride is unassailable by lesser individuals. Other men might, without difficulty, train such an animal; a wage shepherd or a brother without an independent household might easily strut about the village square with a carved shepherd's crook in his hand. But these objects have pride only when a status has been achieved; they merely produce ridicule when it has been usurped.

The migrations between the plains and the mountains (particularly the spring journeys) are important occasions for the display of family pride, for then the entire community is on the road together with their flocks and their horses and mules. This is an opportunity to make a direct physical appraisal of a family, its bearing, and its wealth, in a way that at other times is not possible. 'For pride', on these occasions, horses and mules are decorated with coloured saddle-cloths, the sheep are loaded with large and sonorous bells; and if the spring shearing precedes the journey, one, two, or sometimes three long tufts of fleece (φοῦντες) are left on their backs. One or two late-born lambs that have been adopted as household pets are gaily decorated with lengths of coloured woollen cord. Despite the hardships of the journey, heat and dust in the spring, often continuous rain in the autumn, the men and women also give much attention to their own appearances. The women wear their best skirts, bodices, and shoes, the men are continually combing their hair and straightening their jackets. If a family has taken a new bride during the previous six months, this woman, decked in the finest clothes of her dowry, leads the first mule in the train so that she may be seen and remarked by all.

Similarly, a wedding is a setting for the display of pride. Men show pride in the dance by the dignity of their demeanour; each struggles to show himself first in skill and enthusiasm (μερακλῆς). The visible pride of the riders in the bridegroom's procession brings prestige to his family, but also the individual riders vie with one another in the quality of their horses and accoutrements and the severity of their bearing. For pride, again, the dowry of the bride is formally presented article by article to the assembled guests, first at the bride's home, and afterwards at the home of the groom.

The display of pride is an important element in prestige but it must itself be based on reality. The pride of a Sarakatsanos may always be disproportionate in the view of other men but when it is wholly false it leads only to mockery.

*       *       *

The elements of prestige have been divided into two categories. The first category emphasizes the ideal equality, in the community, of families and individuals of the same sex and age group. Their ideal equality rests on the belief that most Sarakatsani have honour and are honourable, that they struggle to achieve in their lives ideal patterns of conduct. These elements of prestige require of the individual man or woman constant effort and self-discipline. An idea of the essential nobility of the Sarakatsani underlies them. The second category of elements of prestige are factors which to a considerable degree lie beyond the power of the individual, or even the group, to alter. They are all factors (numbers, wealth, leadership of co-operating groups, opportunities to show hospitality, lineage, marriage alliances, and the effective display of pride) which far from positing the ideal equality of families lead inevitably to their differentiation in terms of prestige. And, necessarily, they are caught up in ideas of fate, envy, and the fallen condition of this world.

The two categories of elements of prestige are nevertheless interdependent and both must figure in the evaluation of a family's total prestige. Without the imputation of honour and the quality of being honourable, wealth and numbers only represent a prestige which is, at best, equivocal. And weakness, or poverty, draws in its train doubts about the honour of a family, however socially conformist it may be.

## 6. THE SANCTIONS OF PRESTIGE VALUES

One sanction for the conduct, qualities, and achievements that have been presented as elements in the prestige of an individual, or a family, is the simple fact of the loss of this prestige, a withdrawal of recognition, a kind of social abandonment. But there are also important sanctions related to this withdrawal of social recognition which are internal to the social personality. I refer to the sentiments of self-regard (ἐγωϊσμός)[7] and shame (ντροπή).

Fundamentally, self-regard is the inner necessity and obligation to achieve identity with the image of the ideal self. This image, of course, is a stereotype presented by society, there is little room for individual speculation, nor would it occur to most Sarakatsani to question its traditional content.

We have seen, in chapter seven, how a father instils in his children a sense of responsibility and loyalty to the family. They learn that in all their actions they are judged by others as representatives of their family and that, therefore, they must compete and hold their own with other children of the same age and sex. A boy learns from songs and stories (and later at school) to identify himself with the values of the idealized heroes of the Revolution. He comes to believe in the superhuman deeds of Katsandonis and Kolokotronis, and in the ability of men to repeat them where the cause has sanctity and men possess honour.

At a more prosaic level he learns, from the interminable criticism of other people's failings, what conduct is expected of himself. The significant point about the image of the ideal self is that it is directed towards what must be positively achieved, that is to the ideal of a social personality with particular moral qualities but also certain material attributes. It is not concerned with a code of moral or ritual interdictions that simply must not be transgressed. Failure to achieve what he expects of himself brings self-disesteem and shame.

A man may feel the loss of self-regard even where his dishonourable conduct, or personal inadequacy, is unlikely to become known to others. But more often than not self-regard also has an external point of reference. A man is constantly anxious as to how his actions and qualities will appear

[7] Although the Sarakatsani use the adjective φιλότιμος to describe a person who 'loves honour', they do not use the substantive τὸ φιλότιμο, 'a sense' of this honour, which is a concept of popular thought extremely common in many parts of Greece. It is clear, however, that ἐγωϊσμός is a close analogue.

in the eyes of others, and how their evaluation of himself relates to the ideal image of how he would wish to appear. Clearly, the more the publicity that surrounds any particular area of social life, the greater is the efficacy of the sentiment of self-regard as a sanction of approved qualities and conduct.

A man's self-regard is typically molested where he is insulted or defamed or believes himself to be so treated. When another person suggests by even indirect allusion that a man is dishonourable or weak he molests his self-regard (προσβάλλει τὸν ἐγωῖσμό του). Or when a man by deed, or word, behaves towards another in such a way as to suggest that he is not worthy of consideration and recognition, he again molests his self-regard; for a man only acts in this way towards another when he considers him to be of lesser reputation and, by inference, less honourable. In such circumstances the core of a man's social personality is touched, his manliness and pre-potence are questioned. Then, the only remedy is to attack his detractors with knife or stick.

There are many instances of such a situation. The stoning of a sheep by another shepherd when it has strayed across a boundary. An unguarded public remark which the recipient judges others will consider to be an unanswered insult if he does not retaliate. It is, in part, self-regard which urges the abduction of a girl when a candidate bridegroom has been refused by the girl's father. Christos Kazoukas was refused the hand of the daughter of Paschos. She was too young, the girl's father said, and as she was, indeed, only twenty-two, Christos was prepared to accept this explanation rather than undertake the dangerous business of abduction. But George Carvounis, a second cousin to Christos, heard a different tale that the girl's family had refused Christos because it was said that he was sexually impotent and inadequate. In fact, the girl's mother had dubbed him by a nickname, 'Lame penis' (κουτσοπούτσα), which referred literally to these supposed short-comings. Christos had a smooth skin, fine features and a strikingly high-pitched voice. Simply, he did not look the part of a pallikari. There was, therefore, all the greater urgency that he should reply to these damning allegations; for the alternative was ridicule and shame. His kinsmen offered united moral support and the unspoken threat of abandonment if he did nothing. In due course, the girl was abducted and agreed to marry Christos out of terror at the threats made by the Kazoukas family against her own people if she did not consent.

Self-regard is a subjective and personal sentiment. At the same time the situations which provoke it are socially defined. All those elements of prestige, whether of the individual or the family, affect it and are sanctioned by it. A man's self-regard leads him to conserve his honour, to act honourably, to strive after wealth, to act proudly and arrogantly and so on. Self-regard inhibits any conduct on which an interpretation of weakness may be placed. For instance, the Sarakatsani seldom accept or give apologies. 'A pardon is not acceptable' (δὲν πιάνεται τὸ παρντόν), it is said. Similarly, bargaining between a shepherd and a livestock merchant is extremely difficult because the self-regard of the seller will not allow him to accept a price which he thinks other men will laugh at, even though he may admit to himself that in relation to the state of the market and the condition of his stock the merchant's offer is not unreasonable. For this reason a merchant employs a Sarakatsanos[8] who from his local knowledge advises him how far each man may be pressed in negotiation. It is also his task to assure the shepherd that he has made a good bargain. It is self-regard, again, that prevents a Sarakatsanos from reaching a settlement out of court when his animals have trespassed on other people's land. He prefers to go to law knowing in advance that he must pay double the costs of a private agreement. Any compromise would be an admission of weakness in a personal confrontation. Defeat in the courts, on the other hand, is merely defeat by the power of the impersonal State apparatus, which in any case, it is agreed, is corrupt and inimical to the interests of the community.

Self-regard is a kind of appetitive tension between what a man is and what he ought to be. In this context, however, what a man is depends on the evaluation by the community of what a man is alleged to be, or to have done. The need of a man, socially and psychologically, to identify the community's evaluation of himself with his own ideal image is so great that

---

[8] Known as a κολαοῦζος, a guide.

it leads, very often, to a greater concern with appearances than reality. Or, rather, appearances become reality. In the appearance of being a pallikari, he becomes a pallikari. There is often a kind of unconscious cheating. A man boasts and asserts himself the more when there is little fear that he may be called on to prove himself. And knives are pulled with greater bravado when it is certain that others are present to prevent their use.

If self-regard is the need to achieve an identity with the image of an ideal self, shame is the emotion experienced by an individual when he clearly fails to do so. As in the case of self-regard, although a man may feel shame for short-comings or sufferings that remain secret, it involves at all times some idea of comparison with the achievements of others, and it is all the more acute when a man's inadequacy is publicly exposed. A man may feel shame not only for his own short-comings, but also for those of other persons with whom he is closely identified in any situation. And it may also be a sentiment imputed by others when they make critical comments on a man's behaviour or condition. They may say that his conduct in a particular situation is a matter for shame, that is, if he were an honourable man, his sense of shame would have prevented him from acting in the way that he did.

Like self-regard, shame is a sanction for all those elements that are relevant to the prestige of a family, or an individual. Thus shame relates not only to conduct which is morally bad, but also to any kind of conduct which is only conventionally deviant. And anything which leads to, or is the basis of, low prestige is a matter for shame. Whatever may be the underlying psychological character of shame, its cultural definition amongst the Sarakatsani is the sense or fear of failure. The failure exists to the extent that a man does not possess some attribute required by the image of his ideal self. When a man acts disgracefully he hurts himself. When he is poor or weak, by suffering this condition he condemns himself. And the sense of shame, an essentially internal sanction of action, is related to the external threat of social abandonment, the fear that the community will judge him to be 'lost' (χαμένος).

A number of examples illustrate the relation between shame and failure. When Nasios attempted to seduce a married woman he showed that he was not honourable and, further, by hiding in his hut he revealed his cowardice and exposed his manliness to public ridicule. He failed to measure up to the critical qualities required of a man; this was a matter for shame. The young son of Pistiolis, who possesses only sixty sheep, told me that on migrations the family is so ashamed of its poverty that it delays its departure until a few days after the other Sarakatsani have left the village. 'Otherwise people would see how poor we were and would laugh at us.' Eleutherios has a small son who is subject to fits. His brother admitted that this was a matter for shame because people would say that God was punishing the child for its parents' sins. It is a mark of indelible parental failure if children are spotted by any moral or physical blemish. A modest maiden has shame in two respects. She is aware of the power of her sexuality; in a sense she has already failed by being a woman at all, and for this she 'feels shame'. She is also a girl 'with shame' in the sense that she carefully conforms to a strict code of modest behaviour and movement. This expresses the fear of failure in disciplining sexuality according to the ideal pattern of maidenly conduct. Finally, a little child feels shame before a stranger because it lacks experience of a situation it does not understand. It fears failure and criticism. 'The child is ashamed. He does not understand yet,' says the father.

These different contextual situations in which the concept of shame is used are linked by the notion of failure, or fear of failure, whether the emphasis on inadequacy is internal to the social personality, producing feelings of self-disesteem, or whether, as is more often the case, these sentiments are made more acute through public loss of prestige. The laughter, ridicule, and insults actually experienced, or more often imagined, are the marks of failure so far as the external reference of shame is concerned. Between the two sanctions of right conduct, self-regard, and shame, there is a close affinity. While self-regard is the positive incentive to achieve what is expected, shame is the fear, or the realization, of not achieving it. This difference of emphasis is reflected in the fact that to some extent these two sentiments are sex-linked. The idea of self-regard contains the notion of a positive competitive attitude, especially between men of similar age and standing. Women do not go out into the world and compete with one another. On the contrary, their activities centre round the hearth where they ought to co-operate with their kinswomen and, if they are married, with their sisters-in-law and the wives of the husband's brothers. When a woman is said to have self-regard, this generally refers to a touchy and unco-operative attitude with other women in the extended family or co-operating group; it is, then, not a quality for self-congratulation.

Conversely, where shame is the fear of failure or criticism that demands a careful modest constrained demeanour, it is said that women have more shame than men. The Sarakatsani point out that since it is the sexuality of women which provokes men and not the reverse, women have the greater need to be constantly restrained in their thoughts and actions by a sense of sexual shame. Furthermore, since men must battle with one another in the community and show craftiness in their dealings with prominent and useful people outside its boundaries, it is clear that the restrictive régime, which an extreme sense of shame imposes on an individual, is incompatible with the social role of the head of family who must generally assert himself and on occasion for the sake of his family may even be forced into questionable actions. This is not to say that a man does not equally feel shame when he is judged to have failed. It means, rather, that unlike a woman he cannot remain always in a state of shame, in the sense of guarding against imminent failure by a careful restriction of behaviour and movement.

\*      \*      \*

The fear of gossip and ridicule is closely related to the two concepts of self-regard and shame. The prestige of an individual, or a family, is constantly being evaluated and re-evaluated in the community through gossip about personalities and events. To be gossiped about is in most cases to be criticized adversely, and since people enjoy this recreation they laugh at and ridicule the object of their discussion. The knowledge, or the imagining, of this ridicule and laughter is an important element in a man's feelings of shame. For if the outside world judges him to be a failure he has also failed to live up to his own ideal image of himself which depends on success.

The laughter of other people is invited in all situations where a man, or a group, has failed. 'The world laughs' (ὁ κόσμος γελάει) at a man when he fails to defend his honour; for instance, when he does not reply to an affront. Equally, it laughs at him when he makes some slip in conventional behaviour, or when he is made to look ridiculous. It laughs at him if he does not adequately fulfil his social role. Conversely, the need to conform to social morality and etiquette is often supported by the statement that, if a man does not act in a particular way, 'the world will laugh at him'. To be ridiculous (γελοῖος) is to lack the recognition essential for social reputation.

The ridicule or laughter which a man suffers, or imagines he is suffering, is seldom crudely inflicted to his face. The sanction is more subtle. But he is not slow to sense that he is being ridiculed. A man who is insensitive to the attitudes of others (and among the Sarakatsani such men are rare) will speedily be informed of the situation through some kinsman who, because of their association, is anxious that the ridiculed man should reassert his position, if that is possible, or, in a case of moral delinquency, should mend his ways.

There are, however, certain situations where open ridicule may occur. A man of very low prestige who is 'lost' may sometimes be ridiculed to his face. On the rare occasions when Costas Pistiolis is in any social gathering he is invariably asked to sing, since this ability is one of the many social graces he does not possess. Everybody laughs. Mild as such mockery may seem, no honourable member of this community would accept it passively. Open ridicule may also happen at weddings when men lose their sense of caution. At one wedding a guest who was addled and aggressive from his drinking called for more ouzo. A bottle was brought to him. He poured a glass and drank it, only to discover it was water. A roar of laughter went up, a pointed comment on the weakness of a man unable to drink and retain a measure of self-control. At once his knife was out, but it was quickly wrenched from his hand and the man was thrown bodily from the arbour.

Although the community is dispersed, news travels with rapidity. Any interesting event is widely known throughout the community within two or three days. Weddings and festivals are centres of news exchange, but heads of families, and some older women, are constantly in Jannina for business and shopping. Here, most Sarakatsani eat and sleep at the Korakas Hotel and this establishment is an important clearing-house for business and gossip. The eagerness for news and gossip is intense. The consciousness of being a community stimulates the circulation of news which is all the more urgent because people do not live in a closely settled community. In its turn the very process of evaluating the conduct of other Sarakatsani is a reaffirmation of the solidarity and indeed of the existence of the community as such. Gossip and denigration are carried out in terms of a system of values. Every criticism of a man's conduct, whether it is justified or not, is a restatement of a value.

Gossip within the family is uninhibited and subjective. Fantastic allegations of wrongdoing are levelled against other families of the community on negligible evidence. No doubt this contributes to the group's morale and suggests, by contrast, its own integrity. Public discussion of a man's conduct, for instance in a coffee-shop, is more careful and somewhat more factual. Vicious slander without a foundation of hearsay fact merely destroys the accuser's own reputation for being an honourable man. Slander of this kind might be an answerable provocation if any kinsman of the ridiculed man were present at the time. If there is some, but not conclusive, evidence to condemn a man, a spirited debate will take place and it is in these circumstances that the presence of an articulate kinsman may help to salvage a man's reputation. But where a man's fault or failure seems to be clearly established the whole assembly will unite with obvious pleasure to ridicule a man. In this way they emphasize their own probity and prestige. Then, even the presence of kinsmen will not save a man, and if his shortcomings are sufficiently serious they may be driven to abandon him.

Gossip never ceases and it seizes on the pettiest of details and circumstances. In situations which especially shock or pique the community's imagination satirical songs are sometimes written. Song writing, of course, is the work of individuals but it depends on the community whether the songs will be accepted and remembered. This is a most feared sanction since the ridicule lives on in the song. The song will not be sung to the victim's face, but he will learn of it, and be bitterly shamed.

The songs are not, in fact, particularly daring or insulting in themselves: therein, perhaps, lies their effect. Of Nasios Karapheris the woman chaser it is sung, 'Up at Kouphos where they used to grow corn, Nasios is making a place to lie down. Hidden away in the long grasses, he makes secret eyes. Mitsos draws out his knife to kill Nasios Karapheris.'

A song may be composed about a man who, although he has not erred morally, has been made to look ridiculous. For this, too, is failure. Theodoros Kallis is a physically strong man with a bullying character. He is wealthy and many people fear his violent nature. They were not sorry, therefore, when he suffered the following misfortune.

'On the twenty-first of January went Theodoros, the poor devil, to see his little mother-in-law. But when he arose in the morning, "Oh dear oh dear, they have cut the tail of my horse, dear mother-in-law!" Then cursed the mother-in-law, "May two unmarried boys never live to set up their wedding standards!" '

A man's failure in any respect may also be prolonged in the community's memory by giving him a nickname (παρατσούκλι). Flattering nicknames are sometimes given to members of the leading families. Costas Katsanos in his younger days was known as 'the flyer' (φεύγας) because of his great speed of movement up or down hill. But more often nicknames ridicule a man. Thus a man who was caught in the act of stealing maize from a villager's garden, was named καλαμπόκιος, an adjective fabricated from the Greek word for this grain. The name was not a comment on the morality of theft but the indignity of discovery and failure.

I have said enough to indicate how public opinion functioning through gossip and ridicule acts to sanction the community's prestige values. Gossip and its outcome, ridicule, are in a certain manner the external sanctions which support the internal sanctions of individual action, self-regard and the sense of shame. The subtlety of gossip and ridicule as sanctions is that, since they do not generally operate in his presence, they offer a man no excuse for violent response. He may respond to the insult of an individual, but not to the laughter of the community which he senses, but seldom hears.

## 7. A SYSTEM OF VALUES

Sarakatsan society offers men only three important corporate memberships: in the family, the local community, and the nation. Little conflict arises between the obligations created by these different commitments. The interests of the family are normally contained within the purposes of the community when it faces other communities, those of the community are contained within the aims of the nation opposed to the rest of the world. In war, the actions of a soldier reflect simultaneously on the honour of his family, his community, and his nation. And in each instance the honour and interests of the individual and of the group are mutually implicated.

Honour refers to an exclusive identification. The honour of a group is opposed to the honour of another if only for the reason that there is an implicit comparison between different honours in reference to a pattern of ideal attributes. But honour also reflects on the correct status relations between individuals or groups. When two groups are in communication the behaviour of the persons representing them implies, on either side, a certain evaluation of the other group. If a man suffers treatment that is less than his due, his honour, and the honour of the group he represents, are diminished. But in the experience of the Sarakatsani the interests and prestige of families, communities, and nations are inevitably in collision, and this must lead men to exploit others where they can. Thus relations between different groups always carry the threat of the depreciation of the honour of one for the benefit of the other. Although relations between families, communities, and nations refer, ideally, to an equality in honour, yet at each level those who represent these groups must struggle with all their resources of courage and self-discipline to maintain these ideal status relations. These struggles are intense. And in every significant context of action the world is necessarily divided with dramatic definition into own people and strangers, friends and enemies. Consequently relationship radically affects the forms of approved behaviour. It is a virtue generally to cheat, deceive, and lie to non-kinsmen, but the same conduct towards kinsmen would be shameful and, often, sinful as well. The values of honour and prestige are exclusive and particularist. They have a moral content of their own but they cannot be referred to any universal moral principle.

For the Sarakatsani, family honour is the chief concern. Indeed, the honour of community or nation is, in their view, a projection of the concept of family honour. This honour is shared in two senses; intensively, by those whose reputation is identified by their membership in the same family; extensively, by the community of families sharing in common a system of values by which they judge one another's position and performance. Honour depends not upon the consciences of the individuals in a family whose reputation is under scrutiny, but on the concessions and reluctant approval of other families. Most of these are unrelated and hostile. Since the threat of denigration is continuous, it must be balanced by the repeated exhibition of those qualities that support honour and prestige: self-assertive courage in men, modest virtue in women. In the one case by social convention, in the other by its negative character, the presence of these qualities is more often revealed by attitudes and appearances than substantive proof. There is an emphasis on opinions and appearances, not facts. The consequences of action rather than the intentions behind it are important. This does not mean that private shame for undiscovered failure does not exist. But, inevitably, ideas about individual moral responsibility are blurred, and undiscovered shame is not as morally serious as public disgrace.

Reputation is impossible without strength. Poverty is a mark of failure, not a virtue. Strength in sheep and in men encourages others to respect a family's honour, it attracts dependent kinsmen whose support further extends influence and prestige. Honour and strength are linked. If a family is without sons the call of honour may find a man in the dilemma that if honour is lost the moral existence of the family collapses, or if honour is vindicated his family becomes a leaderless group of women and children dependent on the generosity of kinsmen, a condition which must eventually affect prestige and, perhaps, honour as well. Honour, and the obligation to die for it, is the ideal value, but the sacrifice necessarily weakens the family. Honour remains integral, but becomes more vulnerable. A family needs at least one man in the role of unmarried brother whose unreflecting courage guards its honour, and one man in the role of married leader whose prudence and self-control secures its material strength. This possibility depends on the number of sons in a family and the stage of its development. Yet in the critical and unfriendly view of others a family must always be in a position to defend itself against outrage. Weakness is shameful and circumstances never excuse it. The corollary to this notion is that, within limits, it is normally preferable to insult than to be insulted, to exploit than to be exploited.

The emphasis on strength appears in the importance, in moral judgements, of health, effectiveness (δραστηριότης), skill and cleverness. Skill conserves material strength; animals are less likely to become diseased, inferior pastures are not chosen. A man ought to be 'able' in the sense of able to provide, and he needs cleverness of the kind that foresees future threats in time. Health is imperative in this scheme of things; chronic sickness or deformity is inexcusable. There is little sentimentality. Questions of honour are not complicated by notions of chivalrous conduct. An honour killing is accomplished without warning by a bullet fired from behind cover, or a knife in the back. This does not mean that Sarakatsani are cowards; they are, in fact, immensely brave. But, continually, the accent is on effective action, the achievement of success, the avoidance of failure. Ends matter more than means. Consequently, those qualities and attributes that are necessary for strength tend to be considered as morally good, those that lead to weakness as morally bad. Sarakatsani would condemn any display of excessive altruism on the grounds that it inevitably weakens a person's own family and strengthens the family of another; it would be, at best, imprudent, and in a situation where it clearly damaged the interests of the family it would be immoral.

Strength and prowess, then, matter more than ethical goodness. Indeed a man is only good when he is also by implication, able and strong. Although aimless violence is dishonourable there is no missing the pleasure it gives when a man is forced to kill; nor the prestige which it brings him. For there is no more conclusive way of showing that you are stronger than by taking away the other man's life.

The form of this system of values is related to three features of the social structure: the first of these is the complementary opposition of the sexes. It is consistent with the radical character of this opposition that most virtues are sex-linked. Since the sensuality of sex is a critical flaw in human nature, chastity becomes an important element in honour, around which those complementary virtues, the self-assertive qualities of the men, the modest constricted virtues of the women, are organized in defence. At the same time the moral superiority of the male sex in this opposition allows the main burden of the responsibility for original sin to be borne by the woman in a way that does not compromise the inherent nobility of man which is, necessarily, a premise of a system of values based on ideas of honour. And the complementary opposition of the two sexes and their ideal attributes allows the introduction of those quieter feminine virtues of love, modesty, and a disposition to co-operate, without inconsistency in relation to the self-assertive male values, and in the context of inner family life where they are most necessary to express the moral solidarity of the family and support those who face a hostile and competitive world.

The second relevant feature of social structure is the solidarity of the family, and the categorical nature of obligations between its members. This solidarity is both active and passive. Whatever is done or suffered by one member equally affects the honour and shame of the others. No actor stands in isolation without reference to his membership in a family. He carries always a weight of representative responsibility when his actions are observed or even speculated on by others. And, on the other hand, the family is a small group in which there is no security of anonymity when other members fail. In these circumstances, where there is individual responsibility but no certainty of individual justice, important values are variations on the theme of strength and weakness, success and failure. Without self-confidence, prepotence, and skill, a man is 'lost' (χαμένος), morally as well as practically.

The relationships of hostility between families unconnected by ties of kinship or marriage are the third feature of social structure. They are oppositions consistent with a particular form of bilateral kinship system, and the absence of any forms of political or economic co-operation other than those based on relationship or patronage. These potentially destructive confrontations are reconciled through the acceptance of competition for prestige as the end of individual and family purpose. For it turns men's minds from thoughts of the physical destruction of their enemies to the alternative of their social humiliation, a form of opposition more compatible with the vulnerable quality of the shepherd's life. At the same time these particular values, if they deny the practicability of universal moral principles and individual justice, present an image of man that is in some ways heroic and not ignoble. Men must be brave and women virtuous to achieve ideal, one might say mythical, forms of acting and being. They are encouraged in the need to discipline their weaknesses by the severity of their mutual criticism; roles are few, and values unambiguous in a common field of experience. But judgements concern the effectiveness of the total social personality, an amalgam of virtues, skills, and material attributes; and not abstract qualities of moral excellence.

In competitive institutions, although feelings of hostility may remain unabated, opposition becomes a form of mutual dependence; the more men are opposed in this way, the more they have need of one another. The values of prestige recommend the intense consideration of own interests and honour, accentuating always the exclusiveness and separation of one family from another. Yet they also impose the condition that prestige depends on the attentions and opinions of others. They separate; and, at the same time, they create a necessary and close interdependence in the common membership of a community in honour.

# XI

# THE VALUES OF RELIGIOUS BELIEF

## 1. GOD AND SIN

I DO not propose to discuss in any detail the ritual practices of Sarakatsan religious life, nor the peripheral complex of magic techniques which are sometimes linked to religious beliefs and sometimes not. My purpose is to indicate the general character of Sarakatsan religious conceptions and to show in what way a form of Christian belief may co-exist with the values of honour and prestige that were examined in the previous chapter.

In certain respects the relationship of the Sarakatsani to the Greek Orthodox Church, as an institution, is tenuous. They have never been regular churchgoers. Before 1938 their huts were often far from villages and few adult men and women would have been able to escape from the imperative routines of family and flocks to make the long journey over difficult country. And since they have come to live in or near the villages, the almost open ridicule and contempt of the villagers have discouraged the Sarakatsani from altering this traditional pattern.

When a Sarakatsanos goes to church he normally does so with the intention of taking Holy Communion, and this he ought to do, preferably, twice a year. During Easter week almost every man, woman, and child in the community will find a means of attending one of the services, and the majority will discover an opportunity to communicate again later in the year on the feast day of the Assumption of the All Holy Mother of God on 15th August, or at Christmas, or at one of the other more important festivals of the Church.

The Eucharist, in the simple way that they understand it as the sacrifice of Christ's blood which overcomes the barrier of sin separating man from God, is the central belief of Sarakatsan religious life. Otherwise, when they attend a service they understand nothing of the structure of the liturgy, they do not know that the liturgy is a symbolic representation of the life and sacrifice of Christ. Only the shorter and more frequently repeated phrases of the liturgy are intelligible to them. Yet, although the Sarakatsani are not oppressed by any complexities of religious belief, they have deep faith, and a simple but relatively clear, if sometimes unorthodox, conception of God the Father, Christ the Son, the All Holy Mother of God, and the Saints; the divine archetype family, and those transfigured human beings who through the self-discipline and sanctity of their lives are the appropriate models for the guidance of weaker men, and the natural intercessors between them and God.

I have met no Sarakatsanos who doubts the existence of God. Such a question seems to them unintelligent. A man takes out his watch and asks, 'Somebody made this watch, is it possible that nobody made the world?' God is the creator of the universe and all things in it. And since this is so, anything which is not explicable in terms of simple physical causation tends to be referred to Him: or in the case of evil phenomena to the Devil. He exists in and beyond the boundless space of the sky. He does not descend to earth, yet from on high He is able to see and hear the acts and words of men as well as to know their unspoken intentions. Sarakatsani do not limit their image of God by precise physical definition, He is a 'certain power' (κάποια δύναμη), who is nevertheless personal, concerned with the acts of man, and capable, on a spiritual plane, of the emotions of anger and love.

God has an absolute power to impose His will. God's omnipotence and his own complementary dependence is the simple model of the shepherd's relationship to God. A Sarakatsanos says, 'All our work is with God' (ὅλη ἡ δουλειά μας εἶναι μὲ τὸν Θεό). From God derives life itself. He gives or withholds children from a man, He sends the rain for the essential grass. The sheep itself is in a peculiar sense God's animal, a 'sacred thing' (ἱερὸ πρᾶμα). A Sarakatsan folk myth tells how God was with the All Holy One in a cave when she was bearing Christ. He came out of the cave to find fire, and seeing a flock of sheep and their shepherd He passed silently through, without frightening them or rousing the dogs, approached the shepherd's fire and took a burning ember. As He retraced His steps He blessed the sheep that they should be His own for all time.

God not only provides, He protects. He is the Father of men who are His children, 'God protects the people' (ὁ Θεὸς φυλάει τὸν κόσμο) they say. God is concerned about His creatures and, because they are dependent on Him, He is disposed to have pity and compassion on them. 'Lord have mercy on us', this simple and often repeated petition of the liturgy is well understood. God's mercy is a reflection of His love. And this, since God is all powerful, must be an unmotivated favour, except in the sense that a father loves his children simply because they are his children. When a Sarakatsanos asserts 'We believe in God' (πιστεύομε στὸν Θεό) he means not only that they believe intellectually in His existence, but that they have confidence in Him. He is thought of as being at once distant from men yet close to them. The absolute power of God, and also His absolute goodness, place a great distance between God and sinful men and this, perhaps, is reflected in the notion of His dwelling in the infinity of the sky. But since He created men with the potentiality of divinity, He remains concerned with their affairs. Sarakatsani feel that they are able to approach Him directly with simple petitions pleading for protection from evil, sickness, or want.

But in His concern for the beings He has created God, also, judges and punishes. He is a just God in the sense that no evil-doer ever escapes His judgement, yet the form this punishment assumes frequently appears to men to be capricious and un-predictable. Sometimes vengeance is not immediate but falls on the children of a guilty person. Very often misfortune seems utterly undeserved by the sufferer himself and must be simply ascribed to the will of God which passes his understanding; even other men, who seldom find it difficult to refer a mis-fortune suffered by another to the sin committed, will some-times agree that the measure of God's punishment is hard, particularly when the life of a small child is taken. God the Father, then, appears to the Sarakatsani under two aspects; first as He who provides and cares, He who is merciful, approachable and near at hand; but secondly as the judge and avenger, distant and without pity. Under the second aspect there is a sense of ambivalence, even resentment, in the atti-tude to God, not unlike the tension and strain that enters the relations of a Sarakatsanos with his earthly father. He cannot escape from the omnipotence of God and the futility of resistance, yet his humility is not entirely unconditional.

Man is noble but between him and God there is always a barrier of sin. Sarakatsani express this in the idea of 'a weight' (ἕνα βάρος) which depresses the spirit and in a literal sense draws man downwards away from God. The Sarakatsani, however, make a distinction between two kinds of sin, personal sin (οἱ ἁμαρτίες μας) and ancestral sin (οἱ ἁμαρτίες τοῦ Ἀδάμ). Both divide man from God but while the individual is wholly responsible for personal sins, he feels little sense of guilt for the other kind of sin which he sees as a pre-existing condition of the world into which he was born.

The sins for which a man is individually responsible fall into three categories. The first includes those acts which are wanton and personal insults to God Himself, acts in which a man shows himself to be impious (ἀσεβής) through a denial or mockery of God. Perjury is the greatest of these; for in this act a man calls upon God to witness the truth of his words, that is, he attempts the impossible task of implicating God as a collaborator in his lie. Although the Sarakatsanos lies as a matter of habit and policy at other times, it is only in situations of great difficulty that he will perjure himself.

The second category of personal sins relates to family life, and especially to certain fundamental and axiomatic attitudes and duties on which the moral solidarity of the family institution is based. The family for the Sarakatsanos is not merely a human and social group, it is a complex of relations divinely instituted and sanctioned by God. On a transcendent and spiritual plane, the Holy Family of God the Father, the Mother of Christ, and Christ the Son, is the archetype for all earthly families. As love, respect, compassion, relate the three Holy Persons, so these qualities ought to regulate the relations of the members of earthly families. Where this is not so there is a condition of sin and God's punishment may be expected. Thus this category of sins includes the unnecessary brutality of fathers towards small children; provoking a premature separation of sons' households; laziness or dereliction of duty which leads a family into serious want; in that sense, gambling or chronic drunkenness; public insult to a parent by a son or daughter; maltreatment of aged parents; striking a parent; physical violence between brothers; wanton cruelty to, or neglect of, the family's horses, sheep or goats.

The third category of sins are those which exist in the field of general morality in the behaviour of one man towards another. A man feels little obligation to discipline himself in his conduct towards an unrelated person, but there are limits which ought not to be transgressed, and generally speaking these limits are related to the consequences that immoderate behaviour would have for the victim's family. To exploit a very poor man, or refuse charity to a beggar, is sinful. To slander the name of an unmarried girl is a sin. In these instances there enters a hint of the idea of *hubris*, an arrogance of act, or thought, overstepping bounds set by God and involving wrongdoing to others which threatens the moral or physical existence of a family and is not excusable on grounds of self-interest.

The essence of sin is that, in one form or another, it is wilful rebellion against God and His institutions. And for such an act of personal sin a man may expect to be punished by God through sickness, death, or some catastrophe that leads his family into want. Catastrophe or misfortune is by no means always explained as the punishment of God, but where a man is guilty of a known sin, any misfortune which befalls him, or another member of his immediate family, will certainly be recognized as divine punishment. As I have already suggested, Sarakatsani are skilled in listing the sins of others. The sufferer and his kin, on the other hand, will more often ascribe their ill luck not to God's wrath, but to the evil eye, a manifestation of other men's sinful and envious natures.

It must be stressed that the Sarakatsani visualize the punishment of God as being realized essentially in this world either against themselves, or their children. Hell is a place of vaporous darkness where sinful men suffer in cauldrons of pitch; Paradise is a plain of well-watered grass covered with spring flowers. These conceptions exist, yet seem to make little impression. If an evil man dies unscathed, men are not content with thoughts of the torments he may suffer in Hell; they concentrate their attention on the misfortunes which will certainly overtake his children in this world. The wages of sin is death. But it is not the spiritual death which follows physical death which holds any real terror for the Sarakatsanos, but rather the spiritual death which precedes physical death. For sin interrupts the communion between man and God on whose provision and protection a man and his family are, in the final analysis, entirely dependent. The consistency between this view of divine punishment and the system of prestige values is clear enough. In both cases it is the events of this life, and this world, which are significant.

But the Sarakatsani do not expect to be punished individually in the same way for ancestral sin. For this kind of sin refers to the general human condition not to individual transgression of particular interdictions. The two sins they particularly include under this rubric are sensuality and envy. Both are conditions which imply an attachment to material things which leads man away from God. And it is equally inevitable that every man must succumb, in some degree, to both these sins. However, the attitude to sensuality and envy is not precisely the same. The consequences of sensuality, as we have seen elsewhere, destroy the integrity and honour of the family. Sensuality is a condition which constantly threatens to undermine this institution from within. It must, therefore, be disciplined by all the strength and will of each man and woman. But unlike the protestant puritan who attempts to win his battle by destroying sensuality itself, and feels individually responsible and guilty when he fails, the Sarakatsanos accepts that sensuality is part of the human condition, but that he must struggle to contain and discipline it. The important restraints are essentially external. Unmarried men and women who are not kinsmen or affines have few legitimate opportunities to meet, and none to speak to one another. The unmarried daughter seldom goes to the well alone, and when she passes a man on the path she lowers her eyes. It is a tight prudential control, collectively exercised. For, as the Sarakatsani say, 'If you put your hand in the fire, it gets burnt'. A man of God may win an individual and inward control over the condition of sensuality, but ordinary men need the help of kinsmen and the support of institutions in the unequal fight. Sensuality is part of ancestral sin and as such a man or woman does not feel individually guilty for its existence. But it remains a threat to honour. And in this respect the struggle to control it is so fundamental to the belief in their own nobility that, in a community where masculine values are paramount, it has led the Sarakatsani to a form of sexual dualism in which women must bear the main responsibility for this collective sin; a responsibility, however, which is not to be confused with individual guilt.

Envy does not threaten the family in the same way from within, nor does it conflict with the values of honour and pride. Indeed, the emphasis on competitive values, the need to achieve identity with ideal types of social personality, the competitive opposition of family groups, are social values and relationships which inevitably breed envy. Like the fingers on a hand, all men are not the same, Sarakatsani explain. Those who are less fortunate, or less evidently honourable, must envy those others who surpass them. Envy, they admit, leads directly to deceit and cunning. In the form of the evil eye it is a force of psychic hostility and wickedness that pervades the world, spiritually separating man from man, and man from God. Focused though the eyes of an envious man, it may create physical effects of sickness and destruction. These things, it is agreed, are evil, but they arise from the external conditions of a world of limited resources and contrary human wills, not from the conscious sinfulness of individual men. The force of envy is felt to be so pervasive that it would be futile to struggle to control it, as one must struggle to control sensuality; particularly since a man may put the evil eye on another without conscious knowledge or intention. All that an honourable man can do is to avoid in his conscious actions the consequences of excessive envy. For the observer the difference between the ancestral sins of sensuality and envy is that while the former compromises honour, the latter, in a certain sense, is a consequence of it. Naturally, the Sarakatsani do not see the distinction in quite this form.

The difference between personal and ancestral sin is not unrelated to the distinction between the Sarakatsan senses of guilt and shame. Both guilt and shame are internal states of conscience but whereas shame is concerned with a man's failure to approach some ideal pattern of conduct, the reference of guilt and personal sin is to the transgression of interdicted limits. Shame relates to failure especially in comparisons with the achievements of others. It has an external sanction in the social abandonment which in some degree always accompanies public shame. The sense of guilt, on the other hand, is the consequence of acts which defy the commandments of God, whether they concern the relations between man and God, or social responsibilities that follow from common membership in a group. The external sanction against sin is the punishment inflicted by God and sometimes by a social group. An act may, of course, provoke both a sense of guilt and feelings of shame. Which term will be used depends on whether the act is more generally regarded under the aspect of transgression, or of failure to live up to an ideal pattern of behaviour. Ancestral sin, however, arouses no sense of guilt. Sensuality and envy are not individual transgressions. Yet the first of these sins must be disciplined and the second, at least, prevented from becoming the guiding principle of a man's actions. But this discipline is a matter of relative success or failure, and therefore of shame not guilt.

In this way the Sarakatsani, through their view of ancestral sin, reconcile the nobility of man with his sinfulness. Nobility depends on the struggle of the individual to achieve ideal patterns of being and behaviour. The sins which produce feelings of individual guilt and, therefore, qualify the nobility of his nature, do not constitute an impressive list, and they are transgressions which the Sarakatsani do not easily commit. On the other hand, the ancestral sins recognized by the Sarakatsani are general forms of sin which the Orthodox Church holds to be peculiarly grave and, moreover, sins which the Sarakatsani are continually committing; in the instance of sensuality because they are human, and in the case of envy because the social institutions and values encourage it. Yet the Sarakatsanos avoids any personal responsibility for these sins by insisting that they are exterior to his individual will. They corrupt the condition in which he must live, but not the potentialities of his nature. Sensuality was the consequence of Adam's sin, not his. Envy was the sin of the Devil in his act of rebellion against God. Many Sarakatsani are able to explain these details, all are aware, at least, that these sins have been part of the human condition since the moment of the Fall, a condition against which a man must certainly struggle, but which does not necessarily compromise the nobility of his soul.

Nevertheless these are sins which separate man from God. If they provoke no sense of personal guilt, a man feels a heaviness, a depression of his spirit, when he thinks of his need to be near God, and of this inherited condition of sinfulness. In the previous chapter I mentioned how the Sarakatsani think of the years of youth as the time of moral excellence. Later come responsibilities and the need for cunning, deceit, and lies. There is grudging admiration for the expertise of the shrewd leader but regret that the means to success must be these. 'If only we had trust in one another', is the most common Sarakatsan expression of utopian values. In the face of the many external threats to their way of life they are profoundly conscious of their own disunion. They sense, also, the distance between the heroic quality of their ideals and the often petty quarrels, or hypocritical posturings, of everyday living. But, they say, there is nothing the individual can do to alter the corrupt forms and conditions of life in this world. In this situation sin, for which they are not responsible, separates the Sarakatsani from God. It requires the grace of God, conferred through the sacraments of Baptism and the Eucharist, to make communion possible. Inevitably if a child dies unbaptized, innocent of the world but still implicated in the appalling consequences of original sin, its soul is lost. The baptized Sarakatsanos is free of the original guilt, yet participation in the world of sin again separates him from God and he requires, therefore, the periodical renewal of his state of grace which the Eucharist effects. The related elements in Sarakatsan religious life, then, are simply these: the nobility of the Sarakatsani, ancestral sin in the forms of sensuality and envy for which they are not individually responsible, the consequences of this condition of sin which separates them from God, the sacraments which reunite them to Him.

Ideas about fate are related to these notions of sin. The Sarakatsani, in common with most Greek villagers, believe that on the third night after the birth of a child, the three Fates (Μοῖρες), in the form of three old women, visit the infant's cradle and write the child's fate. What they decree is unalterable. In a number of folk stories the mother overhears the words of the Fates and attempts to prevent some stroke of ill fortune, generally an early death in predicted circumstances. Her precautions, however, are inevitably unsuccessful.

If the Sarakatsani are pressed to give the provenance and authority of these Fates, they reply that ultimately all things are written by God. But it would be incorrect to suggest that the Greek villager or shepherd faces all the events of his life in terms of a simple determinism. They do not think that the Fates arrange every detail of an individual's life. Length of life and amounts of good and ill fortune provide an external framework within which man must still struggle to avoid dishonour. These external circumstances tell nothing of the individual's moral worth; nor within the general limits set by his fate is a man prevented from seeking the help and protection of God. In practice, of course, the individual does not know what the Fates have decided for him. But the knowledge that something has, indeed, been decided encourages him to face dangers with manliness and honour, since no bullet or knife can reach its mark before the appointed hour of death.

When a man suffers misfortune, although different people may variously refer it to God's punishment or the evil eye, all will agree that it was 'written from God' (γραμμένο ἀπὸ τὸν Θεό). Similarly, in commenting on differences of fortune they will say, 'God wills it thus, some are higher, some are lower'. In Sarakatsan thought, existence in a world of external necessity is inevitably involved with ancestral sin. The multiplicity of contrary wills, the division of the sexes, the limitations of time, space, and physical resources lead to acts which are sinful. These conditions imply that the material circumstances of men must be different. Instead of being united in their respect for God, men are divided by their different personal circumstances and their self-interested struggle to improve them. Thus although Sarakatsani would not systematize their thoughts in this way, there is implied a link between ancestral sin and fate. The notion that particular events in life, and the circumstances of an individual's social position are 'written from God' indicates not so much God's detailed pre-arrangement of each individual's life, as His prevision of what will happen to each of His created beings caught up in the contingencies of sin and fate and yet still exercising in the struggle a measure of free will.

We have already seen that the Sarakatsan notion of ancestral sin releases the individual from any considerable personal sense of guilt. The idea of fate is used, but with less success, to release a man from the shame that accompanies certain kinds of failure. In the struggle for social prestige men must have self-regard and supreme confidence in themselves. They must believe that in any situation they will be omnicompetent to meet and defeat their rivals. The one fear of failure is the intervention of the external event, the disease which decimates the flock, the sterility of a wife. In almost every prayer, however short, a Sarakatsanos prays for 'good luck'. And when misfortune strikes, a man's helplessness before 'what has been written' is used to soften the sense of failure both in the presentation of events to outsiders and to himself. The element of external necessity, the restriction of absolute free will, and therefore the idea of fate, were introduced into the world through ancestral sin. By his claim that this kind of sin, or failure, is exterior to his individual will the Sarakatsan attempts to defend and assert his nobility and strength.

## 2. THE DEVIL

Over against God stands the Devil, the agent and first cause of evil. Most Sarakatsani are aware of his angelic origin and his rebellion against God, the consequence of which was expulsion from Heaven. Evil, they think, entered the universe through the contrary will of the Devil, and particularly in the form of envy. When God flings a thunderbolt to earth it passes 40 fathoms into the earth. After 40 days it reappears on the surface. It lies there for a moment, a splendour of gold, only to be claimed at once by the Devil who in his envy and fury urinates on the sacred weapon, turning it black and useless. The sin of the Devil was anterior to that of Adam: already in the form of the tempting serpent he led the first man to his Fall. He knows that he cannot dethrone God, but in his envy he attempts to destroy creation from within by turning human freedom towards evil. His work is always to turn away human souls from their natural path to God. The created world is not evil but the Devil has corrupted it with the infection of his evil. 'The Devil has the earth, God the Heavens', the shepherds often say.

The object of the Devil, then, is the moral corruption of men, or where this is not possible, their physical destruction. 'The Devil has many feet', the Sarakatsani say, that is he works out his evil in many ways, assuming whatever physical appearance is suitable for his purpose. His power is immense, and particularly in the wilderness of the mountains and forests outside the circle of men's homes protected by the grace of God; but even these he sometimes enters. In keeping with his degenerate nature, he appears frequently in the form of an animal, particularly as a black dog, donkey or hare. Sometimes he is half man, half animal, with the horned head of a goat or wild pig. When he assumes human form it is generally as an old man with a face black 'like an Arab's', and lame. In one ‚instance he appeared as an Orthodox priest in red robes. Often he pretends to be a Sarakatsanos.

Some manifestations of the Devil are plural and of either sex. Bands of male demons (σαταναραίοι) with their leader, the black-faced limping Devil, sometimes surround and torment a lonely shepherd. The female demons are referred to as the 'ladies who bring good luck' (οἱ καλότυχες), a propitiatory euphemism which indicates their power. Like their masculine counterparts, these ladies prefer the mountain tops and forests or a lonely meadow in the plain. Very often they join the male demons in an orgiastic feast, the ladies of good luck wearing long white dresses, the men in kilts of the same colour. On a night when there is wind one often hears the Devil's music in the high crags. Otherwise, when they are not feasting or provoking humans, they pass their time eternally spinning and very occasionally one comes across a spindle-weight[1] which one of them has dropped.

Devils come from and disappear into the air which is thickly populated with spirits both good and evil, although in the imagination of the Sarakatsani the evil forms predominate. One of the tasks of Christ on earth was to cleanse the air of evil spirits so that the souls of men could find a way upwards to God. High winds, storms, whirlwinds are manifestations of demonic power. Evil spirits of the air (τὰ ἀερικά) may attack men and animals invisibly or without taking a more definitive

---

[1] On the sites of prehistoric settlements.

form than a passing shadow. Two considerable classes of these spirits are 'the shadows' (τὰ ἰσκιώματα) and 'the things that terrify' (τὰ σκιάσματα)[2]. After dark the former beat men and women about the head and are the cause of pains in the head and teeth. They take hold of your arm or foot and twist it sharply. The latter often attack the sheep which in panic rush in different directions, injuring one another and losing milk.

General disasters such as earthquakes and epidemics may be attributed to the Devil. But his attacks are more often specific. If the Devil falls on the sheep and mounts them, they swell, bleed, and die. If he comes on a shepherd asleep, particularly under a fig or mulberry tree, he presses down with great weight on his chest and attempts to strangle him. The same ladies of good fortune may attack a woman who goes out alone to cut wood, with the possible consequences of paralysis, or loss of speech. But the greatest peril is that you may step, unknowingly, on the table (πατᾶς τάβλα) which a group of male and female demons have laid for a feast. One woman who had this misfortune was found unconscious on the mountainside. She remained in a deep coma, shrinking physically, until she died after 40 days the size of a small child.

But the persons who are in greatest danger from direct attack by the Devil are 'the innocent' (ἀθῶοι), particularly children and young unmarried shepherds. For the innocent person 'does not work in his heart' (δὲν ἐργάζεται στὴν καρδιά), he does not require to plot or scheme against others; his being is not seized by envy and jealousy, he is quiet, detached and free. The Devil unable yet to corrupt them morally, turns in a fury of frustration to destroy them physically. Two years ago a child was found dead with its hands over its face and no mark of injury on its body. It was not wearing a phylactery and nobody doubts that this was the work of the Devil. A young shepherd sleeping on a hillside awoke to see a Sarakatsanos with a mule approaching him from a precipice where no man or animal could pass. There was a moon and he saw that the man's face was black. He said he was Michael Raftis but the shepherd knew he was the Devil. Fortunately he was using

[2] Cf. Chatzimichalis, op. cit., vol. i, Part A, p. ρλθ′

a bag of salt for a pillow, an apotropaic substance of the greatest value. By keeping his head on this pillow and refusing to speak he passed the night in safety. In any appearance of the Devil the essential precaution is to remain absolutely silent whatever the provocation or enticement. Once a man has entered into communion with him through speech he cannot resist his will. The least consequence, then, is the loss of speech; but more probably the shepherd is led to his death over the edge of a precipice. These apparitions of the Devil are relatively common and most shepherds claim to have had at least one experience of this terrifying kind.

Fortunately God has provided the Sarakatsani with a variety of prophylactic means to resist most forms of demonic assault. Some of these are magic substances with apotropaic power, others are symbolic objects, words, or rituals, through which the grace of God confronts and defeats the power of evil. The Devil cannot approach salt or pass through fire. The exorcisms of St. Basil the Great and St. John Chrysostom are read by the priest over possessed persons or animals. Thornbush, a cross of box-wood, incense, are powerful repellants. The red egg that is dyed on the Thursday of Holy Week, or the head of a viper that has been sanctified at forty liturgies in church, is buried in the sheep-fold to protect the animals. A powerful protection for a woman who is approached by the ladies of good fortune is a black-handled knife, particularly when formed as a cross with its scabbard. A shot from a pistol or rifle when fired with the left hand dismisses any apparition. In one instance a child's phylactery contained the dried blood of a priest shot by Communists. But perhaps the most efficient protection, in an armoury which this miscellany does not exhaust, is simply the sign of the cross and the silent repetition of the thought, 'I see Christ, I see Christ, I see Christ'.

The Sarakatsani tell how the Devil hid himself in the Ark of Noah and, when the waters rose, made a hole in the side to sink it. But Noah, warned by God, ordered the snake to block the opening with its head. The Devil knows that he cannot accomplish the external destruction of the world, but he is not convinced that he cannot destroy the relationship between God and man by corrupting it from within. For the salvation of this relationship depends, in part at least, on the desire of

man to maintain it. God and the Devil fight a pitiless and
continuing battle for the souls of men in which the three
elements are the grace of God, the cunning and subtlety of the
Devil, and the will of man.

The Sarakatsani consider man's nature to be a trichotomy
of spirit (πνεῦμα), soul (ψυχή) and body (κορμί, σῶμα). Although
the views of different informants are not always clear about
these conceptions (for instance some people see no difference
between spirit and soul) nevertheless certain simple assumptions
appear to be generally accepted. Spirit and soul together form
a union with the body, yet between the first two elements and
the last there is a degree of tension. The body is a product of
material and sexual generation and is only redeemed when
it is informed by a nobility of spirit and soul. Conversely, when
the spirit and soul are dependent on the values and passions of
the body, honour is lost and communion with God is interrupted.
Spirit refers to the intellect plus the conscience (συνείδηση). Its
natural inclination is to prompt a man's will (θέληση) to lead his
soul upwards to God. It is associated in a man's mind with the
Holy Spirit (Ἅγιο Πνεῦμα) whose nature is imperfectly understood as some divine energy. Evil befalls where for one reason
or another the power of a man's spirit is not guiding his actions.
Of a Sarakatsanos who shot his brother accidentally while clean-
ing a pistol it was said that 'his spirit was not concentrated'. And
it was added, 'the Devil pulled the trigger'. The soul is the divine
element in the individual human personality. Perhaps spirit and
soul are the active and substantive aspects of the same thing.
Both tend in an upward direction, but if the individual as a total
personality does not incline his will towards God they become
corrupted by their union with merely material things; and this
is the end sought by the Devil.

It may be added that where a high value is given to the
related notions of honour, strength, and manliness, the body
cannot be considered as evil in itself,[3] but only under the aspect
of its subjection to sensual passion. Man, then, who is by nature
noble, normally moves towards a closer communion with
God but is held back partly by the sinful condition of the world

[3] In this connexion it is interesting to note that the dualist Bogomil
heresy made little headway in Greece.

in which he lives, and sometimes more seriously by the turning of his free will away from God. God will come to a man's aid when he asks for it with a 'good heart', but he cannot enter the struggle unless a man wills it. It is upon this contingency that the Devil's opportunity and power depend.

The Sarakatsani believe that if a man is willing to deny Christ and surrender his soul to the Devil almost any material favour is obtainable, poor men gain power and wealth, and sterile women have children. The Devil keeps a ledger in which these contracts are signed in blood. This is a somewhat melodramatic image of the general belief that any sudden or extraordinary material success can only be the result of communion with the Devil. In the world as it is, occasional dealings with the Evil One may be unavoidable, but too close a communion represents the surrender of the soul.

Similarly, sexual temptation by the Devil is expressed in the belief that the Devil is able to have sexual intercourse with women in their sleep and that ladies of good luck, who are peculiarly beautiful even if their hair is sometimes in the form of snakes, try to entice lonely shepherds into 'marriage'. These, generally, are the explanations accepted for erotic dreams in either sex.

One of the Devil's chief concerns is to corrupt those relationships of kinship and marriage which are instituted by God. His success is, of course, more likely where there are inherent strains, particularly between the wives of brothers still living in an extended family, and sometimes between the brothers themselves. When a man attacked and nearly strangled his brother, his kinsmen said, 'The Devil has entered into him' (μπῆκε ὁ διάβολος μέσα) and they meant this in a quite literal sense. When the shepherds hear of a case of father-daughter incest among the villagers of Thesprotia, they only understand this enormity as a plot of the Devil.

It must be emphasized that the sins into which a man is led by the Devil's temptation always possess a certain reference to external agency. If a man has sinned in a way not easily understandable it is said, 'The Devil pushed him' (τὸν ἔσπρωξε ὁ διάβολος). A man, by not placing his whole trust in God, inclines his desires towards material and sensual attachments. He is, then, as it were, physically unable to resist the Devil who chooses the sin, and sets the scene of temptation in the knowledge that his victory is assured. But the sin by which the man is corrupted is the work of the Devil. Through these modes of thought the Sarakatsani are able to appreciate themselves as an essentially noble and God-fearing community struggling under the limitations of the human condition which, so far as the physical and political environment is concerned, they are able to represent as being, in their case, peculiarly severe.

The definitive loss of the soul to the Devil is the basis of the appearance of 'βρυκόλακες', the bodies of dead men and women which return from the grave in a hideous distended form often to terrify members of their own family. They are persons whose lives were corrupted in sin, committed suicide, drowned or were unbaptized; or persons whose bodies were not guarded by their kinsmen in the period between death and burial, or whose bodies, although guarded, were leaped over by a cat. In these various ways, and particularly in the first, the soul is lost to the Devil. Instead of departing through the mouth (as some imagine it in the form of a small bird) and rising to God, it passes through the anus to the Devil. And since the body and soul, whatever the internal tension between them, form a unity, the body also falls into the power of the Devil, remains undissolved in the earth, and possessed by his spirit emerges from its grave to mock at the sacred institutions of family life by attacking or terrifying those to whom it owed, in life, the greatest obligations.

But, in a sense, the envy of men expressed in the belief of the evil eye is the great triumph of the Devil; firstly, because it implies a whole complex of vices including enmity, greed, and deceit; and secondly, because without the Devil requiring to set any particular temptations almost all Sarakatsani, in their pursuit of the elusive and competitive ends of prestige with its mixture of spiritual and material values, are necessarily involved in this form of sin. They succeed in avoiding individual guilt for it, but they cannot deny their collective responsibility, nor can they ignore the existence of the barrier which it represents between themselves and God. The witchcraft or sorcery of the evil eye (βασκανία) is recognized by the Church as one of the Devil's weapons; and there are prayers which may be read over the victim by the priest. By the Sarakatsani themselves, it is said that a person known to have the evil eye (τὸ χαχὸ μάτι), 'has an eye infected by the Devil' (ἔχει τὸ μάτι διαβολεμένο).

A family attributes the majority of its misfortunes to this evil force. The range of effects attributed to its activity is wide. The diseases of sheep and other animals, almost all childrens' illness and the sickness of adults, especially when it is accompanied by the onset of sudden pains in the body, may all be referred to the evil eye. A woman is anxious if another sees her kneading the dough for her bread; for then, perhaps, it may not rise. The impotence of a bridegroom may be the result of the evil eye of a woman with an unmarried daughter. The force behind this action of the evil eye is the attraction of things which are envied (ζηλευτὰ πράματα). And it is significant that the two things most important for social prestige, children and sheep, are the two things most prone to attack. It is men who are prosperous, or more especially men, in a sense, too prosperous, or lucky, who stand in particular danger. It does not please a man to be told by another that his sheep are in excellent condition. Praise and admiration, it is thought, indicate the desire of the admirer, which is quite possibly unconscious, to possess what is pleasing to his eyes. And since that is not possible, frustration is followed by envy.

Since the evil eye may be exercised unconsciously nobody is sure that he may not at some time affect other people, their possessions, or even himself. A common and effective precaution is to spit three times at any creature or thing which excites one's admiration. 'Spit on the child that he may not be bewitched' (φτύς'τὸ παιδὶ νὰ μὴν βασκαθῆ), demands a mother of those looking at her small child. In addition, many substances are used as protective charms in the phylacteries of children, or are tied to the tongues of sheep bells. Some of these operate sympathetically such as garlic, thistle, and pubic hairs. Others like a small wooden cross of boxwood, incense, a cross woven from flowers, or a candle taken from the representation of the tomb during Easter week, are objects with sacred connexions that mediate protective power. But even the magic powers of garlic and other substances exist only by the provision of God.

If, despite these precautions, a person (or sheep) is bewitched, relief is generally found in a procedure which first identifies the possessor of the evil eye and then counteracts its influence. A bowl of water is taken and a hair of the bewitched person (or a strand of the sheep's fleece) is placed under the bowl. Small pieces of wood carbon are taken from the fire and after the surface of the water has been crossed three times the first fragment about the size of a small finger nail is dropped into the water. The operator, who is almost always a woman, puts to the piece of carbon the name of a person she may suspect. If the carbon floats the person in question is not guilty, if it sinks one evil eye at least is known. If more than one eye is suspected the process is continued. When the operator is satisfied that the worst has been uncovered, the sick or otherwise afflicted person is crossed with the water in the bowl forty times on the brow, the hands, the feet and the afflicted part if pain or other symptoms are localized. Finally, the patient drinks a little of the water from the bowl.

In putting names to the pieces of carbon the operator is guided by various considerations. Who, to her knowledge, has recently seen the afflicted person or animal? And, of these, who is generally noted for an envious nature, or has a reputation for unconscious bewitching, or is simply disliked by herself and her family? If none of these proves to be guilty, other names chosen at random are put to the carbon. But this rarely happens. From observations on five different occasions and a certain amount of personal experiment it appears that about one fragment of carbon in every five sinks. Therefore the guilty person almost invariably is among those whom the operator considers to be likely possessors of the evil eye. And this confirms the validity of the procedure.

Most people are probably found to be guilty of unconscious bewitching at some time in their lives. If the victim is a relation, the bewitcher will generally co-operate to counteract the influence of his eye by giving a hair which is added to the draught administered to the patient. If the sufferer is unrelated, he will probably not learn of the fact, certainly not in a direct manner. Certain persons are generally believed by the community to have a powerful evil eye which they exercise from feelings of conscious envy. These persons may be of either sex and generally come from poor families of low prestige whose members have an obvious reason to be envious of other people. They may also be persons from respected families who suffer some personal disability or deformity; for instance, a powerful eye is attributed to a prosperous Skamneli villager who has a squint and a club-foot.

Generally, however, the question whether the evil eye of any person is to be attributed to unconscious witchcraft or intentional sorcery depends upon his relationship to the victim. Since small children are often bewitched, it is not remarkable that in extended families the tensions which exist between the wives of brothers are often reflected in the regular presence of the name of the husband's brother's wife among those suspected by the mother of a sick child. But it is always accepted that such bewitching is of the unconscious kind, as indeed are almost all instances of evil eye between kinsmen and affines. On the other hand, where the bewitcher is an unrelated person the victim is ready to ascribe more conscious motives to the possessor of the eye that has hurt him.

It is not, of course, strange that the envy of the evil eye is associated with the Devil. Envy is inherent in the material world of limited resources and numerous contrary wills. Lacking what another possesses and thinking of that rather than of his relation to God, a man is easily led by the Devil to destroy what he himself has not. This tendency is so inherent in the nature of the situation that, as we have seen, even kinsmen and affines bewitch one another, although such is the strength of the moral element in these relationships that the effects are not believed to be produced with conscious intention. And it is interesting to note that of the elements of prestige which were discussed in the previous chapter, those elements, honour and the quality of being honourable, which tend towards the ideal equality of members of the community and the conception of the Sarakatsani as men united in the desire to live in accordance with honour, do not of themselves necessarily lead to envy between men, for they are essentially spiritual values; on the other hand, those elements of prestige which inevitably differentiate men and possess a pronounced material aspect, wealth, numbers, lineage, marriages, dowries, and so on, are precisely the values competition for which must breed envy in those who are not successful.

## 3. THE WAYS TO GOD

That it is important for the Sarakatsani to be in a right relationship with God, hardly needs to be emphasized. The margin of security possessed by each family in its relative isolation is narrow. There are many anxieties; the sickness of children, the diseases of sheep, the scarcity of pasture, social prestige, and personal health. These are matters which concern each family separately, and each family in seeking to enlist God's aid and mercy attempts to establish a particular relation with Him which ignores, in this context, their fellowship with other men. In their simple and frankly pragmatic prayers it does not occur to them to pray for other men, or suffering humanity.

The everyday religious life is essentially a family cult. On a shelf, in the corner of the hut, or in a niche in the wall, are one or often two icons before which stands an open glass oil-lamp. The lamp is lit on the eve of each Sunday or important feast-day and burns through the night. In front of this simple iconostasis each member of the family stands for a moment when he gets up and before he goes to sleep. The adult men, except when they are in trouble, merely cross themselves rapidly three times but the youths and most of the women remain long enough to say a short prayer. Those who know the whole or part of 'Our Father' will recite this to themselves but they will also make some kind of general petition. A mother will say, 'O God protect us, the little ones, and my husband, and give us health and good luck (Θεέ μου νὰ μᾶς φυλάξῃς τὰ μικρά, τὸν ἄντρα μου, νὰ μᾶς δώσῃς γειὰ καὶ καλὴ τύχη).

Through the day a man (or woman) will make the sign of the cross three times when he finds himself in certain situations. A man signs himself when he suddenly confronts some danger; here it is an unspoken prayer for divine aid. He crosses himself before undertaking any important task that without God's protection may not turn out well; an example is the milking of sheep where there is always the fear of a small yield or finding diseased udders; another is the moment of setting out on a journey. After an important task is completed successfully a man again crosses himself to express his gratitude and relief. The sign of the cross is made before the members of the family share in the communion of their common meal. The sign expresses respect when an individual passes a church or any other sacred object. And it is also used to repulse any assault of the Devil whether this comes in the form of physical attack or moral temptation. In the summer when for a few weeks the villages have visitors from the towns, it is not uncommon to see a young shepherd cross himself when he passes a girl wearing a short-sleeved dress.

The sign of the cross is a remembrance (ἐνθύμιον) of Christ. 'If you make the cross, you remember Christ and he protects you', was one view which expresses the general belief. It is a symbol, but also more than this. It is a channel by which God's power and grace descends to man by virtue of the remembrance of Christ's sacrifice, and it is a means through which man's gratitude and respect mount to God. But most Sarakatsani insist that the sign, like the sacraments themselves, is not efficient *ex opere operato*, as the theologians would say; but only if a man repents his sins and has a 'good heart'.

These are the simple everyday acts of direct communion with God which in the main are general petitions for God's protection. But from time to time a man meets serious difficulties or misfortune. He is in great financial trouble, or his honour is affronted; specific and considerable favours are required of God. A direct petition is always possible but here men think of two things; that God is the Father of all men, or at least all Greeks; and that even if his judgements sometimes appear capricious and difficult to understand he is nevertheless, in principle, just and impartial. Yet God is asked for particular benefits, the granting of which may exclude others, in this respect, from the favour of God. It, therefore, seems more prudent to establish a relationship with a lesser but more easily approachable spiritual Being who will make an intercession to God or use his delegated power on behalf of the suppliant. These intercessors are the Mother of God and the Saints. Borrowing from his social experience the Sarakatsanos, who knows how patrons compete for the allegiance of a greater number of clients, believes that the Saints of the Church must be concerned about the number of their followers and the richness of their votives. They have a motive for partiality which God by the definition of his position and nature entirely lacks.

On the other hand, the partiality of the Mother of God has a basis of compassion rather than competition. Her importance, as an intercessor, is her humanity. The idea of her immaculate conception is quite foreign to the Sarakatsani (as also generally to Orthodox theology). The miracle of the Mother of God is that she is one human being who, through an act of her own faith and will as well as the grace of God, has entirely conquered sin despite her human condition. The iconography of the Church shows her self-discipline, her compassion, a person of her sex but drained of its sensuality. For the Sarakatsani Eve and Mary are the two opposed images of Woman. Her humanity and compassion allied to her Holiness makes her the perfect intercessor between man and God. Moreover, the Sarakatsanos, thinking as he necessarily does in terms of his own social forms, finds it natural and sensible that as God's grace to men comes through Christ, men should seek benefits from God through the Mother of the Son. For she is approachable and has influence with her Son. The parallel with earthly systems of patronage is clear.

The All Holy One is naturally the eternal image of motherhood. And although petitions to her are of every kind, prayers for a sick child are especially directed to her. It is felt that however sinful the mother of the sick child may be the Mother of God must feel compassion for her. A man may call directly on his God to protect him in danger but suddenly faced with the horror or shock of some loss, great or trivial, it is the Mother of God who is invoked, Παναγία μου. For the Sarakatsani she is, above all, the comforter (Παρηγορίτισσα). She, too, has experienced loss. And it is to her that the sinner appeals to turn aside the just wrath of God.

The two Saints most popular amongst the Sarakatsani are St. George (feast-day 23rd April O.S.) and St. Demetrius (feast-day 26th October O.S.). These feast-days both punctuate the seasonal calendar at critical moments, in each case just before one of the two annual migrations; both Saints are generally concerned with pastoral life and both are warlike, horsed and armed. On all counts they suit the Sarakatsani admirably. 'We honour them because we are like them', the Sarakatsani say.[4] To St. George especially they are attached, and petitions

---

[4] See Chatzimichalis, op. cit., vol. i, Part A, p. ρλζ´

about diseases of the sheep, pleas to soften the heart of a merchant who will not grant a desperately needed loan are very often made to this Saint. On his feast-day a lamb is always killed in his honour by every family except the very poorest, an honour which is generally only accorded to Christ at Christmas and Easter, and to the Mother of God on the feast of the Assumption (15th August). 'All the Saints look for us to sacrifice a sheep to them', the Sarakatsani explain, 'but St. George protects us'. Sarakatsani respect all the Saints but the only others chosen for particular attention are the Prophet Elias whose chapels are on hill-tops and who is associated with the mountains and the wilderness, St. Theodore another mounted warrior hero, and St. Paraskeve. Individuals, of course, sometimes turn to the Saint whose name they bear and to other Saints who are known to possess specialist powers.

If a man has a very important favour to request from a Saint (or the Mother of God), he will not be content to present it before his own icon of the particular Saint. He will worship before the icon of the Saint in a church, preferably a church or chapel dedicated to him. And in exceptionally serious matters he may not be satisfied with presenting his prayer to the icon of the Saint in his own village if he knows of an icon of the same Saint elsewhere which has a reputation for greater efficacy. The icon is not simply an image which serves to remind the worshipper of spiritual realities, it is a material object in which he believes divine energy is localized. He believes that if he approaches this manifestation of the Saint's power with a 'good heart' and a suitable offering, he will help. He agrees that it is the one Saint present in all his icons but he insists that one revelation is more efficient than another. In these ideas we see the refraction which even divine energy suffers when it enters the material and sensible world.

A suppliant asks of his intercessor favours which are often very specific and material. In return he makes some offering to express his respect and attachment to the Saint; he may also vow a further gift if help is granted. A Sarakatsanos feels free to bargain with a Saint in a way that would be unseemly towards God. The thought here is that even a Saint is open, in some sense, to flattery and honours. He cannot be displeased that he is honoured with more offerings of one kind or another than other Saints. Makryiannis, a hero of the Revolution, tells in his memoirs how, being very poor, he entered the chapel of his patron Saint to offer a silver candlestick if only he might be granted a set of fine clothes and pistols. Sarakatsani behave similarly. Without the least embarrassment the approach is one of *do ut des*. The relations between Saint and worshipper resemble somewhat those of patron and client. But although it is easy to see how the Sarakatsanos projects to some degree the experience of his social relations into his religious life, it is also true that the latter transcends the former. You may bribe a lawyer to act dishonestly but you cannot do this to a Saint. He will not aid in wickedness nor where the suppliant, however great the gift he bears, approaches without a contrite heart. On this point all insist.

Man acquires help and protection not only through personal petitions to the divine Beings in the spiritual hierarchy, although this is the mode of communion which is sought in all critical matters. It is thought that by the grace of God divine power enters and issues from a number of material objects. Contact with or possession of these sacred objects and substances are believed to be defences against attacks of the Devil, the envy of other men and general misfortune. The power immanent in the Word of God is released when the priest reads a passage over an afflicted person or when a worshipper kisses the Book. The incense breathed in church, the possession of a candle which burned on the representation of Christ's tomb at Easter, the sign of the cross on a sick man's forehead when made with oil from a lamp which has burned before an icon, all these have 'power'. Blessed water brought from church at the feast of Epiphany is sprinkled over the sheep. Salt, incense, box-wood when these have been blessed and 'read over' by the priest during the service on the Thursday of Holy Week, are kept throughout the next year—loci of divine strength. *Antidoron*, blessed bread, which is the remainder of the offered loaf after the seal has been cut from it for the communion cup, is similarly conserved. However, these materials are not simply charms. Their efficiency, as with all the manifestations of divine aid, depends on repentance and a 'good heart'.

God is in communion with men not only spiritually through

grace but intelligently through messages, generally warnings of physical danger which may be avoided and premonitions of misfortune or death which may not. Many men claim that just before they escaped some disaster a Saint appeared to warn them of its approach. Dreams, divination of a sheep's shoulder blade, the behaviour of various animals and birds, are all interpreted as messages from God.

In all these modes of communion a man is concerned fundamentally with establishing a relationship with God or His spiritual subordinates in order to obtain help and protection in the many difficulties which his family faces. If he is able, he must raise himself some of the way towards God; for if he succeeds in at least displaying his will in this direction there is the hope that the power of God will descend to him. The means of a poor shepherd to do this, immersed as he is in his material troubles, are slight. He may achieve a small offering and a day's fast and sexual continence before presenting an important petition to a Saint. Always he must represent to himself that he repents his sins: and he must have a 'good heart'. A 'good heart' is the will to strain towards closer fellowship with God. In this context, however, repentance and a good heart imply only weakly and indirectly the idea of fellowship with other men. As in social systems of patronage, so in their everyday religious life each family strives to achieve a particular and exclusive relationship with subordinate spiritual beings and through them to draw down to their aid more of the divine power than other families.

But the grace of God, the favour of God, comes to men only through the sacrifice of Christ. It will not have escaped notice how little His name has appeared in this brief review of cult. Sarakatsani, at least, seem to direct few prayers to Him. In their religious belief God has two hypostases or persons, Father and Saviour. When they refer to God, Θεός, they normally mean the Creator, Father, Protector, and Punisher of men, present everywhere yet separated from them morally by an immense distance. Christ is the Saint, "Αης, or the Master, ὁ 'Αφέντης,[5] that is God in the person of a man like themselves, who sacrificed Himself that other men might overcome the

---

[5] See Chatzimichalis, op. cit., vol. i, Part A, p. ρλζ'.

separating barrier of sin which was the original work of the Devil and Adam. The first of these terms reflects the sanctity of Christ, the second His concern for the well-being of men; both refer to His life under the limitations of the human condition. In their own experience the Sarakatsani see the reflection of the sufferings of Christ. From the moment of His birth He was persecuted and humiliated, yet He did not lose dignity or nobility. Nor in similar circumstances, the Sarakatsani believe, do they. 'Christ is our brother', they sometimes say. He made the first shepherd's flute (φλογέρα). He rounded up the wild goats, beasts of the Devil, and tamed them by placing His seal on the joints of their forelegs. He stands always by their side. They have only to think of Him and make the sign that recalls His sacrifice. Similarly, they believe that the Sarakatsani have always been the followers, worshippers, brothers of Christ. When the gipsy forged the five nails of the crucifixion for the Jews, it was the Sarakatsanos who stole one and drove it up the offending blacksmith's behind.

Christ is the key figure in Sarakatsan religious belief, and the events of the 'Great week' of Easter are the transcendent experiences of religious life. These I shall not attempt to describe in detail, but something must be said of the dramatic atmosphere which makes this complex of rites and customs quite unlike any others in the religious calendar. Normally villagers are exceedingly casual in church, and even the Sarakatsani, who are more devout in the outward respect they show to sacred objects, are quite pragmatic in their attitude and remarks about religious affairs even when they are anxiously presenting an important petition. In contrast, the dramatic intensity of emotion which seizes the community both in church and outside during this week makes an immediate impression on the observer. There is an air both of anxiety and anticipation. The historical events which the liturgy commemorates on the different days of the week are not treated as such. They are re-lived, people participate in them. They know what will happen, He will rise again; yet they are anxious. The women discuss the events in the present or perfect tense as they would the local gossip at other times. As the drama proceeds the women in chorus make their simple and troubled comments, 'They have seized Him', 'He is being judged',

'Now they are crucifying Him'; and finally, at the critical moment of the service on Easter Day, 'Christ is risen'.

The Liturgy on the Thursday has a particular sanctity and significance for this is the day on which Christ is placed on the cross. The older women, particularly the grandmothers who may die during the year, together with the younger children, always communicate on this day; for the Communion which is received on the Thursday 'lasts' for a year. They take with them to the church a sack filled with the various apotropaic substances, some of which will be put into the phylacteries of the children while the remainder is an armoury of divine energy with which the family is able to face and defeat the Devil during the coming year. This sack, which is for 'the living', is blessed and read over by the priest and taken back to the huts. They leave with the priest a second sack which is for 'the dead'. This contains boiled wheat (κόλλυβα), incense, candles, wine. For on this day the Sarakatsani believe that the souls of the dead return to earth. As soon as the older women and children return from church, the younger women knead the dough and bake small breads (ψυχούδια). These are at once taken together with cooked beans and wine and are given to all the neighbouring families, who receive them, one for each person, with an expression of hope that God may forgive the sins of the dead. In this way is symbolized the union of the quick and the dead and their mutual forgiveness of trespasses committed.

On Good Friday the intensity of emotional feeling is scarcely bearable. The effigy of Christ is taken from the cross and placed in the representation of the tomb which is carried round the village and returned to the Church as to the sepulchre. During this service the atmosphere is heavy with grief; tears stream down the faces of the women. Before 1950 the Sarakatsan women used to make their own representations of the tomb and the body of Christ which three of them guarded throughout the day, their black scarves low over their faces, silently weeping, while one of them intoned monotonously the dirge of the Mother of God for her only Son.[6] Finally, the service which begins after midnight on the Saturday is a transformation of joy and exaltation. Christ who was crucified is risen again.

[6] Cf. Chatzimichalis, op. cit., vol. i, Part A, p. ρξδ΄.

The root of the involvement of the Sarakatsani in these dramatic happenings lies in the simple belief constantly re-iterated, especially by the women on the Friday, that 'he died for us'. They identify themselves with the sufferings of Christ because He has identified Himself with them. In becoming a man like themselves He asserted the essential nobility of man. In His death, His blood effected a union between man and God which overcame the separating barrier of ancestral sin. His resurrection has for the Sarakatsani the paradoxical signi-ficance that He lives to die again; for, particularly in the events of the Great Week each year, and more generally in the sacrament of the Eucharist, He continually performs the miracle anew. In the cry, 'Christ is risen', is the knowledge that His liberating blood will always be at hand to save men from abandonment to the Devil.

The role of Christ in this situation, like those of the Mother of God and the Saints in the everyday cult, is that of inter-cessor. But in this instance the act is on the cosmic scale, not merely a partial and external relationship effected by a Saint between a particular individual and God. It is the reconcilia-tion of all men to God and to one another. The fitness of Christ for this role lies in his origin from God the Father on the one hand and His human mother on the other. 'He was a man, then, like us' it is said both in folk tales and in comment upon the events of His life. From His mother the divine Son of God took on a condition in all respects like that of man, except that through His virgin birth he remained outside sin. Born of a virgin, a virgin in His life, it needed the sacrifice of a Being, divine, human, exposed to sin yet untouched by it, to bring man and God together.

The Sarakatsani understand well the efficacy of virginity. It is a condition which, temporarily at least, defies the corruption of age and death. As it has been suggested in the discussion of prestige values, the time of moral excellence in a man's life is the period of youthful manhood before his marriage, when he is free to live by the ideal standards of honour and when, also, he is ignorant of the sexuality of woman which is one conse-quence, in a world of sin, of the division of humanity into two sexes. As the virginity of the Sarakatsan youth or maiden is a partial and individual attempt to deny the consequences of sexuality, so the virginity of Christ suppresses in His person this fundamental division of humanity.

But men are also divided from God and from one another by their mutual envy. This disunion is a more subtle form of corruption which few men attempt or are able to resist. It requires the sacrifice of Christ's blood to redeem this condition and to establish, even briefly, the ideal of the brotherhood of men that makes possible a full communion between man and God. That in their own social experience only an unmarried brother would make this sacrifice of life and blood confirms in the minds of the Sarakatsani the role of Christ as the archetypal brother, in a transcendent sibling relationship where only identification, and never rivalry, finds a place.

The idea of Christ's brotherhood implies, at least, the brotherhood of the Sarakatsani of Zagori, and by extension (though less certainly) the brotherhood of Orthodox Greeks. Christ sacrificed Himself not for one but for all. Not the least miracle of Easter is the measure of social goodwill. There is an easy warmth of greeting and attitude between unrelated men which is entirely foreign to the tense aggressiveness that is the formal idiom of social life at other times. On Easter Monday each family visits, and is visited by, all the Sarakatsan families who live within easy walking distance, whether they are kinsmen or not. Except at the summer festival celebrated by each family (very often the feast of the Assumption) this is probably the only occasion during the year that a man penetrates into the home and receives the hospitality of another unrelated shepherd. On the Saturday of Easter instead of delivering their milk to the cheese merchant the Sarakatsani give it away to villagers or the poorer families of their own community. These simple gestures that might be unexceptional in other communities are an impressive reversal of normal attitudes. The union of men in Christ is reflected at the level of social relations in an expression of ideal solidarity which for a moment breaks down the barriers which isolate family from family and community from community. At other times, the notion that all the ills of the world derive from the view that every man is concerned only for his own family is constantly asserted, and as often deplored. There is always a yearning for unity and goodwill in the community, but it is a yearning accompanied by the knowledge that it can never be.

The Sarakatsani seldom communicate more than twice a year. The most important of the possible occasions for taking communion is, naturally, Easter. It must be stressed that this communion is for the Sarakatsani not something which is taken or received 'at' Easter, it is an integral part, the climactic happening of the week's events. During this time they have watched Christ suffering, they have identified themselves with Him as He in His sacrifice has identified Himself with them. At the end of it all the miracle happens, Christ rises from the dead and they in His blood partake of the life which He has poured out to unite them again to the Godhead.

One can discern three, as it were, related 'indulgences' which Sarakatsani believe are conferred upon them through communion. First they are released from sin. Sarakatsani are not oppressed by a sense of personal sin and indeed, as we have seen, the list of transgressions which constitute personal sins is not imposing. But they are very conscious of the sinful condition of the limited world in which they must live and in which the nobility of men is, to some degree, inevitably compromised. This sinful infusion into human nature, the inevitable meanness of everyday life, depresses their spirit in a very literal sense, it turns their thoughts from God to material things and against their fellow men. 'We are all sinners' they often say with a dispirited shrug of the shoulders. These uncomfortable sentiments are banished by the regenerating blood of Christ. As my friend Aristoteles left the church, he smiled and said, 'A weight has left me' (μοῦφυγε ἕνα βάρος). In saying this he was not referring to personal sin.

The second of these indulgences conferred by communion is that it both expresses the transcendent ideal of the union of all men in Christ and it gives an opportunity, all too fleeting, for unrelated men to show goodwill towards one another. As I have said, the yearning for union with other men is always present but it is inevitable inhibited by attitudes of pride and distrust.

The third indulgence is more pragmatic. By removing the barrier of sin which interrupts the communion between men and God, Christ's sacrifice makes it possible for men to draw down divine aid for their protection in this life against the attacks of the Devil, the envy of other men, and in their struggle for physical survival. A man's state of grace is never static, always dynamic. He strains towards God but is ever pulled downward by the weight of the human condition of sin; yet periodically the saving grace of Christ's blood allows him again to approach nearer to God.

The receipt of the sacrament is not a passive act. Men must give some pledge of their will to turn to God. At the greater religious festivals, Christmas, Easter, St. George, the feasts of Assumption and St. Demetrius, when they may communicate, Sarakatsani sacrifice a lamb or sheep (θυσιάζουν, κάνουν κουρμπάνι). Other occasions when sheep are slaughtered are similarly religious as well as social events, weddings, baptisms, or the dedication (τάξιμο) of an animal to a Saint if men or sheep fall sick. Sheep are never killed for meat but only in the form of sacrifice. Preferably the animal should be male and 'clean', that is a lamb, or a ram that has not mounted a ewe. The sheep is believed to know its fate to which it goes quietly and willingly. In describing forms of sheep theft I have suggested that the sheep which support the life and honour of a family have a spiritual as well as an economic value. Of the white Easter lamb they say, 'we bleed it to honour Christ' (τὸ ματώνομε νὰ τιμήσωμε τὸν Χριστό). A shepherd skins a sheep with swift and confident strokes of the knife but his face is strained and concentrated as he cuts into the artery in the animal's neck. With this sacrificial stroke he gives something of himself. The Sarakatsani are conscious of this element of reciprocity. As Christ pours out his blood to open a way between men and God, so the Sarakatsanos pours out the surrogate blood of his sheep to the same end. And since the sheep is the means of establishing a partial relationship between man and God, those who share its flesh are participating in a form of sanctified communion. And, for the same reason, God chooses to communicate intelligently with men through the shadow markings on the shoulder blade and the condition of the liver.

A man must prepare himself in other ways. He must fast for forty days before the beginning of the 'Great Week', and in this matter the Sarakatsani are more strict than many villagers. Olives, cheese, eggs, milk, meat, fish are not eaten. During Easter week itself even bread is abandoned and the families live for the last few days on vegetable soup, beans, and coffee. For this week, at least, the ancestral sins of sensuality and envy must be suppressed. The community becomes continent and unrelated men behave towards one another with unaccustomed warmth and goodwill. A man must truly repent his personal sins. Whenever a confessor is within reach, he ought to make a confession of his sins before taking communion. He must approach God with a 'good heart'. In these ways a man to a degree, loosens the hold which material things and the senses hold over him and, in some measure, is purified so that he may receive into himself the divine element. The Sarakatsanos believes that if he is properly prepared ritually and spiritually to receive the sacrament, then his sins are forgiven. The wine he drinks is indeed the blood of Christ (the body is seldom mentioned) and it is considered a sin if any man suffers a fit of vomiting in the 40 days which immediately follow communion. It is also described as a remembrance (ἐνθύμιον) of Christ. Thus the wine is at one and the same time a symbol of the first sacrifice and a material substance in which divine energy exists. It represents, and it is, the blood of Christ.

## 4. SOCIAL VALUES AND RELIGIOUS IDEALS

At the risk of some repetition, the problem of the opposition of two systems of values, one social the other religious, has yet to be explicitly considered. This community of Sarakatsani, whose coherent and distinctive traditions suggest, in the absence of any certain historical proofs, that it may have existed since, at least, the late Byzantine period, possesses a body of social values based upon a number of simple and unambiguous concepts of honour, strength, prestige and pride. And in the previous chapter I have emphasized the exclusive and particularist form of these social ideals. Yet throughout this period the community has belonged to an Orthodox Christian civilization. Allowing for its primitive material culture and geographical isolation, it has clearly been profoundly influenced by this wider membership as, for instance, even a cursory examination of Sarakatsan wood-carving immediately suggests. Although it is true that the relationship of the Sarakatsani to the Orthodox Church, as an institution, has been sufficiently tenuous to result in a popular religious life that is a gross refraction of Orthodox dogma and practice, yet the value of the Christian ideal of the fellowship of all men in Christ, with the universalistic ethical values that follow from it, is not to be avoided. How is this opposition of values resolved or accommodated?

There is no great problem of fellowship between Sarakatsani who are related by kinship or marriage. By associating The Father, The Son, and the Mother of God in a Holy archetype Family, the institutions and relationships of the Sarakatsan family, even the concept of honour and the duty to defend it, are given a categorical quality and a divine sanction; and by extension kindred and affinal bonds receive a similar validation. It is true that even within this restricted circle certain Christian values cannot enjoy a general application. Modesty, meekness, humility are values only admirable in women. Some Christian prescriptions have to be entirely set aside. One cannot forgive a kinsman who has betrayed his trust, at least not until he is dead. And one avoids the company of a kinsman who is despised for his poverty; the poor are not blessed. Yet love (ἀγάπη), mutual trust, truth, and altruism are important Christian virtues which are the ideal values of family and kinship life. Men would extend the circle of their application if they could, but the conditions of life in a fallen world prevent this, particularly limited resources, the divinely sanctioned honour and interests of a man's own family, the condition of envy.

Yet in their commitment to the concept of honour as the guiding principle of behaviour, the Sarakatsani cannot admit themselves to be anything but noble; and this must be said not only of the soul but the body also, for honour is related to physical strength and manliness when this is disciplined and spiritualized. The original guilt for sin must be placed elsewhere. This is the role of the Devil. Sensuality was the sin of Adam but only after the sin had been thought of and presented to him by the Devil with the assistance of woman. Envy, the more fundamental sin, was originally the cause of the Devil's rebellion against God. 'The Devil envied God' (ὁ διάβολος ζήλεψε τὸν Θεό), the Sarakatsani say. In this way the Sarakatsani avoid personal guilt for their own implication in these sins. Even in the case of personal sins for which individual guilt is admitted, Sarakatsani would say that the fault of the man was in the act of turning away from God, not in the sin itself. For without the grace of God he cannot resist the Devil who then leads his victim to the sin he has chosen for him.

However, just as children inherit responsibility for the sins of their parents, the responsibility for the sins of Adam cannot be avoided. The condition of sin in which a man lives, although it is exterior to his individual will, interrupts his communion with God on which life and honour depend. It is in this situation that Christ comes to save men, pouring out the sacrifice of his blood to reunite man with God, a salvation, however, which is contingent on man freely turning from the Devil towards God. In a certain sense, then, these forms of sin are a kind of pollution, for which the Devil is originally guilty and responsible, and from which Christ is the saviour. But this analogy must not be pressed too far. This salvation requires moral action on the side of man. In his daily life he must struggle to discipline sensuality and he must avoid the ultimate consequences of envy. For, the fact that all earthly families are imperfect copies of a divine archetype places a limit on the amoral ruthlessness that unrelated men may show towards one another in circumstances where such conduct seriously and unnecessarily endangers the existence of another family. And at certain periods of religious celebration, such as Christmas, Easter, and the feast of Assumption, the sins of Adam must be altogether suppressed through universal continence, goodwill, and the symbolic sharing of food.

Although it is clear that the values of honour are not what they are for any influence of Christian ideals, it would be wrong to suggest, as it has sometimes been said, that Christianity is almost entirely external to Sarakatsan life. Not only are the Sarakatsani deeply conscious of their total dependence on God, whether in the person of The Father or The Saviour, but the family is seen as an image of the Holy Family, and Christian values are the basis of relationships between kinsmen and affines, the people with whom, after all, a man lives and works. And at religious festivals men succeed, momentarily, in living the ideal of a universal brotherhood in Christ. And although, in the periods of profane living which separate these moments of transcendence, men must admire the shrewd and scheming leader and accept the need for lies and deceit, the ideal social personality remains the unmarried pallikari, the 'innocent' (ἀθῶος), alone with his sheep, not yet fully implicated in the ancestral sins of sensuality and envy.

These beliefs indicate, clearly enough, that the Sarakatsani sense that all is not right with their world, a sentiment that is Christian not heroic. When men quarrel and draw their knives, an event that is the breath of life in an heroic culture, the Sarakatsani say, 'The Devil is dancing in the middle' (χορεύει ὁ διάβολος μέσα). Indeed the Devil is the symbol and the efficient cause of all those many tensions and hostilities which prevent the Sarakatsani from living in the values of Christian fellowship. Not only is he the original cause of the miasma of ancestral sin, the provoker of the evil eye and the tempter to sexual lusts, but in his desire to injure physically where he cannot corrupt morally, his action on the spiritual plane parallels the mutual hostilities and social isolation which each family experiences in social life.

When all this is said there remains an opposition between Christian ideals and the values of prestige. Fortunately or otherwise, the Sarakatsani do not see this; partly because the two value systems either appear to be complementary as in family or kindred, or in other areas of social life they are relatively segregated in their incidence; and partly because the individual thinking in egocentric terms cannot see that his own honour, prestige, pride, and self-regard threaten another. It is always the other man, and, behind, the Devil moving and manipulating him, who corrupt society and provoke the anger of God.

# APPENDIX I

## THE WINTER CO-OPERATIVE GROUPINGS OF SARAKATSANI GRAZING THE LANDS OF A ZAGORI VILLAGE (NEOCHORI) IN 1955

| HOUSEHOLDS | The No. of Brothers (if an extended household) | Relation of Head of household to Tselingas* or Leader of the stani | Working males over 13 years of age | Working females over 13 years of age | Sons at secondary school | Wage shepherds working away from family | Children and old people not able to work | Total | Horses and Mules | Sheep | Goats | Total of Sheep and Goats | Notes on Location of Winter grazing, etc. |
|---|---|---|---|---|---|---|---|---|---|---|---|---|---|
| †1. | | | | | | | | | | | | | |
| CONSTANTINE TANGAS | | Tsel. | 3 | 2 | 1 | — | 1 | 7 | 2 | 325 | 40 | 365 | Winter grazing: Grika. Pasture leased with protected rights |
| Vasili | | Br. | 4 | 1 | — | — | 0 | 5 | 4 | 282 | 40 | 322 | |
| Demetrios | | Br. | 1 | 3 | — | — | 2 | 6 | 2 | 229 | 30 | 259 | The families of George Tangas, John Vangelis |
| Evangelos | | Br. | 2 | 5 | — | — | 2 | 9 | 1 | 171 | 30 | 201 | and George Makris each graze their sheep |
| George | | Br. | 4 | 7 | — | — | 0 | 11 | 11 | 255 | 50 | 305 | separately in summer |
| John Vangelis | | Sis.Hus. | 4 | 4 | — | — | 1 | 9 | 5 | 298 | 40 | 338 | |
| George Makris | | Sis.Son | 3 | 4 | — | — | 6 | 13 | 2 | 353 | 30 | 383 | |
| Miltiades Kallis | | Br.Wi.Sis.Hus. | 1 | 2 | — | — | 3 | 6 | 2 | 40 | 15 | 55 | |
| | | | 22 | | | | | 66 | | | | 2228 | |

* In this table I reserve the term Tselingas for the leader of a group with more than 500 animals.
† The numbered groups of households represent sheep management units.

| HOUSEHOLDS | The No. of Brothers (if an extended household) | Relation of Head of household to Tselingas* or Leader of the stani | Working males over 13 years of age | Working females over 13 years of age | Sons at secondary school | Wage shepherds working away from family | Children and old people not able to work | Total | Horses and Mules | Sheep | Goats | Total of Sheep and Goats | Notes on Location of Winter grazing, etc. |
|---|---|---|---|---|---|---|---|---|---|---|---|---|---|
| **2.** | | | | | | | | | | | | | |
| George Zygos | 2 | Tsel. | 3 | 5 | — | — | 1 | 9 | 2 | 355 | 0 | 355 | Winter grazing: Nea Kerasounda. Pasture leased with protected rights |
| ‡ Miltiades Loutsaris | | Mo.Br.Son | 2 | 2 | — | — | 1 | 5 | 1 | 100 | 10 | 110 | |
| Costas Sultanos | | Fa.Br.D.Hus. | 1 | 2 | — | 2 | 2 | 7 | 1 | 45 | 0 | 45 | |
| | | | 6 | | | | | 21 | | | | 510 | |
| **3.** | | | | | | | | | | | | | |
| Gregory Kapsalis | 3 | Tsel. | 5 | 7 | 2 | — | 6 | 20 | 12 | 405 | 70 | 475 | Winter grazing: Mazaraki. Own small property with olive trees. Have right to graze on village common land |
| ‡ John | | Fa.Br.Son | 2 | 4 | — | — | 0 | 6 | 3 | 160 | 20 | 180 | |
| | | | 7 | | | | | 26 | | | | 655 | |
| **4.** | | | | | | | | | | | | | |
| Vasili Charisis | | Tsel. | 1 | 1 | — | — | 4 | 6 | 3 | 320 | 0 | 320 | Winter grazing; Kamarina. Own property for grazing. The families of Kakos and Konakis remain with the stani winter and summer |
| Michael | | Br. | 1 | 1 | — | — | 2 | 4 | 3 | 200 | 30 | 230 | |
| Spiros Kakos | | Unrelated hired | 3 | 1 | — | — | 5 | 9 | 1 | 40 | 10 | 50 | |
| Costas Konakis | | Shepherds | 2 | 3 | — | — | 1 | 6 | 1 | 40 | 0 | 40 | |
| | | | 7 | | | | | 25 | | | | 640 | |

‡ Indicates households in these winter groupings which do not graze at Neochori in the summer.

| No. | Count | Name | Relation | | | | | | | | | Notes |
|---|---|---|---|---|---|---|---|---|---|---|---|---|
| 5. | | ‡ Const. Gogolos | Tscl. | 2 | 2 | — | 4 | 8 | 3 | 160 | 20 | 180 | Winter grazing: Skoupitsa. Pasture leased with protected rights |
| | | ‡ John | Br. | 1 | 1 | — | 0 | 2 | 4 | 170 | 20 | 190 | |
| | | ‡ Thomas | Fa.Br.Son | 1 | 2 | — | 3 | 6 | 2 | 150 | 10 | 160 | |
| | | ‡ Theocharis | Fa.Br.Son | 1 | 2 | — | 2 | 5 | 3 | 170 | 25 | 195 | Detsikas and Chasekis graze their flocks separately in the summer |
| | | Michael Detsikas | Sis.Hus. | 4 | 2 | — | 3 | 9 | 4 | 215 | 60 | 275 | |
| | 2 | Alec Chasekis | § | 2 | 3 | — | 5 | 10 | 3 | 100 | 30 | 130 | |
| | | | | **11** | | | | **40** | | | | **1130** | |
| 6. | 5 | Evangelos Karageorgis | Tscl. | 3 | 2 | — | 0 | 5 | 2 | 220 | 30 | 250 | Winter grazing: Spatharati. Temporary possession of abandoned Muslim pasture |
| | | Athanasios | Br. | 2 | 2 | — | 3 | 7 | 2 | 177 | 20 | 197 | |
| | | George | Br. | 1 | 1 | — | 1 | 3 | 2 | 140 | 50 | 190 | |
| | | Demetrios | Br. | 1 | 1 | — | 3 | 5 | 2 | 167 | 30 | 197 | |
| | | Sister of George's dead wife (Unmarried) | | 0 | 1 | — | 0 | 1 | 0 | 0 | 60 | 60 | This woman lives alone under the stani's protection |
| | | | | **7** | | | | **21** | | | | **894** | |
| 7. | 5 | Theodoros Myriounis | Tscl. | 5 | 5 | — | 7 | 17 | 6 | 396 | 80 | 476 | Winter grazing: Karterion. Former Muslim land now leased to them by the villagers after a compulsory Government order. Raftis grazes separately in the summer |
| | | ‡ Sotiri | Fa.Br. | 1 | 3 | — | 1 | 5 | 1 | 20 | 90 | 110 | |
| | | Pericles | Fa.Br.Son | 2 | 3 | — | 3 | 8 | 2 | 155 | 15 | 170 | |
| | | Theodoros Raftis | Hus. of Mo. first cousin | 3 | 5 | — | 0 | 8 | 4 | 162 | 120 | 282 | |
| | | | | **11** | | | | **38** | | | | **1038** | |
| 8. | 4 | Demetrios Paparounas | Tscl. | 5 | 4 | — | 10 | 19 | 9 | 530 | 60 | 590 | Winter grazing: Karterion. Former Muslim land leased by villagers |
| | | Photios Gogolos | Sis.Hus. | 1 | 1 | — | 5 | 7 | 1 | 50 | 0 | 50 | |
| | | | | **6** | | | | **26** | | | | **640** | |

§ (A cousin of Michael Detsikas married Chasekis' sister)

| HOUSEHOLDS | The No. of Brothers (if an extended household) | Relation of Head of household to Tselingas* or Leader of the stani | Working males over 13 years of age | Working females over 13 years of age | Sons at secondary school | Wage shepherds working away from family | Children and old people not able to work | Total | Horses and Mules | Sheep | Goats | Total of Sheep and Goats | Notes on Location of Winter grazing, etc. |
|---|---|---|---|---|---|---|---|---|---|---|---|---|---|
| 9. CHRISTOS ARVANITIS | 3 | Tsel. | 4 | 4 | — | — | 5 | 13 | 7 | 430 | 60 | 490 | Winter grazing: Karterion. Former Muslim land leased by villagers. Katris grazes his flocks separately in the summer |
| Evangelos Katris | | Mo.Sis.Hus. | 2 | 3 | — | — | 0 | 5 | 4 | 90 | 100 | 190 | |
| | | | 6 | | | | | 18 | | | | 680 | |
| 10. DIONYSIOS BARKAS | | Leader | 4 | 1 | — | — | 0 | 5 | 5 | 190 | 70 | 260 | Winter grazing: Mourton. Fallow land rented from villagers |
| Spiros Arvanitis | | Fa.-in-law | 0 | 2 | — | — | 3 | 5 | 0 | 5 | 60 | 65 | |
| | | | 4 | | | | | 10 | | | | 325 | |
| 11. DEMETRIOS PASCHOS | | Leader | 2 | 2 | — | 2 | 0 | 6 | 2 | 140 | 0 | 140 | Winter grazing: South of Gulf of Arta, fallow land rented from villagers |
| Lambros | | Br. | 1 | 3 | — | — | 1 | 5 | 1 | 20 | 25 | 45 | Theodorakis grazes separately in the summer |
| Demetrios Theodorakis | | Wi.Br. | 1 | 2 | — | 1 | 0 | 4 | 7 | 98 | 30 | 128 | |
| | | | 4 | | | | | 15 | | | | 313 | |
| 12. EVANGELOS LOUTSARIS | | Leader | 2 | 2 | 1 | — | 1 | 6 | 2 | 140 | 0 | 140 | Winter grazing: Grammenitsa. Pasture leased with protected rights |
| George | | Br. | 1 | 1 | — | — | 4 | 6 | 2 | 140 | 0 | 140 | |
| | | | 3 | | | | | 12 | | | | 280 | |

| | | | | | | | | | | | | |
|---|---|---|---|---|---|---|---|---|---|---|---|---|
| 13. GEORGE KAPSALIS | 2 | — | 3 3 | — | 0 | 6 6 | 3 | 180 180 | 0 | 180 180 | Winter grazing: Kanallaki. Shepherds to villagers |
| 14. GEORGE CHARISIS | 2 | — | 3 3 | — | 3 | 9 9 | 5 | 110 | 60 | 170 170 | Winter grazing: Kamarina. Fallow land rented from villagers |
| 15. DEMETRIOS DETSIKAS | | — | 1 | 2 1 | — | 4 4 | 1 | 54 | 0 | 54 54 | Winter grazing: Philippiada. Shepherd to villager |
| 16. THEODOROS ARVANITIS | | — | 1 1 | 2 | 5 5 | 1 | 80 | 15 | 95 95 | | Winter grazing: Kamarina. In winter shepherd to villager. Summer, runs own sheep in one flock |
| 17. DEMETRIOS LADIAS | | — | 2 2 | 4 | 7 7 | 1 | 30 | 10 | 40 40 | | Winter grazing: Preveza. Shepherd to Sarakatsan stani. In summer, shepherd to villager |
| 18. SPIRIDON CARVOUNIS | | — | 2 2 | 2 | 5 5 | 2 | 85 | 20 | 105 105 | | Winter grazing: Mazaraki. Temporary allotment of former Muslim land |

# APPENDIX II

## LAND UTILIZATION IN THE ZAGORI EXPRESSED IN PERCENTAGES

|  | % |
|---|---|
| Cultivated areas (including arable land and orchards) | 2·16 |
| Previously cultivated land, now barren | 3·13 |
| Open pasture land | 25·74 |
| Forest or bush pasture | 26·05 |
| Forests | 36·65 |
| Roads, ditches, village sites, barren land, etc. | 6·27 |
| Total | 100·00 |

Source: Ministry of Agriculture, 1956–7

# APPENDIX III

## A SPECIMEN FAMILY BUDGET 1954–5

This extended family possessed 350 sheep, of which 190 were ewes in milk. They also had 5 horses but no goats. There were 14 members, 7 adults and 7 children.

In these accounts quantities are in okes (1 oke = 1,280 grams) and values are in Drachmas (83 Drachmas to one pound sterling approx.).

| *Expenditure* | *Drachmas* |
|---|---:|
| Winter grazing dues at flat rate of 14 Dr. per sheep, 28 Dr. per horse or mule, on village common land. The stani of which this family is a member grazed the land by virtue of a compulsory Government order which also fixed the amount of payment | 5,040 |
| Owing to the small area and poor quality of this winter grazing the ewes carrying lambs were given supplementary feed in the form of cotton-cake. 17 okes of cotton-cake per ewe, at 3 Dr. the oke | 9,690 |
| Summer grazing in mountain village with citizens' rights of pasturage at the rate of 8 Dr. for the first 150 animals, and 14 Dr. for the remainder | 4,140 |
| Salt for sheep in summer | 400 |
| Flour 1300 okes at 4 Dr. | 5,200 |
| 150 okes of olive oil at 17 Dr. | 2,550 |
| 15 pairs of shoes at 150 Dr. a pair | 2,250 |
| Account with local tailor for the cutting and sewing of 6 jackets, 10 pairs of trousers and various other clothes for children and young girls | 1,500 |
| Share of general expenses of the stani* at 14·54 Dr. per sheep, 29 Dr. per horse | 5,234 |
| Miscellaneous purchases from village shop | 3,066 |
| **Total** | **39,070** |

* This item represented the expenditure incurred by the stani in co-operative undertakings. In this instance more than half the amount was used for gifts and bribes, the remainder representing the cost of lawyers fees, fines for animal trespass, and the travelling expenses of the tselingas. The share paid by each member family is in proportion to the size of its flock.

| *Income* | *Drachmas* |
|---|---|
| 190 ewes produced for sale on average 23½ okes of milk per head at 4½ Dr. in the winter and spring | 20,092 |
| 190 ewes produced for sale on average 7½ okes of milk per head at 5 Dr. in the summer | 7,125 |
| Sale of 173 okes of wool (60 okes were kept for the use of the family), at 26 Dr. | 4,498 |
| Sale of 78 male lambs at an average price of 120 Dr. per beast | 9,360 |
| Total | 41,075 |

This was a fairly satisfactory year for the family. But it has to be taken into consideration that they have a debt of 5,000 Dr. to their winter cheese merchant and a loan of 7,000 Dr. from the Agricultural Bank as well as smaller amounts of debt in two shops.

# A SELECT BIBLIOGRAPHY

1. Ἀραβαντινός, Παναγ.: *Μονογραφία περὶ Κουτσοβλάχων*, Athens, 1905.

2. Capidan, Theodor: 'Saracacianii', *Dacoromania*, 1924–6, vol. 4, pp. 923–59.

3. Γεωργακᾶς, Δημ.: «Περὶ τῶν Σαρακατσαναίων τῆς Θράκης», *Ἀρχεῖον Θρακικοῦ Λαογραφικοῦ καὶ Γλωσσικοῦ Θησαυροῦ*, 1945–6, vol. 12, pp. 65–128, 1947–8, vol. 14, pp. 193–270.

4. Höeg, Carsten: *Les Saracatsans*, Étude linguistique, 2 vols., Paris and Copenhagen, 1925 and 1926.

5. Κασομούλης, Νικ.: *Ἐνθυμήματα Στρατιωτικά*, vol. i, Athens, 1940.

6. Λαμπρίδης, Ἰωάννης: *Ἠπειρωτικὰ Μελετήματα*, Athens, 1887–90.

7. Λουχόπουλος, Δημ.: *Ποιμενικὰ τῆς Ρούμελης*, Athens, 1930.

8. Σκαφιδᾶς, Βας.: «Οἱ Σαρακατσαναῖοι», *Ἠπειρωτικὴ Ἑστία*, 1955–6, vol. 4, pp. 782–92, 892–900, 1004–10, 1101–7, vol. 5, pp. 56–62, 151–7, 276–9, 356–62, 458–65, 564–70.

9. Συράκης, Δημοσθ.: «Ἡ Νομαδικὴ Κτηνοτροφία ἐν Ἑλλάδι», *Γεωργικὸν Δελτίον*, 1925, vol. 12, pp. 651–777.

10. Τζιάτζιος, Εὐάγγελος: *Τραγούδια τῶν Σαρακατσαναίων*, Athens, 1928.

11. Χατζημιχάλη, Ἀγγελική: *Σαρακατσάνοι*, vol. i, Athens, 1957.

12. Wace, A. J. B. and Thompson, M. S.: *The Nomads of the Balkans*, London, 1914.

Note: Although a number of anthropological studies of Greek rural communities have been made in recent years, little of this work has yet been published. Ernestine Friedl, *Vasilika: A Village in Modern Greece*, New York, 1962, is a short but perceptive study of a village in the Boeotian plain. Irwin T. Sanders, *Rainbow in the Rock: The People of Rural Greece*, Cambridge Mass., 1962, is a useful general survey by a rural sociologist.

# INDEX[1]

Abduction, 129–31, 308–9

Adam, 328, 331, 354

Adkins, W. H., 263 n.

Adultery, 152, 169, 199–200

Affinal relations, 124 et seq., 301; consolidation of, 54–55, 134, 136–8; establishment of, 132; ambivalent character of, 135–6, 147; flexibility in range of, 138; the significant relationships in, 139–40; structural implications of, 145–9

Affines, 38; association with, in stani, 17, 93; non-kinsmen as potential, 50, 146; bride's exchange of gifts with, 60, 62–64; co-operation between, 94, 139–40, 143, 146; difficulties between, 105, 141–2; obligations of, 138 et seq.; restraint in behaviour between, 139–40; avoidance of offence to distant, 140; favour returned for service of, 144; breaches of trust between, 145; marriage prohibitions between, 145–6; neither kin nor non-kin, 146; quarrels between, 147; support from, 148; search for suitable, 301–2

Agnatic cousins, 55, 102–5

Agricultural Bank, loans from, 98, 227–8, 238, 253

— Court, cases of animal trespass before, 215, 239 n.

— guard, 209, 226, 227, 234–5; bribes to, 240–41

— officer, 238–40

Agriculture, and pastoralism, 8, 214

Air, evil spirits in, 332–3

Albania, 2; looting by bands from, 13; flight of Muslims to, 15, 89, 282

Albanian Vlachs, 2–3

Animals, theft of, 206–9; as form of wealth, 298; sin of cruelty to, 325; Devil assumes forms of, 332

Aóös, river, 9–10

Apotropaic substances, 334, 338; blessed by priest, 348

Aravandinos, P., 3 n.

Arta, 7, 11, 13, 14, 239

Ascendant kinsmen, 56

Association of Nomad Pastoralists, 217, 265

Assumption, feast of the, 115, 321, 344, 350, 352, 355

Athens, 245–6, 248–9

Aunts, 105–6, 121

Baptism, 218–19, 221, 329

Betrothal, 124–9, 138; rite of, 52, 60, 133; feast, 126–7; refusal of girl's family to enter into, 129; period between marriage and, 132

— contract, 126–7, 134; breaking of, 127–8, 201, 291

Bilateral: filiation, 42; endowment of family, 45; extension, equivalent, 48, 50–51, 71, 93; kinship system, 46, 189, 319

Blood, idea of, 44, 185–6; loss of life seen as loss of, 193, 198; powers of, 197; vengeance for loss of, 198–9; loss of, seen as loss of honour, 269; of Christ, 349, 351–2, 355

— vengeance, see Vengeance killing

[1] I am grateful to Miss H. Jerrold for preparing this Index.

tition, 58, 72, 86; and their wives in extended family, 69 *et seq.*; breach in unity of, after birth of children, 71–72, 78, 141–2; solidarity of, 72, 173–4, 191; different spending habits of, 75; separation of, 79 *et seq.*; their obligations towards sisters, 82, 84, 88, 101, 103, 128, 130, 173, 178–9, 199–201; dependent position of man without, 94, 285; feelings of, towards sister and her children, 103; of bride, 132, 139; permanent estrangement of, 111, 175; danger of rivalry between, 174–7, 184; quarrels between, 174–5, 177–8, 324–5; specialization of technical roles of, 176–7; ties between sisters and, 178–9; trust between, 191; Devil's responsibility for violence between, 336

— unmarried, vengeance obligations of, 84, 172–3, 194–5, 199–201, 317–18; sharing by, 174. *See also* Siblings; Sons; Wives of brothers

Brothers-in-law, 103, 139–40
Burial, 197

Capidan, Theodor, 3–4
Card-playing, 284
Chatzimichalis, Mme., vi, 1 *n.*, 3 *n.*, 5–6, 65 *n.*, 138 *n.*, 281 *n.*, 333 *n.*, 343 *n.*, 346 *n.*, 348 *n.*
Cheese-maker's station, 21, 28, 249; in summer, 23–24; transporting equipment and cheeses from, 205–6; capital needed for, 249–50. *See also* Merchant, cheese
Cheeses, 21 *n.*; made for the family's own consumption, 24, 29, 248–9
Chiftliks, 11, 13–15
Child, interests of, a first priority, 154; relations of, with siblings,

173; fate of illegitimate, 187; choice of name for, 220; fits in, a matter for shame, 311; shame felt by small, 311; fate of an unbaptised, 329; prayers for a sick, 343. *See also* Children
— birth of, conflict of family obligations arising from, 59; change in husband's behaviour to wife after, 70
Childbirth, 165, 289–90
Children, obligations of parents towards, 52, 54, 87, 100 (*see also* Parental obligation); cause of separation of brothers, 71, 73; cause of quarrels between wives of brothers, 71, 77; control of, in extended families, 79, 142; interests of, considered by father in choice of associates in stani, 93; visits of, to mother's family, 103–4; securing adequate kinship support for, 139, 141–2; and parents, 154–72; behaviour of family to young, 154–6, 171, 181–2; unrelated, antagonism between, 155, 171; indulgence towards, 155–6, 171; education of, into community life, 156–8, 171, 181, 183, 281, 307; experience responsibility in representing their families at school, 156, 158, 182, 307; join in family discussions, 157–8; parental responsibility for wrong-doing of, 166–7; God's punishment of parent through, 167, 311, 323, 325; infected by mother's dishonour, 169–70; known by reference to father's name, 186; sin of cruelty to, 190, 324; learn to give evasive answers, 192; dishonourable to insult or assault, 293; Devil seeks to destroy, 333; diseases of, attributed to evil eye, 338, 340. *See also* Boy; Girl

for, 239; in legal difficulties,
240; relations between lawyer
and, 244; ideal attributes of,
282–5; public demeanour of,
283–5; dependence or independence of, 285, 299
— honour, *see* Honour of family
— isolation of, 52, 59, 121, 148;
connexion between prestige
values and, 113; from collateral
kindred, 145; in relation to
patronage, 256–7, 260–61,
263–4
— of marriage, 42 *n*., 53; obligations
within, 49, 53; and family of
origin, conflict of obligations
towards, 53, 70–71, 73, 75, 82,
87, 141–2, 195–6
— of origin, 42, 51, 53; endowment
of family of marriage with
property from, 45; filiation of
man or woman to, 47; and family
of marriage, conflict of obligations towards, 53, 70–71, 73, 75,
82, 87, 141–2, 195–6; effect of,
on social standing, 56; relin-
quishment of obligations to, 59;
bride's departure from, 59–61;
groom's position in, after marriage, 65, 67; wife's visits to,
103–4, 139–40
— prestige *see* Prestige
— solidarity, 148, 185 *et seq*., 212,
319; active and passive, 172–3,
193–4, 198–9, 203, 319; vulnerability of, 174–5, 212; and
vengeance killing, 193–4, 203;
in defence of honour, 203; resides in exclusiveness, 205; in
relation to patronage, 256–7,
260–61, 263–4; outward hostility an expression of, 263
Farês, Bichr, 263 *n*.
Fasting, before Easter, 352–3
Fate and Fates, 329–31
Father, identification of interests
with those of children, 49, 100;
his rights over daughters, 53;

retirement of, from leadership,
68–69, 72, 83–84, 159, 161–3;
indulgence shown to infant
child by, 155–6; authority of,
155–6, 170–72, 180; conditional
indulgence of, to young child,
156–7, 166, 171–2; as disciplin-
arian, 157, 170; relations between unmarried daughter and,
158–9, 171–2, 182; killing of
dishonoured daughter by, 159,
172, 199–200, 271; relations
between adolescent son and,
159–60, 180, 182; relations between adult unmarried son
and, 160–61, 170–72, 212;
weakness of, leading to early
retirement, 162; handicapped
by illiteracy, 162–3; position of,
after retirement, 163–4, 166,
182, 286; attitude of children
to, in old age, 166–7, 171–2;
role of, in elementary family,
170; his duty as protector, 170;
attitude of married daughter
to, 172; limits to authority of,
189; public and private behaviour of, 191; seldom involved in vengeance killing,
194–5; without sons, dilemma
of, 297–8, 317
— spiritual, *see* Godfather
Father-in-law, position of man dwelling in house of, 45, 144–5; relations of man with, 139–40;
powerless to interfere between
daughter and son-in-law, 142
Favours, and obligations, 95 *et seq*.;
gratitude for, 95–96; 'free', 97–
98, 121–2; conditional, 98–99,
121–2, 144; between friends,
102, 122; between affines,
143–4; sought from spiritual
kinsmen, 222; friendship based
on complementary, 223, 229–30;
of village President to shepherd
families, 226, 229, 232; sought
by means of gifts, 234–6, 240,

244; asked of Members of Parliament, 246

Feast-days, celebration of, 115, 343–4; sacrifice of sheep on, 352. *See also* Festivals

Female sex, inferiority of, 56–57, 276, 278; limited male companionship for, 101; under authority of male, 179–80; predisposition to evil inherent in, 277–8; mainly responsible for original sin, 319. *See also* Woman

Festivals, 8; village, 9, 25, 115; of sheep shearing, 30; gathering of kinsmen at, 114 *et seq.*; religious, 115, 352, 355; quarrels at, 216; prohibition of sexual intercourse before religious, 277. *See also* Feast-days

Fights and brawls, 97; at betrothal feasts, 126–7; vengeance for loss of blood in, 198–9; during migrations, 211. *See also* Quarrels

Finances, in extended family, 72–73, 75; within stani, 92. *See also* Debts; Loans; Money

Finley, M. I., 263 *n.*

Firth, Raymond, 48 *n.*

Flocks, 19 *et seq.*; size of, 15, 88, 91, 298; seasonal division of, into four, 19, 21, 88; labour force necessary to manage, 20; following the, 25; dependence on, 31; condition of, and family prestige, 31, 40, 212; co-management of, by kinsmen, 41, 98, 102, 299; partition of, 55, 59, 81, 298; co-management of, by brothers, after partition, 55, 58; common property of family, 72, 187–9, 298–9; common service of brothers to, 173; only kinsmen co-operate in management of, 203; selling produce of, 204, 247 *et seq.*; neighbouring, not subject to theft, 206, 208; on the road

during annual migrations, 211, 305; deception over numbering of, 215; loss of, by disease, 301, 331. *See also* Sheep

Flour, purchase of, 17; credit in form of, 251

Food, preparation of, at weddings, 118; and commensality, 151, 191

Forest guards, 226, 240–41

Fortes, Meyer, 42 *n.*

Fratricide, 188

Freeman, J. D., 51 *n.*

Friedl, Ernestine, 58 *n.*, 261 *n.*

Friendship, between cousins, 101–4, 121, 205; between non-kinsmen, impossibility of, 205; based on complementary favours, 223, 229–30; between villagers, sometimes a form of patronage, 224–38; pressures exerted through network of, 237–8; of lawyer, results obtained through, 243; of merchant, 254–5

Galaria, *see* Milking ewes

Georgakas, D., 4 *n.*

George, St., 343–4; feast-day of, 7, 115, 352; exemplar of male virtues, 272

Gifts, marriage, 60, 62–64, 220; to affines, in return for favours, 143–4; to village President, 234–6; to State officials, 240; to lawyers, 244; to Saints, 342, 344

Gipsy: band at weddings, 117, 120; made nails for Cross, 347

Girl(s), pre-school life of, 156; between school and marriage, 158; relations of, with father, 158–9; pre-marital love affair of, 187; as goatherd, 274; without brother as protector, 297–8. *See also* Daughter; Maiden

Glotz, Gustave, 193 *n.*

Goatherd(s), 22–23, 27, 159; girl as, 274

public knowledge of failure, 307–10; molestation of, 308–9; inhibits display of weakness, 309; and shame, 311–12; a virtue in man but possibly a failing in woman, 312

Settlement of pastoralists, 15–16

Sexes, moral qualities of, 26, 45, 56–57, 274, 277–8; division of labour between, 31–32, 150–51, 274; opposition of, 32, 275–8, 319; male superiority to female 56–57, 276, 278; segregation of, outside family and kindred, 101, 274–5; complementary attributes of, 179–83, 276, 318–19; verbal exchanges between groups of the two, 275

Sexual relations, impurity of, 26, 31, 276–7; between bride and groom, 66–68, 70; illicit, associated with visits to the well, 86; illicit outside marriage, 100–1; between cousins, 110–11; ambivalent attitude towards, 270, 276–7, 280; women's alleged revulsion from, 270, 275–6; shame of, rests on woman, 277; with Devil, 336

— shame, inheritance of sense of, 45, 271; as defence against dishonour, 193, 270; of women, 269, 270–71, 277–8, 312; maiden's cultivation of, 287–8

Sexuality, of women, 31, 271, 277–8, 311–12, 327; man's attempt to discipline, 269, 319, 326, 355; maiden's denial of, 287, 311; spent, of old woman, 290; and sin, 326–8, 354; destroyer of family honour, 326

'Shadows, the', 333

Shame, 310–12; of accepting help from non-kin, 40; bride's feelings of, 62, 65; of family for kinsman's wrongdoing, 112–13; of virtuous maiden, 158, 286–7; 311; of woman, 270; of family

for woman's seduction, 270–71; complementary to manliness, 271–2; a virtue in woman but sometimes a fault in man, 276, 312; woman's redemption by, 278; sense of, in failure to achieve ideal patterns of behaviour, 307, 310–11, 317; and self-regard, 311–12; and ridicule, 312–13; and guilt, 327–8; idea of fate and, 331. *See also* Sexual Shame

Shearing of sheep, 29–30, 33; of goats, 31

Sheep, 19 *et seq.*; number of, 7, 88, 298; wethers as leaders, 19 *n.*; God's animal, 26, 34, 322; characteristics of, 26; bells, 28, 305, 338; protection of, against evil eye, 28, 338; shepherds' solidarity with, 30–31; prerequisite of prestige, 31, 212, 267, 298, 301; care of sick, 31–32, 280; women and, 31–32, 276; ear-signs of, 81, 208; increase in numbers of, in Zagori, 209; trespassing of, on village land, 215, 226; loan for replacing lost, 227–8; counting of, for tax purposes, 229, 232; buying winter feed for, 251; included in dowry, 302–3; decorated 'for pride', 305; attacked by evil spirits or Devil, 333; sacrifice of, 344, 352; spiritual value of, 352

— disease, 28, 277, 301; loss of sheep from, 98, 267, 301; caused by evil eye, 338

— theft, small-scale, 206–7; large-scale, 208–9; during migrations, 211. *See also* Flocks; Milking ewes

Sheep-folds, 20–22, 27, 32

Shepherd(s), 26 *et seq.*; wage, 16, 88, 285, 299; improved conditions of, 17–18; shelters for, 20, 22; summer life of, 24–25, 30; iso-